MW01204801

Reynolds & Reynolds ®

Compliments of The Reynolds and Reynolds Company

CARLAW® III
RELOADED

CARLAW® III
RELOADED

THOMAS B. HUDSON
EMILY MARLOW BECK
and the
lawyers of Hudson Cook, LLP

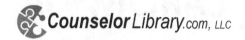

ISBN: 0-9779501-4-X

Printed in the United States of America

Project Director: Thomas B. Hudson
Production Manager: Marlene K. Locke
Production Assistant: Jean Heckhaus
Editor: Janet A. Martin
Cover and Jacket Design: Susan Neighbors
Book Design: Lisa A. Allen
Printer: Victor Graphics

CONTENTS

ACKNOWLEDGMENTS

What a team! Our members have changed a bit for this book. Our new players are Susan Neighbors, who did the cover and jacket design, and Jean Heckhaus, who takes over as production assistant. Marlene Locke has been on the team for our other books, but this time takes the role of production manager. Janet Martin is back as editor, while Lisa Allen once again handles book design.

INTRODUCTION

Tom: The Chinese have a saying: "One hand washes the other."
That's the essence of teamwork.

So, when I considered the writing of **CARLAW**® *Reloaded,*
I wanted some help—hands on deck, you might say—to make
the latest legal trends in car dealership real, relevant, and, yes,
maybe even riveting to readers.

First, I looked next door. It was the logical place to begin . . .

Before Emily Beck joined our firm, I thought I knew quite
a bit about how dealerships work. I actually worked as a salesman
in an Atlanta Chrysler dealership and in an Athens, Georgia,
motorcycle and MG dealership, and as a callow youth I had
managed a mobile home lot for a prominent mobile home
retailing company for two years.

The problem with this practical experience was that it was
all a few decades old. My subsequent knowledge of dealership
operations I learned second-hand, either through reading legal
opinions or by talking with dealers and advising them about
legal problems. One of the best ways to learn stuff is to actually
do it, and I haven't "done" a great deal of dealer stuff, at least
not recently.

Enter Emily. She was right out of law school when we first
started working together, and she didn't know a great deal of
law. But she had grown up in a dealership family in the
Shenandoah Valley of Virginia, and she had done every job there
is to do in a dealership.

Emily: Tom likes to tell people that he keeps me around because of the practical knowledge that I gained from years of hands-on experience. Frankly, I always thought that was a little bit like the pot calling the kettle black. After all, in over 30 years of practice, Tom has "been there" for the development, enactment, and evolution of almost every federal consumer credit law. Talk about practical experience!

Tom: Emily struck me as professional and savvy. She knew the jargon, and she knew the tricks of the trade. Quickly she became my teacher.

Emily: Tom's record of advising clients on how to navigate the regulatory landscape governing car sales and finance makes you realize that working with him is like consulting a virtual dealer law encyclopedia. Yet, he manages to translate complicated laws and regulations into a language that industry folk can understand and apply to their day-to-day operations. Frankly, I think it's one reason why dealers and auto industry professionals like him.

Tom: Over time, I've soaked up as much of Emily's background as I could, but she's still ahead of me when it comes to live, on-the-ground knowledge of how dealerships work. When Emily does dealership compliance audits, you have to pity the dealership personnel she talks to who think that she's "just a lawyer" (and a young one at that) that they can fog stuff by.

Emily: Early on in my practice, I made it my job to absorb everything I possibly could from Tom. Sure, like any young lawyer, I spent my fair share of hours with my nose in some law book. But, I also spent a slew of hours monopolizing Tom's time trying to put a "why" with the laws and regulations I was learning. And, for me, it was time well spent.

Tom: Emily's experience keeps me from giving too much pointy-headed lawyer advice. A good example was her admonition not long ago to back off my criticisms of dealers who charge documentation fees. I had carped for years that the practice constituted nickeling and diming customers, and that it drew more legal fire than it was worth. Emily basically told me that I was howling at the wind, that dealer doc fees were a fact of life, and that I should concentrate on making sure that dealers knew how to do it correctly.

I know good advice when I hear it. And that's why I needed Emily Beck to help write this book.

Emily: Anybody can read up on the nuts and bolts of consumer credit law requirements. But, even the biggest books in the best libraries can't compete with what's in Tom's head. I hope someday I'll be able to draw from my own, personal, 30-plus years of "hands-on," "in-the-trenches" consumer credit lawyering experience to provide color and context to the advice I give and the articles I write—just as he does. But, today, fortunately, I've got Tom in the office next door.

And, that's why I needed Tom Hudson to help write this book.

From Emily and Tom:

An American version of the Chinese proverb "One hand washes another" could be "Many hands make light work."

In that spirit, looking for creative handiwork for this book, we just looked out our office doors and down our office halls . . .

The lawyers in our firm are all consumer financial services lawyers. That's all our firm does.

You'd think that would mean our lawyers concentrate their practices to a small area, and they do. But the area is even smaller than that description indicates, because over the course of time, most of our lawyers have ended up concentrating on an even narrower area of practice. Those lawyers devote a substantial percentage of their practices to the Truth in Lending Act, the Equal Credit Opportunity Act, the Fair Credit Reporting Act, the Uniform Commercial Code, the Consumer Leasing Act, or the many more federal and state laws and regulations that bedevil dealers on a daily basis.

Because of their intense immersion in their practice areas, these lawyers can offer timely, pertinent, and insightful articles on breaking developments in their practice areas without breaking a sweat. They made our job a lot easier.

We hope you enjoy the result of our efforts.

WHICH BOOK SHOULD I BUY?

We've done four books so far, and we're frequently asked, "Which one should I buy?"

Our ready answer, of course, is that you should buy them all! But the right answer for you might be a little more complicated.

The first book, *CARLAW®*, is a collection of Tom Hudson's articles from 10 years of his industry observations. Tom is irreverent and corny, but if you want a pretty thorough chronicle of legal developments in auto sales, financing, and leasing from 1997 through 2007, this one's your book.

Our next effort was the *F&I Legal Desk Book,* written by Tom and the other lawyers at Hudson Cook, LLP. The *F&I Legal Desk Book* is more like a reference book for F&I professionals, arranged in a Q&A format around the main federal laws that govern the sales and F&I process. Because Tom didn't write as much of it, it isn't as corny. If you can buy only one book, here it is.

CARLAW® II: Street Legal came along in 2008. It's a collection of articles that continues the original *CARLAW®* theme. This one's a multi-author effort as well, so if you like different voices (and if you want a book with a super cool dust jacket), toss this one into your shopping cart.

The book you're holding, *CARLAW® III: Reloaded,* is another series of articles, mostly written by Tom and Emily

Beck—and occasionally joined by their colleagues at Hudson Cook.

Emily and Tom have similar writing styles, and similar ideas about what's funny, so if you enjoy their style and if you want the very latest and greatest, here it is.

But like we said, you ought to buy them all.

MEET THE AUTHORS

Following are the authors and editors who wrote the articles featured in this book. They are among the 32 attorneys at the law firm of Hudson Cook, LLP, and together represent a vast amount of experience in consumer finance.

Thomas B. Hudson
Phone: 410.865.5411
E-mail: thudson@hudco.com

Emily Marlow Beck
Phone: 410.865.5438
E-mail: ebeck@hudco.com

Catharine S. Andricos
Phone: 202.327.9706
E-mail: candricos@hudco.com

Michael A. Benoit
Phone: 202.327.9705
E-mail: mabenoit@hudco.com

Catherine M. Brennan
Phone: 410.865.5405
E-mail: cbrennan@hudco.com

Thomas J. Buiteweg
Phone: 734.222.6025
E-mail: tbuiteweg@hudco.com

Dana F. Clarke
Phone: 714.263.0427
E-mail: dclarke@hudco.com

Patricia E.M. Covington
Phone: 410.865.5409
E-mail: pcovington@hudco.com

Lisa C. DeLessio
Phone: 410.865.5437
E-mail: ldelessio@hudco.com

Rochelle B. (Shelley) Fowler
Phone: 410.865.5406
E-mail: rfowler@hudco.com

Michael A. Goodman
Phone: 202.327.9704
E-mail: mgoodman@hudco.com

Maya P. Hill
Phone: 410.782.2356
E-mail: mhill@hudco.com

Elizabeth A. Huber
Phone: 714.263.0424
E-mail: eahuber@hudco.com

Daniel J. Laudicina
Phone: 410.865.5435
E-mail: dlaudicina@hudco.com

Emily G. Miller
Phone: 410.865.5418
E-mail: emiller@hudco.com

Nicole F. Munro
Phone: 410.865.5430
E-mail: nmunro@hudco.com

Meghan Musselman
Phone: 410.865.5403
E-mail: mmusselman@hudco.com

L. Jean Noonan
Phone: 202.327.9700
E-mail: jnoonan@hudco.com

Geoffrey C. Rogers
Phone: 518.383.9591
E-mail: grogers@hudco.com

Alicia H. Tortarolo
Phone: 714.263.0425
E-mail: atortarolo@hudco.com

DEDICATION

This book is dedicated to the memory of our friend and colleague,
Teresa Rohwedder, who inspired, and continues to inspire,
much of the writing we do.

Teresa Rohwedder
1963–2006

C h a p t e r   1

Basics

Maybe it's because it is football season as we write this, but "basics" brings to mind the sorts of things that good coaches have their teams work on constantly. A team that consistently blocks and tackles well, one that can avoid penalties and turnovers, can often have a pretty good season, even when it isn't loaded with talent. Those basic maneuvers form the underpinnings of the plays, from simple quarterback sneaks to double reverses. If a team doesn't have the basics down pat, very little in the game will go right.

A dealership's business also has its basics. A dealership that understands the legal structure of the transactions it engages in with its customers is, in our experience, more likely to understand which federal and state laws apply to its sales, lease, and financing transactions; how those laws apply; and how to avoid violating them.

Probably the most basic concept for dealers to understand is that when they sell and finance a vehicle, they are creditors. Dealers like to talk about "loans" and "lenders" when they discuss the sale and financing of vehicles, but in a typical sales and financing transaction at a dealership, the dealer and its customer enter into a "retail installment sales contract." When they do, the dealer is a "credit seller," and the customer is a "credit buyer." The extension of credit occurs when the dealer hands over the keys to that bright, shiny new car in exchange for a contract by which the customer agrees to pay, say, $600 per month for 60 months. In such a transaction there has been no "loan," and there is no "lender." There exists just a credit seller and a credit buyer.

Dealers who are not "buy-here, pay-here" dealers typically do not want to service and collect these contracts. Instead, they want liquidity so they can buy more cars and engage in still more credit sale transactions. As a result, they immediately sell their contracts to banks, credit unions, or sales finance companies. In the process they lump these institutions into a category that they erroneously call "lenders." But think about it—these "lenders" have not engaged in any "loan" transactions, they have simply purchased contracts from the dealers.

Many dealers don't understand this most basic of legal concepts that underpin their business. They would have a clue to this structure if they spent an hour or so reading the retail installment contracts they use in their transactions, and if they read the dealer agreements they enter into with their banks, credit unions, and sales finance companies. Those contracts pretty clearly spell out the fact that the customer is buying a car from the dealer on credit, and that the dealer is then selling the contract to another entity. Federal and state laws recognize the difference between loans and credit sales, and the pointy-headed lawyers like us who create those contracts fashion them to comply with those credit sale laws, and not with loan laws.

A similar discussion applies to leasing. Most leasing programs involve the dealer as the original lessor, with a subsequent sale of the lease contract and the vehicle by the dealer to a bank, credit union, or leasing company. For purposes of these introductory comments, though, we'll stick to credit sales.

Why does all this matter? Why is the concept of "dealer as creditor" the most basic thing that dealers need to understand about their business?

Well, simply, it is the concept of "dealer as creditor" that determines which state laws apply to dealers and how those laws apply. It is the concept of "dealer as creditor" that determines how the federal credit disclosure laws apply to the transactions the dealer engages in. It's the concept of "dealer as creditor" that Congress uses when it ropes dealers into the scope of the Equal Credit Opportunity Act, the Fair Credit Reporting Act, the

Gramm-Leach-Bliley privacy laws, the Red Flag requirements, and other laws and regulations.

A dealer who engaged only in cash sales transactions would operate in a vastly simplified world. Perhaps not as simple as running a bait shop—after all, state licensing restrictions, tag and title requirements, MVA rules and regulations, advertising laws, and some federal requirements like the Magnuson-Moss Warranty Act, the Federal Odometer Act, and the FTC's Used Car Rule would still apply—but still much simpler than a credit sale operation.

The articles that follow deal with this most basic of legal concepts, along with some other introductory topics that dealers should try to get their arms around. Those who don't want to go to the trouble might want to consider closing their doors and opening that bait shop.

Great Whites and Sand Sharks

November 2007
By Thomas B. Hudson

There are more than 360 types of sharks in our Earth's oceans, but most people hearing the word "shark" immediately think of the great white, an aggressive monster some 20 feet in length, weighing almost 5,000 pounds. That species is the main character in Peter Benchley's "Jaws" and the subject of tall tales and real nightmares. At the opposite end of the shark spectrum there is also the sluggish sand shark, which most frequently appears as a small 2- or 3-pound bait-snatching nuisance to surf fishermen. One variety habitually cruises the oceans; the other commonly buries itself in ocean sands. One is the world's largest recognized predatory fish, known to attack humans; the other, while also a predator, is not known to attack humans and surfs mainly for smaller fish.

So, why are we talking about sharks, you ask? Well, because they are on my mind . . .

At this year's Leedom dealer 20 groups conference in Vegas, Emily Beck and I had a chance to talk with a number of dealers about the legal risks they face in their everyday operations. During an "Ask the Experts" panel presentation, Chuck Bonanno tossed out an opening question: "What's the biggest development that you've seen in the last year or so for dealers?"

I didn't have to think very long about my answer. The emergence of "predatory litigators" (a term coined, as far as I know, by Chris Leedom) is easily the most significant legal trend in the dealership legal arena.

Chris defines "predatory litigators" as lawyers who are beginning to make it their business to sue car dealers over their sales and F&I practices. Now, lawyers suing car dealers isn't exactly news. And class action lawsuits against dealers aren't news either.

For years, lawyers have been filing lawsuits on behalf of consumers, and, for years, they have been tossing in class action claims, mostly to bolster the settlement value of the case for their clients and to increase the attorneys' fees that are usually part of the settlement agreements in consumer cases. Usually, however, these cases were not filed by experienced class action lawyers with pockets deep enough to withstand a protracted legal battle against a dealer or finance company that decided to really make a fight of it.

That's changing.

A decade or more ago, we began to see class action lawsuits alleging violations of consumer protection laws, like the federal Truth in Lending Act, filed against sales finance companies and banks by really experienced and well-heeled class action lawyers.

At least some of these cases dealt with retail installment sales contracts bought by the sales finance companies and banks from car dealers.

Litigating these cases against the buyers of retail installment contracts taught these lawyers a great deal about the laws that regulate the sales and financing practices of dealers. This knowledge turned out to be just as useful against dealers as it had been against the bigger targets.

As court opinions dealing with these cases were reported, other lawyers began to take note. In a very short time, a new law firm specialty arose—consumer actions against car dealers.

And these lawyers weren't the typical lawyers that dealers had seen for years, often willing to accept a quick settlement in order to earn enough to pay the next month's rent. Many of these lawyers had been engaged in heavyweight class action lawsuits against big companies for years. They had the experience to recognize and effectively pursue good class claims, they had learned enough car sales and finance law to be truly dangerous, and they had accumulated enough of a war chest from their prior lawsuits to go chin-to-chin with the largest defendants for as long as it took to negotiate a favorable settlement, with big attorneys' fees attached.

In short, these guys are about as closely related to yesterday's plaintiffs' lawyers as great white sharks are to sand sharks.

Y'all be careful swimming in the consumer protection ocean, you hear?

Is Your Buyer Able to Enter Into a Contract?

December 2007

By Thomas B. Hudson

A dealer sells a car to a buyer, only to have the buyer's parents return with the buyer the next day to advise the dealer that he must unwind the deal because the buyer is developmentally disabled and under the legal guardianship of his parents.

What should a dealer faced with these facts do?

Wait a minute! Let's reverse that. Let's take a look at what he shouldn't do, as illustrated by a recent Alaska court opinion. Keep in mind that there may be more to the story than appears from the court's decision.

Kenai Chrysler Center Inc., sold a new car to David Denison that he bought in part by trading in his old vehicle. At the time of the sale, Kenai apparently did not detect Denison's developmental disability or the fact that Denison was under the legal guardianship of his parents.

When his parents tried to return the car the day after the sale, claiming that Denison's disability rendered the contract void, the Kenai manager refused to take it back, saying that the dealer sold cars to "a lot of people who aren't very smart."

Question 1: Don't you suppose a little sensitivity training might be in order?

Kenai also demanded restitution to rescind the contract.

Question 2: Do you suppose the manager called his friendly local lawyer before rejecting the parents' request out of hand?

The parents repeatedly brought the car back to Kenai, and Kenai employees kept giving the car to Denison. Despite the knowledge of the guardianship and the parents' claim that the guardianship voided the contract, Kenai continued its efforts to enforce it.

Question 3: See Question #2.

Kenai sold the contract to GMAC, without informing GMAC of Denison's disability or the guardianship, and sold Denison's trade-in vehicle.

Question 4: Do you suppose the dealer gave any thought to the representations and warranties that it makes to GMAC when it sells them contracts?

Question 5: See Question #2.

GMAC eventually repossessed the car and sold it, resulting in a deficiency judgment. However, when GMAC learned of Denison's disability, it wrote off the debt.

Kenai then asked the probate court to modify Denison's guardianship order so that Denison could purchase the car, claiming that it was "a person interested in [Denison's] welfare."

Question 6: Where do you get that kind of gall?

The probate court denied the petition and awarded the parents attorneys' fees, expressly deeming the petition frivolous and without good cause. The parents ultimately sued Kenai to void the contract. The parents also sought damages under the state unfair and deceptive trade practices act.

The trial court granted the parents' motion for summary judgment, voided the contract, and awarded actual and treble damages. The trial court subsequently awarded the parents an additional amount that partly covered their attorneys' fees. Both the parents and Kenai appealed.

The Alaska Supreme Court affirmed the trial court's decision. The high court noted that it is a black letter law that the existence of a legal guardianship precludes the formation of a valid contract with the guardianship's ward. Further, restitution is only appropriate when a party who entered into a contract with a ward lacked knowledge of the ward's incompetence. Here, Denison was subject to a formal, public guardianship that gave

Kenai constructive notice of the guardianship. The Denisons also told Kenai repeatedly about the guardianship after the sale, and Kenai continued to ignore that information.

Kenai argued that the parents abandoned Denison's guardianship, as evidenced by their inability to control his spending. The high court rejected this argument, noting that the parents' alleged inability to control their son's spending did not suggest abandonment.

The high court also upheld the award of damages under the state unfair and deceptive trade practices act, finding that the jury reasonably found that Kenai's attempts to enforce the contract blatantly disregarded the parents' rights and amounted to unethical conduct. The parents also argued that the trial court erred in reducing their attorneys' fees. The high court rejected the claim for additional attorneys' fees, finding that the trial court correctly assessed the fees against Kenai under the circumstances.

So, now you've seen what we say a dealer shouldn't do. To find a better way, simply sum up your own answers to Questions 1 through 6. Then, read Question 7. You'll find your answer.

Question 7: Is it easier to sit on an empty wallet or a full one?

Kenai Chrysler Center Inc. v. Denison, 2007 WL 2745193 (Alaska September 21, 2007).

Time to Toss Out That Buyers Order?

December 2007

By Thomas B. Hudson

We do legal audits for car dealers, and, in the process, we look at all the documents that the dealerships use to document transactions with customers. One problem that we see consistently is that the various forms used in car credit transactions contradict one another.

This problem pops up most often with the buyers order and the retail installment sales contract. Because both of these documents are contracts of sale (more on this below), they both cover much of the same ground.

Usually, though, the buyers order and the retail installment sales contract have different parentages. Very often, the buyers order comes from the state auto dealer's association or independent auto dealer association. Sometimes, the dealer has a custom-made buyers order. Sometimes, the dealer is using a buyers order from a forms company.

If the dealer has a custom-made buyers order, its quality can range from good to somewhere beyond terrible, depending on where it came from. If a knowledgeable car finance lawyer drafted it, likely it will be fine. If, however, the dealer built it with scissors and tape from several other buyers orders that the dealer has scrounged up to avoid spending money on lawyers, then it likely will be full of problems. The buyers orders produced by the dealer associations and the forms companies are usually well done and complete.

But the quality of these buyers orders, and their level of compliance with state and federal law, isn't the issue. The problem is that they are used with retail installment sales contracts that often have nothing in common with the buyers orders. Not only have these documents not been "married" to each other, they often haven't even been introduced.

As a result, they often contain terms addressing the same topics, and the terms are different, or even contradictory. The legal term for this mismatch is "oops."

Mismatched documents are fertile ground for plaintiffs' lawyers. As an example, a New Jersey dealer used several documents that each contained an arbitration agreement. The dealer was using the arbitration agreements to try to protect against class action lawsuits. Because the arbitration agreements in the various forms contradicted each other, the court refused to enforce any of them.

So, I have a solution for you. Toss out your buyers order when you are selling a car on credit!

However, before you do, make sure that your state's law doesn't require the use of a buyers order, or require your buyers order to contain certain disclosures. Those sorts of requirements, and perhaps some other considerations (such as, for example, the fact that your buyers order contains your spot delivery arrangements and those arrangements are not addressed in your retail installment sales contract), may lead you and your lawyer to decide that you can't pitch the form. Also, you will need a buyers order for your cash transactions.

If you can't pitch the form (or if you need the buyers order to meet finance companies' or manufacturers' requirements), you can reduce the chance that its contents will contradict your retail installment sales contract by taking everything out of it that is contained in your retail installment sales contract and that isn't required by law.

And if you decide you have to keep your buyers order for your credit transactions, consider adding language to it that says, "If the terms and conditions of this buyers order and the terms and conditions of the retail installment sales contract you sign are different, the terms and conditions of the retail installment sales contract will control." Also consider adding a term that says, "This buyers order does not become effective until the buyer signs the retail installment sales contract."

A warning is in order. Even though I think that pitching the buyers order for credit transactions could be a good idea, your state law or your particular operations and documents might make it a bad idea. So, as usual, schedule some time with your lawyer before you do anything. Otherwise, contradictions in car credit transaction forms could unhappily complicate your life.

Here We Go Again ...

January/February 2008
By Thomas B. Hudson

Where is my trusty soapbox?

At nearly every industry meeting I attend, I have to bite my tongue while the presenters and attendees talk about "loans" and "lenders" when they really mean "retail installment contracts" and "sales finance companies" or "banks." When I'm one of the presenters, I drag out my soapbox and spend a few minutes railing about the danger of mis-describing the way indirect auto finance works.

When I start my diatribe, it doesn't take long for the audience to fall asleep. They've heard me rant and rave on this topic so many times before that you can almost see their lips forming the words before I say them. When I'm done, as often as not, the next presenter will take the podium and start talking again about "loans" and "lenders." They think I'm crying wolf.

But periodically we see lawsuits that attack finance companies and dealers by alleging that the retail installment sales contracts that dealers enter into with car buyers and then assign to sales finance companies and banks are not retail installment sale transactions at all; they are, instead, goes the theory, disguised loan transactions. The plaintiffs' lawyers claim that the company that buys the retail installment contract is a "lender" and that the dealer is merely the "lender's" agent in completing the "loan documents." The lawyers then contend that the "lender" and the dealer violated a variety of laws that govern loans—laws that were never intended to govern retail installment sales.

We call these lawsuits "recharacterization" suits. The suits are seldom successful, but they can be very costly to the defending sales finance company and dealer. Let's look at a very recent "recharacterization" attack.

Todd and Martha Hunt bought a 2001 Dodge Caravan from Pierce's Lincoln Mercury, Inc., a Montana dealer. In the process of buying the car, they signed a retail installment sales contract with a rate of 20.99% per annum. Pierce's assigned the contract to TranSouth Financial Corp., which was later acquired by CitiFinancial Auto, Inc.

When the Hunts failed to make the payments required by the retail installment contract, Citi repossessed the Dodge and sold it at auction. Citi then sought a deficiency.

The Hunts responded by filing an answer and counterclaim, with the counterclaim taking the form of a class action. The Hunts ended up amending their answer and counterclaim several times, but the gist of their claim was that the retail installment sales transaction was a disguised loan.

The Montana trial court wasn't buying. It threw out the Hunts' usury claim, flatly stating, "[a] retail installment contract is not a loan . . . ." It then bounced the remaining claims on the ground that they were not filed within the time period of the applicable statute of limitations. "So," you say, "No big deal." The recharacterization attack failed.

That's true, but look at what the finance company and the dealer had to go through. The defendants in this case had to file several motions (I'm sure at considerable expense) to get rid of these claims. The finance company and the dealership both lost the time and attention of their business people who were involved in the case. The dealership also probably got a bit of bad press out of the suit.

Look at what could have happened, however. If the trial court had bought the claptrap being sold by the plaintiff's lawyer, Citi and the dealership would be looking at the time and expense of one or more appeals. While I have no doubt that the appellate court in Montana would have eventually decided the issue correctly (as have the courts in many other jurisdictions), those appeals aren't cheap.

Now, while the loose talk at industry conventions probably didn't provoke this lawsuit, I still believe that we in the industry need to correctly describe our business. When we, as well as the media that follow our industry, are sloppy with these descriptions, we contribute to misunderstandings that lead to suits like these. When dealers, finance companies, and others correctly describe the business, we educate consumers, regulators, legislators, and, yes, even plaintiffs' lawyers, and perhaps we deter them from actions that harm the industry.

The American Financial Services Association and the National Auto Dealers Association have produced a booklet that accurately describes the indirect financing of motor vehicles. It is titled *Understanding Vehicle Finance* and is available from the websites of both organizations. It bears the seal of the Federal Trade Commission, which reviewed it before it was published. It is available in both English and Spanish.

If I were a dealer, I would make everyone who works for my dealership read it as part of his or her training. I would display copies of *Understanding Vehicle Finance* at my dealership in the showroom and on the coffee table in the service area waiting room, right beside *Motor Trend*. I'd put a copy in every financed customer's deal documents. I'd donate a bunch of them (with my dealership's business card attached) to whoever teaches personal finance at the local high school, and I'd take a bunch of them to the local Hispanic Community Center, if my community had one. I'd mail one to whatever reporters cover the local business scene. Finally, I'd take one to every legislator and regulator in my state.

The booklet will do a good job of explaining the basics of indirect auto finance. And you won't find any erroneous references to "loans" and "lenders" in it.

CitiFinancial Auto v. Hunt, Cause No. DDV-06-041(B)(C) (Mont. Dist. January 16, 2008).

Are Your Bootstraps Tied?
March 2008
By Emily Marlow Beck

If you've read as many complaints filed by consumer credit plaintiffs' lawyers as we have, you know that plaintiffs' attorneys have developed "throwing it against the wall to see what sticks" into an art form. They will try long shot claims on the possibility that some judge will agree with whatever cockamamie claim they're pushing.

One common argument they advance is that the violation of one law constitutes the violation of another law. In some states, depending on how a state's "unfair and deceptive acts and practices" or similar law is worded, this argument can work. We call this little trick "bootstrapping."

Here's a situation where the plaintiff's attempt to bootstrap a violation of one state's law into a violation of another law didn't work. (I know that this case involves housing credit, but trust me, motor heads of the world, the theories and analysis carry over to car sales and financing as well!)

Rose Stith was delinquent on several bills. Fabian Thorne

approached her and offered to assist her with her financial problems by refinancing her home. Thorne referred Stith to Sterling Palmer with American Credit Solutions, a credit repair company.

Palmer developed a plan whereby Stith would sell her home and transfer title to a third party referred to merely as "Friday" for one year. (No, we don't make this stuff up!) During that time, Stith would remain in the home and work with ACS to improve her credit so that at the end of the year, she would be able to obtain a better loan to buy the house back from Friday.

Friday obtained two loans to buy the house from Stith. According to Stith, the parties agreed that Thorne would receive much of the proceeds of the loan in order to pay Stith's debts during the one-year period. But Thorne never paid the debts, and eventually Friday sought to evict Stith from the home.

Stith sued Southern Central Title, L.L.C., the closing company, for violating federal and Virginia law, arguing that defects in the closing documents should have alerted SCT to this alleged predatory lending scheme. Stith moved for summary judgment on many of her claims, including her claim that SCT's violations of Virginia's Consumer Real Estate Settlement Procedures Act (CRESPA) and Mortgage Lender and Broker Act constituted a violation of the Virginia Consumer Protection Act (VCPA). The U.S. District Court for the Eastern District of Virginia denied Stith's motion with respect to all claims except for the CRESPA and MLBA claims because they presented "material issues of fact."

But, that's the boring part. The really interesting claim was the VCPA claim. With respect to the VCPA claim, Stith argued that the provision of the VCPA prohibiting "any other deception, fraud, false pretense, false promise or misrepresentation in connection with a consumer transaction" is a catchall provision under which a violation of any consumer protection statute in the Virginia Code constitutes a violation of the VCPA. (And that, my friends, is what bootstrapping looks like!)

Unfortunately for her, Stith's bootstrapping tactics proved unsuccessful. The court held that the language of the statute did not support Stith's argument that a violation of any consumer statute is also a violation of the VCPA. Further, neither the CRESPA nor the MLBA provides a private right of action. Thus, the court dismissed Stith's VCPA, CRESPA, and MLBA claims.

So, no "bootstraps" in Virginia. As noted above, though, this claim might work in other states. (We've seen it before, folks!) We've also seen plaintiffs' lawyers use it to bootstrap a violation of a federal law that didn't permit private lawsuits into a state law violation that did, so the theory can be dangerous.

One more reason to run your dealership on the up-and-up!

Stith v. Thorne, 2007 WL 4246097 (E.D. Va. November 26, 2007).

Buyer (That Means Dealer) Beware!

March 2008

By Thomas B. Hudson

So, subprime and buy-here, pay-here (BHPH) are the fastest growing segments of the retail marketplace and, perhaps, the most lucrative. Maybe that's why vendors are targeting these dealers with all sorts of additional finance and insurance (F&I) and other products to sell to customers.

Lately, we've seen programs that we haven't seen before, including:

- Rent-to-own programs, supposedly designed to avoid state usury limits, sales taxes, and other unpleasantness

- Lease-here, pay-here programs that offer some of the same advantages as the RTO programs
- Offers to tap the buyer's bank account every other week for 1/2 of a payment, resulting in 26 payments per year and thereby a shorter repayment cycle and quicker equity buildup
- Offers to take manufacturer rebate cash and bank it, applying it to the buyer's payment, resulting in lower payments for a specified period
- Programs that offer to prepare the buyer's income tax returns and apply refunds to the down payment on a car
- Skip-tracing programs that offer to find buyers by pinging their cell phones or following their Internet activities

These are programs that we have seen and heard about. In some cases, we've done legal work on such programs. I really don't take a position on whether the programs work or not from a legal standpoint, unless we've actually reviewed the programs and given opinions on them. All of these programs may be perfectly legal. But (you knew this was coming) I've seen many that aren't.

When dealership clients actually bother to ask us about these programs, we usually get a glimpse of the marketing materials and sometimes the documents that the buyers sign. Very often, these materials raise more questions than they answer.

From the way that many of these documents are constructed, it's evident that whoever drafted them is either (1) way smarter than we are, or (2) has not done the necessary legal due diligence on the products.

When we get an inquiry from a dealer about a product, our response is always the same. We advise the dealer to ask the product vendor for a copy of the legal opinions that the vendor has gotten that say that the products are legal. We then suggest that the dealer ask the vendor if the vendor will indemnify the dealer if the program gets the dealer into legal hot water and whether the vendor will put that promise in writing. Finally, we suggest that the dealer determine whether the vendor has enough jingle in its jeans to make the indemnification worth having.

Our experience so far is that very few vendors will produce the requested legal opinions and that even fewer will agree to indemnify the dealer if trouble arises. Where does that leave the dealer?

Right back where the dealer usually is—on his own. A dealer will rarely be able to escape legal liability by arguing that a product or service sold by the dealership is that of a third party. For that reason, if the dealer wants to offer these products or services without risking serious legal liability, it will be up to the dealer, or the dealer's lawyer, to do the legal due diligence on these offerings. Time for another golf date with your friendly local lawyer?

Trade Ya!

March 2008

By Emily Marlow Beck

It's nearly springtime where I live, and my husband and I just got our season tickets for our local major league baseball team. While I should be getting psyched for the crack of the bat and stadium dogs, my mind is stuck on one thing—trades.

No, I'm not thinking about trading in that rookie Babe Ruth card for your retirement fund. I'm not even talking about trading your star southpaw for a bunch of no-names. So, what, you may ask, could possibly put my spring fever on the bench?

A couple of months ago, I saw another one of those TV

exposé programs that hammered on car dealers. According to the news story, a sales manager was charged with theft after he refused to return a customer's trade-in vehicle to her. A jury convicted the sales manager and ordered him to pay a $400 fine (plus court costs), to perform community service in lieu of three days in jail, and to write a letter of apology to "his victim."

According to the news story, a customer went to the sales lot, filled out a credit application, handed over the keys to her car to be appraised, and spoke to the salesperson "for several hours." But, when the customer went to the finance office, the customer decided not to buy the new vehicle. According to the testimony of the customer, moments later the sales manager walked in, and then "he got very irate and threw up his hands, no, no, it's a done deal, it's a done deal, no, no, no, there's no going back, it's a done deal." When she asked for her trade-in back so that she could drive home, the sales manager allegedly responded, "Your car is not even here," and then added, "I don't care [how you get home], that's your problem, get home any way you can, your car is gone."

I don't even know where to begin with this one. If the alleged facts are true, this dealership (particularly the sales manager) may have some pretty big problems and may need to work on its "people skills" (or, maybe just sit down and have a few cold ones).

But, for me, the sales manager's actions raise the issue: Do you know your dealership's obligations with respect to trade-in vehicles?

For starters, are you required to hold the vehicle for a certain number of days before you can sell it? If you do sell it, do you have to account for the value of the trade-in to the customer if the transaction unwinds? If you do have to account for this value, may you deduct any storage and repair costs?

Sometimes, these obligations are spelled out under state law. Other times, the forms and paperwork you use at your dealership (particularly your buyers order or spot delivery agreement) will dictate your obligations with respect to trade-in vehicles. (When was the last time you read that stuff, anyway?) Finally, regardless of whether your state laws or your documents address this issue, you still need to worry about those unfair and deceptive trade practice laws. If you are careful, you will run the trade-in policies by your friendly local lawyer, too.

Once you figure out what your trade-in practices are, you need to train everyone who deals with customers so that they know the policy, too. You should also consider prominently posting your policy at the dealership and on your website so that customers will be informed about your practices as well.

So, whattaya say? If you buckle down on your trade-in practices now, just maybe you'll give yourself the gift of an AG-free 2008!

And I can relax and enjoy baseball.

The View From the Other Side of the Table

March 2008

By Thomas B. Hudson

Gotbucks, LLP, is a venture capital outfit. It was formed, just recently, to find worthwhile ways to employ capital in the vehicle retailing sector. It has done its marketing and is beginning to get dealer applicants for various sorts of potential investments.

Slipshod Motors, Inc., has responded to Gotbucks by calling its sales rep, and the sales rep has sent out Gotbucks' application materials and a list of documents that Gotbucks wants to see and has scheduled an interview between Slipshod and Gotbucks.

Slipshod shows up for the interview, as scheduled, and has

brought along some of the requested documents. Slipshod was able to produce a copy of the form of retail installment sales contract that it uses. Unfortunately, it is a form from a local business stationery firm that Slipshod has used for years because the firm's prices are the cheapest in town, and it doesn't comply with federal or state law.

Slipshod's buyers order is, if anything, worse than its retail installment sales contract. It is a "cut-and-paste" effort that started life 10 years ago as a buyers order that came from another dealership, but has had so much stuff grafted onto it over the years that it is internally inconsistent and full of problems.

When Slipshod was asked to produce its Privacy Policy, its Privacy Safeguarding Procedures, and its OFAC procedures, Slipshod's president's answer was, "Say what?"

When asked to describe the training that its salespeople received, Slipshod could only point to a two-year-old sales training course.

Finally, when asked for copies of all of Slipshod's lawyer's legal opinions blessing its forms and operations, Slipshod came up empty.

Square Corners Motors, Inc., also in need of capital and liquidity, likewise responded to the sales pitch of Gotbucks. That's about all that Square Corners had in common with Slipshod, though.

Square Corners produced copies of three different forms of retail installment sales contracts that it regularly uses to enter into credit sales with customers. The dealership also produced legal opinions, updated periodically, in which Square Corners' lawyers OKed the forms. To top it off, Square Corners described the procedure it uses to assure that the versions of the forms it uses are the most recent versions.

Square Corners' buyers order is one that was produced by

the state association. It's a recent document, but Square Corners has had it reviewed by counsel anyway and produces the lawyer's opinion addressing the form.

Square Corners produced training records for its F&I personnel, who had all been certified by the Association of Finance and Insurance Professionals. Square Corners also described its ongoing compliance-training program.

Not only does Square Corners have a Privacy Policy, a Safeguarding Policy, and an OFAC Procedures Manual, it had implemented a first draft version of a Red Flag Policy, months before the FTC's Red Flag Regulation became final. Square Corners also has named a Privacy Officer, as required by federal law, and has named that same person as its compliance officer.

To top it off, Square Corners has had a dealership compliance audit and has scheduled periodic updates of the audit. It also has obtained its lawyer's opinion that all of its forms, policies, and procedures are in compliance with applicable federal and state law.

Now, pretend for a moment that you are sitting not on the dealer's side of the table, but on Gotbucks' side. If you are an investor thinking about putting money into one of these two dealerships or buying contracts from them, which one are you going to choose?

Wouldn't it be nice if everything in life were this easy?

Death and Taxes
April 2008
By Emily Marlow Beck

Nobody likes tax season. Nobody, of course, except maybe special finance and buy-here, pay-here dealers. If you're like many special finance or buy-here, pay-here dealers, you know that tax season could mean big profits. All those tax refund checks make some pretty juicy down payments and can go a long way toward turning your inventory.

But, in the ultimate quest to increase down payments and sales volume, there are a few things you should keep in mind.

Underwriting. With images of all those tax refund checks dancing in your head, it's easy to get carried away and toss out sound underwriting principles. Now, I don't pretend to know anything about how to underwrite deals to get the "sweet spot" for your buy-here, pay-here portfolio, and I don't know squat about underwriting for profitability. But, I do know a thing or two about underwriting to avoid lawsuits. I also know that one of the potential side effects of the so-called "subprime mortgage crisis" is that regulators and plaintiffs' lawyers will be critical of creditors that put borrowers on the hook for more debt than the borrower can afford.

If you qualify customers based purely on down payment, you'll have to keep yourself in check to make sure that the customers can realistically afford to make the payments for the car you put them in. For example, a hefty tax refund might help a Dodge Neon customer qualify for a Lincoln Navigator, even though the customer doesn't have the income stream to realistically make payments on the Navigator. It might be worth keeping an eye on your default rates during tax season to see if you are at increased risk of accusations that your underwriting practices are predatory.

Tax Preparation Services. Often, we hear of dealerships that offer point of sale tax preparation services during tax time. These programs vary (and, accordingly, the regulatory restrictions may vary too), but they usually involve allowing the dealer to calculate a customer's tax refund based on information provided by the customer. The dealer then uses the tax refund as a down payment for the purchase of a new vehicle.

Like all programs marketed to car dealers, some of these programs are sound and some are not. There are some basic questions you need to ask yourself before you jump on board with any particular program.

For starters, if you sell your contracts to a third-party finance company, you'll need to check and make sure that offering these programs would not violate any dealer agreements you have in place with these finance companies. For example, some of these agreements will require the dealer to warrant to the finance company that any down payment reported on the contract represents an amount actually received by the dealer in cash. To the extent the down payment is comprised, in full or in part, of an assignment of loan proceeds, you might be in violation of your dealer agreement. In most instances, this will mean that you might well have to repurchase the paper.

Further, these sorts of programs are not necessarily exempt from the other "nuts and bolts" laws and regulations that govern the credit sales of your vehicles. For example, does your state have a "single document rule" that requires all credit terms to be included in a single document? Does state law require a particular license to originate or broker a refund anticipation loan? How do you disclose the refund on the installment contract? What happens when the refund doesn't come back as expected? You'll want to think through the answers to these questions before you jump in, hook, line, and sinker.

The increased volume you experience during tax season may give you the shot in the arm you need to carry you into the summer months. But, in all the excitement, you'll need to make sure you don't lose sight of compliance basics. After all, the side effects of some mishaps can linger long after Uncle Sam and the taxman have packed up and moved on.

What's That Smell?

May 2008

By Emily Marlow Beck

This article isn't for the faint of heart or the weak of stomach.

I discovered something at my desk today that made me queasy. It wasn't a plaintiff's brief for a class action lawsuit. It wasn't a new AG complaint bashing a dealer's "over the line" mail piece. It wasn't even another lame article written by a "car guy turned whistleblower" about the "latest and greatest" car dealer tricks.

Nope. Not today. Today's surprise was a three-month-old salad, tightly sealed in Tupperware and hidden away in my desk drawer. (What were you expecting?) Strangely, while the container remained surprisingly odorless, its contents would have been the pride of any second grader's science project. I quickly and embarrassingly tossed it out (clearly, along with my feminine mystique).

I could credit this little homemade batch of penicillin to time spent out of the office on business travel. I could blame it on time spent out of the office recovering from the flu. But, truth be told, the real reason for the grotesque disaster is that I thought I had taken care of that dish already.

Now, what does this have to do with dealership compliance? Well, before you think my train of thought has derailed, stay tuned for the point.

Most dealerships have "sleeper issues"—things going on right under the dealer's nose that the dealer doesn't notice (or ignores) until everything goes bad. These are things that the dealer thought he took care of, or didn't notice when implementation and procedures fell by the wayside. In most of these cases, the source of the stench results from the dealership's failure to communicate its expectations to the sales team and collectors.

I'm fortunate that many of our clients keep themselves informed about compliance issues. In fact, one dealership client I visited retained all of Tom Hudson's articles "three-hole punched" and in binders in his office. (This was clearly back in the "dark ages" before Tom published his first *CARLAW*® book!) But, our most well-informed clients can often be the most shocked to learn about the compliance issues festering in their dealership.

Of all my favorite compliance review stories, one involved a dealer who assured me that it was impossible for his employees to be payment packing because his dealership had purchased a menu software program. But, when I met with the dealership's employees in the finance office, they told me that they weren't using the menu software the dealer bought. In the words of one employee, "Yeah, I know that we're supposed to be using that stuff, but it's really not my style."

Another dealer client I visited was aware that the Federal Trade Commission had been cracking down on companies and individuals for allegedly violating the requirements of the National Do Not Call Registry (by late 2007, the actions had already resulted in six settlements imposing nearly $7.7 million in civil penalties). This same dealer told me that his dealership didn't need a Do Not Call policy because his employees "don't make cold calls." Imagine his surprise when he learned that his sales employees routinely try to generate business by calling and soliciting names and numbers provided as "credit references" on customer applications.

I also recall meeting with a dealer engaged in the lease-here, pay-here business who had done his homework in structuring his lease transactions to comply with federal and state leasing and tax laws. In the process, the dealership didn't train its employees on the proper way to "sell" a lease to consumers. When I spoke to collectors at that dealership, I learned that the collectors frequently called customers who believed they had purchased a new vehicle and didn't know they had, in fact, leased a car. In the words of the collectors, this mistake happened most often "with the senior citizens." Yikes!

So, here's the question for you: What sleeper issues are lying in wait at your dealership? Maybe it's time you go and do a little digging.

Consider "spot checking" your deal jackets to make sure your employees are completing forms correctly and retaining records properly. Consider compliance audits or mystery shoppers. Revisit your written policies to make sure they reflect your current operations, and then incorporate the revised policies into your new hire and periodic employee training. Review and update your compliance training efforts. Keep records of all your training and compliance efforts. Roll up your sleeves and dig in, and the odds improve that you stumble upon those unsavory problem areas before a consumer lawyer or AG does!

Ahh! Now, breathe in that fresh air!

An Ill Wind

May 2008
By Thomas B. Hudson

An ancient saying holds, "It's an ill wind that blows no one good." It is generally thought to mean that regardless of how bad events are, often there's a silver lining for at least some of us.

That thought crossed my mind recently as I was listening to a couple of investment types talking on the radio about the mortgage mess. One of them made a pretty good point—one that I think may apply to buy-here, pay-here operations. His point was that the incentives in the mortgage system, or the lack of them, led in a predictable way to the wave of defaults and delinquencies.

He noted that the way mortgages have been made in the recent past had people—brokers—creating mortgages and selling them to banks and other financial institutions, which, in turn, either sell them to other entities or "securitize" them. When the mortgages are securitized, they lend themselves to being sliced and diced into various instruments that aren't even mortgages, but that are "derivatives" of mortgages. At the end of the day, the person who is owed money under the mortgage or derivative is far, far removed from the person making the underwriting decision. He suggested that if the entities doing the underwriting had intended to keep the mortgages and collect them, their incentives and their underwriting standards would have been vastly different.

That gave me an "aha!" moment. I thought, "I know an industry where the debt obligations stay with the originator. It's called the buy-here, pay-here industry."

Now, I'm not saying that buy-here, pay-here dealers won't suffer in a number of ways because of the mortgage meltdown. I am saying, though, that if ever the incentives were in the right place for creditors to get paid in this or any other market, they are in the right place for buy-here, pay-here dealers.

Among the ill effects buy-here, pay-here dealers could feel from the credit crunch would be a tightening of credit, as many lenders to the industry see liquidity problems of their own. I have no doubt that delinquencies and repossessions will creep up for buy-here, pay-here dealers as well, and perhaps significantly, just not to the degree that we're seeing on the housing side.

Another problem that the housing mess will create for dealers will come from the legislative backlash that we will see as our elected representatives fall all over each other in their attempts to "fix" the housing problems. In their attempts to address housing woes, legislatures may propose fixes that are so broad that they impact vehicle financing as well.

Finally, the plaintiffs' lawyers have already smelled the blood in the water and are filing lawsuits against the mortgage brokers and lenders as fast as the trees can be chopped down to make the paper for the complaints they are filing.

They will be using many of the arguments that have been developed over the years for suing creditors, but they will be coming up with new theories that, in many cases, can be used to sue subprime car creditors. One of my personal favorites is that the broker/initial lender made the borrower a loan that was "unsuitable" for the borrower. (This is the "The devil made me do it" claim, and we are already seeing that one on the car side.)

But, after all this digression, I need to get back to the title of this article because there is some good news in all the housing bad news. That comes from the fact that legislators, regulators, and plaintiffs' lawyers have only so much time and only so many resources.

If their time and their treasure are devoted to going after housing creditors, they will have less time to devote to the sorts of mischief that they might otherwise be visiting on car dealers and finance companies.

So, we get at least a little good out of this ill wind.

Why Be Nice? Millions of Reasons

May 2008

By Thomas B. Hudson

A recent article in the *Washington Post* caught my eye. The title of the article was "Foreign Courts Wary of U.S. Punitive Damages."

The article recounted the experience of an Alabama woman whose son was killed when he was thrown from his motorcycle and the chinstrap of his helmet failed. An Alabama court awarded her $1 million, at least part of which (and probably most of which) consisted of punitive damages.

When the helmet manufacturer, an Italian company, refused to pay, the mother sued the company in an Italian court to force it to do so. The matter worked its way to the Italian Supreme Court, which refused to enforce the Alabama court judgment on the grounds that the concept of punitive damages was offensive to Italian notions of justice. The Italian court did not comment on the practice of certain Roman emperors feeding human beings to lions, but I digress.

The court's revulsion to the idea of punitive damages led me to think about other ways that the U.S. judicial system differs from those in other countries, and what those differences mean to car dealers.

In some countries, a person who brings a lawsuit is required to pay the defendant's legal expenses, including attorneys' fees, if the suit is not successful. The prospect of perhaps having to pony up such amounts, which in the United States sometimes run to six figures in even fairly straightforward cases, imposes a considerable damper on cases that don't have much merit.

I am told that in Canada, class action lawsuits are quite rare. A Canadian attorney friend also pointed out that a Canadian jury's idea of punitive damages might be $5,000.

These civilized approaches to the dispensation of justice are quite a contrast to the U.S. system. Here, in the good ol' USA, plaintiffs can bring even very flimsy suits without worrying about the huge legal fees that the defendant may have to incur in defending a frivolous claim.

Plaintiffs are actually encouraged to sue dealers and finance companies by the many federal and state laws that provide that a prevailing plaintiff is entitled to court costs and attorneys' fees. Many state laws that prohibit unfair and deceptive acts and practices go even further and provide that the successful plaintiff may recover some multiple of (double or triple) his or her actual damages.

And finally, there is the specter of punitive damages. The U.S. Supreme Court has tried to rein in freewheeling juries that make some plaintiffs lottery winners by imposing a cap on punitive damages measured as a multiple of the plaintiff's actual damages. Even so, there's still plenty of room for a defendant, and particularly a car dealer defendant, to get seriously whacked with a punitive damages award.

A lawyer friend of mine has frequently said that there are really no Truth in Lending lawsuits. He says that customers with car problems that are not resolved by dealers end up going to lawyers who assert every claim the lawyer can think of, and that includes all the disclosure, fraud, and discrimination claims provided by the various state and federal consumer protection laws.

These laws provide for consumer recoveries, but, as we've often pointed out, the plaintiffs' attorneys' fee awards will often dwarf any actual damages awarded by the court. And that's before the jury gets to an award of punitive damages. And before the dealer pays his or her own lawyers.

Car dealers, and particularly dealers in the subprime space, deal with people who have little bargaining power and who are desperate for wheels. While most dealers we know are honest, ethical businesspeople, there are still too many dealers who use these customers' weaknesses as an opportunity to engage in predatory practices. When this sort of bad treatment is aired before a jury, the "ca-ching" you hear is the sound of punitive damages dollars.

Where does all this take us? Dealers need to be alert to customer complaints, even relatively minor ones, and they need to address them fairly and promptly. Doing so isn't only good business—it is one of the best forms of risk management. It is also a worthwhile practice to train the dealership's representatives to expect that everything they say to a customer will be repeated in court.

A Compliance Program That Won't Break the Bank
June 2008
By Thomas B. Hudson

Sales and profits down? Business off? Guess who doesn't care?

Attorneys General and plaintiffs' lawyers, that's who.

Car dealers are more and more frequently the targets of lawsuits and enforcement actions.

Why? Because most of them are very easy targets. The legal requirements imposed on car dealers are staggering.

Consider the message I got from a dealership lawyer a couple of days ago. He asked whether I had a list of all the federal laws that applied to dealer car sales, lease, and financing transactions. Here's my quick rundown of some of the federal laws and regulations that came to mind:

- The Truth in Lending Act and Federal Reserve Board Regulation Z

- The Consumer Leasing Act and Federal Reserve Board Regulation M
- The Equal Credit Opportunity Act and Federal Reserve Board Regulation B
- The Fair Credit Reporting Act (including the new Red Flag Rules)
- The Federal Trade Commission's Used Car Rule
- The FTC's Preservation of Consumer Claims and Defenses Trade Regulation Rule
- The FTC's Credit Practices Regulation
- The Magnuson-Moss Warranty Act
- The Federal Odometer Act
- The Gramm-Leach-Bliley Act and the FTC's Privacy Regulations (including the Safeguarding Rule)
- The Internal Revenue Service's Cash Reporting Rules
- The Treasury Department's Office of Foreign Assets Control (OFAC) Specially Designated Persons (Bad Guy) List Requirements
- The USA PATRIOT Act
- The FTC's Do Not Call and Do Not E-mail Rules
- The Federal Communication Commission's Telephone Rules

That's a list of federal laws, mind you, and it isn't complete. However, it does illustrate my point. Many state laws also apply to dealers' activities.

All of these laws and regulations have some degree of impact on a dealership's forms and procedures. How many dealers are aware of them all? My bet is not many.

Large dealer groups and dealerships can afford the substantial costs involved in trying to comply with this maze and keep their people current and trained regarding the requirements imposed on the dealership, but smaller dealers often simply lack the resources to do so. What are such dealers to do?

It seems to me that the choice is either to throw in the compliance towel, try to fly under the radar and hope for the best, or try to come up with some compliance solutions that don't cost an arm, a leg, and a first-born child.

I've given some thought about how to have a compliance program that doesn't break the bank. Here's what I've come up with:

1. Name a Compliance Officer. This person can, and probably should, be your Privacy Officer (the requirement for dealers to name a Privacy Officer has been around for several years). This person should report to the highest person in the dealership organization.

2. Send the Compliance Officer to the Association of Finance and Insurance Professionals (or other such organization) for F&I training and certification. The Compliance Officer can then train others in the dealership.

3. The Compliance Officer will need some resources. Some worthwhile ones will be provided by AFIP as part of its training program. Others should include at least the following (all of which are free or very inexpensive):

- *Understanding Vehicle Finance*—a pamphlet available from the websites of the National Automobile Dealers Association (NADA) or the American Financial Services Association (AFSA). It's free and isn't copyrighted. Download and print.
- The FTC website—there is a treasure trove of information on this site, including materials on advertising, the Used Car Rule, warranties, and more. Free.
- State consumer protection agency and Attorney General websites—some of these are good, some not so helpful, but the Compliance Officer needs to check them out. Free.

- State dealer associations—these run the gamut from great to awful. Many have compiled very helpful materials on topics like advertising that can make the Compliance Officer's job much easier. You will probably have to join the association to get beyond a firewall. Free if you are already a member.

- National dealer associations—the ones that spring immediately to mind are NADA and the National Independent Auto Dealers Association (NIADA). NADA, for example, offers dealer guides on a number of subjects such as adverse action notices and the FTC's safeguarding requirements. The guides are available to members and to nonmembers at a slightly higher price. Even for nonmembers, the guides cost less than $100, and they are well worth it.

- Professional consultants and trainers—there are some good ones out there. You should get references, and you should be very nosy about the source of the legal materials these folks use. These resources can be pricey, but the good ones are worth their fees.

- Vendors—here, you need to be very careful. I've seen some vendor training that is as good as it can get, and I've seen vendor training that made me reach for my 10-foot pole. Again, get references, and ask for the source of their training materials. The cost here is usually the business that the vendor hopes to get from you.

After the Compliance Officer avails himself or herself of as many of these resources as possible, he or she should begin to create written policies and procedures (note that such written programs are required by the FTC's Safeguarding Rule and the new Red Flag Rules). These need not necessarily be elaborate documents, but they do need to reflect accurately the legal requirements that the dealership faces. For that reason, the dealership's lawyer should review them, if at all possible. That won't be free.

So, there you are. If you have the money to create a comprehensive compliance program, ignore this article and go do your thing. If you don't have the long green, use this article as a recipe for a rudimentary compliance program that can be developed over time into something more comprehensive.

Compliance Atrophy

June 2008

By Emily Marlow Beck

You won't see it coming. You won't know how it got there. Then one day, when you least expect it, it will hit you right between the eyes. I'm talking about compliance atrophy. Merriam Webster defines *atrophy* as "a wasting away or progressive decline." A degeneration. And, if you're not careful, it will happen to you.

It's not enough to bring your operations into compliance. The real challenge is in keeping them that way. There's a tale I hear a little too often. It goes something like this . . .

After hearing stories from other dealers in his 20 group, Dealer gets serious about compliance and coughs up the dough to send some of his employees to get compliance training from a reputable trainer. Employees go to training and quickly learn that some of the techniques that they have used for years aren't exactly above board. In fact (Holy Smokes!), some of the techniques are flat out illegal.

Employees and Dealer have an emergency meeting, and Employees rehash everything they learned at training. Dealer is thrilled he spent this month's balloon money to send Employees to training. Dealer and Employees agree that these illegal practices must stop, and Dealer sends Employees back to their posts. Dealer feels like he dodged a bullet.

Employees reel in the questionable behavior and try their best to do things by the book. However, it becomes quickly (and readily) apparent that Employees don't have the skills they need to be both compliant and profitable. Penetration rates fall. Employee commissions fall. Employee paychecks shrink. Employees panic and go back to old habits. Noncompliance reigns supreme.

Let's face it folks—the car business has been around a lot longer than most of the laws and regulations that have crept into our industry in the last several years. To top that off, very few lawmakers have spent time on the tower or in the finance office. The result? Compliance isn't natural or intuitive. It takes work to avoid sliding back into old habits.

So, how do you keep compliance atrophy from setting in at your dealership? Here are some thoughts:

Provide the right tools. Equip your employees with the right resources to make the changes you're suggesting. Bad habits are hard to break, and, in most cases, employees will need to re-learn the way they do things. Consider compliance-minded trainers who can teach employees new techniques to close deals and increase profitability with menu sales. The good trainers will be able to help employees take the leap from the old way of doing things to the new. (How 'bout that? Make money and avoid lawsuits!)

Hold steady. Change isn't easy or quick. You'll need to make sure your employees understand that you support them in their efforts to take compliance up a notch. Support them through the short-term bumps in order to achieve long-term gain. If your employees don't feel that you support the change, they'll go back to the old way of doing things.

Put your money where your mouth is. Don't forget about compliance when establishing employee compensation plans. Too often, compensation plans are set up to reward employees who produce quantity, but not quality. If compliance is a dealership priority, the dealership should reward employees who are thorough, deliberate, and conscientious in working deals.

Now is just as good a time as any to start flexing those compliance muscles. Act fast before the atrophy sets in!

Just Because You're Paranoid Doesn't Mean They Aren't Following You

July 2008

By Thomas B. Hudson

If you are a dealer, you may take some comfort from the fact that your customers seldom get upset enough to haul you into court. That comfort disappears, though, when you find out that your customers are being encouraged to sue you.

Lawyers aren't supposed to solicit clients to sue others. It's called *barratry*. From *Black's Law Dictionary:* Barratry: Vexatious incitement to litigation, esp. by soliciting potential clients. Barratry is a crime in most jurisdictions.

I think a lot of barratry goes on in connection with suits against auto dealers. I have seen reports of instances in which lawyers use various means to identify a dealership's customers in order to rustle up new clients willing to sue the dealer.

And we've seen dealers who fight back. A couple of years ago, a West Virginia car dealer sued a law firm that wrote letters to the dealership's customers in an attempt to stir up litigation. The dealer's lawsuit was based on a common law tort theory and not on a statute.

A recent case illustrates how easy it would be for a law firm to find an army of plaintiffs to sue a particular dealer. Let's take a look.

The law firm of George, Hartz, Lundeen, Fulmer, Johnstone, King and Stevens, P.A., obtained personal information from motor vehicle registration records of 284,000 Florida residents, including Colin Thomas. Thomas sued the law firm and attorney Charles Hartz, claiming they violated the federal Driver's Privacy Protection Act by knowingly obtaining and using personal information contained in motor vehicle records.

The trial court granted summary judgment to the defendants. Because the defendants obtained the vehicle records in order to identify potential witnesses to testify in unfair and deceptive trade practices lawsuits against car dealerships, the trial court found this use to be permissible under an exception for "investigation in anticipation of litigation" (the DPPA provides 14 "permissible uses," one of which allows for the information to be used in connection with "investigation in anticipation of litigation").

The U.S. Court of Appeals for the Eleventh Circuit affirmed the trial court's grant of summary judgment to the defendants. The appeals court agreed with the lower court that Thomas bore the burden of proving that the defendants' use of the personal information was not permissible under the DPPA and that he did not satisfy this burden.

Now, in the absence of anything suggesting the contrary, I have to assume that this law firm was operating on the up-and-up and gathered this information in good faith for the purposes it described.

But, what if some scoundrel lawyers gathered this information, claiming that they were interested in finding witnesses to testify in ongoing unfair and deceptive trade practices cases, but instead were really interested in the possibility that, once contacted, these potential witnesses would decide that they would rather become plaintiffs than be witnesses? Would the fact that some of the witnesses had converted to plaintiffs be enough to convince a court that the law firm's use of the information was an improper one?

I think that a dealer challenging the scoundrel law firm's practices would have a hard time of it. As long as the law firm could assert with a straight face that it had gathered the information for the purpose of identifying witnesses, and there weren't any smoking guns around (like an ex-employee of the firm testifying that the scoundrels were lying through their teeth), I think that the scoundrels would get away with their scheme.

After all, the practice of barratry has been around at least since the 15th century.

Thomas v. George, Hartz, Lundeen, Fulmer, Johnstone, King, and Stevens, P.A., 2008 WL 1821238 (11th Cir. (S.D. Fla.) April 24, 2008).

Lease Payoffs and 10-Foot Poles
July 2008
By Thomas B. Hudson

OK, you take a trade-in vehicle, you call the lienholder for a payoff, and you do the deal based on the number the lienholder provides. What happens if it turns out the lienholder quoted you a number that is lower than the actual balance due from the customer?

Hey! No prob. You've got that great language in your buyers order where the customer agrees that if the payoff amount is wrong on the low side, he or she will pay the difference, and that if the payoff is wrong on the high side, you'll pay the difference.

So, what could go wrong? Anybody know a guy named

Murphy who has a law? Let's take a look.

Normand and Brandy Inkel bought a truck from Pride Chevrolet-Pontiac, Inc. As part of the transaction, the Inkels traded in a truck with high mileage leased from Chittenden Bank. The Inkels alleged that a salesperson at Pride told them the amount of the lease payoff allegedly received from Chittenden and also told them that they were not required to pay over-mileage charges on the trade-in. The parties' purchase agreement provided that if the amount of any lien quoted by Pride or the lienholder covering a trade-in is not correct and the amount necessary to satisfy the lien exceeds the amount calculated in the purchase agreement, then the purchaser agrees to pay any such deficiency upon demand.

So far, so good.

Pride later informed the Inkels that Chittenden understated the payoff amount and the Inkels needed to pay the difference. The Inkels refused.

Oops.

At some point, Pride offered to give the Inkels back their trade-in if they returned the new truck to Pride. The Inkels refused.

Oops again.

The Inkels sued Pride, alleging violations of the Vermont Consumer Fraud Act. The parties moved for summary judgment. The trial court granted summary judgment for Pride, and the Inkels appealed.

The Vermont Supreme Court reversed the trial court, finding summary judgment inappropriate. The Inkels argued that Pride engaged in unfair and deceptive trade practices in violation of the VCFA by demanding additional money beyond the amount due on the contract and harassing the Inkels to pay the additional money.

The court stated that practices such as hiding the negative

equity in the trade-in, failing to pay off the lien on the trade-in, lowering the agreed price of the trade-in, or otherwise raising the cost of the vehicle after the consummation of a deal are widely accepted deceptive practices. The court noted that a number of reasons existed why a dealer would want to hide negative equity in a leased trade-in, including that the consumer might back out of the deal upon realizing the amount needed to purchase a new car.

The court stated that, although the trial court found that Chittenden gave Pride an incorrect payoff amount for the Inkels' trade-in, Normand testified that a Chittenden employee told him that Pride had asked Chittenden for the wrong payoff amount (somebody needs to explain to me how you can ask for the wrong payoff amount).

Thus, the appellate court found the circumstances surrounding the transaction between the Inkels and Pride unclear and, therefore, concluded summary judgment was inappropriate. The court stated that the inclusion of a provision in the parties' agreement whereby the Inkels promised to pay any deficiency amount resulting from the use of an incorrect payoff amount in the contract did not preclude a jury from finding that consumer fraud existed under these circumstances. The court also rejected Pride's argument that the Inkels affirmed the contract by refusing to accept Pride's offer to return the trade-in after learning of the parties' mutual mistake.

All in all, a real cluster-fiasco. Are there lessons here for a dealer? As always in litigation, yes.

First, it probably isn't a real good idea to tell customers trading in a leased car that they are not required to pay over-mileage charges on the trade-in without having that in writing from the leasing company, signed in blood.

Second, when the so-called "trade-in" is a lease, get out your 10-foot pole. A lot of people think that a lease is just another form of financing. In the broadest sense, that's correct, but leasing is a different animal. For one thing, the leasing company owns the car, not the customer "trading" it in. The customer has nothing to trade, unless he exercises his or her right to purchase the car, assuming that the lease has a purchase option. If it is the end of the lease term, chances are the customer will owe excess mileage charges, excess wear and tear charges, and, perhaps, a disposition fee and even taxes assessed on the vehicle during the lease term. If the lease term has not ended, the lessee's liability will be calculated under a formula in the lease that can be so complicated that one court has referred to the language as "Byzantine." Given the varying ways that fees and charges can be due under a lease, it may be possible to ask for a "wrong" payoff.

The final lesson? The boilerplate provisions in your buyers order aren't bulletproof.

Inkel v. Pride Chevrolet-Pontiac, Inc., 2008 WL 162464 (Vt. January 18, 2008).

Group Mentality?

August 2008

By Emily Marlow Beck

I live in Washington, D.C.—the land of power, pride, and personality. I have a friend who refers to Washington, D.C., as "Hollywood for ugly people." After all, if the egos walking around this city had moderately good looks, they would have gone to claim their fame and fortune in Hollywood, and not Washington. It doesn't take too many strolls down Pennsylvania Avenue on a warm summer night (especially during summer intern season!) to know that this city has its share of folks who are at risk of being very out of touch.

The smart ones spend some time "outside the beltway," touching base with folks whose nine to five doesn't depend on which side of the aisle they sit on. They spend time making connections with real people who "tell it like it is," hold them accountable, and push them to be their best. The not-so-smart ones nurture their fiefdoms and surround themselves with "yes men" who tell them what they want to hear.

So, let me ask you this: With whom do you surround yourself? I've had the privilege of speaking to many 20 groups over the last few years, and I've always been amazed at some of the conversations that dealers and managers have had among themselves in these meetings.

I think the best conversations I've heard are stories of dealers holding each other accountable for the compliance (or lack thereof) of their operations. I've heard stories about dealers sharing new, consumer-friendly complaint resolution techniques. I've heard dealers talking about offering consumer-friendly programs, like warranties, and new and better ways to handle deficiency balances. And, I've heard dealers sharing personal stories about how they got into trouble, how they responded, and what they'd do differently next time.

While not everyone will agree with me, my experience has been that dealers who participate in 20 groups and other similar experience-sharing programs tend to be better informed about the legal climate that they live in and better equipped to deal with it.

Now, let me ask you this: Where do you get your information? Do you know about the new developments involving compliance?

Have you heard about the new Red Flag Rules and the requirement that dealers develop identity theft prevention programs?

Have you heard that, yes indeed, many state Attorneys

General are cracking down on dealership advertising? Recently, Attorneys General in Washington State, Maine, and Florida put the hammer down on some deceptive vehicle advertising practices. Washington State settled with an ad firm over deceptive auto ads, a Maine court ordered a dealer to sell vehicles at the advertised price, and Florida issued a lengthy consumer advisory about misleading car advertisements. These are just a few of the states where AGs are on the rampage—perhaps they are in your state, too?

Have you heard that plaintiffs' lawyers across the country have learned how to make a bunch of money suing merchants (yes, that means dealers) for their failure to "truncate" certain credit card receipts so that the receipts display only the last five digits of the customer's credit card number and don't show the card's expiration date? Have you checked your credit card slips?

You see, sometimes it pays to have a group mentality. There are no cave dwellers in Dealer Compliance-ville, and you can't put a price tag on good information.

Don't know where to start? If you're reading this article, you're ahead of the game! Consider joining a 20 group, if you haven't done so. Consider subscribing to compliance-oriented newsletters. Consider sending your employees for compliance training.

No matter where you live—either side of the beltway or anywhere else in the country, for that matter—it just might be time to join the herd and move forward!

Why Write It Down?

August 2008

By Thomas B. Hudson

We urge dealers to create written policies and procedures for their sales and financing operations. Why? Because at least some policies and procedures are required to be in writing; written procedures can impose needed discipline; written policies and procedures are better than ones made up on the spur of the moment; and people are people, memories are fallible, and dealers get sued.

Sometimes it's required. The federal privacy laws and regulations require that dealers have written safeguarding policies. Even though these requirements have been in existence since before the invention of fire, I'm still flabbergasted at the number of dealers we see who haven't complied with these requirements.

The new federal Red Flag Rules will require dealers to have a written identity theft prevention policy. If the level of dealer compliance with the Red Flag requirement is as low as it has been so far with the privacy requirement, there will be a substantial number of dealers out of compliance for the next few years.

Do it the same way, every time. Written policies and procedures impose a discipline on the dealership's activities and prevent problems. We saw a court opinion not long ago about a dealership employee who had stolen the identities of several of the dealership's customers and had applied for credit using the stolen information. The dealership had hired the guy only a couple of weeks before and guess what? The fellow had a criminal record of defrauding people! If the dealer's hiring policies and procedures contained a checklist of things to do when hiring new employees, including running a criminal background check, this dealer would have nipped this problem in the bud. This requirement should go into the dealership's Red Flag policy as well.

The time to come up with an emergency plan is before the emergency. If a dealership is forced to sit down and think about what its policies and procedures should be (a necessary step in writing them down), it will be able to devote the necessary time and thought to its business practices instead of having to make them up on the fly in the heat of the moment. An example of this is the question we frequently receive of whether the dealership should refuse to do a deal if the customer balks at signing an arbitration agreement. Without getting into the merits of whether the dealership should or should not insist on a signed arbitration agreement, the time to determine dealership policy is not when the first customer objects. Instead, these decisions should be made, and written down, well in advance.

People are people. And occasionally a dealership finds that, despite its best efforts, it has bad apples working for it. If the Attorney General, Channel 4, or the plaintiffs' lawyers come calling, alleging that the dealership's employees have engaged in bad acts, defrauding customers, or flimflamming the dealership's banks and finance companies, the first question that will come up is whether the bad conduct involves the entire dealership or is the work of just one or two bad individuals. In other words, are they dealing with bad apples or a bad orchard?

Consider how much more easily the dealership can persuade those who need persuading that it is the apples and not the orchard if the dealership can point to written codes of conduct prohibiting the conduct in question and signed by the employees, as well as providing periodic refresher training for those employees. The policies and procedures can spell the difference between an attack on the entire dealership and the arrest of a couple of employees.

Memories are fallible. Dealers who have been involved in lawsuits often face the unpleasant prospect of having to give depositions or testimony in court about transactions with their customers. Customers are at a distinct advantage here because a customer likely has had only one car buying experience in the last couple of years, while a dealership may have had hundreds.

When it comes to proving or disproving whether a particular document was placed before the customer or included in the deal jacket, the dealership's representative is unlikely to have a specific recollection of a particular transaction and may be unable to contradict the customer's testimony. If, though, the dealership's written policies and procedures spell out the dealership's requirements for documenting a transaction, the dealership's representative can testify that, in closing deals, he or she follows the dealership's written requirements.

Dealers get sued. And when they are, those dealerships with written policies and procedures will do better than those without. If your dealership doesn't have written policies and procedures, you should create them. When you do, be sure to involve your attorney and, if you can, your insurer.

After they are created, DO NOT three-hole punch them, throw them in a notebook, and stick them on your office shelf. Use them to train and periodically re-train all your employees. And remember that your policies and procedures need periodic review as laws and regulations, business practices, technology, and everything else in the dealership environment changes.

Unintended Consequences

September 2008

By Thomas B. Hudson

My wife is fond of telling a story about time travelers. Before the time travelers are permitted to strap themselves into the time machine, they are first given a lecture, the gist of which is, "When you go back in time, you must not change anything that you see, lest that change have unintended consequences in the future. Furthermore, there are no changes that are too small to matter." Of course, one of the time travelers travels back in time several eons, and when he is outside the time machine, he steps on a butterfly. When he returns to the present, he notices several changes—some minor, some profound.

That tale comes to mind when I read the trade press and see the following:

- Finance companies exiting the business of buying contracts from dealers
- Leasing companies bailing out of leasing altogether
- Companies that sell GAP increasing their premiums
- Driving in the United States off 3% in terms of mileage, with anecdotal evidence that speeds have decreased
- Hybrids and "plug-in" electric cars are touted as the answer

The mortgage mess has spilled over into the car arena. The credit markets appear to be temporarily (we hope) shell shocked and reluctant to assume any risk. Finance companies that lived on the securitization model can't find people willing to provide the liquidity that is their lifeblood. Others won't be buying as deeply. Dealers may well be tempted to assist customers in fabricating evidence of creditworthiness in order to get deals "bought" by the more selective buyers.

The shock of oil pushing $150 a barrel has put the value of big cars, trucks, and SUVs in freefall. The companies that have leased those vehicles now find themselves facing huge potential losses as those gas hawgs roll off lease. The consumers who have leased the big vehicles find themselves in the enviable position of not incurring the losses that those who purchased identical vehicles will now face.

Companies that sell GAP protection for a car buyer for any shortfall between the amount owed on the vehicle and the amount the vehicle is worth when it is totaled are scrambling to try to figure out how to pay claims when the GAP widens for the big vehicles. I suppose that some of those potential losses might be made up when gas sippers are worth more than projected.

Companies whose products, prices, and profits are predicated on assumptions about vehicle mileage or the likelihood of vehicle accidents—providers of service contracts and insurance companies come to mind—are likely to be chuckling all the way to the bank if vehicle use and vehicle speeds continue to be depressed.

The hybrids and the yet-to-be-seen mass production plug-in electric cars may well bring smiles to the faces of those early adopters who get a thrill when they whirr by gas stations, but those smiles may well turn to frowns when those batteries finally give up the ghost, leaving them with a battery bill that might equal the value of their cars.

What does all this have to do with legal stuff, you ask?

Well, all of the relationships described involve legal arrangements of some sort, and all of those arrangements anticipate certain payments and certain returns on behalf of those participating in the arrangements. When contracting parties fail to get the benefit of the bargains they have struck, the resulting disappointments can work their way into the courts.

And there's no telling what the consequences of that will be.

Why Conference?

October 2008

By Thomas B. Hudson

By my count, there are approximately seven and a half million conferences for car dealerships scheduled for the next 12 months. You can't attend all of them, so how do you decide which ones to go to?

If you go to conferences primarily to play golf, the answer's easy. Attend the one that is in the city with the best golf courses.

If you go to conferences to get better at what you do and to improve your dealership, don't be a vegetarian—go for the meat! Look over the programs of the competing conference sponsors and see who is presenting and on what topics. It's just a personal preference, but I don't need to hear political analysis, patriotic speeches, or lessons on how to improve my memory at a car conference. I want to hear about the car business. Some folks who put these conferences together are a lot better at including serious and focused topics than are others.

Don't expect every presentation at the conference to be fascinating, interesting, and current. In my experience, most conferences will have a couple of clunker presentations. While speakers who are vendors can give really great presentations, the worst speakers I've ever seen are the vendors who give you a 30-minute or hour-long infomercial on their products or services. Use that time to check out the pool or spa.

You're paying to go to the conference, so you have a right to expect value for your money. Ask around and find out who has attended conferences put on by the organizer of the one you are considering. Find out whether those previous attendees thought the presentations were worthwhile or not. Ask the sponsor of the conference if there are speaker ratings available and if they would be willing to share those with you. Think hard about attending a conference sponsored by an organization with no conference track record. A newbie conference sponsor can hit a home run the first time at bat, but that isn't easy to do. Generally speaking, veteran conference promoters do a better job.

Once you sign up, make it a point actually to attend the sessions. I've been to conferences where it seems that most of the attendees have come for the golf, the gambling, or some other nonconference attraction. You can't take back much to your dealership if you aren't in the sessions.

When there aren't presentations, you should spend time in the exhibit hall. The companies represented in the exhibit hall have all spent pretty serious money to get themselves in front of you, which indicates that at least they believe they have something to offer you.

Most do, but take your salt shaker with you because you will need to take what some of the vendors tell you with a few grains of salt. Especially when the vendors are offering things for you to sell to your customers, you need to put on your "due diligence" hat and start asking questions.

Most vendors will not object at all to a few pointed questions aimed at determining whether the vendor has done its homework in creating a legally compliant product or service. Reputable vendors should be able to guide you through the steps that they have taken to assure compliance and show you proof of those steps, if asked.

We know of one vendor offering a franchise-type product that has been saying for several years that lawyers have reviewed its national program and that it passes muster in every state. We have encouraged our dealer clients who have shown interest in the program to ask the vendor for copies of the lawyers' opinion letters, which the vendor always promises to deliver but never does.

But I have digressed. Most vendors have valuable services and programs for the attending dealers, and you will almost certainly learn a lot in the exhibit hall.

Plus, if you happen to pick a conference that we've chosen and you stop by our booth, we'll chew the legal fat with you!

Can You Make the Cut When Money Gets Short?

October 2008

By Thomas B. Hudson

I awoke this morning to the news that a major dealership group had filed for bankruptcy, the victim, apparently, of a decision that its lender made to stop lending it money. The particular dealership involved in this headline was one that had been in regulatory hot water for years, as Attorneys General on many occasions found fault with the dealership group's various sales and financing practices.

The various AG claims were all settled with the dealership group admitting no fault. So, there's no way to know from the various charges leveled against the group whether it was actually involved in bad practices. Perhaps the group ran a spotless operation, and the AGs were pursuing their various operations unfairly. Or perhaps not.

In any event, the thought crossed my mind that as money gets tight, and as banks and finance companies decide to cut back on their activities, they will need to use some criteria to determine which dealers they will continue to finance and which ones they will cut off. Note that there is no assertion here that this particular dealership group lost its financing for any particular reason—the event just got me thinking.

If I were in the decision-making chair for the bank or finance company, and the choice of which dealers I would continue to finance came up, I believe I'd take a look at the way the dealership behaved.

- First, I'd consider how well the dealership had honored its dealer agreements with my institution. For example, if I've been buying retail installment contracts from this dealer, I'd evaluate whether the deals have been "clean," with complete deal jackets, and whether the dealer has been responsive to requests to fix problems, even when those requests involve the repurchase of a troubled deal.

- Second, if I'm floor-planning the dealership, I'd try to remember how many times I have not been able to find cars I've financed on the dealer's lot and, when I couldn't locate them, how helpful the dealer was in resolving my questions.

- Finally, I'd want to know if the dealership treats its customers legally and ethically. If the dealership has been thrown out of the Better Business Bureau because of its questionable practices, is regularly featured on those hidden camera consumer protection "gotcha" features, and has been called on the carpet by state regulatory authorities year after year after year, I'd be thinking, "Do I want to buy the paper that this dealer is producing?"

Maybe life won't work out this way, but I've got to think that dealers who "do it right," treating their customers and their finance sources well and staying out of hot water with their state sales and credit cops, are going to get the nod over ones who don't.

Another reason to run a legally and ethically compliant shop—survival!

Compliance Standards of Learning!

October 2008

By Emily Marlow Beck

"No more pencils. No more books. No more teachers' dirty looks!" You know how the old song goes and maybe you are glad those school days are behind you.

But, don't get too cheery. Back where I grew up, we had these things called "Standards of Learning" tests or SOLs. My memory is a little fuzzy on the details, but I remember that the SOLs tested us on the basic things that some bureaucrats in the state education department determined we should know for our appropriate age group. In other words, we passed the minimum standards of learning deemed essential to us and to our peers. We spent an awful lot of time preparing for them. After all, if we failed, it was Summer School City! (Not to mention we were in big trouble!)

Sometimes I think we should adopt a similar approach when it comes to dealership compliance. There are some things that all dealers simply should know. You know—the basics.

What are these things, you may ask? Well, you know what they say about opinions, but I have them—definite opinions about what I believe all dealers should know. So, sharpen your pencils! And, whip out your protractor! (OK, so you might not need your protractor). It's time to take some notes!

Yes, Mr. Dealer, you are a creditor! If you've been reading Tom Hudson's articles for any length of time now, you know that dealers typically sell cars on credit to buyers, and these transactions are called retail installment sales, with the dealer as the creditor. Not loans. Not lenders. 'Nuff said.

Don't get your legal advice from your marketing company. Advertising is a hot issue in Dealer Compliance-ville. (Think white, steamy hot). We've read lots of cases about dealers getting in trouble after buying a marketing company's ad program. I've never read cases about the marketing company stepping in to take the bullet when the regulators and plaintiffs' lawyers come knocking at the dealership door.

When it comes to compliance, the devil is in the details. When developing a compliance program, don't ever underestimate the ability of plaintiffs' lawyers to trip dealers and other creditors up on technical violations of the law. Some examples? Think about adverse action, firm offers of credit, and, heaven forbid, even truncation cases. If you think the details don't matter, think again.

Adopt consumer friendly policies (i.e., think "conflict avoidance"!). Most lawsuits against dealers start with a customer who feels like he or she got a raw deal. Imagine how much dealers could save in legal fees if they just found a way to keep the customer out of the comforting arms of the plaintiffs' lawyer or Attorney General! And remember that the first check you get a chance to write to settle a customer complaint will be the one with the fewest zeroes.

This ain't your granddaddy's dealership. My, my, my, times have changed. The dealership practices that were commonplace just a decade ago could put a dealer out of business today, and the thoughts of what tomorrow might bring are frightening! The dealers who are able to survive in this brave new world of dealer compliance will be the ones that find a way to adapt to changes. And, the ones who don't? Well, you know what happened to the dinosaurs, right?

So, back to those school days . . . yes, they've changed. But students today still learn the basic ABCs, and car dealers are no different. The smart ones memorize the compliance basics. That way, passing dealership SOLs for success is a cinch.

So, What's NAAG-ing You?

December 2008

By Emily Marlow Beck

You didn't know you had a lot in common with your local Attorney General, did you? Just think about it. You're both very driven and ambitious (we don't call them "AGs," or "Aspiring Governors" for nothin', ya know). You both care about your public image. And neither of you is a stranger to phone calls from angry customers. (OK, so that was a joke . . . sort of!)

One key similarity between dealers and AGs is that ever so often, AGs, like dealers, travel far and wide to hang out with their industry brethren and compare notes; that is, successes, failures, trials, and tribulations. Dealers call these groups "20 groups." AGs call this group the National Association of Attorneys General or (the appropriately named) NAAG.

Like a 20 group, NAAG members set goals, analyze benchmarks, and compare notes. AGs walk away from NAAG meetings with new ideas of bigger and better ways to bring claims and levy fines against all sorts of unsavory critters . . . including car dealers.

Forgive me, but I can't shake this image of a stiff-looking suit high-fiving his little pocket protector-sporting buddy, saying, "Hey, Cecil! I just busted this one store for payment packing! That's a hundred-fifty-pounder for me! What did you do last month?"

In all seriousness, we may never know what really goes on in NAAG meetings. But, we've been clued in a bit from time to time. Just last month, NAAG released its Top 10 Consumer Complaints List for 2007.

According to the NAAG website, the list of consumer complaints is a compilation of reports provided by the various AG offices nationwide.

So, what consumer complaints made the coveted NAAG list?
Drum roll, please! The winners are
1. Debt Collection
2. Auto Sales
3. Home Repair/Construction
4. Telecommunications/Slamming/Cramming
5. Automotive (General)
6. Telemarketing/Do Not Call
7. Financial/Investments
8. Retail Sales
9. Internet Goods and Services
10. Contests/Sweepstakes/Prize Promotion

According to the press release, these findings are based on a
"non-scientific survey from the top complaints" from across the
land and provide a "snapshot of trends and enforcement activities"
occurring in the states. The release also boasted that, "Attorneys
General are a leading consumer protection force in the nation and
can be found in the forefront of defending senior citizens from
telephone and mail fraud and home repair fraud, protecting
consumers from fraudulent practices as the practitioners migrate
from the 'bricks-and-mortar' to the 'online' world."

So, this "top 10" list got me thinking.

First of all, I was shocked and amazed by how many of these
top 10 items apply to the car business. I know of dealers that have
been busted doing things that could easily fall into eight of the 10
categories listed above. (For those curious folks, I've yet to see a
dealer get nailed for a home construction project, and, while I've
seen a lot of slamming and cramming in my day, the AGs seem to
use this term to refer to telecommunications abuses.)

What's also interesting is that the AG enforcement actions
against dealers in 2008 have been so reflective of the abuses
reported in 2007. Don't believe me? Those of you who have

been reading the news in 2008 will know that AGs nationwide have come down like a hammer on dealerships running "special" sweepstakes and price promotion ad programs this year. We've also read about AGs nailing dealers for everything from payment packing to failing to pay off the liens on trades.

So, what should a dealer do?

It's time to pay attention to those AG radar detectors, folks! What that means for you is that you should clean house where the AGs have indicated that they are most likely to look.

Making sales calls? How does that Do Not Call policy of yours look? Thinking about running one of those third-party marketing company "win a prize" ads? Maybe it's time to pass or pay your local dealer lawyer to give it a thorough scrub. Selling cars on the Internet? Have you and your lawyer reviewed your online sales procedures lately? Maybe it's time to pay attention to the things that the AGs are paying attention to. After all, there are some "top 10" lists you just don't want to be on!

The Nanny Commission

December 2008

By Thomas B. Hudson

A year or so ago, as the mortgage mess began to spin seriously out of control, I was asked to do an article on the topic of how the mortgage meltdown would affect the auto finance industry. At that time, before $4-plus gasoline and a steep recession, it seemed like the answer was "not much," and that's more or less what I said.

In a later article on the same topic, I got a little closer to the mark, pointing out that because of the emerging credit crisis, it might become a lot tougher for dealers to find banks and sales finance companies willing to buy the retail installment contracts the dealers were producing.

Still later, I wrote that some of the abuses that were evident in the defaulting consumer mortgages might stir legislators to re-regulate the industry to ban some of the more egregious practices.

Finally, I predicted that if the Democrats gained control of both the executive and the legislative branches of the federal government, we could expect to see legislation aimed at particularly business-friendly parts of the federal code, such as the Federal Arbitration Act.

But I didn't see this one coming.

Two Democratic congressmen have introduced bills that would create a federal agency to oversee the safety of consumer financial products, including mortgages, credit cards, car loans, and other types of credit. Car dealers will be covered by the measure because they enter into credit sales of vehicles with their customers using retail installment contracts.

Rep. Bill Delahunt (D-Mass.) and Sen. Richard Durbin (D-Ill.) recently introduced bills in the House and Senate that would establish a Consumer Credit Safety Commission (CCSC). The CCSC, as envisioned by these bills, would oversee any category of lender that extends credit to borrowers.

To this point, federal law has generally been directed at regulating the entities that offer credit, rather than credit products themselves. Content to let the states regulate actual substantive limits on credit products, the feds focused mostly on how creditors disclosed the terms and conditions of those products.

As envisioned by Delahunt and Durbin, the CCSC would focus on whether financial products offered to consumers are "safe."

The Delahunt/Durbin bill provides for a five-member bipartisan agency that would oversee mortgages, credit cards, auto loans, savings accounts, checking accounts, and other consumer credit. The CCSC would "prevent and eliminate unfair practices that lead consumers to incur unreasonable, inappropriate or excessive debt" and would focus on practices and product features that are abusive, fraudulent, deceptive, or predatory.

In addition, the CCSC would also collect data on the most harmful products, providing consumers with information to help them avoid "dangerous" financial products.

Specifically, the bill provides that the CCSC's objectives are to:

- Minimize unreasonable consumer risk associated with buying and using consumer credit. Who could argue with minimizing unreasonable risk? But do we want government telling us what level of risk is reasonable and what level of risk isn't reasonable? Will the feds prohibit the financing of negative equity?

- Prevent and eliminate unfair practices that lead consumers to incur unreasonable, inappropriate, or excessive debt, or make it difficult for consumers to escape existing debt, including practices or product features that are abusive, fraudulent, unfair, deceptive, predatory, anti-competitive, or otherwise inconsistent with consumer protection. The first part of this mandate sounds like federal underwriting. The second creates a redundant enforcement mechanism since the FTC and most states already prohibit unfair and deceptive acts and practices. And we will have a federal agency that will make it easier for consumers to escape existing debt. Is a 120% LTV "excessive" debt?

*[**Editor's note:** An LTV is an underwriting term—"loan-to-value." If you're financing a house appraised at $500,000, and the bank's maximum LTV for good credit customers is 90%, the bank will lend you $450,000.]*

- Promote practices that assist and encourage consumers to use credit responsibly, avoid excessive debt, and avoid unnecessary or excessive charges derived from or associated with credit products. The bill doesn't say whose practices it intends to promote—those of consumers or those of creditors, but here again, we'll have a federal agency determining what is "excessive" debt and "unnecessary or excessive" charges. More federal underwriting? Is a $495 doc fee an "excessive" charge?

- Ensure that credit history is maintained, reported, and used fairly and accurately. I thought that this is what the Fair Credit Reporting Act did. Will prescreening and "firm offer" mail campaigns constitute "fair" use?

- Maintain strong privacy protections for consumer credit transactions, credit history, and other personal information associated with the use of consumer credit. Don't the Gramm-Leach-Bliley Act and the FTC's privacy regulations address these concerns?

- Collect, investigate, resolve, and inform the public about consumer complaints regarding consumer credit. This would replicate duties of the FTC and state consumer protection agencies.

- Ensure a fair system of consumer dispute resolution in consumer credit. This is poorly disguised consumer advocate code for eliminating the ability of creditors to use binding arbitration agreements to reduce the risks and costs of class action lawsuits.

- Take such other steps as are reasonable to protect consumers of credit products. This catchall provides the commission members with plenty of discretionary room to make mischief.

Just how the consuming public would be protected by the

CCSC isn't spelled out at this early date. Would we have an FDA-type approach, where companies that want to offer financial products must have them approved by the CCSC? Or would it be a "crash-test" rating system, with the CCSC awarding five stars to the financial products deemed safest and no stars to the ones that would eat a hole in your wallet? The intrusiveness of the CCSC could depend a great deal on the implementation details.

The bills have been referred to committees in the House and Senate and won't be going anywhere in this session. But you can look for them to be revived next year.

Just what we need. A nanny in Washington to keep all those mean old creditors in line. Time to give a call to your trade associations and crank up those lobbying machines.

What's in YOUR Dealer Agreement?

January/February 2009
By Thomas B. Hudson

Looked at your dealer agreement with your financing sources lately, Bunkie? I'll bet you Mama's cornbread recipe that, in that agreement, your dealership makes a representation and warranty that it has complied with all state and federal laws in connection with the retail installment sales contracts that you sell to the financing source.

Did you ever wonder why such language appears in those contracts and how a financing source might use the language to make the dealer take back a contract? In times like these, after all, you can bet that financing sources will be examining the files containing defaulted contracts with a fine-toothed comb to find ways to avoid taking losses.

Well, wonder no longer. Here's a perfect example of how those provisions work.

First National Bank of Ottawa sued Rosemary Dillinger, Clifford Mounts, and Rub Chevrolet Buick Oldsmobile, Inc., in connection with the sale of a vehicle. The undisputed evidence at trial established the following facts. Mounts and Dillinger contracted to buy a truck from Rub Chevrolet. Mounts told a Rub Chevrolet employee that he made $9 per hour at his job. The employee was also told that Dillinger had income of about $1,200 per month from Social Security disability benefits. Nevertheless, the employee had Mounts and Dillinger sign a blank credit application and falsified the application by misrepresenting the annual incomes of Mounts and Dillinger as $21,600 and $30,000, respectively. The falsified application was faxed to the bank, and the bank agreed to buy the financing contract from Rub Chevrolet. Mounts and Dillinger defaulted on their monthly payments, and the truck was repossessed.

The bank filed a five-count complaint against the defendants. Count I alleged that Mounts and Dillinger breached their contract with the bank. Counts II and III alleged that Rub Chevrolet fraudulently misrepresented the incomes of Mounts and Dillinger. Counts IV and V alleged that Rub Chevrolet breached its contract with the bank, which contained a warranty by Rub Chevrolet that the sale of the vehicle "was completed in accordance with all applicable federal and state laws and regulations." Counts IV and V also alleged that the sale of the vehicle violated a section of the Illinois criminal code that provided that one commits wire fraud when one "devises or intends to devise a scheme or artifice to defraud or to obtain money or property by means of false pretenses, representations or promises" and transmits a document in furtherance of the scheme. The bank alleged that Rub Chevrolet participated in a scheme to defraud the bank of money based on its misrepresentations of the incomes of Mounts and Dillinger.

The trial court found that Mounts and Dillinger breached their contract with the bank. In finding Rub Chevrolet liable on two counts of fraudulent misrepresentation, the court found that the Rub Chevrolet employee had Mounts and Dillinger sign a blank credit application and then falsified the incomes of Mounts and Dillinger to induce the bank to buy the financing contract. However, the court found that Rub Chevrolet did not partake in a "scheme or artifice to defraud" the bank as defined in the Illinois criminal code and, therefore, did not breach its contract with the bank. The bank appealed from the judgment for Rub Chevrolet on Counts IV and V.

On appeal, the bank argued that the trial court erred when it found that Rub Chevrolet was not liable to the bank on two counts of breach of contract. Specifically, the bank argued that the trial court erred when it found that Rub Chevrolet did not partake in a scheme to defraud the bank as defined in the criminal code.

The Appellate Court of Illinois reversed the trial court's decision that Rub Chevrolet did not partake in a "scheme or artifice to defraud" the bank. The appellate court noted the undisputed evidence of falsification and faxing of the application presented at trial. The court observed that no argument was made that the employee acted outside the scope of his employment or that Rub was otherwise not liable for his conduct. The court stated that it believed that Rub Chevrolet's plan constituted a "scheme" to defraud the bank through false representations, violating Illinois law, and that by engaging in such a scheme, it breached its contractual warranty to the bank that the sale of the vehicle "was completed in accordance with all applicable federal and state laws and regulations."

This lawsuit involved only the civil claims of the bank. Facts like the ones alleged in this civil case often interest state and federal prosecutors and, when they do, can lead to criminal charges. In fact, a dealer from the Carolinas with more than 50 years of experience recently learned that lesson the hard way and has pled guilty in a plea deal that will cost him more than $1 million in penalties and will require him to stay away from his dealership for approximately two years.

You might want to post this article in the break room. Knowing the score about your dealer/financing source agreements might just keep some of your folks from having to wear those orange jumpsuits.

First National Bank of Ottawa v. Dillinger, 897 N.E.2d 358 (Ill. App. October 23, 2008).

"Best Practices" for the Use of Starter Interrupt Devices

March 2009
By Thomas B. Hudson

Like many of you, I am a member of several "listserv" groups. One of the groups consists of dealership lawyers who, lately, have been chattering about the bankruptcy of this or that manufacturer or the discontinuance of this or that brand. I tend not to have much to contribute on those subjects, but occasionally I'll see a question asking about something that I actually know something about.

That happened a few days ago when one of the listserv participants asked whether anyone had a "best practices" guide for buy-here, pay-here dealers and finance companies using starter interrupt devices. That request sparked a distant memory—I thought I had written something like that years ago.

I dug out my old article and read through it. Most of it looked current and useful, so I used it as the basis for this article.

First, a little history. Starter interrupt devices are gizmos that dealers and finance companies—primarily those operating in the subprime part of the market and frequently those doing buy-here, pay-here financing—attach to financed and leased vehicles to encourage the drivers of the vehicles to make their payments on time. The devices first came to the attention of most of us in the late 1990s when consumers sued a Detroit-area dealer, claiming that the devices stopped their cars while they were running. The suit was quickly settled.

Other suits (fewer than 10 reported cases nationwide) have been filed since then, with most dealing with how a creditor using the devices must act when the car buyer goes into bankruptcy and the "automatic stay" goes into effect. There have been no reported cases dealing with whether the devices are legal under state law ("reported cases" are federal trial court cases, some state trial court cases, and appellate cases) dealing with the devices. If cases have been filed, they have been settled, or at least have not percolated up to a court that publishes its opinions.

Meanwhile, there are signs that the use of the devices is becoming more widespread. Several companies now sell them, and their use is a frequent topic at dealer meetings and on website chat rooms. A few state authorities have issued favorable or semi-favorable opinions dealing with the devices.

Does the fact that most states have been silent concerning the devices mean that there's now a "green light" for the use of the devices as far as their legality goes? Hardly.

The devices are still very controversial. Some state authorities really dislike the devices and have issued letters saying that they are illegal to use in their states. Consumer advocates denounce the use of the devices, darkly hinting that they may be used in dangerous, illegal, or discriminatory ways.

Authorities in other states, some of whom initially opposed the use of the devices, have determined that dealers can use the devices legally if certain safeguards are met.

Our view of the devices hasn't changed a lot since we initially wrote about them years ago. We've always said, for most states, "no red light, no green light, but, instead, a flashing yellow light" should be the proper signal as far as the use of the devices is concerned. The following are a few "dos" and "don'ts" that we think are worth considering:

- Do determine before you start to use the devices what your state consumer protection authorities and/or your state AG have to say about the devices.
- Do your "due diligence" on the company selling the devices. See if the company has done its legal homework. Some of the companies have gotten themselves pretty far up the curve on legal issues, especially disclosure requirements, while others are just beginning to grapple with these topics.
- Do alert your insurance carrier that you intend to use the devices, and get confirmation in writing that risks arising from the use of the devices are covered by your policy.
- Do have the personnel who will install the devices properly trained, or use properly trained third-party installers.
- Do have the use of the devices and all paperwork dealing with the devices reviewed by your lawyer. Have him or her check that the use of the devices complies with both state and federal law.
- Do consider using an arbitration agreement in connection with your financed sales and leases. It will go a long way

toward keeping you out of class actions and will reduce your exposure to runaway jury verdicts.

- Do fully disclose to the customer that the device is on the vehicle, how the device works, emergency procedures, if any, and anything else your lawyer tells you to disclose.

- Do contact your state legislators and consumer protection authorities, and educate them on how the devices work, how you intend to use them, and how they benefit you and your customers—if you let the consumer advocates tell the story, you won't like the result. If at all possible, get the device manufacturer to assist in this process. Tell the authorities that you want to be alerted if any regulations or bills are introduced dealing with the devices.

- Do contact the folks at your state auto dealers association, and tell them that the devices are an important issue for you. Tell them that you expect them to watch for any state legislative or regulatory activity concerning the devices.

- Don't try to pass the cost of the devices along to the customers whose cars are to be equipped with the devices. Treat the cost as a general item of overhead, like the dealership's electricity bill. And on a related issue, the legal problems that arise when you require the installation of the device and then try to market it as an anti-theft system give us heartburn.

- Don't make claims about the supposed advantages of the device to the customer—this is a payment collection device, pure and simple. Tell the customer exactly what the device does. Be especially careful in those states that have so-called "credit repair" statutes—courts in some states have held that car dealers that find financing for their customers, or that offer to help the customers improve their credit ratings, fall within such statutes, triggering disclosure, licensing, and other requirements. Don't tell the customer that installing the device will improve the customer's credit rating.

- Don't discriminate in requiring the devices in a manner that violates federal or state anti-discrimination laws. If you discriminate on a "neutral" basis, such as credit scores, be alert to the possibility that, at least under the federal Equal Credit Opportunity Act (ECOA), discrimination on a neutral basis can violate the ECOA if such discrimination has the "effect" of discriminating on a protected basis.

More "dos" and "don'ts" will no doubt emerge as the use of the devices spreads. As far as the future of the devices is concerned, a lot is riding on how they are used. If dealers and finance companies use the devices with care and in connection with finance and lease programs that are fair in every sense, including the price of the car and the cost of financing, then the devices may well become more "mainstream" and acceptable by those who currently criticize them.

If, though, sharp operators (or careless ones) use the devices in ways that are overreaching or are perceived to be overreaching, look for courts and regulatory authorities to seek to curb or prohibit their use.

Washington Run Amok

April 2009

By Michael A. Benoit

In these tough economic times, the last thing your business needs is an unreasonable impediment to your ability to sell your products and services on credit. Hasn't all the bailout and stimulus spending been focused on unfreezing credit markets so folks can spend money and boost the economy? I thought so. Yet, our leaders persist in confounding their own efforts.

A recent bill introduced by Sen. Durbin (D-IL), though filled with good intentions, has the potential to devastate installment sale financing if passed in its current form. At first blush, it doesn't seem too worrisome—it simply seeks to impose a national usury cap of 36% on all consumer credit transactions. How often have you had a transaction that even came close to that percentage? I'd suspect for most of you, not often—if at all.

But, like most things that come out of Washington, the devil is in the details. Were the calculation to determine whether one hit the 36% cap identical to the current calculation for an Annual Percentage Rate (APR) under the Truth in Lending Act, only a scant number of you would give this a second thought. Unfortunately, the APR calculation is irrelevant for Sen. Durbin's bill. What matters is a new "fee and interest rate" (FAIR) calculation he proposes.

The FAIR calculation includes all of the things a current APR calculation does, plus some significant additions:

- Optional credit insurance premiums (excludable from the APR if properly disclosed) are included in the FAIR calculation.
- Currently, the cost of ancillary products (GAP coverage or debt cancellation agreements, property insurance, service contracts, theft deterrent devices, tire and wheel coverage, etc.) is excluded from the APR calculation. These amounts would all be included in the FAIR calculation.
- "All default fees" are included in the FAIR calculation. These include late fees in excess of $20 and NSF fees in excess of $15. The FAIR calculation can also include

costs of repossession and attorneys' fees and other collection costs passed on to the consumer.

Where the APR calculation is a snapshot in time, i.e., the cost of credit at a point prior to the consummation of a transaction that assumes all payments will be made in accordance with the terms of the contract, the FAIR calculation is a moving target. It will change from time to time during the life of the transaction, based on the customer's behavior. For example, a vehicle sale that includes a service contract might result in a 30% FAIR calculation at the time the customer signs the contract. But that percentage will rise every time a late charge or NSF fee is imposed on the transaction if such fees exceed the proposed caps. In addition, if the assignee of the contract adds collection and repossession costs to the amount owed after the customer defaults, all of those costs become part of the new FAIR calculation. And once the calculation exceeds 36%, the customer can sue you, and you can go to jail.

That being the case, what respectable finance company will want to buy subprime paper (or any low dollar paper for that matter) that could become subject to attack as a result of the collection charges passed on to a defaulting consumer? Who will be able to sell a service contract or credit insurance or other ancillary products requested by the consumer if the very sale of those products will put the seller at risk of both civil and criminal violations of law? What finance company will be willing to raise its rates on everyone to subsidize the costs of collection and repossession that it will no longer want to add to a defaulting customer's bill? I can't think of any.

Most everyone I know in the credit industry (including myself) hates predatory lending and lenders and supports legislation to stop them. Predatory lending is bad for consumers and, by logical extension, bad for business. Hence, Sen. Durbin's bill goes too far. It throws the baby out with the bathwater and assumes that all ancillary products and default fees are predatory. It takes the extraordinary step of assuming that consumers, even with appropriate disclosure, cannot judge for themselves the value various products and services provide them.

In essence, Sen. Durbin is buying the consumer advocates' position that risk-based pricing is bad and that everyone should pay the same for credit, no matter what. Consumer advocates would like to see folks with stellar credit pay more to subsidize the risk posed by borrowers with less than stellar credit. But we all know that won't happen. The reality is that folks with less than stellar credit—the very folks the consumer advocates are trying to protect—will be denied access to credit so the low-risk borrowers can get credit at an appropriate price. Less credit availability means less business for you (and that's good for the economy how?).

I mean, really, is it worth going to jail for selling a service contract to someone who both wants it and would benefit from it? I'd hate to say that Sen. Durbin thinks so, but his bill has me scratching my head. At the very least, he needs some education.

Time for a Compliance Self-Test?
May 2009
By Thomas B. Hudson and Catherine M. Brennan

The sky is falling. Manufacturers are going under. There's no floor plan money, and franchised dealers are going away. Nobody's buying retail installment sales contracts from you.

That's all true, but plaintiffs' lawyers, state Attorneys General, and the Federal Trade Commission aren't going away.

So, if you are one of those fortunate dealers who will be able to ride out the current storm with your business intact, you can count on having to deal with this second crowd. They've been sharpening their teeth on mortgage companies and banks, so you need to be ready.

With these developments in mind, we thought a compliance self-test might be in order. The following one is by no means complete, but it covers enough ground to give you a good idea of how vulnerable to attack your dealership might be.

If you pass with flying colors, you might be able to rest easy. If you score badly, maybe it's not too late to consider a second career.

So here we go—let's see how you do.

1. You have named a privacy officer, as required by the Gramm-Leach-Bliley Act and the FTC's Privacy Regulations.
   ❑ Yes (+2)   ❑ No (–2)

2. You have named a Compliance Officer (not required, but a really good idea).
   ❑ Yes (+2)   ❑ No (–2)

3. You have a written privacy safeguarding policy that you actually follow and keep up to date, and you have trained your employees about the policy.
   ❑ Yes (+2)   ❑ No (–2)

4. You check all of your customers against the Specially Designated Persons (SDP) list maintained by the Office of Foreign Assets Control (OFAC), and you scrub your portfolio against the OFAC list every time the SDP list changes.
   ❑ Yes (+2)   ❑ No (–2)

5. You provide adverse action notices as required by the Fair Credit Reporting Act and the Equal Credit Opportunity Act.
   ❑ Yes (+2)   ❑ No (–2)

6. You have had your application form reviewed by counsel within the last 12 months.
   ❑ Yes (+2)   ❑ No (–2)

7. You have a complying Red Flag program in place and you've named a Red Flag Program Coordinator.
   ❑ Yes (+2)   ❑ No (–2)

8. You have written policies dealing with do not call, do not fax and loan closing and collection procedures, and you periodically train your employees on these policies.
   ❑ Yes (+2)   ❑ No (–2)

9. You have your advertisements reviewed by counsel every time you change the content and periodically even when you don't.
   ❑ Yes (+2)   ❑ No (–2)

10. You have implemented a mandatory arbitration program for consumer complaints to protect against class action lawsuits and large punitive damages awards.
    ❑ Yes (+2)   ❑ No (–2)

So, how did you do?

If you scored 20 points, call up your state association and offer to teach the next course it offers on compliance.

If you scored from 10–19 points, consider yourself in need of a compliance tune-up.

From 0–9 points, you need serious repairs.

If you scored from 0 to −10, consider a complete frame-off restoration.

If you hit a perfect −20, it's time to close the old dealership and open a bait shop.

That Thing Swinging This Way Might Be a Pendulum

June 2009

By Thomas B. Hudson

I've been at this legal stuff since 1973, long enough to have seen several cycles of de-regulation, under-regulation, and over-regulation. We've enjoyed a pretty good run of de-regulation and under-regulation. That period is slamming to an abrupt halt.

If even half of the stuff presently pending in Congress passes, and if the newly energized federal agencies start cranking out regulations like I think they are going to, we're in for one of the most extensive periods of re-regulation that I've ever seen.

Consider some of the initiatives floating around Washington at the moment.

A federal usury cap? Typically, states have set the maximum rates that car dealers and sales finance companies can charge for consumer credit in general and car credit in particular. Congress now wants to get into the rate regulation game.

Maximum cap rate? A bill (S 500) has been introduced that would impose a maximum rate cap of 36% on auto credit, with a truly goofy formula for calculating interest that, unlike the APR calculation we are all familiar with, includes things like voluntarily purchased credit life insurance. It also includes amounts that are impossible to determine when credit is extended, such as late charges above a specified amount. I sense the hands of young and idealistic congressional staffers without any business or even practical experience here—they are blindly following the playbook of the more radical consumer activists without regard for the impact of such a course.

Creditors' loss? Another bill (S 257) doesn't establish a maximum rate, as such. Instead, it provides that if a creditor charges a rate in excess of a specified amount (the lesser of 36% or 15% plus the 30-year T-bill rate, a formula that would today equal 19% or so), the creditor will essentially lose its ability to present a secured claim in a bankruptcy proceeding. Same destination, different route.

Bye, bye arbitration? Many creditors, including many in the car sales, finance, and leasing business, have turned to the use of mandatory arbitration agreements as a first line of defense against professional plaintiffs' lawyers and their use of class claims as a way to "up the ante" and leverage a plain vanilla consumer complaint into a claim that a dealer must settle for big bucks if he doesn't want to "bet the dealership" that a court will render a huge award. So-called "trial lawyers" and consumer advocates have railed against arbitration more loudly with each passing year, and the din is now just about intolerable. My bet? You can kiss arbitration goodbye—Congress will either repeal or amend the Federal Arbitration Act. HR 1020 is a pending measure.

A Consumer Financial Products Safety Commission? I really don't know what to think about this idea. Its burden on creditors will depend on what the final arrangement looks like. Perhaps the idea is to have some sort of governmental body that looks at consumer financial services products the way that the Consumer Products Safety Commission looks at car safety. It would hand out ratings for financial products—rating, say, a 30-

year, fully amortizing first mortgage with five stars and a variable-rate mortgage with a negative amortization feature and a balloon payment with no stars.

Or perhaps the model is more like the Food and Drug Administration, with creditors submitting their proposed financial products for governmental approval before they can be offered to the public after a review period of a decade or two. That one makes my hair hurt. It is S 566.

A new sheriff in town? Another pending bill (HR 2309) would greatly expand the enforcement authority of the Federal Trade Commission, specifically directing the FTC to engage in rulemaking that would impose a cooling-off period on car financing transactions and that would regulate or eliminate spot delivery transactions, dealer finance charge markups, and the sale of F&I products, among other things. Do you recall the "Car Buyers' Bill of Rights" legislation that we've seen in the last few years at the state level? Here it is again, this time gussied up as a federal regulation.

So, boys and girls, buckle your chinstraps because we're in for a rough ride. Sorta makes you long for the days of gridlock, doesn't it?

Calling the Cops at Repo Time? Maybe Not.

June 2009

By Thomas B. Hudson

The brother-in-law of your finance company's manager is a member of the local police force. Occasionally, when you have a repo that looks like it might get dicey, you send him over a dozen Krispy Kremes and invite him to drop by the debtor's house at the time the repossession is to take place.

Just a prudent precaution? Or a violation of law? Let me tell you a little story.

After Carlos Albertorio-Santiago defaulted on his auto financing agreement with Reliable Financial Services, Reliable conducted a self-help repossession of Albertorio-Santiago's 2000 Ford Explorer, the subject of the financing agreement. Reliable's agent, Ricardo Acevedo-Correa, conducted the repossession with a police officer escort.

Albertorio-Santiago's son, Feliciano, who was present during the repossession, protested and told Acevedo-Correa to wait for his father. When Feliciano began to walk toward Acevedo-Correa to get his attention, one of the police officers approached Feliciano and told him to calm down.

Albertorio-Santiago sued Reliable under federal law, specifically 42 U.S.C. § 1983, alleging a violation of his right to due process under the Fourteenth Amendment. Albertorio-Santiago argued that Reliable was a state actor for purposes of Section 1983 by virtue of Acevedo-Correa's joint action with the police officers in effecting repossession.

Albertorio-Santiago also asserted a negligence claim on the grounds that the repossession was not effected without a breach of the peace. Applicable Puerto Rico law allows self-help repossession provided there is no breach of the peace. Reliable moved for summary judgment.

The U.S. District Court for the District of Puerto Rico denied Reliable's motion. The court found that the presence and involvement of the police officer in the repossession precluded a finding that Reliable was not a state actor as a matter of law. With respect to the negligence claim, the court noted that "if law enforcement is needed, then a breach of the peace has occurred, and the creditor must secure judicial intervention to carry out the repossession."

We can think of a couple of additional arguments that Reliable might have faced on these facts, but the court identified all the reasons you would need to keep the Krispy Kremes for yourself next time.

Albertorio-Santiago v. Reliable Financial Services, 2009 U.S. Dist. LEXIS 37982 (D.P.R. May 4, 2009).

Read Those Documents!

July 2009

By Thomas B. Hudson

When dealers finance cars for customers, they use a number of forms to do so. It isn't unusual for a dealer to use a buyers order, a retail installment contract, a credit application form, forms relating to required insurance, and forms reflecting ancillary products sold in connection with the car transaction, such as service contracts, GAP contracts, and the like.

These forms very often have different sources, and it isn't unusual, in our experience, for one form being used by a dealer to vary from, or conflict with, other forms used by the dealer in the same transaction.

Forms that don't agree with one another or, worse yet, that contradict one another can lead to unexpected, and unpleasant, legal problems. Here's an example.

Kristyn and Michael Krueger bought a used truck from Heartland Chevrolet Inc. In the process, the Kruegers signed a buyers order, an addendum to the buyers order that required arbitration of disputes, and a retail installment contract.

When the Kruegers learned the truck had prior damage that Heartland did not disclose, they sued the dealership for fraud and other claims. Heartland moved to dismiss or, alternatively, send the matter to arbitration. The trial court denied the motions and Heartland appealed.

The Court of Appeals of Missouri agreed with the trial court's decision. Heartland argued that the court erred in refusing to compel arbitration because the Kruegers entered into an arbitration agreement. The appellate court noted, however, that the Kruegers entered into a retail installment contract that made no reference to either the buyers order or the arbitration addendum.

The retail installment contract included a "merger clause" that specifically stated that it represented the complete and exclusive agreement of the parties. Thus, the appellate court found that Heartland was bound by the terms of the retail installment contract as the complete and exclusive agreement with the Kruegers. Because the contract included no arbitration agreement, the appellate court agreed with the trial court's decision to allow the litigation to proceed.

Other courts, dealing with similar facts, have reached different results. Those courts got to a different answer by reasoning that when a number of documents are signed at the same time in connection with the same transaction, they should be read together, where possible.

But you can't count on that sort of common sense reasoning by all courts, as this Missouri court demonstrates. So, read those documents! Better yet, get your dealership lawyer to read them, looking for traps like this one.

Krueger v. Heartland Chevrolet Inc., 2009 Mo. App. LEXIS 498 (Mo. App. April 21, 2009).

Don't Blink

July 2009
By Emily Marlow Beck

Don't blink. Don't even think about it. Trust me. I know.

My husband and I recently had our first child. Like many first-time parents, I spent a short time in a postnatal daze of sleepless nights and frantic days where finding time to brush my teeth was an accomplishment. And, frankly, for the period of time where my days and nights swirled together, the ebb and flow of the regulatory tide washing over the American auto industry was almost lost on me.

Now, for those of you who don't know me, let me put this into context. I'm the third generation in my family to work in the car business, and I'm about as glued to the political and regulatory mish-mash underlying the retail auto industry as one could be. Quite frankly, you might as well pour Pennzoil on my pancakes because I eat, sleep, and breathe this stuff.

But, somewhere in my sleep-deprived haze, I blinked. And, while I did, a whole bunch of stuff happened. To borrow some words from Tom Hudson, the compost hit the cooling system.

Auto manufacturers' bankruptcies made mincemeat of state franchise laws. Now, some of my clients and long-time friends are no longer in the new car business.

Congress dreamed up a variety of bills that could turn the auto industry on its head. Some of these pending bills are a federal usury law, a bankruptcy bill that has essentially the same effect as a usury law, and a bill that will outlaw the use by dealers of mandatory arbitration agreements with their customers to protect against class action lawsuits.

Lawmakers are considering giving the Federal Trade Commission new and broader powers to obtain civil penalties for any unfair or deceptive act or practice in connection with consumer credit or debt. These powers would expand the FTC's ability to collect civil penalties for any unfair or deceptive act or practice in connection with consumer credit or debt if the company "had actual knowledge or knowledge fairly implied on the basis of objective circumstances" that the practice was unfair or deceptive. To top that off, the bill would also give AGs power to bring suits in state or federal courts under any law enforced by the FTC or any rule relating to consumer credit or debt.

Yet another measure directs the FTC to address the practices of dealer participation and spot delivery. Think about that. Congress is telling the FTC (1) to eliminate an important source of dealer income at a time when dealers need every dime they can generate, and (2) to eliminate a dealership's ability to quickly deliver cars to some customers. This one has progressed from a subcommittee to the full Committee on Industry and Commerce and really bears watching.

And (Surprise! Surprise!), the FTC has delayed enforcement of the Red Flag Rules (again!), giving dealers and some other folks a little more time before the FTC starts bringing enforcement actions for noncompliance.

And, all of this is just for starters. There's much more. It's amazing what can happen when you blink.

But, I'm lucky. You see, I've got a great team of attorneys at my firm who make sure nothing slips past me when I'm not looking. They provide me, and folks who subscribe to some of the products we publish, with monthly, weekly, daily, or even hourly updates on the status of Uncle Sam's latest and greatest attempts to rein in folks like car dealers. They've got my back, and they keep me straight.

So, let me ask you this—who's got your back? Who's

keeping you in the loop? Where are you getting your information? Who's your wingman?

In the current economy, it might be tempting to pass up on that conference, cancel that magazine subscription, drop out of your state dealer association, or bail out of the upcoming 20 group meeting. Don't make that mistake. Doing so would be penny wise and pound foolish. Things are changing at a pace that is faster than most of us have ever seen. Smart dealers will take advantage of as many resources as possible, educate themselves, and "plug in" to the variety of resources available to them.

So, got your toothpicks ready? It's time to pry your eyes wide open. Don't blink. Some things you just can't afford to miss!

Court Enforces RISC Language
Holding Consumer Liable
July 2009
By Thomas B. Hudson

Newspaper editors will tell you that "dog bites man" isn't news, but that "man bites dog" will sell papers every time.

We see suits by car buyers against dealers all the time, but we rarely see suits involving dealers against car buyers. It's even rarer to see such a suit that results in the dealer winning. This case is one of those rare instances, although, even in this case, the dealer didn't win on all points.

David Serian bought a new truck from Dan's Carworld, LLC. As part of the transaction, he traded in his old truck.

A salesman at Carworld called Wachovia, the lienholder on the old truck, to get the payoff amount. Wachovia told the salesman that the payoff amount was $2,320. Wachovia also told him that it had a lien on a different car owned by Serian and the payoff amount on that car was $4,357.

The salesman used the $2,320 figure as the payoff amount for the old truck. The retail installment contract that Serian signed when he bought the new truck contained an express requirement that Serian would pay Carworld any balance owed on his old truck if the payoff amount turned out to be higher than expected.

Carworld sent Wachovia a check for $2,320. Wachovia told Carworld that the payoff amount was actually $4,357. Oops.

Carworld sent the balance due to Wachovia and then tried to collect the balance from Serian. Serian refused to pay. Double oops.

Carworld sued Serian for unjust enrichment (this legal term means just what it sounds like—a claim that the defendant got something to which he was not entitled). Serian countersued Carworld under the West Virginia Consumer Credit and Protection Act (WVCCPA) for allegedly trying to collect a "claim" from him that he did not owe.

Both parties moved for summary judgment. The trial court granted Carworld's motion. The trial court held that the transaction was not a "claim" subject to the WVCCPA because the transaction at issue involved Carworld's purchase of Serian's trade-in, not Serian's purchase of the new truck, and Carworld did not "buy" Serian's old truck for "personal, family, or household" purposes.

Serian, unhappy with the trial court's verdict, appealed.

The West Virginia Supreme Court reversed the decision in part and affirmed it in part. The appellate court held that the underlying transaction at issue was Serian's purchase of the new truck, which Serian bought for "personal, family, or household" purposes. Although Carworld may have taken Serian's trade-in truck and satisfied the lien on it, the court reasoned, the trade-in transaction was incidental to the underlying transaction. Because Serian bought the new truck for "personal, family, or household" purposes, the appellate court held that the entire transaction, including the disagreement over the trade-in truck, was subject to the WVCCPA. Because the WVCCPA applied to Carworld's collection efforts, the appellate court overruled the trial court's grant of summary judgment to Carworld on this issue.

The appellate court affirmed the trial court's holding with respect to Carworld's argument that the retail installment contract obligated Serian to pay the difference, noting that the contract language requiring the repayment was unambiguous.

We see dealer contracts containing a provision like this all the time. We're sure that your contract has such a provision, right? Right? RIGHT????

Dan's Carworld, LLC v. Serian, 2009 W. Va. LEXIS 41 (W. Va. May 13, 2009).

The Head-Butt Bill

July 2009
By Thomas B. Hudson

Sometimes I'm asked if I'm a pro football fan. My stock reply is, "No, I follow the Washington Redskins." I respond this way because the Skins are more of a soap opera than a sports team, with an owner who chases each "star of the moment" the way that politicians seem to be chasing skirts.

I was reminded of "the team I love to hate" when I read through a measure, S 500, presently pending in the Senate. Once upon a time, the Skins had a young quarterback named Gus Frerotte, who, a few years back, decided to celebrate after a successful play by head-butting a wall. Even with his helmet on, the blow knocked him silly and injured his neck. Watching, my first thought was, "Gus, you really didn't mean to do that . . . ." Reading S 500, I had the same reaction—"Hey guys, do you really mean to do that?"

What is "that," you ask?

First, the bill, if enacted in its present form, would wipe out the payday lending business. That's because the bill imposes a 36% rate cap. Sen. Durbin (D-IL), the bill's sponsor, evidently believes that imposing that generous rate on the amounts will adequately compensate those who make typical short-term loans.

Let's see now. If I'm a payday lender and I charge 36% on a $100 loan for one week, that's 36% x $100 = $36 divided by 365 = .098 cents per day, or about 70 cents for a week. Who in his right mind would lend someone with challenged credit $100 for a week and charge 70 cents for the loan? Would Sen. Durbin make that loan? I'm thinking maybe not. Will banks step in and service this market at these rates? Not on your life.

The problem for payday lenders and other short-term, small dollar lenders is that any sensible return that reflects the cost of the transaction and the risk involved results in APRs that are through the roof. Those high APRs offend Sen. Durbin and others, so their response is to eliminate an industry.

"Hey guys, do you really mean to do that?"

Payday lenders will have some company as they slide down the chute. Title lenders are also typically short-term lenders, with economics that look a lot like those of payday lenders. Ditto for pawnshops. So that's three industries wiped out.

Do the proponents of measures like this think that the demand for these financial services is going to disappear? When S 500 wipes out these companies, which are regulated in many states and by a host of federal laws, who do you suppose will satisfy the demand for short-term credit?

Maybe S 500 should be called "The Organized Crime Relief Act." And you know how careful the Mob will be to give proper disclosures, maintain their customers' financial privacy, refrain from discriminating, and adhere to all those other pesky consumer protection laws.

Now let's turn from those businesses your government wants to destroy and focus for a moment on the ones it merely wants to maim. "Who's that?" you ask? Why you, dear dealer.

S 500, as I said, caps rates at 36%. If that 36% was calculated using the formula that is used to calculate the currently required APR disclosure under the federal Truth in Lending Act, there wouldn't be a large objection to it from car dealers.

Sen. Durbin wants to calculate the rate another way, however. In addition to those amounts that would properly be included in the finance charge under present TILA and Reg. Z rules, Sen. Durbin wants to include fees and charges that are excluded from the finance charge under current law. His additions include optional credit insurance premiums and all charges for ancillary products sold in connection with or incidental to the credit transaction. This sweeping language will pick up charges for things like GAP coverage and perhaps even service contracts. In addition, his formula would include default fees, as well as late fees and returned check fees in excess of certain amounts, in effect imposing a federal maximum on late fees and NSF charges (someone will need to explain to me how you include in a calculation a fee or charge that may never materialize).

S 500 will essentially eliminate dealer income from the sale of F&I products that can't be accommodated in the 36% finance charge calculation. Dealers really need that kind of pressure on profits in this economy.

"Hey guys, do you really mean to do that?"

Gus would be proud of this bunch.

Can't You Just Give Me a Form?

August 2009

By Thomas B. Hudson

As we finish our compliance review of a dealership, we brief the dealership owners and managers on the compliance deficiencies we've identified. Often, we'll note that the dealership has no privacy policy, has no Safeguarding Policy, has no Red Flag policy, doesn't use adverse action notices, or has a defective buyers order or application form.

Often the response from the dealership is, "Can't you just give me a form?"

Usually the answer is "No."

"Why is that?" you ask. Here's why.

Many laws and regulations govern auto sales, finance, and leasing. These laws aren't particularly hard to understand (after all, we understand them, and rocket scientists we aren't). But dealers using forms, especially forms prepared by others, need to be familiar with the laws and regulations that require the form to be used, that require specific content to appear in the form, or that require the form to be used in a particular way or at a particular time. Having forms—even good, compliant forms—won't result in a compliant operation unless the form users know the underlying law and regulations.

First, forms need to be completed properly. There are correct ways, and incorrect ways, of completing a form. For example, the FTC Buyers Guide must be completed by identifying the "Systems Covered" by a warranty. You cannot use a general descriptor, such as "drive train," to complete the form, but you must name the components of the drive train that are covered. Unless the dealership personnel are familiar with the FTC's regulation, they might have a perfect form that, when improperly completed, results in a $16,000 fine.

Other documents that we deal with are not "one size fits all." If you need a privacy statement and we "just give you a form," that form must accurately describe your dealership's privacy policy. If we "just give you a form," you will need to conform your dealership's privacy policies to satisfy the description of the policies appearing in the form. That's a serious case of the tail wagging the dog.

Some forms must be provided to your customers at specific times. Again, the privacy policy serves as a good example. It must be provided annually to customers with whom you have a continuing financial relationship, such as your buy-here, pay-here customers. The content of repossession letters is highly regulated. We can give you a perfect one, but if the law requires that it be mailed by registered mail within 10 days of the date of repossession, and you don't know that, the complying form becomes a compliance problem.

So, no, we can't just "give you a form." First, we need to learn enough about your operation and how you intend to use the form before we know what form to provide. That involves some legal work. Then, either you have to take the time to learn to complete the form and use it properly, or we have to instruct you regarding those things. That involves more legal work. And the best forms on the planet can be rendered obsolete overnight when a law or regulation changes, so any form you have must be periodically reviewed to make sure it remains in compliance. Still more legal work.

If you want to run an operation that complies with all those federal and state laws and regulations that govern how you must do business, you can't just buy yourself an "off-the-shelf" solution. There is simply no way to get there without some serious skull work.

If all this studying and learning about the laws and regulations that affect your business is too much trouble for you, maybe it's time you thought about getting out of the car biz and opening up that bait shop.

Worms are pretty simple.

Take a Lesson From Judge Judy
August 2009
By Emily Marlow Beck

The other day, an episode of "Judge Judy" was playing in the waiting room of my doctor's office. I couldn't help but get drawn in (don't you dare laugh—you know you've done it!). The drama involved some young 20-somethings in a case of "former roommates turned hostile." Both parties claimed that the other party owed them money. Neither party had read their lease agreement before signing it. Judy gave them a good talking to in typical Judge Judy style and bashed those jokers for not reading the lease before signing it.

Dumb kids. No responsible adult would make that same mistake. After all, only an irresponsible youngster would sign a legal document without at least reading it, right?

Recently, I had the opportunity to attend a manufacturer-sponsored training class. The class was small, with about 15 attendees, most of whom were from large, urban area, multi-point franchise groups. Most of the class participants were general managers or controllers. All of the participants had at least 15 years of experience in the car business (some significantly more). So, this wasn't a class full of green peas, but a class filled with veteran car folks.

I tried to wear my "student hat" and not my "lawyer hat" that day, so I hid in the back of the class and tried to absorb as much information as possible. Unfortunately, my cover was blown when we were asked to introduce ourselves and provide our various backgrounds. Now, I don't know if any of you have experienced this, but something happens to the "feel" of a crowd when folks learn that a lawyer is in the room. I can't explain it, but people just act differently. (My good friend, a pastor, says he experiences the same thing. A guilty conscience, perhaps?) For far too much of the remainder of the class, the moderator turned to me and said, "Let's ask the lawyer."

So, here's where it gets good. At one point in the class, I mentioned that many of the legal obligations dealers have arise because of the role of the dealer as creditor in the transaction (blank stares). It was clear to me that I had lost some folks, so I explained to the group that in a typical retail installment sale transaction, the dealer exchanges a shiny car for a promise to pay over time in the form of a retail installment sale contract, and the dealer then typically assigns this contract to a third-party financing source (blank stares). One general manager shot me a look that could kill and said, "I find that very hard to believe."

As I continued talking, it became clear to me (as many attendees began to confess) that very few folks in the room had actually read the documents they had been signing for all these years. Not the retail installment sale contract. Not the dealer agreement setting forth the terms between the dealership and the finance company. Zip. Zero. Nada.

Sounds like these folks need to watch a bit more Judge Judy.

Now, I'm not writing this article to poke fun at anyone, but time and time again we see dealers get themselves into trouble because they don't understand the business they are in. We see it in advertisements that refer to "loans" and "lenders" when the dealership is originating plain vanilla retail installment sale contracts. We see it in dealerships where employees boast that they'll get customers the "best rate" or lead customers to believe that the dealership is their agent assisting them to obtain financing.

And, yes, my friends, we see it later in courtrooms and during depositions, where veteran car folks trip all over themselves when trying to explain how they do business. There's no Judge Judy to read them the riot act, but often these situations end with a car guy feeling and looking foolish.

Well, here's a question. When was the last time you rolled up your sleeves and read through your deal documents? Have you ever? Do you know what you're agreeing to day in and day out with every car that drives off your lot? It's the thing that you don't know (or thought you knew) that just might jump up and bite you. After all, I'm sure we'd all prefer to keep the courtroom drama on TV and out of our dealerships.

The Federal Trade Commission

The Federal Trade Commission (FTC) is a federal agency created by Congress. It both makes rules and enforces them, but it also enforces federal laws and rules made by other agencies. The FTC is the top federal cop for nearly all of the federal laws and regulations that apply to dealers. That's bad news, good news, and bad news, as we shall see . . .

It's bad news because, in our experience, FTC staffers tend to be short on experience, particularly business experience, and long, often very long, on zeal. They tend to have never met an honest merchant or a dishonest consumer, if you catch my drift.

It's good news, because the FTC's jurisdiction is vast. The agency is responsible for enforcing all those federal laws and regulations for all merchants, not just car dealers. Consider how many department stores; jewelry stores; furniture stores; appliance stores; home improvement companies; pawn shops; payday and title lenders; boat, RV, and motorcycle dealerships; and the like that are all selling stuff on credit, and you'll get some idea how thinly the agency is spread. The agency probably focuses a bit more on the car business than on other areas, simply because car transactions tend to end up on its radar as a result of consumer complaints; however, the likelihood that you will end up with an FTC SWAT team swarming over your shop is pretty small.

That aside, it's bad news because, other than being on the pointy end of a serious class action lawsuit, about the worst possible experience a dealership can have is an FTC investigation of its practices and charges of violating the law.

So, you're unlikely ever to see an FTC enforcer in your shop. If you do, however, it's gonna be a bad day, unless he's there to buy a car.

Dealer Fraud—Not on the FTC's Radar Screen?

March 2008

By Thomas B. Hudson

The FTC has released the list of top consumer fraud complaints received by the agency in 2007. The list is contained in the publication *Consumer Fraud and Identity Theft Complaint Data January–December 2007.*

I always find this list to be fascinating. If you follow the rants of consumer advocates like the so-called "Public Citizen" report about F&I practices titled "Rip-Off Nation," you'd believe that consumer fraud by car dealers is the number one problem in this country, ahead of global warming, the Iraq war, and Al Gore's diet. Listen to industry critic Duane Overholt, and you'd believe that a consumer isn't safe within five miles of a car dealership.

But where do "dealership fraud," "auto fraud," or even "auto repair fraud" fall on the FTC's Top 20 List? Nowhere— that's where. There isn't a single reference to cars in the Top 20, and note that a mere 1,900 complaints would land you in the Top 20. Now, granted, some of the other categories might implicate dealers along with all other retailers. Examples are Internet Services and Identity Theft.

Indeed, the Identity Theft category really leads the pack. The report showed that for the seventh year in a row, identity theft is the number one consumer complaint category. Of 813,899 total complaints received in 2007, a whopping 258,427, or 32%, dealt with identity theft. Surely some of these complaints involved car dealers.

Sadly for Public Citizen and Overholt, that wasn't the case. The report states that credit card fraud was the most common form of reported identity theft at 23%, followed by utilities fraud at 18%, employment fraud at 14%, and bank fraud (the FTC doesn't define this term, but it appears to deal with fraud related to consumers' bank accounts, and not fraud by, say, dealers on banks) at 13%. Those four categories involved about two-thirds of the identity theft complaints.

There are, of course, dealers who are unethical and who regularly rip off consumers. No one defends dishonest business people like these, and the sooner the Attorneys General and the plaintiffs' lawyers shut them down, the better. But the vast majority of dealers are honest and ethical business people, and the FTC's report bears that out. Still, there is some learning in the FTC's report for dealers, and that involves identity theft.

The fact that the FTC has identified identity theft as the top consumer problem should get dealers' attention. The FTC's Red Flag Rules are designed to combat identity theft by increasing the likelihood that a dealer is actually dealing with a buyer who is who he or she claims to be. The Rules impose a number of duties on dealers that further this aim.

I don't intend in this article to set out the details of the Red Flag Rules—that has been done in other articles—but instead I want to urge you immediately to turn to the job of assuring that your dealership will be in compliance with those rules. Many dealers were literally years late in complying with the FTC's Safeguarding Rule dealing with privacy, and some have never complied. Such noncompliance runs the risk of significant fines and other legal difficulties.

You don't want to let the Red Flag Rules sneak up on you.

If the Government Comes to Call, Make Sure You Answer the Door Politely!

June 2008

By Lisa C. DeLessio

I'm sure you have all heard stories about the dreaded knock on the door from the Attorney General, the state regulator, the Federal Trade Commission, and maybe even the District Attorney. You probably figure that the only time these heavy hands knock is when some business has done something terribly wrong. And since you are on top of your compliance obligations, you probably think it's never going to happen to you. But it can happen even to good companies. And if it does, what will you do?

In a seminar sponsored by the Federal Trade Commission and the Better Business Bureau of Metropolitan Dallas in May 2008, some regulators shared their "thoughts" on things you should keep in mind if you are the target of an investigation. Here are a few tips I took away:

1. Keep this in mind. The government doesn't call without a reason. By the time a government agency contacts you, the agency has already received complaints about you. You might be surprised to know that these complaints often come from your competitors, not just consumers.

2. Get a lawyer. Right away. The panel, which included representatives from the AG's office, the DA's office, and the FTC, unanimously agreed that they would far prefer to work with your lawyer than you. And this is true at every stage of the process.

3. Cooperate. This one might seem too obvious to write down, but the panel revealed that after the agency makes a request—usually for documents or information about a product, service, or advertisement—they are often met with long, unexplained delays or no response at all. They all found this to be frustrating. They also made it clear that government agencies don't like to deal with company reps who are defensive or argumentative. Intimidation will not make the government back down. In fact, it has the opposite effect. If you are argumentative or defensive, the government will believe you have something to hide even if you don't. The lack of cooperation occurs most often with the company that doesn't hire a lawyer. So don't skip tip #2.

4. Share information. That is, about your business. The rep from the AG's office candidly stated that he is always surprised when a company provides documents or an initial response and then never contacts his office again. I think there might be several reasons for this silence. One, the government's power is daunting—it can fine you or put you out of business. You figure if the government wants something, it will ask. Two, you might think that the less the government knows about you, the better off you are. Three, maybe the AG speaking at the conference is a lot more open-minded than lots of other regulators. So, you and your lawyer will need to decide on the best strategy for your circumstances. Keep an open mind.

5. Sometimes the government will see your side of the story. And when it does, it will close the investigation. Some of the panelists were more enthusiastic about this point than others. For example, the DA rep said that the DA's office frequently drops cases after hearing the other side of the story. But the DA's office needs to hear the whole story first. This was not necessarily the view of the FTC.

6. An investigation is not litigation. You don't have rules of evidence or the benefit of procedural requirements. In fact, when I asked if the agencies could share any protocol or guidelines (preferably written), the answer was no. These government agencies have loose and flexible guidelines when investigating complaints about bad practices. This means you are not playing on a level field. The government agencies can ask you for all sorts of things, but you can't ask them to tell you everything they have against you.

So, keep these tips in mind if you ever receive a request from a regulator. If you are on top of your compliance obligations and put your best foot forward, maybe you (and your lawyer) can convince the regulator that the complaints are unfounded or isolated—and he or she didn't really need to knock on your door!

FTC Used Car Buyers Guide to Receive Overhaul

August 2008
By Elizabeth A. Huber

In the words of Billy Joel, "Don't go changin' ...," but we're not talking about your appearance here.

We mean the Federal Trade Commission's Used Car Buyers Guide, the form that must be prepared, filled in (as applicable), and displayed prominently and conspicuously (in English and, in some cases, also in Spanish) on every used motor vehicle for sale on a dealer's lot. The FTC form for this purpose must be exactly as required by the FTC Used Motor Vehicle Trade Regulation Rule, 16 C.F.R. Part 455. We've heard some dealers' personnel have been changing the form, and generally that's a "no, no" (it is a violation of the FTC Used Car Rule to fail to comply). Only changes discussed in the Rule are permitted.

Note, however, that this situation may change. In 2008 the FTC published a "Request for Public Comment" on a number of issues in the Used Car Rule as the Rule was last updated 13 years ago. (More on this later.)

The basics: The basic provisions in the FTC Used Car Rule

make it an unfair or deceptive act or practice for any used vehicle dealer, in connection with the sale or offer of sale of a used vehicle, (1) to misrepresent the mechanical condition of the vehicle, to misrepresent the terms of any warranty offered, or to represent that the vehicle is sold with a warranty when this is not true; or (2) to fail to disclose prior to sale that a used vehicle is sold without any warranty, or to fail to make available the terms of any written warranty offered. A Buyers Guide in the exact form, size, and text as in the Rule must be prepared and placed prominently and conspicuously in any location on a vehicle so long as both sides are "readily readable."

Part of the Buyers Guide required by the FTC Used Car Rule concerns whether a warranty is being given in connection with the vehicle or whether the vehicle is being sold "AS IS—NO WARRANTY." For the purposes of this Rule, a "warranty" is a written undertaking by a used car dealer, in connection with the sale by that dealer of a used vehicle, to refund, repair, replace, maintain, or take other action with respect to such used vehicle that is provided at no extra charge beyond the price of the used vehicle. "Warranty" does not include third-party extended warranties or vehicle protection plans offered for optional purchase by consumers, where the extended warranty or vehicle protection contract is between the consumer and a third party (not the dealer selling the vehicle).

If, as a used vehicle dealer, you offer the vehicle with a warranty, the form must describe the warranty terms in the space provided, including:

- Whether the warranty offered is "full" or "limited."
- Which of the specific systems are covered (for example, "engine, transmission, differential"). You cannot use shorthand, such as "drive train" or "power train" for covered systems.

- The duration (for example, "30 days or 1,000 miles, whichever occurs first").
- The percentage of the repair cost paid by you (for example, "The dealer will pay 100% of the cost of labor and 100% of the cost of parts").
- If the vehicle is still under the manufacturer's original warranty, you may add the following paragraph below the "Full/Limited Warranty" disclosure:

MANUFACTURER'S WARRANTY STILL APPLIES. The manufacturer's original warranty has not expired on the vehicle. Consult the manufacturer's warranty booklet for details as to warranty coverage, service location, etc.

If you offer a service contract (noninsurance states) on the vehicle, you must add the following heading and paragraph below the "Full/Limited Warranty" disclosures and mark the box provided:

[X] Service Contract
A service contract is available at an extra charge on this vehicle. If you buy a service contract within 90 days of the time of sale, State law "implied warranties" may give you additional rights.

If you offer the vehicle for sale without any warranty, you will select that option in the Buyers Guide: "AS IS—NO WARRANTY." Note that some state laws limit or prohibit "AS IS" sales of used motor vehicles (for example, Connecticut, Hawaii, and New York). In these states, state law overrides the FTC Used Car Rule. The Rule indicates that the heading "AS IS—NO WARRANTY" and the accompanying two sentences must be deleted from the Buyers Guide in these cases, and the following heading and paragraph must be substituted:

> Implied Warranties Only
>
> This means that the dealer does not make any specific promises to fix things that need repair when you buy the vehicle or after the time of sale. But, State law "implied warranties" may give you some rights to have the dealer take care of serious problems that were not apparent when you bought the vehicle.

Under some state laws (for example, Arizona), an implied warranty will apply if the dealer does not make certain disclosures and obtain the buyer's acknowledgment. Other states may require additional disclosures in the retail installment sale contract. (Consult your legal counsel.)

FTC Request for Public Comment: On July 16, 2008, the FTC released a request for public comment. Interested parties may submit written comments (by mail or electronically) related to the FTC Used Car Rule on a number of issues, including,

- Whether the pre-printed list of 14 major systems and the defects that may occur in those systems should be revised or eliminated;
- How well the current method for disclosing unexpired manufacturer's warranties on the Buyers Guide is working;
- Whether the Buyers Guide should include information about used car warranties provided by manufacturers (for example, in connection with a certified used vehicle program) or third parties; and
- The effect of the FTC Used Car Rule on deception in the used car market, including the continuing need for the Rule and its economic impact.

The FTC's announcement can be found at www.ftc.gov/opa/2008/07/ucr.shtm. Public comments are being accepted through September 19, 2008 (FTC File No. P087604; the staff contact is John C. Hallerud, FTC Midwest Region, Chicago, 312-960-5615).

As a closing reminder, there are still other issues regulated by state law not addressed by the FTC Used Car Rule or Request for Public Comment that relate to the sale of a used motor vehicle. Examples include safety or emissions inspection issues, nonoperation of vehicle provisions, content of extended warranties or vehicle protection coverage, title or registration disclosure requirements, prior use and damage disclosures, and contract cancellation options and disclosures. Furthermore, both Maine and Wisconsin have received an exemption from the federal rule as each state has in place its own Buyers Guide rules.

At the time this book went to press in 2010, the FTC had not issued the expected Proposed Rule updating the costs, benefits, and effectiveness of the Used Car Buyers Guide. The FTC initially received 21 comments, from (among others) the National Automobile Dealers Association, the National Association of Attorneys General, and the National Consumer Law Center. In April 2009, the FTC reopened the comment period for a period of 45 days as a result of having received supplemental comments from the National Automobile Dealers Association and the National Independent Dealers Association in response to comments made by other interested parties during the initial comment period.

Whether Billy Joel's lyrics, "Don't go changin'" had anything to do with the extension or not, well, we can't really say.

Something New for the Used Car Rule?

September 2008

By Emily Marlow Beck

Yeah, I'm one of those people. I have a tough time setting boundaries between my work and my, ahem, arguably nonexistent personal life. After all, who needs a life when your job is as fun as mine?

Don't believe me? More than once on a recent road trip vacation "Out West," I asked my husband to "drive slower" or "pull over" so I could catch a quick glimpse of the window stickers at the local used car dealerships. Of course, he wasn't the least bit surprised—I've asked him to do this a zillion times before.

So, it made my heart flutter to learn that the FTC is considering making some changes to the very law that has provided me with barrels of fun on my family road trips. The Federal Trade Commission is seeking public comments on the effectiveness and impact of the FTC's Used Motor Vehicle Trade Regulation Rule, commonly known as the Used Car Rule. As many of you know, the Rule has been around for quite a while (1984) and got a little "refreshing" in 1995. This is the Rule that requires used car dealers to, among other things, disclose on a window sticker (i.e., Buyers Guide) whether they are offering a warranty and, if so, the terms and conditions of any such warranty.

According to a July 16, 2008, press release, the FTC seeks comments on a range of issues including, among others, whether a bilingual Buyers Guide would be useful or practicable as well as what form such a Buyers Guide should take. It also is seeking comments on possible changes to the Guide to reflect the various types of warranties that are available today—like certified used car warranties. According to the press release, comments on the possible revisions will be accepted through mid-September.

But, the release made me think—with possibly increased attention being placed on the beloved Used Car Rule, maybe it's about time we all give a quick look-see and figure out how our compliance with the present version of the Used Car Rule measures up. Need some help? Here are the most common mistakes we see dealers make when trying (or not trying) to comply with the Used Car Rule.

Not affixing the Buyers Guide before offering the vehicle for sale. I think you know how this story goes. Your buddy's customer just traded in the car one of your customers has been looking for. You know this cream puff won't last long, so you dial up your customer. "Good news, Mr. Customer! We just got that car you've been looking for!" You encourage your customer to move fast, and you take him "out back" and make sure he sees the car before anyone else—and also before a completed Buyers Guide has been affixed to the vehicle.

Not good. The Federal Used Car Rule requires that dealers affix a properly completed Buyers Guide on the vehicle before offering it for sale. Taking customers "out back" to see the car before it's been tagged is, in lawyer-speak, dead wrong.

Size, format, color, font. I sometimes see dealerships that have attempted to "spice up" the Buyers Guide, using creative fonts, colors, sizes, or even pictures. Unfortunately, the FTC didn't seem too interested in invoking the spirit of your inner Picasso when it scribed the Used Car Rule. Instead, the Rule is painstakingly specific about what the Buyers Guide is supposed to look like. Anything that differs from the exact formatting requirements described in the Rule misses the point. Resist the temptation to play with it.

Spanish-language transactions. My husband will tell you that I like to pull over at dealerships that display "Se Habla Español" signs to see if the dealers who have spent money to advertise in Spanish have also taken the time to learn the laws that govern these transactions. Unfortunately, I still see many dealers who fail to affix a Spanish-language version of the Buyers Guide to the used car before offering it for sale. Using a "Spanglish" version or handing the customer a Spanish-language version when you deliver the car doesn't cut it. ¿Comprende? If you've been reading this publication long enough, you know that we've beaten this issue like a piñata.

Proper completion of the Buyers Guide. Federal law is specific about what may and what may not be included in the Buyers Guide. The dealer must disclose which of the specific systems are covered (for example, "engine, transmission, differential"). You cannot use shorthand, such as "drive train" or "power train," for covered systems. It might be tempting to breeze past these steps to get the car on the lot, but cutting these corners may come back to bite you.

Proper integration of the Buyers Guide into the buyers order. The FTC didn't limit itself to the contents and display of the federal Buyers Guide. No Sir-ee! In fact, the Rule requires that your sale document (bill of sale, purchase contract, buyers order, you get the point) contain "magic language" informing customers to refer to the Buyers Guide affixed on the vehicle for more information about any warranties. And, just how "magic" is this "magic" language? Well, for my purposes, this language is magic because it is given to you directly from the pens of the FTC and is printed verbatim in the Rule. In other words, this is language that you should "cut and paste" directly from the statute into the sale document. Unfortunately, I don't have to review too many forms to see that a dealer or forms provider has monkeyed with the "magic language." From the eyes of the compliance lawyer, monkeying with "magic language" is seldom a good thing.

No discussion of the Used Car Rule would be complete without a discussion of the penalties for noncompliance. The FTC has the authority to tag you with a $16,000 per violation penalty for your dealership's failure to comply. In a worst-case scenario, that could be $16,000 per violation, per car, per day. (You do the math!) And, don't forget—as easy as it is for me to drive around looking for Used Car Rule culprits, think about how it would be just as easy for federal regulators to do the same. So, let's all hope that the next car that pulls on your lot barking about the Used Car Rule is mine and not a federal regulator's!

A 'New' Used Car Rule? AGs Get in the Act

December 2008

By Dana Frederick Clarke

A gaggle of Attorneys General (that's 42 if you are counting), with time on their hands after the last presidential election and the winds of change at their backs, have collaborated on a comment urging the Federal Trade Commission to revise the 23-year-old Buyers Guide, more commonly known as the "window sticker," required by the FTC's Used Motor Vehicle Trade Regulation Rule. To be perfectly fair, the FTC encouraged the gaggle by its July 21, 2008, solicitation of public comments on the proposed revised Used Car Rule as part of its "systematic review" of all FTC regulations and guides. So what are the AGs urging the FTC to do and, equally important, how will that affect used car dealers?

The AGs are requesting that the FTC amend the Buyers Guide to include two additional pieces of information—the vehicle's history and prior use, including title branding, damage history, and occurrence of a manufacture repurchase under a state lemon law. The AGs state in their comment that these two components are "the most material information consumers need to consider and, indeed, do consider in deciding whether to purchase [a used car]."

Curiously, the AGs concede that they are advocating for the addition of this information to the Buyers Guide even though such information is already being considered by consumers to make a purchase. In fact, the AGs specifically reference various sources by name, such as CARFAX and AutoCheck, that provide consumers with vehicle history information. Although these are pay services, the AGs note that a soon-to-be established federal database, the National Motor Vehicle Title Information Service, would provide free "public access to critical information about the reliability and safety of used motor vehicles." Further, the AGs observe that several states already require disclosure of one or both pieces of information under separate statutes or regulatory authority. In fact, the AGs offer the Wisconsin version of the Buyers Guide as a potential model for a revised FTC version.

This brings us to the second curiosity in the AGs' comment: If Wisconsin could enact legislation providing for a more robust form of Buyers Guide, then why can't the home states of these AGs enact similar legislation? The FTC Used Car Rule includes a specific provision that sets out the standards for granting statewide exemptions from the rule—the state rule has to apply to any transaction to which the FTC rule applies, and the state rule has to have an overall level of protection to consumers that is as great as, or greater than, the protection afforded by the FTC rule. That thought, however, might fall under the heading of "be careful what you wish for" because the task of having to administer numerous state versions of the Buyers Guide might be far more expensive than simply adopting a "new" uniform version from the FTC.

KA-BOOM

July 2009
By Thomas B. Hudson

I couldn't get the image out of my head. I had imagined a fellow lost inside an ammunition factory. The lights had gone out, and he was striking matches to try to find the door.

I was conducting an on-site dealership compliance audit of a buy-here, pay-here (BHPH) store, looking over the dealership's sales and F&I process from A to Z in an effort to decrease the dealership's potential liability for violations of state and federal law. It's a good thing that it was only little ol' me probing this dealership's operation—if, instead, an FTC SWAT team had descended on the car lot, the dealer would be out of business.

What was so wrong with this dealer's operations, you ask? Let me give you a few examples.

There were perhaps 50 used cars on the lot. Three were displayed for sale without the required FTC Used Car Buyers Guides. If I'd been the boss of an FTC inspection team, I'd have written the dealer up for three violations, at up to $16,000 per violation. A cool "up to" $48,000 penalty.

Looking over the inside of the dealership, I saw customer files containing personal information protected by federal privacy laws and regulations that were not under lock and key or otherwise protected from prying eyes. More fines.

The dealership's buyers order was a "cut-and-paste" job that the dealer had dummied up a decade ago. It contained a required federal notice, but did not present the notice "conspicuously" as required by the federal regulations. That little omission creates a potential liability of $16,000 for every deal created using that form.

When I asked for a copy of the dealership's privacy Safeguarding policy—something that federal regulations have mandated for several years—I was met with blank stares. "How about your Red Flag policy?" I asked. "We've heard about that," they answered. More fines.

The dealership's application form had not been redone in ages. It, too, was a "do-it-yourself" form that had obviously been constructed with no lawyer assistance. Score two blatant Equal Credit Opportunity Act and Regulation B violations. These were violations that would have appeared in every customer file that this dealership had ever done—a class action waiting to happen. Also, more fines.

The dealership's Internet ads boasted prices that were "for cash buyers and good credit buyers." A little questioning elicited the admission that the dealer would not honor these prices if the buyer had credit bad enough to necessitate the sale of that buyer's contract to a sales finance company that bought the contracts at a discount or if the buyer were a BHPH buyer. That practice, at least in the way this dealer operated, violated the federal Truth in Lending Act and Regulation Z and probably violated state motor vehicle department advertising regulations as well. Yep. More fines, as well as potential class actions.

All in all, an FTC posse would have put this dealership out of business in about five seconds flat. And, like the guy in the ammunition factory lighting the matches, the dealership was blissfully oblivious to its exposure.

If any of the examples here cause any warning bells to go off, you need to consider scheduling a compliance audit for your business. Many law firms, including our own Hudson Cook, do such audits, as do many qualified consulting firms. The best place to start is with your own lawyer, who might be able to do the audit himself or herself. If not, he or she can assist you in choosing someone who can.

Now blow out that match, OK?

The Dumb Lawyer Made (Another) Mistake
August 2009
By Thomas B. Hudson

In a recent article titled "KA-BOOM," I likened a dealer's compliance operation to a fellow wandering around a dynamite factory, striking matches to try to find the way out. It was a disaster waiting to happen. In the article, I toted up all the fines the dealer would be exposed to if the FTC happened to come calling.

My partner, Jean Noonan, noticed that I had gotten a bit too enthusiastic totaling up the fines. She should know, since she served as Associate Director for Credit Practices of the FTC's Bureau of Consumer Protection for five years. Her response:

Just read your KA-BOOM article. A great article, and the overall point is spot-on. But remember, all Federal Trade Commission rules are not created equal. There are no fines for violations of: Privacy Rule, Safeguarding Rule, Red Flag Rules, and Truth in Lending. These rules are enforced administratively by the FTC. The FTC issues a cease-and-desist order; fines are an option only for subsequent violations of the order. In contrast, the Used Car Rule (Buyers Guide) and the Holder in Due Course Rule are trade regulation rules (TRR), and violations of a TRR involve penalties for the first violation. Ditto for violations of the ECOA's Regulation B.

It's nice to have partners who are smarter than I am. At least she was willing to agree I had a point, despite my error regarding the fines.

Here are the real risks for dealers violating those laws and regulations Jean identifies as not resulting in an FTC assessment for the first violation. First, having the FTC investigate your operation and write you up for violations is no picnic, with or without a fine. Second, we've seen plaintiffs' lawyers bring lawsuits in which they allege that a dealer's violation of a federal law or regulation constitutes a violation of a state unfair or deceptive act or practices law, essentially bootstrapping a state claim onto a federal violation.

OK, I blew it regarding the fines. The bottom line is that poor compliance can be costly. I'll try to do better next time.

Chapter 3

The Federal Truth in Lending Act

The federal Truth in Lending Act (TILA) is what it sounds like—a federal law. In the late 1960s, Congress enacted TILA to curb abuses in the credit industry. The basic idea behind TILA is that consumers shopping for credit ought to be able to obtain the same information regarding the cost of credit from each potential credit provider, and that the cost of credit quoted by each creditor should be computed in the same way.

TILA and Federal Reserve Board Regulation Z, which implements it, have largely achieved these goals, but along the way, they have been discovered by plaintiffs' lawyers, who have turned the often very technical and arbitrary federal disclosure rules into a series of potential "gotchas," with significant civil, and even potential criminal, liability for trivial as well as serious violations.

Our friend Gene Kelly, a grizzled warhorse of a Chicago litigator, who has defended many creditors in suits alleging violations of TILA and Reg. Z, once said at a conference of credit lawyers representing dealers and finance companies, "There are no Truth in Lending lawsuits." That statement stopped the audience cold, and Gene went on to explain what he meant.

Gene said that TILA suits arise not when the buyer goes home after a car purchase and plows through his contract and disclosure statement looking for violations, but rather when the buyer has a problem with the car or with the credit transaction that, in the buyer's mind, has not been adequately addressed by the dealer. At that point, the buyer is fed up with trying to resolve the matter, so he seeks the help of a lawyer. The lawyer then peruses all of the paperwork provided to the buyer, looking for TILA violations, as well as violations of the many other federal and state laws and regulations that applied to the transaction between the dealer and the buyer.

We agree with Gene's observation. Most of the TILA and Reg. Z lawsuits we've seen have arisen after the buyer has become unhappy with the car or with other aspects of the transaction.

So, when you have an unhappy buyer, and you are trying to run a cost-benefits analysis to determine whether it's worth giving her X, Y, and Z to satisfy her complaint, you might want to factor in the benefit of avoiding the TILA suit that might well result if the customer decides to take her deal papers to her friendly local lawyer.

Not All Violations of the Truth in Lending Act Result in Statutory Damages

October 2008

By Thomas B. Hudson

Several years ago, a bad Fourth Circuit Court of Appeals decision sparked a wave of class action lawsuits claiming violations of the federal Truth in Lending Act. That case, *Polk v. Crown Auto, Inc.,* 228 F.3d 541 (4th Cir. (W.D. Va.) June 28, 2000, dealt with the timing and delivery of Truth in Lending disclosures by a car dealer. The court wrongfully decreed that the car buyer was required to receive a completely filled in copy of his TILA disclosures before signing the retail installment contract.

Some of the courts that dealt with the mini-wave of lawsuits followed the Polk court's flawed reasoning, while others got it right. Eventually the staff of the Federal Reserve Board revised its Truth in Lending Commentary to clear up the confusion by stating that a dealer could comply with the TILA timing and delivery requirements by handing the filled-out retail installment contract to the customer for review, completely relinquishing control of it, then taking it back and having the customer sign it.

I hadn't thought of Polk for quite some time—the revised Commentary has provided enough guidance to keep alert dealers out of mischief. But a recent case dealing with the timing and delivery of TILA disclosures by a payday lender caught my eye. Plaintiffs suing under TILA can claim actual damages, attorneys' fees, and court costs, plus, for some TILA violations, so-called "statutory damages," or damages provided automatically, without proof that the plaintiff has been damaged. This case dealt with the issue of whether a violation like the one in Polk gave the plaintiff the right to recover under TILA, absent a showing of actual damages.

Bobby Ferrell, Jr., got a payday loan from Checks-N-Advance, Inc. After Ferrell filed a Chapter 13 bankruptcy petition, the trustee in the bankruptcy, Kathleen McDonald, sued Checks for violating the Truth in Lending Act by failing to provide required disclosures prior to consummation of the transaction, in violation of 15 U.S.C. § 1638(b)(1), and failing to disclose the finance charge and annual percentage rate properly and conspicuously, in violation of 15 U.S.C. § 1632(a). McDonald sought damages, attorneys' fees, and costs.

Checks did not respond to the complaint (Note to Checks' lawyer—generally not a recommended legal maneuver), so the bankruptcy court disallowed Checks' proof of claim and found that Checks violated TILA.

The court, however, refused to award statutory damages to McDonald and concluded that McDonald did not prove actual damages. The bankruptcy appellate panel affirmed the decision of the bankruptcy court, as did the U.S. Court of Appeals for the Ninth Circuit in this opinion. The circuit court agreed with the lower courts that 15 U.S.C. § 1640(a) limited liability for statutory damages to certain TILA violations, and the list of TILA violations did not include Section 1638(b)(1) or Section 1632(a). Moreover, the circuit court agreed that the trustee was not entitled to actual damages where she did not prove that Ferrell detrimentally relied on the faulty loan documents.

You shouldn't draw too much relief from a decision like this, however. The court did determine that the creditor had committed a TILA violation. If the plaintiff had been able to show actual damages (an admittedly tough thing to do in many TILA cases), she'd have been entitled to those damages, plus attorneys' fees (which often dwarf any damages award) and court costs.

Also, plaintiffs' lawyers have been known to bootstrap violations of federal law into claims under state unfair and deceptive acts and practices laws, the theory being, "You had an obligation to obey federal law, and the failure to obey that federal law is an unfair practice under state law."

In re Ferrell (McDonald v. Checks-N-Advance, Inc.), 2008 WL 3876602 (9th Cir. (9th Cir. BAP (Bankr. D. Nev.)) August 22, 2008).

A Basic Lesson Relearned

January/February 2009
By Thomas B. Hudson

I bought my first few new cars in the '60s. I recall paying $1,700 or so for a new VW Bug, $1,964 for a 1964 Ford Falcon, and about $2,100 for a 1965 Chevrolet Biscayne with nothing on it but the paint.

I think about those numbers every time I speak to a group of dealers and mention the fact that the federal Truth in Lending Act and Regulation Z do not apply to transactions in which the amount financed exceeds $25,000, an amount established in 1968 and never adjusted for inflation.

That statement always elicits a startled reaction from the audience. Most dealers, as well as most consumer lawyers and an alarming number of judges, seem to believe that TILA and Reg. Z apply to all car finance transactions. 'Tain't so.

Pay careful attention to the way TILA describes the transactions to which it applies. The $25,000 number doesn't apply to the price of the car, to the price of the car plus the finance charge, to the total of payments, or to any formulation other than the "amount financed."

That makes life pretty easy because every federal disclosure statement or combined disclosure statement and retail installment contract includes a disclosure of the amount financed. All you need to do is look at the number that appears in the "amount financed" disclosure space and compare it to $25,000. If it is $25,000 or lower, TILA and Reg. Z apply; if it's over $25,000, the federal disclosure laws don't apply.

Despite this black-and-white test, plaintiffs' lawyers still occasionally argue that the law applies, even when it clearly doesn't. A recent opinion illustrates another such attempt.

Gail Schultz bought a car from Burton-Moore Ford, Inc. She traded in a car on which she still owed money. Burton-Moore added the negative equity to the cash price of the new car and financed the entire amount. The contract listed the amount financed as $30,618.

The contract did not separately itemize the negative equity, the purchase price of the new car, or the sales tax charged by Burton-Moore. The application for title completed by the parties contained a disclaimer by Burton-Moore of all express and implied warranties except any warranties provided by the manufacturer. The Buyers Guide for the car did not indicate whether it came with a warranty.

Schultz sued Burton-Moore, alleging violations of the Truth in Lending Act (TILA), the Magnuson-Moss Warranty Act (MMWA), and the Michigan Motor Vehicle Sales Finance Act (MMVSFA). Schultz moved for summary judgment on these claims. Her argument regarding whether TILA and Reg. Z applied was, apparently, that the amounts allocated to negative equity should not be included in the amount financed for the purpose of determining whether the amount financed exceeded $25,000.

The U.S. District Court for the Eastern District of Michigan granted Schultz's motion as to the MMVSFA claim, but not as to the TILA and MMWA claims. Burton-Moore moved for reconsideration of the MMVSFA claim and for summary judgment.

The court granted Burton-Moore's motion as to the TILA and MMVSFA claims, but denied it as to the MMWA claim. The court affirmed its earlier finding that TILA did not apply because the amount financed exceeded the $25,000 jurisdictional limit.

This seems to be one of those lessons that has to be taught repeatedly, and you can probably make book that we'll see it again.

*[**Footnote:** A couple of words of warning. State disclosure laws may apply regardless of jurisdictional amount, and some of these, such as California's, require TILA disclosures regardless of the amount financed. Also, we advise our dealer clients to comply with TILA even when it doesn't apply and to use the same documents and procedures for high-dollar deals that they use for low-dollar deals. Things are just less complicated that way.]*

Schultz v. Burton-Moore Ford, Inc., 2008 WL 5111897 (E.D. Mich. December 2, 2008).

A Finance Charge Is a Finance Charge Is a Finance Charge ...

March 2009

By Thomas B. Hudson

We frequently hear from dealers who believe that they have come up with a brand-new way of charging finance charges without having to go through those nasty little technical steps of actually disclosing the finance charges to the customer. Occasionally, we'll hear a dealer say, "It isn't a finance charge, it's a service charge!" or "It isn't a finance charge, it's an origination fee!"

The dealer in a recent case decided the he would impose a "set-up charge." He then evidently concluded that because he did not elect to call the charge a finance charge, it wasn't one.

Oops.

Tomeka Wiley bought a 1991 Oldsmobile Cutlass from Scott Englund, who was operating under the name A & K Auto Sales. Jamal Al-Awamie held the dealer license for A & K Auto Sales.

Wiley's retail installment agreement included a $450 "set-up charge." Wiley returned the Cutlass because of problems with the heater, and she bought a Ford Escort.

The retail installment agreement for the Escort included a $750 set-up charge. Wiley quit making payments on the Escort and wrote to Englund stating that she was withholding her payments because of Englund's failure to transfer title. Englund repossessed the Escort.

Wiley sued Englund and A & K Auto Sales for violations of the federal Truth in Lending Act and the Minnesota Consumer Fraud Act (CFA). Al-Awamie and A & K Auto Sales failed to file an answer. Wiley moved for summary judgment. Englund did not contest liability, but did argue about the appropriate measure of damages.

Wiley argued that she paid Englund $2,000 out of pocket for the two cars. The U.S. District Court for the District of Minnesota found that Englund was liable for $2,000 in actual damages pursuant to the CFA. Wiley further argued that, pursuant to TILA, she was entitled to twice the amount of any finance charges she paid, and claimed that the set-up charges were finance charges.

Englund argued that the set-up charges were not finance charges because they were not labeled as finance charges.

The court concluded that the set-up charges were finance charges and that Wiley was entitled to twice the amount charged.

To get to this conclusion, the court correctly ignored the label that the dealer stuck on these charges and focused instead on whether the charge met the very detailed and technical definition of "finance charge" in the federal Truth in Lending Act and Federal Reserve Board Regulation Z. In the court's view, the charge met the definition. The dealer could have called the charge a cumquat, and it would have made no difference.

The lesson here for the dealer? Actually, there are several.

First, I'm willing to bet that no lawyer signed off on the dealer's pricing scheme. The issue of whether the set-up charge is a finance charge or not is about as elementary a question as you could pose. I've got to believe that even a not-too-experienced lawyer would have flagged the problem.

Second, the dealer might want to get a bit of F&I training. A very few hours of class time would have tipped the dealer at least to the fact that there was an issue with his pricing.

Finally, the dealer could have simply taken a look around. I doubt that he could have found any other dealers using this pricing scheme. That's what we in the detective business call "a clue." If no one else is doing it, there might just be a reason.

Wiley v. A & K Auto Sales, 2008 WL 5244614 (D. Minn. December 15, 2008).

The Equal Credit Opportunity Act and the Fair Credit Reporting Act

The Equal Credit Opportunity Act (ECOA) is a federal law that prohibits certain kinds of discrimination by, and imposes certain duties upon, creditors. The Federal Reserve Board has promulgated Regulation B to further spell out the requirements of the ECOA.

The Fair Credit Reporting Act (FCRA) is also a federal law. It spells out how credit reporting agencies and those who use credit reports, generated by the credit reporting agencies, must behave.

The ECOA and Reg. B have, we believe, generally been successful in reducing discrimination by creditors. That has occurred despite the fact that lawsuits under the ECOA and Reg. B have been much less frequent. The lawsuits that have arisen, however, often have been big-dollar, dangerous class action lawsuits. Nearly all of these lawsuits settled, but the amounts of the settlements sent chills through the credit community. As a result, creditors with good compliance programs run scared when they consider the potential for discrimination in their credit programs.

Although the big-money cases in the discrimination area have involved large sales finance companies and banks, they all began life as lawsuits that included dealers as defendants. Dealers need to pay attention to this!

Many credit the FCRA with driving down the cost of credit while making it more widely available. Both are likely true, but like most federal enactments, the FCRA is a very technical and complicated law. The FCRA doesn't have an implementing regulation, so those trying to comply with it have no guidance beyond the law itself. Most of the FCRA deals with duties and requirements that apply to credit reporting agencies, but dealers get swept up in a few of its provisions. Over the last few years, litigation has erupted in several areas that dealers need to know about. These include so-called "firm offer" prescreened advertisement programs, the requirement to provide "adverse action" notices to credit buyers, and requirements that apply to the content of credit applications, among a few others.

Department of Justice Brings First ECOA Discrimination Cases Against Dealerships
October 2007
By Thomas B. Hudson

On August 21, 2007, the Justice Department announced that it had reached settlements with two Philadelphia-area car dealerships, resolving claims that the dealerships engaged in a pattern or practice of discriminating against African-American customers by charging them higher interest rates on car "loans" (these were likely retail installment sales transactions—it would be nice if the Justice Department lawyers would learn the difference).

The DOJ's announcement says that these are the first two cases alleging discrimination by a car dealership filed by the Justice Department under the Equal Credit Opportunity Act. You can bet they won't be the last.

In two complaints, the Justice Department claimed that Pacifico Ford Inc. and Springfield Ford Inc. violated the Equal Credit Opportunity Act by charging systematically higher "markups" on car "loan" interest rates to African-American customers. The DOJ announcement stated: "In the auto industry, it is common practice for banks and other lenders to set a base interest rate or 'buy rate' and then for the auto dealership to 'mark up' the interest rate to the final rate on the loan for the car." As an aside, again, it would be nice if the DOJ lawyers knew enough about the car business not to call companies buying retail installment contracts from dealers "lenders."

But I digress. The complaints allege that Pacifico Ford and Springfield Ford charged African-American customers higher interest rates than similarly situated white customers for at least three years from 1999–2002.

The dealerships agreed to so-called "consent orders"— orders filed in court under the terms of which Pacifico Ford and Springfield Ford are prohibited from discriminating against customers on the basis of race in connection with auto "loans."

"Racial discrimination in lending is wrong and will not be tolerated," said Wan J. Kim, Assistant Attorney General for the Civil Rights Division. "The lawsuits filed today are part of a continuing effort by the Department of Justice to vigorously enforce the Equal Credit Opportunity Act. We commend Springfield Ford and Pacifico Ford for working cooperatively with the Justice Department to reach an appropriate resolution in these cases."

If the charges are resolved as announced, Pacifico Ford will pay up to $363,166, and Springfield Ford will pay up to $94,565, plus interest, to African-American consumers who were charged higher interest rates. The dealerships have also agreed to change the way they set markups to prevent discrimination. The dealerships will follow the same procedures for setting markups for all customers, and only good faith, competitive factors consistent with ECOA will influence that process. Both dealerships will also provide enhanced equal credit opportunity training to their officers and employees who set rates for automobile "loans."

The cases arose from an investigation conducted by the Civil Rights Division of the Department of Justice, in conjunction with the Pennsylvania Attorney General's office. I don't know, but would bet, that mystery-shopping techniques were employed in the investigation.

The Pennsylvania Attorney General's office announced in an August 23, 2007, press release that it had resolved its related state law claims through separate agreements with the dealerships. The tab was $40,000 for Pacifico Ford and $15,000 for Springfield Ford.

The ECOA has been around for several decades. Private lawsuits—some of them big, noisy, class action lawsuits—have alleged practices of this sort for nearly a decade. So why is the DOJ just now waking up to the problem?

I don't know the answer to that question, but I can tell you that the DOJ is likely to find a lot of low-hanging fruit if it continues its investigations. Dealers typically charge whatever they can charge when they sell cars, financing, insurance products, and all the other stuff that gets moved by the F&I department. Any time a dealership permits its people to exercise discretion in the pricing of these goods and services (and most do), the possibility will arise that some people will pay more than others. And some of the people who pay more will be members of protected classes under the ECOA.

The DOJ is not likely to limit its inquiry to the cost of credit. The ECOA prohibits discrimination in "every aspect" of a credit transaction. Look for the DOJ and plaintiffs' lawyers to argue that the cash price of the car and the price for other goods and services are "aspects" of the credit transaction. If they are successful, dealers will be pressured to charge everyone the same price for everything—the car, the service contract, GAP, you name it.

I'll bet you didn't know you were running a utility, now did you?

Direct Mailings—Where Did That List Come From?

October 2007

By Thomas B. Hudson

In 2001, an Illinois car dealer sent out a mailer to potential customers whose names had been obtained from a credit bureau. The practice of getting lists of potential customers is one that is pretty heavily regulated.

Under the federal Fair Credit Reporting Act (FCRA), you cannot get such a list to use in any manner you please, but you can get a list of people who meet certain criteria (for instance, a credit score of 550–650 who live in a particular geographic area) if you are willing to make them a "firm offer of credit." That gives you a "permissible purpose" in FCRA-speak.

The Illinois car dealer (or some marketing company) came up with the bright idea of obtaining such a list and then sending out a mailing making a "firm offer of credit" in the amount of $300. Now, $300 isn't much credit when you're talking about buying a car, but the FCRA didn't specify a minimum amount—it just required that the offer be "firm."

One of the recipients of the mailing sued, claiming that the dealer's offer of $300 in car purchase credit was not a firm offer but rather was an excuse to pull her credit report and market to her. After a trial and an appeal, the courts concluded that the car dealer's "firm offer" wasn't "firm" enough, and ruled for the consumer.

When the court's decision was reported, the plaintiffs' lawyers smelled blood in the water and started to circle car dealers, mortgage companies, and banks that had used these "firm offer" direct mail pieces. They attacked not only those mailings in which the "offer" was for a low amount, but also the solicitations that failed adequately to describe the offer.

Before you could say "contingent fee," more than 250 "firm offer" class action lawsuits were pending around the country, many of these against car dealers. These cases have been winding their way through the courts, with some courts generally following the first appellate court to address the issue and generally finding for consumers, and other courts injecting a breath of fresh air into the mix by finding for creditors.

A recent case illustrates the limitations on these sorts of attacks. Barbara Reynolds received a pre-approved offer of credit from LeMay Buick-Pontiac-GMC-Cadillac, Inc., a car dealership. LeMay had retained a marketing company to create and send a mailer to potential customers who were emerging from bankruptcy. The list of names was obtained from a source that created and maintained the list solely for direct marketing purposes and not for use as a factor in establishing eligibility for credit.

Reynolds sued LeMay, alleging that LeMay obtained her consumer report without a permissible purpose because the mailer was not a firm offer of credit. LeMay moved for summary judgment.

The U.S. District Court for the Eastern District of Wisconsin found that the list was not a consumer report under the FCRA. The mailer stated that information from a consumer reporting agency was used to pre-qualify the mailer recipients, but the prescreening opt-out disclosure containing this statement was printed on the mailer by mistake. It seems there was a miscommunication between the marketing company and the printer.

The source that provided the list maintained the list only for direct marketing purposes and not for establishing eligibility for credit. Moreover, LeMay did not use the list to determine eligibility for credit. The court also found that neither the list provider nor the marketer qualified as a consumer-reporting agency.

Because LeMay did not use a consumer report from a consumer reporting agency, the FCRA firm offer requirements did not apply to its marketing. Accordingly, the court granted LeMay's motion and dismissed the case.

If a marketing company selling lists approaches your dealership, you may be able to use a list safely if it is derived from a source other than credit reports, and if you are using it correctly. But this is a very, very tricky area. Determining the pedigree of such a list can be hard, and perhaps in some cases impossible. You should get your lawyer involved with the marketing company to make sure the list and your use of it are outside the scope of the FCRA.

If the list is one that is subject to the FCRA, crafting the message to the recipients of the mailers in a manner that will comply with the FCRA's firm offer requirements is also a job for your lawyer, not a marketing firm.

In the South, the instructions for planting kudzu are, "Throw it on the ground, and run like hell." While that's not what I'd do if a marketing company approached me with a list for solicitations, I'd at least be extremely cautious.

Reynolds v. LeMay Buick-Pontiac-GMC-Cadillac, Inc., 2007 WL 2220203 (E.D. Wis. July 30, 2007).

Clearly Inconspicuous

April 2008

By Michael A. Benoit

A friend of mine once described the federal legislative process as akin to performing open-heart surgery in the backseat of a careening taxicab. That's the reason, he contended, that Congress often leaves the details of implementing legislation to federal agencies with expertise in the subject matter. Such was the case with the Fair and Accurate Credit Transactions Act of 2003 (FACTA), which amended and revised a number of specific areas of the existing Fair Credit Reporting Act (FCRA), and added several new, fairly broad provisions with instructions to a number of federal agencies to write implementing rules.

After deliberating for four years, the federal agencies have issued a final rule implementing the new FACTA proscriptions on sharing consumer reports and other information for marketing purposes. At first glance, this "Affiliate Sharing Rule," as it's called, seems pretty straightforward. But as many of us have realized, the rule is much more complicated than it appears, and it is already creating compliance challenges.

As background, the FCRA has long provided that certain communications are not "consumer reports" even though they technically meet the statutory definition. These "exceptions" include communications of one's transaction and experience (T&E) information regarding a consumer, and information other than T&E information as long as the consumer is given a clear and conspicuous opportunity to "opt-out" (i.e., tell you not to communicate the information).

The Affiliate Sharing Rule has narrowed these exceptions by prohibiting affiliated parties from using this information to solicit consumers, unless the consumers are first given a clear and conspicuous notice of the proposed use and the opportunity to opt-out of such use. Seems simple enough, given that we're used to opt-outs already in place under the FCRA and the Gramm-Leach-Bliley privacy rule (GLB). But as always, the devil is in the details, and the particular detail I'm concerned with today is the abandon with which the federal agencies throw around requirements that consumer notices be "clear and conspicuous."

I'm not sure a lot of thought was given to the interplay between the Affiliate Sharing Rule and the GLB privacy rule. Under GLB, you are required to include FCRA-mandated opt-out notices in your privacy policy. This means that if you need to provide two FCRA opt-out notices (i.e., the existing notice, which now applies to sharing information with affiliates for nonmarketing purposes, and the new Affiliate Sharing Rule notice, which applies to sharing credit eligibility-related information with any party for marketing purposes), they both need to show up, clearly and conspicuously, in your privacy policy.

Here's the rub. We have one rule, GLB, requiring your entire privacy policy to be clear and conspicuous, and further mandating that the opt-out notice it requires to appear within your privacy policy for sharing nonpublic personal information with nonaffiliated third parties also be clear and conspicuous. Then you have the FCRA mandating that the opt-out notice for nonmarketing purposes (which must also appear in your privacy policy) be clear and conspicuous. Now the Affiliate Sharing Rule adds another opt-out notice (which must also appear in your privacy policy) to be clear and conspicuous. In other words, your entire privacy policy must be clear and conspicuous, and, if applicable, three additional notices within that privacy policy must be independently clear and conspicuous. If everything is clear and conspicuous, can anything really be clear and conspicuous? Or are there degrees of clarity and conspicuousness that apply? I guess we'll see.

At the end of the day, it will be interesting to see how many consumers actually opt-out. My understanding is that relatively few have actually taken advantage of existing opt-outs, leading one to believe that these opt-outs are often more about politics and lip service than providing actual benefit.

Maybe Congress should think about putting sunset provisions in consumer legislation to eliminate rules in which consumers are clearly and conspicuously not interested. Wouldn't that be something?

Not-So-Firm Analysis

April 2008

By Michael A. Benoit

There are many ways to entice a potential buyer into a dealership. One is a marketing technique familiar to many of you—the direct mail solicitation. This involves working with a third-party finance company, or lender, that obtains a consumer reporting agency list of potential customers who meet certain credit-worthiness criteria, also known as a "prescreened list." The finance company will make a firm offer of auto finance credit to anyone on the list who applies, and continues to meet, the credit criteria established before the list was generated.

The Fair Credit Reporting Act heavily regulates this particular marketing method, and there has been much confusion about what exactly constitutes a "firm offer" of credit, sufficient to comply with the FCRA. The confusion has sprung up fairly recently. Before the case of *Cole v. U. S. Capital, Inc.,* came along in 2004, direct mail solicitations were literally flying out of every post office in the country. *Cole* imposed a "validity and value" standard on these mailings. The Seventh Circuit Court of Appeals is responsible for this standard, which essentially provides that a "firm offer" of credit is valid only if it contains sufficient terms to permit the consumer to determine whether the offer is of value and therefore worth accepting.

I thought the *Cole* case was decided wrongly when it came out. Why? Because nowhere in the FCRA does it mention any kind of "validity and value" standard, at least not to the extent imposed by the Seventh Circuit. Despite this fact, a number of vendors found themselves in hot water in Illinois, Indiana, and Wisconsin (the states comprising the Seventh Circuit), because their "firm offer" solicitations did not adequately disclose all of the material terms of the credit offer (for example, the term, amount financed, APR, etc.), and may not have provided for enough credit to make it worth the consumers' while in the eyes of the Seventh Circuit. There is no language like this in the FCRA, and I thought the court read a paternalistic/big brother kind of duty into the statute that Congress never intended.

Well, I'm happy to say that a number of courts have agreed with me and have rejected the Seventh Circuit's approach. For example, the court hearing two recent cases from the Southern District of Texas (*Hoffer v. Landmark Chevrolet Ltd.* and *Hoge v. Parkway Chevrolet, Inc.*) refused to apply the Seventh Circuit's standard because it could find no basis for it in the FCRA.

What does all this mean for you as dealers? It means that a disagreement in the courts is brewing, and it is possible that the *Cole* case may one day be overturned. Of course, it won't happen overnight, so you'll have to be sure you continue to follow the rules that apply in the jurisdictions where you solicit using prescreened lists from consumer reporting agencies. *Cole* still rules in Indiana, Illinois, Wisconsin, and some other areas of the country, but reasonable minds differ in others. Check with your counsel so you know the rules that apply where you want to market.

Truncation, Anyone?

April 2008

By Thomas B. Hudson

An article in the June 2007 issue of *Spot Delivery*® summarized a new and serious problem for car dealers. An often-overlooked provision of the Fair Credit Reporting Act amendments became effective on December 1, 2006. It says that the electronically printed credit and debit card receipts you give your customers must shorten—or truncate—the account information. You may include no more than the last five digits of the card number, and you must delete the card's expiration date. For example, a receipt that truncates the credit card number and deletes the expiration date could look like this:

ACCT: **********12345

EXP: ****

Most electronic card machines have been modified to truncate the account number. But quite a few merchants are still handing out receipts that include the card's expiration date. That's a violation of the FCRA, say a number of courts that have considered these cases. Attorneys have filed class actions all across the country seeking up to $1,000 per credit card receipt for this mistake. The FCRA allows consumers to receive a statutory damage award from $100 to $1,000 for each willful violation of the Act, and each receipt can be a separate violation.

Congress added this provision to the FCRA in 2003, as part of its effort to prevent identity theft. It was concerned that a consumer's credit card slip could fall into the wrong hands, letting a thief use the account number and expiration date for fraudulent purchases. But this provision was phased in gradually. Merchants using newer machines had to comply by December 2004. Merchants with older machines had until December 2006. Since that time, all merchants using electronic machines have to truncate account information, including masking the expiration date.

In addition to class action and individual suits from customers, dealers also must worry about the Federal Trade Commission. The FTC has hinted that it may bring enforcement actions against companies whose credit card slips are showing a little too much information. When the feds come calling, the penalties jump to as much as $16,000 per violation.

Our warning about class actions turned out, if you'll pardon the pun, to have been "spot-on." We've seen seven reported 2007 opinions in these cases—all filed as class actions, by the way. So far, we've seen three 2008 opinions—again, class actions. The defendants in the cases include typical "deep pocket" companies like restaurant chains, but "Mom and Pop" businesses are being hit as well. So far, there have been no reported cases dealing with car dealers, but believe me, it's just a matter of time. There is some good news to report from the opinions. Plaintiffs file lawsuits seeking class relief, but it's up to the court to permit the matter to proceed as a class action. Defendants in these cases have been resisting class "certification," and, for the most part, they've been successful. The judges writing most of the opinions have evidenced a nearly palpable dislike for the plaintiffs and their claims, and most of the judges have refused to certify a class, leaving the defendants with manageable, but still troublesome, individual lawsuits.

The judges have cited several reasons for refusing to grant class certification. In some cases, the courts have concluded that the "named plaintiff" is not representative of the class. In other cases, the courts have cited the potential for attorney abuse in filing highly technical suits when there have been no alleged damages on the part of the class.

But the eye-popping reason that some of the courts have relied on really got my attention, and it should get yours, as well. Some courts have refused to certify a class because of the potential for damage awards that are so high the defendants would be put out of business!

The bad news is that not all courts have refused to certify classes in these cases. That also should get your attention.

Now, a typical dealership doesn't generate the sheer number of credit card transactions that a fast-food store or a hotel would generate, but when you count the number of parts and service credit card transactions in a typical dealership each day, when you realize that there are potential violations with regard to every such transaction every day, and when you realize that each violation is a potential $1,000 award, you start to realize that it might not be a real bad idea to comply with the law.

Auto Finance Marketing—Seventh Circuit Makes U-Turn on "Firm Offer" Requirements

May 2008

By Jean Noonan

Car dealers, their marketing companies, and auto finance companies got good news last month from a court that has been creating legal havoc for the past three years. In *Murray v. New Cingular Wireless Services, Inc.*, the U.S. Court of Appeals for the Seventh Circuit did a major about-face on its opinions regarding pre-approved credit offers—opinions that have been making plaintiffs' lawyers rich and tormenting dealers and auto finance creditors.

For more than 30 years, sellers have used pre-approved credit offers to encourage customers to come in and shop. Congress officially blessed this practice in 1996, when it amended the Fair Credit Reporting Act (FCRA) to set out the rules for using credit bureau information to identify potential recipients of pre-approved credit offers. In exchange for getting a peek at consumers' credit information, creditors must follow the FCRA's "firm offer" rules.

This generally worked well for dealers and other merchants that extend credit, until the Seventh Circuit decided one company took the firm offer rules too far. In *Cole v. U.S. Capital, Inc.*, the court objected to a company's use of prescreened credit lists to make $300 offers of credit to finance a car purchase. The court said that the credit offer must have "value" to the consumer in light of the merchandise the consumer must purchase to use the credit. By itself, this opinion was not a disaster; few people wanted to defend using prescreening to make worthless credit offers. But courts around the country, and especially those in Illinois, Wisconsin, and

Indiana, quickly extended the *Cole* opinion. The Seventh Circuit seemed to go along when, in *Murray v. GMAC Mortgage Corp.,* it said that all material terms of the credit offer had to appear in "the four corners of the offer."

More than 300 class action lawsuits were filed against companies that made firm offers of credit. Some of them were settled for millions of dollars each. Companies faced being put out of business by judgments that could be from $100 to $1,000 for each piece of mail containing a pre-approved offer. It didn't matter that companies were making legitimate, valuable credit offers. Courts were often siding with plaintiffs just because the pre-approved offer did not spell out every credit term.

The *New Cingular* decision restored some sanity to the firm offer rules. The best part of the opinion is the court's clear rejection of the notion that the firm offer rules require a company to include all material terms of the offer when using prescreening. The court noted that the FCRA's "firm offer" definition simply does not include such a requirement. We are pleased the Seventh Circuit has learned how to read. This decision should bring a swift end to the class action lawsuits seeking millions simply because an auto finance offer did not promise a specific credit amount, interest rate, or other credit term.

Our celebration over the newly found literacy skills of this court is not unqualified, however. The court clung to its earlier holdings that sales finance offers must have "value" as credit offers. We might have hoped that the court would extend its reading ability to this issue, too, because the judges would quickly see that the FCRA's "firm offer" definition nowhere mentions the concept of "value." For now, however, companies using prescreening must still be prepared to justify their sales finance credit offers as having value.

In the wake of this decision, we are left with two questions:

1. What must we do to show our auto credit offers have value to consumers?

There is no bright line for a value test, which is why we cannot be completely happy with the *New Cingular* decision. Financing of only $300 for a car sale does not have value, the court has said. But how much is enough? Your minimum offer apart from prescreened solicitations should be a good guide. For example, if a sales finance company's usual minimum credit amount is $5,000, and the dealer has cars available in that price range, a $5,000 minimum offer should be sufficient. The best way to show an offer has value is to show that previous customers have accepted and used credit on those terms.

2. Is there any legal reason to include credit terms in our prescreened credit offers?

Even though the court has confirmed that the FCRA doesn't require including all material credit terms, there are still good reasons to provide them, or at least as many of them as you can. By putting the terms of the credit offer in the mailer, you let consumers (and their class action lawyers) see just by reading it that the offer has value. That makes any FCRA challenge much easier and cheaper to defend. Even better, it means you, as dealers, are much less likely to be sued in the first place.

You sometimes will not have enough information to provide the precise credit terms. Those terms may depend on information the consumer provides after accepting the offer, such as income, and on the car selected for purchase. Providing ranges for some terms will usually be enough to demonstrate the offer's value. Avoid using only the most favorable end of the offer range, however, such as, "You are pre-approved for up to $25,000" or "Down payments as low as $1." The point is to show that even the least favorable offer has value to some consumers.

The Seventh Circuit's U-turn on firm offers is a welcome development, even though the court is still not entirely on the right path. The road for dealers who use prescreened lists for pre-approved credit offers has now become much safer.

Murray v. New Cingular Wireless Services, Inc., 2008 WL 1701839 (7th Cir. (N.D. Ill., N.D. Ind., E.D. Wis.) April 16, 2008).

Mail Offers—Firm and Not So Firm

May 2008

By Thomas B. Hudson and Michael A. Goodman

Dealers around the country have been beset by class action lawsuits challenging a particular sort of mailer—specifically mailers in which the dealer makes a "firm offer of credit" to the customer as an inducement to pay a visit to the dealership. These "firm offers" are made for the purpose of permitting dealers to obtain prescreened lists of consumers from credit reporting agencies, a practice that would be prohibited but for an exception for "firm offer" mailers.

The cases involving firm offer mailers have some dealer lawyers we know so spooked that they would rather pick up a live rattlesnake than give an opinion on whether a particular "firm offer" mailer is inside or outside the law. Those lawyers, and the dealers they represent, should be able to breathe a bit easier now, at least in some states.

All this mischief started with the case of *Cole v. U.S. Capital, Inc.* In *Cole*, the U.S. Court of Appeals for the Seventh Circuit found that a dealer's mailing offering $300 in credit toward the purchase of a vehicle was not a valid firm offer of credit under the Fair Credit Reporting Act (FCRA). Many lawyers disagreed with the *Cole* decision, pointing out that the court had read requirements into the FCRA that were not there.

In two recent decisions regarding prescreening under the Fair Credit Reporting Act, the U.S. Court of Appeals for the First Circuit affirmed district court decisions rejecting consumers' class action challenges to creditors' firm offers of credit. Both decisions concluded that the FCRA's "firm offer of credit" definition does not require the disclosure of any specific terms of the offer in the initial communication to consumers.

On March 19, 2008, in *Sullivan v. Greenwood Credit Union*, the court affirmed the district court's award of summary judgment to the creditor. Greenwood Credit Union sent its credit offer to a prescreened list of prospects provided by a consumer-reporting agency. Sullivan argued that a valid firm offer of credit must satisfy the FCRA's definition of that term and must also constitute a valid "offer" as that term has been interpreted by common law. Sullivan further argued that the credit union's mailing was not a valid "offer" because it did not provide credit terms with enough specificity to allow for acceptance by consumers.

The court found no basis for looking beyond the statutory definition of "firm offer of credit" and explained that this definition does not require the disclosure of any particular terms in the initial mailing. Rather, the court reasoned that a firm offer of credit is valid as long as the creditor will not deny credit to any consumer who meets the creditor's preselection criteria—that is, the criteria established before the prescreening process was conducted. The FCRA allows the specific terms of the offer to be provided to interested consumers once they have expressed interest in learning more from the creditor.

In reaching this decision, the *Sullivan* court distinguished the *Cole* opinion. In *Cole*, the U.S. Court of Appeals for the Seventh

Circuit found that a dealer's mailing was not a valid firm offer of credit. The *Cole* court found that the mailing was an insufficient "guise for solicitation" in part because specific terms of the offer were missing and because it was unclear whether the mailing was, in fact, an offer for credit or a sales pitch for a car dealership.

[***Editor's note:*** *Distinguish: To call attention to differences; to illustrate why a cited case in legal argument is applicable or inapplicable.—Gilbert Law Summaries*]

The *Sullivan* court had no problem concluding that Greenwood's offer was for credit. The court also noted that the "minimal invasion of privacy" created by prescreening was offset by the value of the information provided in the credit union's mailing.

On April 3, 2008, in *Dixon v. Shamrock Financial Corp.*, the same court affirmed the district court's decision to grant the creditor's motion to dismiss Dixon's challenge. As in *Sullivan*, the court applied the FCRA's "firm offer of credit" definition and declined to look beyond that definition for any additional requirements for a valid firm offer. Because that definition does not require the disclosure of any particular terms in the initial mailing, the court concluded Shamrock's mailing did not need to contain any such terms.

Once again, the court distinguished *Cole*. In this case, this distinction was based on the fact that in *Dixon,* unlike in *Cole,* the consumer did not allege that any consumer was, or would have been, denied credit despite meeting Shamrock's internal criteria. Finally, the court noted that consumers' "remedy" in response to the "invasion of privacy" created by prescreening is to opt out of prescreening rather than to sue the creditor.

So, things are a bit less dicey in the First Circuit (that includes Maine, Massachusetts, New Hampshire, Rhode Island, and Puerto Rico ¡Muchas gracias!).

Maybe we won't have to pick up that rattlesnake after all. *Sullivan v. Greenwood Credit Union*, 2008 WL 726135 (1st. Cir. (D. Mass.) March 19, 2008). *Dixon v. Shamrock Financial Corp.*, 2008 WL 902200 (1st. Cir. (D. Mass.) April 3, 2008).

It's Enough to Make a Grown Man Cry

June 2008

By Thomas B. Hudson

For the last few months, we've been warning car dealers about a really serious danger posed by a measure enacted by Congress in 2003. That law, the Fair and Accurate Credit Transactions Act (FACTA), contained two provisions dealing with credit cards and designed to fight identity theft.

One measure required merchants who accept credit cards (yes, that includes many car dealers) to display only the last five digits of the customer's credit card number, or a "truncated" number, on the customer's receipt. Another measure prohibited merchants from displaying the card's expiration date on the customer's receipt.

News about the truncation requirement spread more effectively than did news about the expiration date requirement, though, and, before long, we began to notice class action lawsuits challenging merchants who had failed to get the word about expiration dates. The suits claimed statutory damages of $100 to $1,000 per customer receipt. Under FACTA, there is no requirement that a consumer show that he or she has been damaged in any way—statutory damages are available just by showing that the consumer's receipt isn't truncated or that the receipt displays the expiration date.

Many of the suits were against small businesses, such as

restaurants, but many were against larger chains as well. Every car dealer that accepts credit cards became a potential target.

Responding to these suits, the businesses argued that a class action was not the best way for the lawsuits to proceed because of the potential that massive damages awards could bankrupt the businesses. While a few courts bought this argument, most did not, and certified the suits as class actions.

The truncation and expiration date parts of the FACTA legislation turned out to be the worst sort of "gotcha" legislation. An obscure (at least for those who are primarily in the retailing business) credit law imposes potentially massive damages against businesses when no one has been damaged. The resulting legal trap was a plaintiff's lawyer's dream.

And remember where these incredibly awful provisions came from? Yup, your good old elected representatives in Congress.

So imagine my reaction when I got a press release from a House committee announcing that the House had passed H.R. 4008, the Credit and Debit Card Receipt Clarification Act, authored by Florida Congressman Tim Mahoney, by a unanimous vote of 407-0. The bill would amend FACTA to "ensure that it is not abused by frivolous class action lawsuits against businesses." Part of the House press release stated:

H.R. 4008, the Credit and Debit Receipt Clarification Act, addresses the unintended consequences of FACTA and makes clear that if a company truncated a consumer's credit card number, but did not remove the expiration date, then the company did not willfully violate FACTA and cannot be sued for statutory damages. It is important to note that there is no evidence that the failure to redact an expiration date has ever resulted in a consumer being harmed and not one of the lawsuits currently filed alleges any actual harm to an individual's account or identity. The technical correction, however, would preserve a consumer's right to sue for negligence in the event someone experiences actual harm or account fraud as a result of having their expiration date printed on their receipt.

I looked through the rest of the press release in vain for any sort of admission that Congress, by not doing its job, had created this mess and was responsible for the hundreds of class action lawsuits against businesses across the country.

Instead of crowing about their wonderful accomplishment in removing a threat that it created in the first place, wouldn't you think that the members would at least say, "Our bad"?

As I finished writing this, I learned that the measure had just passed the Senate, as well. They didn't apologize either.

Congress Slips up on Slip Fix
July 2008
By Shelley B. Fowler

If you are a diligent *Spot Delivery*® reader, you know what information is not allowed on the electronically printed credit and debit card receipts you give your customers. In the June 2007 issue, Jean Noonan reminded you about amendments to the Fair Credit Reporting Act, phased in over a two-year period, that required merchants to shorten—or truncate—the account information on receipts. The amendments prohibited merchants from including more than the last five digits of the card number and from printing the card's expiration date on the credit or debit card receipt.

Although many merchants complied with the first requirement by eliminating all but the last five digits of the card number, many merchants slipped up by continuing to print expiration dates on receipts after the effective date of the amendment—December 2004 for merchants using newer machines and December 2006 for merchants with older machines. This mistake turned out to be costly for many businesses, as plaintiffs' attorneys began filing suits, mainly class action suits in droves, seeking statutory damages of up to $1,000 for each receipt printed with an expiration date.

In last month's issue, Tom Hudson expressed outrage that Congress, in connection with legislation it introduced to stem the tide of class action lawsuits over the failure to redact a card's expiration date on the copy of the receipt given to the customer, did not admit that it made a mistake in causing the problem in the first place.

The legislation Tom mentioned was signed by President Bush on June 3, and dealers should collectively breathe a sigh of relief. The bill, H.R. 4008, provides that if a merchant properly truncated the account number but printed the expiration date on a receipt, that merchant did not willfully violate the FCRA and cannot be held liable for statutory damages.

Unfortunately, however, the sigh of relief you just took is only temporary. Congress did not eliminate the prohibition against printing a card's expiration date on the receipt, even though it recognized that "[e]xperts in the field agree that proper truncation of the card number, by itself &, regardless of the inclusion of the expiration date, prevents a potential fraudster from perpetrating identity theft or credit card fraud." Instead, the law merely provides that if the card's expiration date was printed on a receipt between December 4, 2004 and June 3, 2008, but the receipt did not include more than the last five digits of the card number, then the merchant is off the hook unless there is proof that a customer suffered actual harm from the printing of the expiration date.

What does this mean for you? It means that, as of June 4, if you include a card's expiration date on an electronically printed receipt, you're probably going to have a tough time persuading a judge that you shouldn't be liable for statutory damages. I can just hear the plaintiffs' attorneys' argument to the judge— Congress gave businesses a two-year phase in of the law and just gave them another three-year reprieve, so enough is enough!

As Jean recognized a year ago, and it's even more important now, you'd better make sure your slip isn't showing more than it should!

Just the FACTA, Ma'am

July 2008

By Michael A. Benoit

Back in 2003, Congress got busy and made a number of substantive amendments to the Fair Credit Reporting Act when it passed the Fair and Accurate Credit Transactions Act (FACTA). FACTA imposed some significant rulemaking requirements on the federal agencies, and more than four years later, those regulations are still trickling in.

Last fall saw the arrival of the Affiliate Marketing Rule and the Red Flag Rules, with initial mandatory compliance dates of October 1, 2008, and November 1, 2008. Both are hot topics in the auto finance community. The Affiliate Marketing Rule limits the ability of a creditor's affiliate to use "eligibility" information (e.g., information related to the customer's creditworthiness or history with the creditor) about the creditor's customer for marketing purposes. The Red Flag Rules require all creditors, including auto dealers, to develop and implement a written Identity Theft Prevention Program.

On May 8, 2008, the Federal Trade Commission and the Federal Reserve Board issued their long-awaited proposed rule on "risk-based pricing," another hot topic for the credit community in general. We've all been waiting to see what the FTC and the fed would do with this rule required by FACTA, given that FACTA seems to require a notice that says something like, "Welcome to XYZ Finance Company, and by the way, you're not one of our most desirable customers (and here's why)." This may be a well-intentioned attempt to get consumers focused on information in their credit files that negatively impacts their cost of credit, but it is not necessarily the best way to establish good customer relations.

The proposed "Risk-Based Pricing Notice Rule" generally requires a dealer to provide a specific notice to a consumer when the dealer uses a consumer report to grant or extend credit to the consumer on material terms that are "materially less favorable" than the most favorable terms available from or through that dealer to a substantial proportion of its consumers. It's a vague standard, no matter how you view it. The proposed rule seems to indicate a preference for a 40% standard, i.e., the top 40% of the customer base would not get a notice, but the lower 60% would. Of course, it's more complicated than that.

Fortunately, the proposed rule provides for two alternative means by which creditors can determine when they are offering credit on material terms that are "materially less favorable." These are by use of a credit score proxy or the use of credit tiers. The proposed rule also includes certain exceptions to the general rule, including exceptions for creditors that provide a consumer with a disclosure of the consumer's credit score in conjunction with additional information that provides context for the credit score disclosure.

The bad news is that the proposed rule specifically places the burden on dealers, as opposed to the finance companies that purchase auto paper from dealers; also, it specifically excepts purchasers and assignees of credit obligations from the requirement to provide the notice. The good news is . . . well, there is no good news.

As always, stay tuned. This is only the proposed rule, and the comment period is open through early August. I expect the comments will be many and varied.

Have You Defused the "Truncation" Bomb in Your Credit Card Sales?

December 2008

By Thomas B. Hudson

If you live in a yurt on the steppes of Mongolia, your Internet service is out, the battery in your cell has died, and your *New York Times* subscription has expired, you might not have heard about these "truncation" class action lawsuits. If that describes you, and if you don't subscribe to *Spot Delivery®* and you are still giving your customers credit card receipts showing more than the last five digits of the card, or showing an expiration date, you need to stop, and you need to stop right now.

Here's why. Giving your customer a credit card receipt showing an expiration date or more than the last five digits of the credit card number violates federal law and exposes you to class action lawsuit damages that are potentially so large that they will ruin your business, and that's no exaggeration. Here's what we said in a *Spot Delivery®* article in June 2007:

An often-overlooked provision of the Fair Credit Reporting Act amendments became effective on December 1, 2006. It says that the electronically printed credit and debit card receipts you give your customers must shorten—or truncate—the account information. You may include no more than the last five digits of the card number, and you must delete the card's expiration date. For example, a receipt that truncates the credit card number and deletes the expiration date could look like this:

CCT: ***********12345
EXP: ****

Most electronic card machines have been modified to truncate the account number. But quite a few merchants are still handing out receipts that include the card's expiration date. That's a violation of the FCRA, say a number of courts that have considered these cases. Attorneys have filed class actions all across the country seeking up to $1,000 per credit card receipt for this mistake. The FCRA allows consumers to receive a statutory damage award from $100 to $1,000 for each willful violation of the Act, and each receipt can be a separate violation. Since our warning, the cases haven't stopped. The case discussed in this article is just the latest of many similar cases filed against all sorts of businesses that accept credit card payments.

Benjamin Beringer received a credit card receipt from a terminal at the parking garage at O'Hare International Airport that contained more than the last five digits of his account number and the expiration date of his card. Beringer sued Standard Parking Corp., which operated the parking facility, for violating the Fair and Accurate Credit Transactions Act amendments to the Fair Credit Reporting Act.

Beringer moved for class certification (this is just what it sounds like—he wants the court to confirm that he can bring a claim on behalf of himself and others who are "similarly situated"). The U.S. District Court for the Northern District of Illinois certified the class.

The court found that the numerosity (is the class big enough?), commonality (are the class members' claims enough alike?), and typicality (is Beringer enough like the class?) requirements of Rule 23(a) of the Federal Rules of Civil Procedure were satisfied and that Beringer and his counsel could adequately represent the class.

The court also found that common issues predominated over individual ones under Rule 23(b)(3). The court rejected the argument that some consumers might prefer to seek actual damages or that individual determinations were necessary to set an amount of statutory damages. The court found that there were no individual issues at the liability stage, and it was unlikely that there would be individual issues at the damages stage.

Standard tried to defeat class certification by arguing that a class action was not superior to individual actions, because the damages to it could be ruinous. The court noted that there was a potential for a damages award so large that it violated the company's due process rights, but concluded that such considerations should be taken into account only if the class were certified and prevailed on liability.

The only real issue left, it seems, is how many zeroes the settlement check will have.

If you accept credit cards and you haven't taken steps to assure that your receipts don't show more than the last five digits of the credit card number and don't show the expiration date, your dealership is a sitting duck for one of these class action lawsuits. Better hustle on down to the bookkeeping department, and make sure you know what's going on.

Beringer v. Standard Parking Corp., 2008 WL 4390626 (N.D. Ill. September 24, 2008).

Firm Offers and Prescreening: Dealers Get a Break

June 2009

By Jean Noonan

You have cars you need to sell. There are potential customers out there who need your cars. But some of them cannot qualify for credit, and some others can qualify but don't know it. Dealers have found that prescreened lists from credit bureaus have provided a valuable solution to this problem. Some dealers purchase prescreened lists of consumers who have good credit. Other dealers, who can sell subprime contracts to finance companies, look for consumers with damaged credit or recent bankruptcies.

Dealers who use prescreened lists must make a "firm offer of credit" to each consumer on the list. Most dealers hire a marketing company to obtain the prescreened lists, create the promotional flier, and mail it to consumers. They sit back and wait for the customers to come streaming into their showrooms.

So what is wrong with this arrangement? The Federal Trade Commission staff and some plaintiffs' lawyers have insisted that marketing companies cannot buy prescreened lists. They argue that the law permits only creditors to purchase these lists. This argument ignores the fact that a dealer making a credit sale is a creditor. As we've said many times, just because the dealer plans to sell the contract immediately to a bank or finance company doesn't mean the dealer is not the original creditor in the deal. A dealer should be able to hire a marketing company to buy lists on its behalf, so long as it fulfills its duty to make a firm offer to everyone on the list.

A federal court recently weighed in on this arrangement, and the outcome was good for dealers and their marketing companies. Here's what happened.

Jerrod Harris received a flier that offered him a pre-approved line of credit to purchase a car from Foreign Motors Suzuki. It also said he had won "one of the following prizes": a Sony flat screen TV, a $1,000 shopping spree, $4,000 in cash, or a Sea-Doo watercraft. The flier stated it had been issued by "Auto Credit of America," a fictitious company. In fine print, the flier listed the requirements for credit qualification, including debt-to-income and payment-to-income limits and a requirement that any bankruptcy be discharged.

The dealer did not buy the prescreened list directly from the credit bureau. In fact, there were at least three intermediaries between the credit bureau and the dealer. Harris happily sued them all. He claimed that the credit bureau violated the Fair Credit Reporting Act (FCRA) by selling a prescreened list to someone who did not intend to make a firm offer of credit. He claimed the marketing companies also violated the FCRA by obtaining the list without making firm credit offers.

Harris eventually dismissed his claims against the marketing companies and pressed his case against ChoicePoint, which had acted as Experian's agent in selling the list to the marketing companies. He argued that ChoicePoint knew the company purchasing the list was a marketing firm, not a creditor.

The court ruled for ChoicePoint. The FCRA only requires a credit bureau to have a "reason to believe" the list buyer will use the list to make firm offers of credit. The marketing companies certified that they would use the lists for legitimate business purposes. The court was not troubled that ChoicePoint knew the marketing company was not a creditor. ChoicePoint knew the marketing company was acting as a middleman for entities that made firm offers, and that was sufficient, the court ruled.

Not every court can make its way through complicated business arrangements and come out with the correct answer, as this one did. That is especially true when the issue involves a law as knotty as the FCRA's prescreening rules. The questionable aspects of the offer, including the free prizes and phony lender name, also did not sidetrack the court.

Despite this good ruling, I'm sure we haven't seen the end of challenges to selling prescreened lists to marketing firms who work for dealers. Here's some practical advice for using marketing companies who buy prescreened lists.

- Pay close attention to the terms of the firm offer, and be prepared to honor them. The FCRA protects you by permitting certain qualifications to the offers. But if the consumer meets the qualifications, you must offer credit, even if you discover you cannot sell the contract.

- Use a reputable marketing company, and review the mail piece carefully. Avoid questionable come-ons, like "free prizes," that sound better than they are. There is no point in beating an FCRA lawsuit if you wind up losing a deceptive practices case.

- Treat your customers well. As often happens, Harris found a lawyer originally for another reason entirely. His initial concern was not about a firm offer of credit; he was upset because the dealer made him return the car to the dealership two days after he bought it and offered no explanation. When he lost his lawsuit against the dealer for breach of contract and deception, his enterprising lawyer came up with an FCRA case.

This opinion should help turn down the heat on dealers whose marketing companies use prescreened lists. It is a good idea, though, to review the mailings and your firm offer compliance procedures with your attorney.

Harris v. Database Management & Marketing, Inc., 2009 U.S. Dist. LEXIS 34947 (D. Md. April 23, 2009).

Red Flags, OFAC, and Privacy

We are lumping these topics together because they treat the same general topic—personal identity—albeit in different ways. Because they all deal with personal identity, dealers and creditors sometimes confuse them. Here's a good way to keep them straight:

Red Flags—The FTC's Red Flag Rules attempt to make sure that the person a dealer or other creditor is doing business with is who he or she says he or she is. Think, "Are you really who you say you are?"

OFAC—The Treasury Department's Office of Foreign Assets Control puts out a list of people with whom dealers and other creditors are prohibited from doing business. Think, "Are you a bad guy with whom I can't do business?"

The Gramm-Leach-Bliley Privacy Law and the Federal Trade Commission's Privacy Rule require dealers and other creditors to maintain the confidentiality of customer information. Think, "How will I keep what you tell me from getting into the hands of those who will misuse it to hurt you?"

In all three areas, the federal government has, in effect, deputized dealers and other creditors into policing the activities and personal business of citizens in an effort to accomplish various public objectives—fighting identity theft, fighting terrorism, and protecting privacy.

Make sure you keep that Deputy's badge polished, you hear?

Red Flag Warning

December 2007

By Michael A. Benoit

In the fall of 2007, Southern California had a spate of devastating wildfires, and residents experienced the hot Santa Ana winds and the "red flag warnings" that accompany them— that is, warnings of the potential for such a catastrophe.

With the recent publication of the Red Flag Rules and Guidelines (the "Rule") mandated by the Fair and Accurate Credit Transactions Act of 2003 (FACTA), the federal government has now announced its own "red flag warning" as a means of combating identity theft. The Red Flag Rules are effective January 1, 2008. The initial mandatory compliance date for auto dealers was set for November 1, 2008, but that date has been extended more than once. This may sound like there is time to get your house in order, but don't dally—there's a lot to do.

The Rule requires auto dealers who engage in financing activities to establish an Identity Theft Prevention Program that is designed to detect, prevent, and mitigate identity theft. For most dealers, this means creating a written Program with respect to new credit accounts. For those of you in the buy-here, pay-here community, your Program will need to address your existing accounts as well. All consumer accounts are covered by the Rule, as well as business accounts to the extent you determine that there is a reasonably foreseeable risk to the business customer or yourself from identity theft.

Your Program must be composed of four distinct elements containing reasonable policies and procedures to:

1. Identify relevant "red flags" (patterns, practices, or activities that indicate the possibility of identity theft) relevant to the credit origination process;

2. Detect and evaluate these "red flags" in connection with individual customer transactions;

3. Respond to red flags you detect in an appropriate way to prevent identity theft; and

4. Ensure your Program is updated periodically to reflect changes in risks to customers from your experiences and new identity theft activity.

The term "Red Flag" refers to a pattern, practice, or specific activity that indicates the possible existence of identity theft. There are some examples in the Rule as to what these might be, but you will need to make a determination for yourself as to what these are in the context of your business.

The Rule does contain a list of potential red flags you may consider for incorporation into your Program. The list is provided for guidance to help you identify relevant red flags. While you will not need to justify to the Federal Trade Commission your failure to include a specific red flag from the list in your Program, you may find yourself having to account for the overall effectiveness of your Program. So, if a particular red flag makes sense in the context of your business to include in your Program and you didn't include it, you may still find yourself in hot water if you experience an identity theft incident.

The Rule also provides final guidance regarding actions a user of consumer reports must take when a consumer-reporting agency sends the user a notice of address discrepancy. When you receive such a notice, you must use policies and procedures you have designed to enable you to form a reasonable belief that the consumer report relates to the actual person standing in the dealership or otherwise applying for credit. To the extent you furnish information to consumer reporting agencies, you must also furnish a corrected address for the consumer.

This new Rule is involved and complicated, and, as always,

such things create opportunities for commerce. You'll soon be set upon by vendors with snappy technology that will take care of all your obligations and allow you to go on your merry way. But remember that if something sounds too good to be true, it usually is. While there are certainly some technological solutions that will help you comply with your obligations, my view is that there will be some amount of training and effort you will have to undertake in order truly to comply.

So, do yourself a favor—carefully vet new technologies with your compliance counsel. While certain parts of the Rule lend themselves to technological solutions, other parts may require some good old-fashioned subjective thinking. Be sure you know which parts are which, and you'll keep the regulatory wildfires to a minimum.

What Are You Putting in YOUR Dumpster?
January/February 2008
By Thomas B. Hudson

A car dealership that left credit documents with buyers' sensitive personal and financial information in and around an unsecured dumpster has agreed to settle Federal Trade Commission charges that it violated federal regulations.

The FTC's complaint alleges that the dealership violated the Disposal, Safeguards, and Privacy Rules by failing to properly dispose of credit reports or information taken from credit reports, failing to develop or implement reasonable safeguards to protect customer information, and failing to provide customers with privacy notices.

"Every business, whether large or small, must take reasonable and appropriate measures to protect sensitive consumer information, from acquisition to disposal," FTC Chairman Deborah Platt Majoras said. "This agency will continue to prosecute companies that fail to fulfill their legal responsibility to protect consumers' personal information."

According to the FTC's complaint, the dealership collected personal information about consumers, including Social Security Numbers, bank and credit card account numbers, income and credit histories, and consumer reports. Since at least December 2005, the dealership engaged in a number of practices that, taken together, failed to provide reasonable and appropriate security for consumers' personal information. Among other things, the company allegedly failed to implement reasonable policies and procedures requiring the proper disposal of consumers' personal information, including consumer reports; to take reasonable actions in disposing of that information; and to identify reasonably foreseeable internal and external risks to consumer information. The company also allegedly failed to develop, implement, or maintain a comprehensive written information security program.

As a result of the company's failures, the complaint alleges, on multiple occasions the dealership's documents containing consumers' personal information were found in and around a dumpster near the dealership that was unsecured and easily accessible to the public (does that sound like your dumpster?). In February 2006, for example, hundreds of such documents were found, including consumer reports for 36 consumers, many of which were in open trash bags. In March 2006, FTC staff notified the company in writing about this situation, and, on at least two occasions afterward, more such documents were found in and around the same dumpster.

The complaint charges the dealership with violating the FTC's Disposal Rule, which requires companies to dispose of credit reports and information from credit reports in a safe and appropriate manner, and the FTC's Safeguards Rule, which requires financial institutions (remember, that term includes car dealers) to take appropriate measures to protect customer information. The complaint also alleges that from July 1, 2001, until March 2006, the dealership failed to provide its customers with a privacy notice describing its information collection and sharing practices with respect to affiliated and nonaffiliated third parties, as required by the FTC's Privacy Rule.

The stipulated judgment and final order requires the dealership to pay a $50,000 civil penalty for violations of the Disposal Rule and prohibits the company from further violations of the Disposal, Safeguards, and Privacy Rules. The settlement also requires the dealership to obtain, every two years for the next 10 years, an audit from a qualified, independent, third-party professional to ensure that its security program meets the standards of the order.

This is the FTC's first Disposal Rule case and its 15th case challenging faulty data security practices by companies that handle sensitive consumer information.

The FTC action described in the previous few paragraphs didn't happen. But the text is a paraphrase (actually a near-quote) of an action that the FTC announced in mid-December involving a mortgage company. I changed the mortgage company's name and any references to it to "dealership" and tweaked a couple of other details for the purpose of getting your attention.

So, I lied, and you're probably thinking that the FTC might go after a mortgage company, but it wouldn't go after a mere car dealership. You'd be wrong. We've seen a number of recent indications from the FTC that it is very, very interested in car dealers. If your privacy and safeguarding compliance isn't what it should be, let this be a wake-up call.

Copies of the complaint and stipulated judgment and order (the real one, involving the mortgage company) are available from the FTC's website at www.ftc.gov.

Change Your Clock; Keep Your Customers' Private Information Secure
April 2008
By Catharine S. Andricos

Have you ever heard the saying, "change your clock, change your battery"? Twice a year, when you change your clock for daylight savings, you should also take the opportunity to change the battery in your smoke detector. Or, so the saying goes. The idea is to get people to associate two things that they may not otherwise consider related.

Bearing this saying in mind as you embark on implementing an Identity Theft Prevention (ITP) Program at your dealership as required by the new Red Flag Rules. It is worth associating your new ITP Program with your existing privacy, information security, and anti-fraud policies and procedures.

The Red Flag Rules requires you to implement an ITP Program at your dealership. As part of your ITP Program, you must identify and detect "red flags" that may indicate the possibility of identity theft at your dealership. Doing so will involve a thorough examination of every aspect of your handling and use of customer information.

Implementing your ITP Program gives you a prime opportunity to consider ways to improve your dealership's existing privacy, information security, and anti-fraud policies and procedures as they also relate to your handling and use of customer information. (Think information security program, privacy policy, record retention policy, customer service policy, customer authentication procedures, anti-fraud procedures, etc.)

Just as taking the opportunity to change the battery in your smoke detector will help to keep your loved ones safe, taking the opportunity to improve your existing privacy, information security, and anti-fraud policies and procedures will help to keep your customers' private information secure.

To begin your ITP Program implementation, we suggest the following steps.

First, take the opportunity to increase the general awareness at your dealership of the importance of protecting private customer information. You can use the Red Flag Rules' compliance requirements to draw your employees' attention not only to your ITP Program implementation efforts, but also to your dealership's other privacy, information security, and anti-fraud policies and procedures. Doing so will underscore your view of the importance of protecting private customer information within your dealership.

Second, use your ITP Program implementation as an opportunity to detect specific substantive gaps in your dealership's existing policies and procedures. For example, let's say that during your ITP Program implementation you notice that the submission of an out-of-state license with a credit application would raise a red flag, requiring you to verify that the out-of-state license is a valid license. Such an alert also may trigger concerns about your dealership's general anti-fraud procedures. For example, do you currently have a mechanism in place by which to verify that an out-of-state license is valid? Associating red flags with potential gaps in your existing privacy, information security, and anti-fraud policies and procedures will build a secure dealership environment, minimize the risk of identity theft, and increase protection of private customer information.

Third, during your ITP Program implementation, consider ways to tighten up your privacy and information security practices. The Red Flag Rules require you to incorporate your own experiences identifying red flags at your dealership. Have you ever experienced theft resulting from someone stealing a photocopy of a credit applicant's driver's license? If so, note that incident as a red flag in your dealership's ITP Program. Also consider revising your dealership's information security program to identify and assess the risk of unauthorized access to a customer's driver's license. Driver's licenses may contain your customers' Social Security Numbers and other personal information you are required to protect by the FTC's Safeguards Rule and Disposal Rule.

Fourth, as you evaluate the above red flag, consider requiring your employees who copy a customer's driver's license to promptly safeguard that information. For example, make it your dealership's policy that upon a customer's submission of a driver's license, to immediately copy and store the photocopy in a secure place. Thus, you have control over who may access it and where it will remain until the expiration of any required retention period. Review your record-keeping policies to ensure that, once any required retention period expires, you have procedures to properly dispose of the information. Restricting access to private customer information will make your dealership less vulnerable to a security breach in the future (which, by the way, potentially subjects your dealership to a host of onerous security breach notification duties).

The relationship among the laws governing your handling and use of private customer information is significant. Rules governing information privacy and security are written to offer dealerships flexibility to best protect private customer information within the circumstances present at each dealership.

So, consider your existing privacy, information security, and anti-fraud policies and procedures in light of the Red Flag Rules. As you identify red flags during the implementation of your ITP Program, find ways to improve procedures for collecting, using, storing, and disposing of customer information in order to minimize security risks and guard against identity theft.

Whack-A-Mole Compliance

April 2008

By Emily Marlow Beck

As a kid, I remember begging my parents to give me quarters so I could play games in the mall arcade. I'd run right past the skee ball and pinball games, and I'd mosey up to the game of champions—Whack-a-mole.

The challenge in Whack-a-mole is to club the "moles" in the head when they pop up. If you're too slow or fast—"whoosh!" You'll miss! You'll only be successful if you can react to the "moles" when they show their mischievous smiling faces.

As much fun as that can be, adopting the Whack-a-mole technique just isn't the way to go when developing a company-wide Safeguards Policy.

What do I mean? Well, many dealerships I see have never stepped back and developed an information security program, or "Safeguards Policy," that is appropriate for the size and complexity of their particular dealership. Instead, many dealers merely react to what they perceive as their risks on a day-to-day basis.

For example, it is not unusual for me to visit a dealership that doesn't have a written Safeguards Policy, has not appointed a program coordinator, or hasn't attempted to identify reasonably foreseeable risks to their dealership (all of which are required under the federal Safeguards Rule). Instead, the dealership tries to scare the employees into "lock-down" mode. It posts signs all over employee areas, saying things like, "If it doesn't go in a deal jacket, it gets shredded!" or, my personal favorite, "If the FTC fines us, it's coming out of your paycheck!"

I could write a complete article about the legal misinformation communicated in these signs, but I won't. (Not today, at least.)

So, what's the problem with taking this approach? Well, other than potentially giving your employees ulcers, these messages simply don't reflect the requirements of the Rule. The Rule doesn't say that "everything must be shredded" or even that your dealership has to be as tight as Fort Knox. When it comes to Safeguards compliance, there is no substitute for following the express requirements of the Safeguards Rule.

Let's take a look. The Rule requires the following:

- Designate a program coordinator
- Identify reasonably foreseeable internal and external risks to the security, confidentiality, and integrity of customer information handled by the dealership that could result in its unauthorized disclosure, misuse, alteration, destruction, or other compromise; and assess the sufficiency of any safeguards in place to control these risks
- Design and implement safeguards to control the risks you identify through the risk assessment, and regularly audit the safeguards to ensure their effectiveness
- Oversee service providers
- Evaluate and adjust your Information Security Program

The FTC intended these requirements to be as flexible as possible. As such, your dealership's safeguards don't have to be perfect, but they must be appropriate for the size and complexity of your dealership and its operations, the nature and scope of your dealership's finance and lease activities, and the sensitivity of the information you handle.

So, what does all this mean?

It means that when it comes to developing a Safeguards Policy, you need to be proactive, not reactive. So, as you go through the process of tackling the whopper requirements under the Red Flag Rules this spring and summer, take some time to make sure that your Safeguards Policy is as proactive and responsive to the Rule's requirements as it should be.

You'll rest easier once you've gone through the steps. After all, whacking those moles can wear you out!

Has Your Compliance Program Got Game?
May 2008
By Michael A. Goodman

In the April 2008 issue of *Spot Delivery®,* Emily Beck's Whack-A-Mole Compliance article presented a short and sweet summary of the Safeguards Rule and a plea to readers to get into compliance with that Rule now, before they have a security problem. As Emily explained, addressing data security one issue at a time is the undesirable Whack-a-Mole compliance technique. To avert compliance folly, I suggest you model yourself after another arcade classic: Pac-Man.

Let me remind you that Pac-Man's goal in life was to eat all day while not being caught by one of the four ghosts stalking him. By eating a "power pellet," Pac-Man got to turn the tables on his pursuers and rule the maze.

In today's environment, where nearly any lapse in data security can become a headache, a news story, or even a lawsuit, you are a lot like Pac-Man—trying to go about your business so as to avoid getting gobbled up by the ghosts of paperwork, bad press, or unwanted law enforcement attention. A good compliance program is your power pellet, giving you the ability to protect yourself from these ghosts. This article will tell you a little bit more about the law enforcement and private plaintiff ghosts on your trail—the legal standards regulating data security and the people who can sue you when there's a problem. Emily's article addressed the Safeguards Rule, but when protecting yourself from the ramifications of data security breaches, there are other ghosts for you to worry about—namely the FTC Act as well as other legal theories wielded by private plaintiffs and state law enforcement.

The FTC Act. Emily was right to emphasize the Safeguards Rule in her article, but your data security compliance obligation does not begin and end with the Safeguards Rule. In two data security cases recently announced by the FTC, there was no allegation of a Safeguards Rule violation. Rather, the FTC alleged that the defendants' inadequate data security violated Section 5 of the FTC Act, which prohibits unfair or deceptive trade practices.

In contrast to the Safeguards Rule, which lays out a clear and succinct list of compliance requirements, the FTC Act's more general "unfairness" standard presents a thorny data security compliance challenge. This standard is necessarily vague: It has to be flexible to give the FTC agility to target an infinite variety of potentially improper practices as they emerge in the marketplace.

There are three general elements to the FTC's unfairness standard. A practice may be considered "unfair" if it is (1) likely to cause substantial injury to consumers, (2) one that consumers cannot reasonably avoid, and (3) one in which the injury is not outweighed by countervailing benefits to consumers or to competition. In recent years, the FTC has targeted inadequate data security as "unfair" under the FTC Act. Although the FTC has not provided and cannot provide a complete list of specific practices that could violate this standard, the agency has said that it will use this authority only with respect to the most clear-cut data security violations.

In light of that, as you check and recheck your compliance with the Safeguards Rule, you should also look at the questionable practices that prompted the FTC's most recent cases. Simply put, if you're doing what the FTC charged its defendants with doing, you should think about ratcheting up your data security. The practices challenged by the FTC included the following:

- Storing and transmitting personal information in unencrypted form
- Failing to implement readily available security for wireless networks
- Failing to require the use of "strong" passwords
- Failing to use readily available security measures, such as firewalls and suspending accounts after unsuccessful log-in attempts
- Failing to employ sufficient measures to detect and prevent unauthorized access, including conducting security investigations, using patches, and updating anti-virus software

Because elements of the Safeguards Rule are so flexible, such as the required risk assessment and measures to address identified risks, you may find yourself wishing for some guidance to let you know you're on the right track. The FTC's data security lawsuits can help. The complaints describe a targeted company's allegedly unlawful practices, and the settlements can be a good resource for best practices.

Private Plaintiffs. In addition, a recent data security breach involving a supermarket chain shows another reason why proactive data security is essential. In March, Hannaford Bros., revealed that a hacker had reportedly installed malicious software on scores of its computers, allowing the hacker to receive the same information that the company received as consumers checked out. It further announced 1,800 fraud cases among the millions of consumers affected by the breach.

By early April, consumers had filed 16 class action complaints based on this security breach, charging Hannaford with negligence in failing to protect data, breach of fiduciary duty, unfair trade practices, implied breach of contract, and conversion. State law enforcement authorities can also pursue some of these claims in response to a data breach. You can imagine the scope of potential damage.

The Safeguards Rule, the FTC Act, additional claims from private plaintiffs, and perhaps state law enforcement—these are your ghosts. They stalk any company that possesses sensitive consumer information. On the other hand, you are Pac-Man! Robust, proactive compliance efforts are your power pellets! These will allow you to thrive in the complicated maze of data security.

Your Privacy Policy Is an Advertisement!
June 2008
By Lisa C. DeLessio

Over the last several years, the Federal Trade Commission has partnered in a training workshop with local Better Business Bureaus in cities around the country in an effort to educate businesses about advertising practices. The workshop—"Green

Lights & Red Flags: FTC Rules of the Road for Advertisers"—focuses on how advertising practices can get companies—and their individual officers, employees, and directors—into big trouble. One mistake struck me as rather painful, so I thought I'd share it here.

According to the FTC, one "advertising mistake" a business can make is to send out a privacy notice to consumers and then not follow its own policies described in the notice. If the FTC learns about a mistake, the FTC has and will bring an action under the FTC Act for unfair and deceptive acts and practices.

In 2002, the FTC filed a complaint against the pharmaceutical company, Eli Lilly. The FTC alleged that Eli Lilly advertised, promoted, and marketed an e-mail reminder service known as "Medi-messenger" so that consumers could receive alerts for drug prescription renewals and other information. Consumers who subscribed received the company's privacy notice, which stated that Eli Lilly respected the privacy of visitors to its websites and promised to maintain guests' privacy as they took advantage of this resource. The privacy policy also promised consumers that there were layers of security to protect their personal information.

Unfortunately, this wasn't exactly true. According to the FTC's complaint, a company employee sent an e-mail to 669 subscribers notifying them that the Medi-messenger service would be discontinued. Instead of putting the consumers' names and e-mail addresses into a blind copy line, the employee included the information on the "To:" line of the e-mail—thereby disclosing personal and confidential information to everyone on the list. Although the privacy policy promised that there were layers of protection in place, that wasn't true or this "mistake" would not have happened. Thus, according to the FTC, Eli Lilly had engaged in unfair or deceptive acts and practices.

Are you cringing? You should be because this is an easy mistake to make and one that could be costly. Although the FTC acknowledged that no one believed Eli Lilly meant for this to happen, the FTC used this as a prime example of how mistakes can get you into trouble if you make a promise in your privacy policy that isn't true.

The practice tip: Check your privacy policy and look at your company's website on a regular basis. Can you, and do you, deliver on your promises? If the answer is "no," take steps to fix the problem immediately. Mistakes happen—but don't let that mistake be one that the FTC will view as unfair or deceptive!

Where's the Thief?

August 2008

By Emily Marlow Beck

A couple of years back, I wrote an article about a little experiment I conducted using "Google E-Mail Alerts." As part of this nifty program, I typed "car dealer fraud" and some similar search terms in "Google E-Mail Alerts," and Google e-mailed me daily about any Internet news articles discussing dealer fraud. ('cause if it's not on Google, it doesn't exist, right?).

Those of you who have been reading *Spot Delivery*® for a while will recall that this little experiment resulted in a flood of e-mails with news stories about dealer fraud—fraud against customers, fraud against finance companies, fraud against the state—you name it, I read about it.

And, yes, I've tracked those stories for the last couple of years, and the stories continue. Interestingly, I've seen an increase in news reports alleging fraud by car salespersons charged with stealing customers' identities.

Take, for example, a recent story coming out of Niceville, Florida. According to a report on www.nwfdailynews.com, authorities charged a not-so-nice 31-year-old male with stealing the identities of more than 30 customers while he worked at a Florida dealership. According to the news release, fraud investigators from seven credit card companies told police that the employee made 73 applications and was issued 20 cards. The employee allegedly went on a little shopping spree, charging nearly $8,000 at Overstock.com and nearly $7,500 at a hotel chain. That is one case. Read on . . .

Another employee at an Omaha, Nebraska, dealership allegedly used customers' information while working at a local car dealership to open a credit card account. According to a statement provided by the Omaha Police Department to the reporters on www.ketv.com, the employee had been stockpiling customers' names, addresses, phone numbers, and Social Security Numbers, and he carried this information with him for years.

Those kinds of stories leave me with more questions than answers. For example, I wonder whether the dealer knew about the theft. If so, how did he or she respond after learning about it? Did the dealer have a Safeguards Policy that limited access to certain nonpublic personal information to only those employees who needed access to it? Had the dealership trained employees on their responsibilities with respect to customers' private information? The answers to these questions could mean the difference between a judge or jury viewing the situation as the misbehavior of a "bad apple" employee who didn't follow instructions or a "bad orchard" dealership that tolerated or even encouraged such misdeeds.

Whether the increase in news articles reflects an increase in identity theft or whether the media has simply cranked up its efforts to write about it, dealers will need to step up their efforts to ensure that information within their dealerships stays safe and sound. Don't forget that while state and federal regulators have identity theft on their radar and can come after dealers with hefty fines and penalties, the mighty pen of the news media can be just as devastating.

The effects of a negative news article about identity theft in your dealership may linger long after you've paid the fines, fired the rogue employee, and made any restitution to the customer. Who wants that kind of free advertising?

Red Flag Lemonade?

November 2008

By Thomas B. Hudson

I went into lawyering because I didn't have the nerves of steel that I think business people, and particularly car dealers, have to have. That doesn't stop me from occasionally having a business idea that gets mixed into the legal stuff about which I customarily write.

I had one of those ideas as I drove to work recently, and I'll share it with you. It has to do with the Federal Trade Commission's Red Flag Rules.

The Red Flag Rules are a new compliance requirement for dealers. It has been in effect for several months, and dealers could comply with it if they wished, but were not required to do so. The FTC was to begin enforcing the Rule against dealers on November 1; however, this date has been pushed back more than once.

I'm not going to describe in this article the requirements of the Red Flag Rules—many others have written articles setting forth the details of the Rules' requirements. Suffice it to say for the purposes of this article that the Rule is the federal government's attempt to deputize car dealers and other businesses into assisting in the fight against identity theft. Dealers must have in place a program that is designed to detect the "red flags" that often signal a fraudulent attempt to steal someone's identity and to prevent and mitigate identity theft in the dealership's financial transactions.

The design and implementation of a Red Flag program will involve a bit of hassle to a dealer, but, at the end of the day, a good Red Flag program will also benefit the dealer by reducing the odds of a scamster perpetrating a successful fraud on the dealer. But might there not be other benefits to the creation and implementation of a Red Flag program? And since the dealer really has no choice but to comply, are there ways to leverage on the requirement and create some additional dealer benefits? I think perhaps so.

If I were a dealer (hint—here comes the business advice), I would make a big deal out of the fact that my dealership had designed and implemented its Red Flag program, and, while I was at it, I'd ballyhoo my Privacy Safeguarding Program as well. I would announce the programs to my customers and would explain the programs to them in broad terms. I'd get with my marketing folks and have them create marketing materials that would tell the world that my dealership was on the front line in the fight against identity theft, helping to make sure that we were doing everything we could to protect the financial privacy of our customers and to reduce the possibility that our customers might be victimized by those nasty identity thieves.

Maybe I'd create (or borrow from other sources that have already done the creating) some consumer education materials as well. Of course, since my main mission is car sales, I'd liberally mix in my marketing materials with the educational stuff.

Be careful, though, that before you get your marketing people involved, you've actually got good, compliant Red Flag and Safeguarding Programs in place. You don't want to be talking the talk if you aren't walking the walk. And, as with most things that your dealership provides to your customers, it's probably not a bad idea to put this in front of your lawyer before you pull the trigger on it.

The feds have handed dealers another lemon with the Red Flag Rules. Might as well make a little lemonade!

Why You Shouldn't Delay Your Red Flag Program
November 2008
By Thomas B. Hudson

The Red Flag Rules, announced by the Federal Trade Commission in November 2007, had a mandatory effective date of November 1, 2008. On October 22, 2008, the FTC announced that it would suspend enforcement of the Rule, moving the official enforcement date to November 1, 2009. That move gave financial institutions and creditors subject to the FTC's jurisdiction (that means car dealers) additional time to get their Red Flag programs in place without incurring FTC sanctions.

"Hooray!" you say—"more room to breathe." And while I can't disagree with your elation, I am obliged, regrettably, to burst your bubble. Hear me: The additional time won't do you any good unless you get to work on your program now.

From our vantage point, the vast majority of dealers did not have a complying Red Flag program in place by November 1, 2008, and that was after they were given nearly a year to put the program in place.

We are urging dealers to move quickly to get their Red Flag programs in place—long before the end of the six-month enforcement grace period granted by the FTC. Why? Three reasons, and they may apply to you.

If you procrastinated before, you'll do it again. If your dealership didn't have a program in place with a year's notice of the mandatory effective date, what is going to change? We think that it's likely that those dealers with a bad case of procrastination aren't going to be magically cured by the FTC's medicine of additional time.

There may still be risk in not having a program. The FTC has announced that it won't prosecute violators for six months, but there's an argument that the Rule is mandatorily effective now, notwithstanding the FTC's statement that it will forego enforcement, and that after November 1, dealers must comply with it. Think about it like this—your town lowers the speed limit on the main drag, but the cops announce that they won't hand out speeding tickets for less than the old limit for a couple of months so that people can adjust to the new limit. That enforcement timetable by the cops won't stop a plaintiffs' lawyer from suing if someone exceeds the new limit and causes injuries or damages. Look for those lawyers who make their livings suing dealerships to argue that the federal requirement is in force notwithstanding the FTC's enforcement policy and that the dealer's failure to comply with the federal requirement constitutes an unfair or deceptive act or practice under state law. Lest you think such a "bootstrapping" attack is far-fetched, think again. We've seen just this argument in connection with federal Used Car Rule claims.

It's good for you! Finally, the Red Flag Rules are a bit unusual in that the principal effect will be to benefit the dealer by making identity theft more difficult. If an identity thief strikes your dealership, it's hard to imagine a situation in which you don't end up with the resulting loss. That being the case, why wouldn't you rush to get your program in place?

There you are, three reasons. Get to work!

[Editor's note: As we went to press, the FTC granted yet another enforcement delay, this one until June 1, 2010. Our admonition stands. Get your policy in place now.]

Treasury Department Warns Dealers— Keep a Wary Eye Out for Scamsters
November 2008
By Thomas B. Hudson

As if car dealers didn't have enough to worry about, the U.S. Department of the Treasury's Office of Inspector General is investigating instances in which people are using fraudulent Treasury-related financial obligations or accounts to buy, or attempt to buy, vehicles from car dealerships or to pay debts.

Treasury gave the following example of the scam:

In September 2008, Treasury learned that someone tried to buy a $67,000 car at a Phoenix dealership using a bogus promissory note and bond. The value of the note was supposedly $75,000, and the bonds were purported to represent government obligations of $150,000 and, in another instance, up to $900,000,000.

Treasury has alerted dealers to the use of these types of notes and bonds, which might or might not be called "U.S. Treasury" bonds or promissory notes; however, they are identified as "personal promissory notes" and/or "private offset bonds" and often contain the name of the Secretary of the U.S. Treasury, currently Henry Paulson, on the document.

Treasury warns that Paulson's name would not appear on any document listed as a private bond or promissory note since these items are not backed or guaranteed by the U.S. Treasury. And, warns the Treasury, the only type of paper bond issued by the U.S. Treasury that a citizen can buy today is a U.S. Savings Bond. All other Treasury Bonds are electronic—the buyer does not receive an actual document.

A similar scheme in Indiana involved unauthorized people providing car dealerships and other retail businesses with bank routing and account numbers to buy vehicles or other property and/or to pay off personal debts. They represented these account and routing numbers to be personal grant or bank accounts and directed the dealerships to electronically debit the accounts to fund payments for their purchases. In this instance, the account was a Treasury account for vendors to electronically transmit payments to the Treasury Department.

Treasury urges dealers with any information regarding such Treasury-related scams to contact the Department of Treasury, Office of Inspector General, Office of Investigation's Hotline at 1-800-359-3898 or via e-mail at hotline@oig.treas.gov.

Additional information regarding this scam can be found at www.treasurydirect.gov/instit/statreg/fraud/fraud_bogussight draft.htm.

With the car business deep in the fertilizer, dealers can be desperate for sales. The scamsters know this, so when times are bad, they slither out from under their rocks and show up in your showroom. In this market, the last thing a dealer needs is to lose $100,000 or so to one of these crooks.

Selling Road Tack Dispensing Systems
and Other Goodies
January/February 2009
By Thomas B. Hudson

I participate in a very interesting online "listserv" sponsored by the National Association of Dealer Counsel. It's interesting in a couple of ways.

First, the sheer variety of legal topics covered by the participants will make you blink. From franchise issues to tax questions to labor issues to lemon laws to my area—compliance—the list goes on and on.

But sometimes the questions themselves are riveting. Here's a recent example (I've slightly edited it).

Buyer wants to purchase a Nissan Armada, but wants it slightly modified first (Kevlar, bulletproof glass, run-flat wheels, shocking door handles, soup to nuts on the 007 stuff). He also is willing to pay the sales tax on all this and then plans to ship it to Nigeria himself.

There are a ton of issues in the above scenario, I know, but my question is, is there a duty to report or notify any government entity that a car is being armor plated? Also are we (the United States) allowed to do business of this type with Nigeria or are they on some watch list?

To make it even more outrageous, here is the actual list of items:

- Kevlar on roof and doors
- 6mm AR500 steel on walls, fuel tank, and battery
- Wire mesh for the radiator
- Siren w/ P/A
- Red/blue lights
- Smoke dispenser

- Dual battery system
- Automatic engine fire suppressant system
- Explosafe tank
- Road tack dispensing system
- Shocking door handles
- Ram bumpers (front and back)
- Run-flat tires
- Tail pipe protection
- 39/40 mm thick glass—windshield and rear
- Installed fire extinguisher
- (The best for last)—"Undercoat spray-on protection against corrosion"

I'm not making this up!

The letter was signed, John F. Walsh, Esq., General Counsel, AMSI, Automotive Management Services, Inc.

When I read John's letter, my immediate reaction was to think about the federal "bad guy" list and the new Red Flag requirements. I e-mailed him, mentioning these but saying that I was not familiar with any other provisions of federal law that might apply to his bizarre facts.

NADC has nearly 500 lawyers, though, and I had confidence that someone out in Internet-world would actually know this area. I wasn't disappointed because, within an hour or so, an authoritative answer landed in my inbox. Russell P. McRory, Esq., of the New York firm of Robinson Brog Leinwand Greene Genovese & Gluck P.C., penned the following:

John:

From an export perspective, you basically have two sets of regulations to worry about—EAR (Export Administration Regulations) and ITAR (International Traffic in Arms Regulations). EAR, which governs so called "dual-use" items, is run by the Department of Commerce and ITAR, which covers military articles, by the Department of State. Actually, it's your buyer who has to worry about it because he is the one exporting the truck. But, in order for him to export the vehicle in compliance with these regulations, your buyer will need information from the dealer and the dealer will, in turn, need information from his parts suppliers.

With respect to EAR, you first need to determine whether a specific ECCN (Export Control Classification Number) covers the vehicle or if it is classified as EAR99 (which is a generic classification meaning the item is governed by the EAR but does not fall under a specific ECCN). In this case, the described vehicle may be classified under ECCN 9A018.b or as EAR99 depending on the level and sophistication of the modifications. You should carefully review Export Administration Regulations §770.2(h), which governs just this situation. Then, depending on the country of destination, a Commerce Department license may be required for that ECCN or even for EAR99. There are government websites that can walk you through the determination whether a given ECCN classification can be exported to a given country. While not in the category of North Korea, I suspect Nigeria is pretty high on the control list and there's a good chance your buyer will need a Commerce Department export license.

The ITAR area is more complicated because it goes down to the component level. Thus, you will need to find out from the suppliers providing the components and parts for the armored vehicle if any of the things they are selling you are military articles (sometimes it's phrased as being on the "Munitions List"—the term "munitions" is a term of art and means much more than bullets). In all likelihood, the components are not covered by ITAR, but the dealer should ask the manufacturer. If the manufacturer of a particular component informs you that an item is a military article, then a

State Department export license will be needed to export the vehicle. An example of a component requiring a State Department export license would be radio frequency jammers to interfere with the remote detonation of roadside bombs.

Bear in mind that the obligation falls on the exporter, not the dealer, but the customer will likely need to get the relevant information from the dealer, who in turn will have to get it from the manufacturer.

Moreover, it would probably be an excellent idea to have the customer sign an acknowledgment that the vehicle may be or is subject to export controls under EAR and ITAR and it is his responsibility to obtain any necessary licenses prior to exporting the vehicle.

Feel free to call with any questions.

Regards,
Russell P. McRory, Esq.
Robinson Brog Leinwand Greene Genovese & Gluck P.C.

The e-mail exchange brought home to me in a very big way how devilishly difficult it is for dealers to even be aware of, much less be really knowledgeable about, all of the arcane laws and regulations that can apply to their transactions. Good lawyers, like John, "know what they don't know" and have the smarts to float questions that are off the beaten track past all of the other lawyer members.

Sorta makes you feel sorry for those dealer lawyers who haven't joined NADC and don't have access to the listserv, doesn't it now?

Anybody know where I can have a road tack dispensing system installed in my Roadmaster?

A Man Walks Into a Dealership . . .

January/February 2009

By Maya P. Hill

A man walks into a dealership and applies for financing through the dealer to buy a car. He provides a driver's license as a form of identification that shows City A as his residence. His credit report, however, shows City B as his residence. Moreover, the picture on the driver's license looks nothing like him, and the license reflects that he is five inches shorter and 40 pounds heavier than he actually appears to be in real life.

Maybe the guy moved at some point, which would account for the address discrepancy. Maybe he's wearing platform shoes today, and that's why he seems taller. And maybe the South Beach diet is working for him, which would explain why he's 40 pounds lighter. But are there any bells going off in your head? Or better—any Red Flags?

The dealer should recognize that this customer might not really be the person he claims to be and should take some further steps, in accordance with the dealership's written identity theft prevention policy, to verify the man's identity before continuing with the sale and financing. The federal Red Flag Rules, as you know, require these steps.

But these days, identity theft and obtaining credit under false pretenses aren't just limited to someone pretending to be someone else, using a stolen driver's license, or obtaining someone else's personal information from dumpster diving. Identity theft appears to be hitting closer to home.

Take, for example, the case of Everett Frank in Chester County, Pennsylvania. Frank was accused of repeatedly using his estranged wife's personal information to obtain financing to buy six cars and trucks from a Chester County dealership. The vehicles or consent of Michelle Frank, who learned about the purchases when she was contacted by a collection agency after several of the accounts were reported as delinquent in January 2008. According to the criminal complaint, Frank allegedly agreed to buy the vehicles but did not have sufficient credit to purchase them himself. He allegedly asked dealership employees if he could take the documents home in order to have his wife sign them.

We'll ask you again—any Red Flags going off in your head? Husbands and wives buy cars together all the time. In some cases they apply jointly for credit, and in some cases only one spouse applies. Nothing too alarming there.

But what about the customer wanting to take the paperwork home to have his wife sign it? There may be an occasional state law that requires that certain documents be signed at the dealership (and dealers should check with their lawyers to make sure), but for the most part, there is no such requirement. Allowing a customer to sign paperwork at a place other than the dealership without verifying his or her identity can be a little bit risky. Seeing the customer and comparing the picture on the customer's driver's license with how he or she actually appears in real life are among the good ways to determine with whom you are really dealing. By allowing a customer to sign paperwork sight unseen, however, you put yourself in danger that the signatory isn't really the applicant for credit.

So, the next time a man walks into your dealership and asks to take some paperwork home for someone else to sign, think twice about the implications of permitting this kind of practice.

While "a man walks into a dealership" may sound like the beginning of a joke. It's no laughing matter when the result is identity theft.

The List of All OFAC Lists

August 2009

By Michael A. Benoit and Catharine S. Andricos

We recently received a client inquiry regarding a dealer's obligations with respect to the Specially Designated Nationals and Blocked Persons list (SDN list) of the Office of Foreign Assets Control (OFAC). In making his inquiry, our client explained that he had pulled a credit report on a potential customer. The report came back indicating that the customer's name was on a "Watch List." The client called the information provider. He discovered that the potential customer's name appeared on the CIA's Politically Exposed Persons list. Did this mean that the client needed to do any further investigation? He knew that he would need to do further checking if a name appeared on OFAC's SDN list, but he wondered whether there was a "master" list of all the lists about which dealers should be concerned.

As our client was aware, car dealers must ensure that they do not enter into a transaction with an individual or entity on OFAC's SDN list. OFAC's SDN list contains more than 5,000 variations on names officially "designated" by OFAC as foreign agents and front organizations, as well as terrorists, terrorist organizations, and narcotics traffickers around the world.

All car dealers must check the names of new and existing customers against OFAC's SDN list regularly to ensure that a customer's name does not appear on the list. Often, car dealers rely on credit bureaus to run customer data against OFAC's SDN list and to render a determination with the customer's credit report. Because different entities (e.g., banks) have different due diligence obligations when it comes to their customers, the credit bureaus do not just run customer data against the SDN list, but they also run the data against other listings as well. These other listings include the CIA's Politically Exposed Persons list, the Denied Persons List and Entities List, the FBI's Most Wanted list, and the Debarred Parties list.

If a customer's credit report includes a "hit" against an OFAC listing, the dealer must determine whether the "hit" is actually against OFAC's SDN list or whether, as in our client's case, the hit is actually against another list, such as the CIA's Politically Exposed Persons list.

If the "hit" is against a list other than OFAC's SDN list, the dealer should contact the "keeper" of whichever other list the match is "hitting against," as indicated by the contact information included below:

- The Denied Persons List and Entities List—please contact the Bureau of Industry and Security at the U.S. Department of Commerce at 202.482.4811.
- The FBI's Most Wanted list or any other FBI-issued watch list—please contact the Federal Bureau of Investigation at www.fbi.gov/contact/fo/fo.htm.
- The Debarred Parties list—please contact the Office of Defense Trade Controls at the U.S. Department of State at 202.663.2700.
- The Bank Secrecy Act and the USA PATRIOT Act (including information on the CIA's Politically Exposed Persons list)—please contact the Financial Crimes Enforcement Network (FinCEN) at 800.949.2732.

Unless a dealer is contractually obligated to do so, it is not required to undertake any further investigation if a customer's name appears on any list other than OFAC's SDN list. If the dealer determines that a customer's name matches a name on the SDN list, the dealer must contact OFAC's hotline at 800.540.6322. In addition, the dealer may be required to stop the sale and/or block the customer's account and file a report with OFAC within 10 days.

For more information on a dealer's compliance obligations under the OFAC regulations, please see www.ustreas.gov/offices/enforcement/ofac/.

Chapter 6

Warranties

Warranties are promises. In the car world, they are dealer promises that say that the car you buy is the car you think you have bought, or the dealer will make it so. It is a guarantee of product integrity; also, it is the assurance of a maker's responsibility for the repair or replacement of defective parts. This short, simple paragraph paraphrases the definition of "warranty" in *Webster's Ninth New Collegiate Dictionary.*

In the real world of dealer's warranties, however, the subject is more complex. And, as you will quickly learn in the pages that follow, warranties not only can be more inclusive than you'd ever expect, but also, their application and impact constitute much more territory than a briefly worded paragraph.

Warranties are regulated in several ways. The federal government gets into the act by regulating warranties under the Magnuson-Moss Warranty Act (MMWA). The MMWA basically says that a warranty either must be a full warranty, meeting certain standards, or a limited warranty, meeting lesser standards.

States get into the act as well. Every state has adopted a version of the Uniform Commercial Code (UCC). Article 2 of the UCC deals with sales, while Article 2A deals with leases. Both articles deal with warranties; however, the provision of each article that probably gets the most play in litigation against dealers is the one dealing with the disclaimer of implied warranties (or warranties that arise as part of the transaction, even when they are not spelled out). The UCC describes two such implied warranties—the implied warranty of merchantability (these goods are in good enough condition to be sold) and the implied warranty of fitness for use (these goods are the kind that will do the job the customer told the dealer the customer wanted them to do).

In most states, these implied warranties can be "disclaimed" by manufacturers, dealers, and other sellers, but there are technical requirements for such disclaimers, and unless the seller disclaims the implied warranties in strict accordance with the rules, the implied warranties will apply.

Some states go further than the UCC and impose additional warranty requirements, so you'll need to check your state's law to make sure you know the rules.

Yep, warranties can be complicated. We guarantee it.

Did You Take Proper Care of That Car I Sold You?
June 2008
By Thomas B. Hudson

Many dealers offer express warranties in connection with the cars that they sell. When car buyers have enough trouble with their cars to drive them into the hands of a lawyer, you can almost bank on the fact that the lawyer's complaint will contain a "breach of express warranty" count.

The question of whether there has been a breach of an express warranty is usually pretty straightforward. The warranty is, after all, a contract, and the dealer's promises are either in the contract or they aren't. If the contract is ambiguous, courts will generally resolve any ambiguity against the dealer, since it was the dealer who drafted the contract and created the ambiguity.

So it is interesting when a case comes along in which a warrantor (in this case, Volkswagen of America in its capacity as manufacturer and lessor) is able to successfully assert a defense against a consumer in connection with a breach of express warranty claim. Here's what happened.

Jane Roman entered into a four-year car lease with Volkswagen of America, Inc. Volkswagen provided an express written limited new vehicle warranty and a limited power train warranty on the car in which it agreed to correct, by repair or replacement, most manufacturer's defects that might occur.

Roman's car experienced engine damage, and she made a claim under the limited warranty, which Volkswagen denied. Roman sued Volkswagen in state court for breach of warranty.

Volkswagen moved for summary judgment, arguing that the warranty did not cover the engine damage, because Roman failed to prove she maintained the car as required by the warranty. Volkswagen argued that the sludge buildup that caused the engine damage stemmed from a lack of proper maintenance and regular oil changes.

The trial court granted Volkswagen summary judgment. Roman appealed to the Court of Appeals of Ohio, arguing that she had done the required maintenance, but she could not present proof of some of the maintenance appointments because the shop performing the maintenance had closed. Roman also argued that requiring her to present such proof imposed an unreasonable duty on consumers.

The appellate court noted that Volkswagen made Roman aware of her duties to properly maintain the vehicle and provide documentation, which was reasonable when warranting goods that can sustain severe damage when not properly maintained. The court also noted that Volkswagen established that there were no genuine issues of material fact and affirmed the trial court's decision to grant Volkswagen's motion for summary judgment.

What's the lesson here for a dealer offering an express warranty? Based on this case, I'd add language to my express warranty that would obligate the customer to maintain the car as required by the owner's manual, and to retain proof, in the form of service receipts, of having done so. That way, if there is any issue about whether the problems with the car are the fault of the dealer or due to improper (or no) service by the customer, the dealer will be well positioned to raise such a defense.

Warning: Not all courts will be as receptive to this defense as this one was, but it's always good to have one more argument to use in your defense.

Roman v. Volkswagen of America, Inc., 2008 WL 1921717 (Ohio App. May 2, 2008).

Court Rules Warranty Claim Too Late, Reverses Judgment

October 2008

By Thomas B. Hudson

Some legal positions are pretty simple. In this recent case, the manufacturer and its dealer posited the not-exactly-shocking position that a breach of warranty claim must accrue during the warranty period in order for the claim to be valid. A California court actually agreed and overturned an award of over $220,000 against the defendants. Let's look at what happened.

Robert Shtofman bought a new car from Calstar, a Mercedes-Benz dealer, in January 1997. The written warranty on Shtofman's car provided that any authorized Mercedes-Benz dealer would make any repairs or replacements necessary to correct defects in material or workmanship and that the warranty expired after 48 months or 50,000 miles, whichever came first.

Over the next five years, Shtofman returned his car to Calstar 12 times for repairs of a recurrent brake light problem. According to Shtofman, Mercedes-Benz and Calstar told him in September 2003 that "they were unable to fix the problem" with the car. Shtofman claimed that it was at that moment when he "realized" the problem with his car would never be fixed permanently.

In August 2004, Shtofman sued Mercedes-Benz and Calstar, alleging breach of warranty, negligent repair, and fraud, among other claims. Mercedes-Benz and Calstar moved for summary judgment, arguing that Shtofman's warranty claims were timed-barred.

The trial court denied their summary judgment motions and granted summary judgment to Shtofman on the breach of warranty claim, finding that, as a matter of law, Mercedes-Benz and Calstar failed to properly service or repair the vehicle after a reasonable number of opportunities to do so. With respect to the breach of warranty claim, the trial court awarded Shtofman approximately $87,250 in compensatory damages plus attorneys' fees in the amount of $136,000 *[Editor's note: Ouch!]*. Mercedes-Benz and Calstar appealed.

The California Court of Appeals reversed the trial court's judgment on the breach of warranty claim, finding that the breach of warranty claim was time-barred by the four-year statute of limitations in California Uniform Commercial Code Section 2725. By April 1999, Shtofman had driven his car more than 50,000 miles, and thus the warranty on his vehicle expired no later than April 1999. As such, the appellate court determined that if Mercedes-Benz had breached the warranty on Shtofman's car on the last day before the warranty expired, then Shtofman had until April 2003 to sue the defendants on the breach of warranty claim. By filing his complaint in August 2004, Shtofman filed more than a year too late.

The appellate court also rejected Shtofman's argument that, because he did not discover the breach of warranty claim until September 2003, he had until September 2007 to file his suit against Mercedes-Benz. The appellate court reasoned that Shtofman's analysis would lead to an unacceptable conclusion that a breach of warranty cause of action may accrue at any point in time, without regard to whether or when the warranty had expired.

The appellate court remanded the case to the trial court with directions to vacate its order granting Shtofman's summary judgment motion on the breach of warranty claim and enter a new order denying Shtofman's motion and granting both Mercedes-Benz and Calstar's summary judgment motions on the breach of warranty claim. Because Mercedes-Benz was successful on appeal, the appellate court also reversed the trial court's award of attorneys' fees to Shtofman.

Shtofman v. Mercedes-Benz of North America, Inc., 2008 WL 3984219 (Cal. App. August 29, 2008)

A Warranty Is a Warranty Is a Warranty

April 2009

By Emily Marlow Beck and Catharine S. Andricos

We recently received a request from a dealer to convert the dealer's service contract into a warranty. Upon receiving this request, we discussed with the dealer the differences between warranties and service contracts. We wanted to ensure that the dealer understood that warranties and service contracts are entirely different critters that were governed by an entirely different set of rules.

This confusing issue comes up quite a bit. Unfortunately, car folks all too often use the word "warranty" to describe both warranties and service contracts. While both can be similar in their scope of coverage, they have key differences that can spell big trouble for dealers who don't properly distinguish between the two.

On one hand the federal Magnuson-Moss Warranty Act

(Mag-Moss) primarily governs written warranties. Mag-Moss generally defines "written warranty" to include a written affirmation, promise, or undertaking relating to the material or workmanship of a motor vehicle, if such affirmation or promise becomes "part of the basis of the bargain" between the dealer and the customer. To be a "part of the basis of the bargain," the warranty must be conveyed at the time of sale, and the customer must not give any consideration (payment) for the warranty beyond the purchase price of the vehicle.

On the other hand, state laws primarily govern service contracts. A service contract is a contract relating to the maintenance or repair of a consumer product. However, unlike a written warranty, a service contract is not included in the price of the consumer product, and the consumer must provide something "extra" for it. The best way to think about a service contract is as an agreement that would constitute a warranty but for its failure to satisfy the "basis of the bargain" test, because the consumer paid above and beyond the price of the car for it.

Mag-Moss does impose some broad limitations on service contracts, but service contracts tend to be heavily regulated by state laws. For example, in some states, a service contract may be treated as insurance subject to insurance laws. In other states, a service contract may be subject to specific laws governing automobile service contracts.

So, here's a quick review. The product will generally NOT be a warranty if either (1) the buyer pays additional consideration beyond the purchase price of the vehicle to obtain the benefits under the warranty, or (2) the agreement is entered into some time after the date of sale.

Here's an example. Let's say, at the time you sell a car, you provide to your customer free of charge a written promise to repair any defective car parts. Applying the test described above, your written promise will constitute a warranty subject to Mag-Moss, because the buyer did not give any additional consideration and because the promise was made at the time of sale. However, if you stick a price tag on that "warranty" and charge the customer $1,400 for it, the "warranty" would likely be regulated as a "service contract."

Easy enough, you say. You'll just call this written promise a "service contract" and not worry about all this Mag-Moss hogwash, right? Not quite. A promise that meets the definition of "warranty" under Mag-Moss will be treated as such, even if you call it a "service contract."

Furthermore, as a written warranty subject to Mag-Moss, your written promise must comply with the Mag-Moss disclosure requirements. These requirements provide, among other things, that the promise be clearly designated as a "Full Warranty" or a "Limited Warranty," not as a "Service Contract." In addition, unless the repairs made under the warranty would be made at no charge to the customer, the warranty can't require all repair work to be done at your dealership. Such a requirement would violate the Mag-Moss prohibition on "tying" arrangements.

Mag-Moss also has a thing or two to say about communicating the warranty terms to the customer. The law requires you to make the warranty available for examination by your customer before the customer decides to buy. You can do this by displaying the warranty in close proximity to the warranted car or by furnishing the warranty upon request prior to the sale. You also must provide a copy of the written warranty to the customer after the sale.

Finally, if you sell used cars, don't forget that your decision to offer a warranty or a service contract (or both) will impact what information the federal Used Car Rule will require you to disclose on the Buyers Guide. Noncompliance with the Used Car Rule can have some pretty hefty penalties, too.

So, why does all this matter? Well, dealers must know whether they are offering a service contract or a warranty to determine which state or federal law(s) govern the transaction. And, as is so often the case in the consumer credit world, the terms and features of the product—not the title on the top of the paper—will determine the governing law. Plus, you want your warranty or service contract to keep your customers happy and avoid lawsuits, right?

Internet Sales and Electronic Commerce

As more and more dealerships turn to the Internet to sell cars, more lawsuits arise that deal with these "electronic commerce" activities. Most of the cases we've seen so far fall into two categories.

The first category deals with locale. Dealerships that sell cars over the Internet to residents of other states have found themselves facing the question of whether a disgruntled customer can bring a lawsuit against the dealership in the customer's home state. The courts that have addressed this issue have come down on both sides, with roughly half saying that the dealership is subject to such suits, and the other half coming out the other way. The opinions that these courts have rendered are very "fact specific," as the lawyers like to say, with a lot of ink being spilled to describe the extent of the dealership's activities in the customer's state, the details of the contacts of the parties leading up to the sale transaction, and the specifics, including the documentation of the transaction.

The second category deals with communication and advertising. These cases don't really involve "electronic commerce" issues, but are, rather, cases that involve dealer actions that don't have anything to do with the manner in which the dealership communicates with the customer. For example, a customer might sue a dealer for a fraudulent, false, or misleading eBay advertisement. Dealerships advertising in newspapers have faced similar suits for decades. These advertising suits are based on legal theories that have long been applied to print and other media, and really don't involve any new law dealing with electronic commerce.

We are waiting for a third category of suits to arise. It is only a matter of time before plaintiffs' lawyers begin to challenge the substantive aspects of interstate Internet transactions. We believe that we will see allegations that dealers are subject to dealer licensing in states in which their customers reside, and that the transactions that they enter into with their out-of-state customers are subject to regulation by the sales and credit laws of the customers' jurisdictions.

Beyond these, it isn't hard to imagine the legal theories that might be brought to bear as dealer's blogs, Twitter, and engage in social networking in their efforts to move the metal. You can bet that state and federal laws won't evolve as quickly as will these new ways of communicating. As old legal theories meet new technologies and applications, we predict that a lot of judges will find themselves trying to pound square pegs into round holes.

Interstate + Internet = Trouble
October 2007
By Thomas B. Hudson

Unless you live in a cave, it's not news that dealers are selling cars over the Internet. When the dealer and the Internet buyer are both in the same state, it's usually the case that the Internet is simply a shopping medium, like a newspaper, and that any resulting transaction takes place at the dealership. From a legal standpoint, that's pretty vanilla.

When the dealer and the buyer are in different states, it's a whole new ballgame. The business models we have seen range from the safest to the more dangerous, from a legal standpoint. The safest are those in which the out-of-state buyer is required to come to the dealership to take delivery of the car and sign the paperwork. The more dangerous are those in which the dealer delivers the car, along with the paperwork for execution, to the buyer's home state.

The more dangerous programs are more dangerous because they raise many legal questions that legislatures and courts have hardly touched upon. Lawyers worry about whether the dealer can be sued in the customer's state, whether the dealer needs a used car or new car dealer license from the customer's state, and which laws—that of the dealership's state or the customer's state—apply to the dealer's documents and the terms of the sale (for instance, the dealer's state might permit an as-is sale, while the buyer's state might prohibit it).

So far, very few courts have addressed Internet interstate sale issues, and most of the cases so far have dealt with the first point—can the dealer be sued in the buyer's state? The half-dozen or so cases that have addressed the issue are conveniently split in their conclusions, providing ammo for both the buyers and the selling dealers

We have been warning that courts will eventually address the remaining issues. They have started to do so, albeit in a different consumer industry—payday lending. That's unfortunate because payday lending is not, shall we say, a particular favorite of state regulators and consumer advocates. Pro-consumer judges don't care much for payday lenders either (sorta the same way they feel about car dealers). Their opinions are likely to reflect that fact.

So it came as no real surprise when a federal court recently sided with the Kansas banking commissioner's office in a case against Internet payday lenders. The court ruled that the state has the right to impose consumer protection laws on Internet financing companies. The decision will likely prohibit Internet lenders from operating in Kansas without a license, regardless of whether or not they have an office in the state. That wasn't the end of the payday lender's headaches. In a separate proceeding, the Kansas regulators are suing, demanding a $5 million fine and $445,000 in refunded money.

Ouch.

What does this have to do with car dealers, you ask?

This payday lender was peddling money (loans) over the Internet. Car dealers sell cars over the Internet. When a court says that the payday lenders are subject to the laws of the states where their borrowers live, you can bet that the case is going to be thrown in the face of any car dealer doing interstate Internet business when he tries to argue that he's obligated to comply with only the laws of his home state.

There are ways that car dealers can reduce the legal risk inherent in interstate Internet transactions. If you are a dealer engaging in these activities, be sure you've gotten a thorough legal review from your lawyer about how to best bulletproof your program. You can't actually get to "bulletproof," but you can load the deck a bit in your favor.

Unless you have an extra $5.5 million burning a hole in your pocket.

Internet Lending: License ... What License?

October 2007

By Nicole F. Munro

You have a great idea! You want to make loans over the Internet. Located in Utah, you know the laws of your state. And why wouldn't you—you worked for a local loan company for the past 20 years and you already applied for your Utah lender's license. How hard could it be? You'll hire someone to create a web page that is easy to use and enticing. You'll market the loans through mailers sent to potential borrowers requesting that they visit your website. Borrowers who cannot resist your impressive advertising campaign will complete an online application. You will send them Utah-compliant loan documents that they will sign and return to you. Or, they will complete the online loan forms and sign them electronically. You're all set.

After a month of doing business, and consummating more than 200 loans across the country, you are contacted by the Kansas Office of the State Bank Commissioner. The regulator, who had received a complaint from one of your customers, wants to know why you are not licensed to do business in Kansas. You say, "License? What license?" You are licensed in Utah—the loan was made in Utah; ergo, you don't need a license under the Kansas Consumer Credit Code. Or, do you?

In a recent case, an Internet-based payday lender challenged the constitutionality of a licensing requirement under the Kansas Consumer Credit Code. The U.S. District Court for the District of Kansas found that the statute requiring Internet-based payday lenders to be licensed in Kansas did not violate the dormant Commerce Clause or the Due Process Clause of the U.S. Constitution. That's lawyer-speak for the court said the payday lender had to be licensed if it solicited potential borrowers in Kansas and made loans to Kansas residents via the Internet.

Quick Payday, Inc., was a Utah company that offered payday loans over the Internet. Quick Payday was registered as a lending entity in Utah, and its loans complied with Utah law. From May 2001 to January 2005, Quick Payday made payday loans to Kansas residents. Kansas consumers found Quick Payday by Internet searches, lead generators, and, for prior Quick Payday customers, e-mail solicitations. Kansas consumers applied for loans online. Quick Payday approved their applications. Contracts were executed online or by fax. Quick Payday funded the loans by direct depositing the payout to borrowers' bank accounts. Upon default, Quick Payday began collection efforts against Kansas residents in the form of e-mails, telephone calls, or letters to the debtors.

After receiving a consumer complaint, the Kansas Office of the State Bank Commissioner sanctioned Quick Payday for making loans in Kansas without a license. Quick Payday filed suit, claiming that the Kansas Consumer Credit Code's licensing requirement was unconstitutional under the dormant Commerce Clause and the Due Process Clause. In other words, Quick Payday claimed that the licensing requirement placed an undue burden on interstate commerce, regulated conduct that occurred completely outside of Kansas, and subjected payday lending to inconsistent state law requirements. Further, Quick Payday argued it didn't have sufficient contact with the state of Kansas to warrant the regulation.

The U.S. District Court for the District of Kansas granted the Office of the State Bank Commissioner's motion for summary judgment on both claims. The court found that the Credit Code does not discriminate against or unduly burden interstate commerce. The court reasoned that Kansas had a significant consumer protection interest in regulating credit transactions with Kansas consumers. That interest outweighed the impact that required licensing had on interstate commerce. Further, any argument that Quick Payday's conduct occurred wholly outside of Kansas likewise failed. Like many states that have enacted a Consumer Credit Code, Kansas law provides that loans are "made" in Kansas if they involve a Kansas resident and are induced by solicitation in Kansas. Quick Payday's transactions were made with Kansas residents, directly solicited by Quick Payday, and could not be construed as occurring wholly outside the state.

The court also rejected Quick Payday's argument that application of state laws to Internet lenders subjected Internet payday lenders to inconsistent state regulation. While Quick Payday cited cases holding that the nature of the Internet requires uniform national regulation, the court found that Quick Payday's cited cases related only to the content of the Internet and not to commerce conducted through the Internet.

Quick Payday also argued that the required licensing violated its rights to due process, claiming that it had no "contacts" in Kansas. Although Quick Payday did not have an office or employees in Kansas, the fact that it solicited borrowers in Kansas and made loans to Kansas residents made the contacts sufficient to warrant regulation.

While the Quick Payday case is unusual, Kansas isn't the only state that has a lender licensing law applicable to out-of-state lenders. By my research, some 37 other states apply their licensing provisions to out-of-state lenders. If an Internet loan is deemed "made" in Kansas or one of the other 37 jurisdictions, a lender would likely be required to obtain a license. Making a loan without a license subjects a lender to civil and criminal penalties, and could potentially affect the validity of the loan. Lenders should give due consideration to state licensing provisions before conducting an Internet loan with a borrower who resides outside of the lender's home state.

Note, too, that licensing is just the tip of the iceberg when dealing with Internet-based transactions. In addition to licensing, lenders should worry about ESIGN (the Electronic Signatures in Global and National Commerce Act), state unfair and deceptive acts and practices laws, state-specific disclosures, jurisdictional issues, tax laws, and, if the agreement is secured, state titling and repossession laws. Because the choice of law in an Internet-based transaction is unsettled, making Internet consumer purpose loans without complying with multi-state consumer protection laws is risky business.

Internet Sales—Once Is Not Enough for Jurisdiction

March 2008

By Thomas B. Hudson

Jacqueline Susann wrote a book titled *Once is Not Enough*. Although I doubt if she had Internet interstate vehicle sales in mind, it turns out that she was right.

The question is whether a vehicle seller who sells a single car to someone in another state using the Internet can be sued in the buyer's state when the deal turns sour. Two recent cases deal with this scenario.

Steve Malone, an Ohio resident, bought a 1968 GTO convertible from Thomas Berry, who is not a resident of Ohio, on Racingjunk.com, an online auction website. Berry had posted an advertisement on Racingjunk.com that stated the car was ready to drive and had a new engine and transmission.

After Malone submitted the winning bid, he arranged to have the car shipped to him in Ohio. During this time, Malone and Berry had several discussions by telephone and e-mail. Malone received the car, was not happy with its condition, and sued Berry in small claims court in Franklin County, Ohio, for misrepresenting the vehicle's condition. The Franklin County magistrate found for Malone, and Berry challenged that judgment on appeal, arguing that he was not subject to personal jurisdiction in Ohio.

The Ohio Court of Appeals noted that determining the reach of Ohio's long-arm statute is a factual inquiry and will vary in each case. The appellate court compared Racingjunk.com to eBay and found that where an individual posts an advertisement on an auction site and makes a single transaction, the individual does not purposefully avail him- or herself of the privilege of doing business in the state where the buyer resides. In reaching this conclusion, the appellate court focused on the fact that Berry did not operate the auction website and that sellers on Internet auction websites have very little control over who will ultimately submit the highest bid. Thus, the appellate court concluded that Berry's contacts with Ohio were not sufficient to subject him to personal jurisdiction.

A similar case actually involved an eBay posting. Nathan Wratislaw, a Montana resident, posted a car for sale on eBay. Robert Marschke, a South Dakota resident, saw the car on eBay but did not bid. Instead, Marschke called Wratislaw about the car and negotiated an agreement to purchase it.

Marschke arranged to wire funds to Wratislaw's bank account in Montana, and Wratislaw mailed the contract to Marschke in South Dakota. Marschke arranged to have the car transported to South Dakota. After the car arrived, Marschke decided that the car was not in the condition he expected and sued Wratislaw in a South Dakota court.

Wratislaw moved to dismiss based upon lack of personal jurisdiction. The trial court dismissed the case, and Marschke appealed.

The South Dakota Supreme Court affirmed dismissal for lack of personal jurisdiction. The high court found that since Marschke did not bid on or buy the car through eBay, the contact created by use of the Internet was no different than if Marschke responded to a print ad. The high court pointed out that it had not previously addressed a nonresident defendant's use of the Internet as a basis for establishing personal jurisdiction, and because the actual sale in this case did not take place on the Internet, the court would not reach that issue.

The high court turned to a traditional analysis of sufficient contacts and found that, based upon the following factors, Wratislaw did not have sufficient contacts with South Dakota:

Wratislaw had no physical contact with South Dakota before, during, or after the sale of the car; this was a "one-shot" deal; Marschke initiated the telephone calls and negotiations; Wratislaw sent a solitary e-mail into cyberspace to obtain Marschke's contact information to mail him the contract; and Wratislaw did not have an office, employees, real estate, or a bank account in South Dakota and did not distribute or sell products within the state.

These cases are the latest we've seen dealing with interstate Internet vehicle transactions. So far, there have been perhaps 10 or 12 of these cases, and most have involved car dealers. The others, like these cases, involved individuals. The cases have split on the issue of whether the buyer's state has jurisdiction over the seller for purposes of a lawsuit. Although these cases would seem to favor the seller, dealers shouldn't take much comfort from them.

First, both of these cases involved a single sale. It's very likely that the courts would come out differently if the seller were a South Carolina dealer selling several hundred cars a year over the Internet to Georgia residents. The Ohio court might come out the same way, but it's unlikely that the South Dakota court, with its emphasis on the "one-shot deal," would.

Second, as the courts note, their analysis of the issues in these cases is very heavily dependent on the facts in front of them. Smart dealers who do their homework will be able to assure that the facts describing their transactions are ones that would support a decision that they cannot be sued out of state.

Third, the interstate Internet cases so far have involved only the issue of jurisdiction—can the seller be sued in the buyer's state. It is only a matter of time before plaintiffs begin to assert more claims, alleging, for example, that the selling dealer needs a used car license in the buyer's state, that the selling dealer's buyers order violates the law of the buyer's state, that a finance transaction, even though legal in the seller's state, violates the maximum finance charge limits in the buyer's state—the issues that can be raised are limited only by the imaginations of the plaintiffs' lawyers.

If you have your own website that can be accessed by potential buyers, or if you are actively selling cars on eBay or other websites, you probably have been careful and have had a legal review of the way you are conducting business online. That sort of review will reduce the possibility that you can be sued in other states or that you are otherwise violating the laws of your buyers' states.

If that legal review is something you've been meaning to do but have simply not gotten around to yet, this might be the time.

Malone v. Berry, 2007 WL 4261679 (Ohio App. December 6, 2007); *Marschke v. Wratislaw,* 2007 WL 4277436 (S.D. December 5, 2007).

Who Is Watching Your Internet Sales Transactions?
March 2008
By Thomas B. Hudson

The old saying goes something like, "Just because you're paranoid, it doesn't mean that they aren't following you." If you're a car dealer, and you are selling cars over the Internet, there's a pretty good chance that they are following every move you make. And "they" means the Attorney General or other consumer protection folks in your state.

We've been warning for the last several years that the AGs are taking an increasingly active interest in car dealership advertising practices and that the advertising practices that they are interested in include Internet activities. We weren't surprised when a recent Pennsylvania AG press release underscored our point.

On February 8, the Pennsylvania Attorney General's Bureau of Consumer Protection announced that it had reached a civil settlement (called an Assurance of Voluntary Compliance or AVC) with LoCastro and Associates, doing business as All Pro Auto Mall, a used car dealership, concerning consumer complaints arising from the dealership's sale of vehicles on the "eBay Motors" auction website.

Attorney General Tom Corbett said that from 2004 to 2007, the Bureau of Consumer Protection received 51 consumer complaints related to eBay vehicle auctions conducted by All Pro. The complaints included disputes about the accuracy of vehicle descriptions, differences between the advertised condition and the actual condition of the vehicles, conflicting information about warranties, and the refusal to return consumer deposits for cancelled sales.

Under the AVC, All Pro must pay $6,600 in civil penalties, along with $5,000 for consumer education and future public protection services. On top of that, the AG's release noted that the dealership has already paid over $20,000 in restitution to complaining consumers. Not included in these numbers are whatever amount All Pro had to pay its own lawyers and the loss of management time dealing with the AG.

The AG said the settlement also requires All Pro to take steps to comply with Pennsylvania's Consumer Protection Law and state auto sales regulations for all future transactions. Specifically, All Pro must do the following:

- Clearly identify vehicles being sold "as is"
- Not extend or suggest any warranties that conflict with "as is" sales
- Honor all warranties that are offered

- Not sell vehicles that are unroadworthy
- Return deposits for cancelled transactions unless consumers have agreed that those funds are nonreturnable
- Disclose the All Pro dealership name in all sales and promotional materials
- Notify Pennsylvania authorities of any proposed name or structure change in the company

If you are a dealer in a state other than Pennsylvania (OK, Pennsylvania's actually a commonwealth instead of a state, but that's another article), you might think that you don't need to be concerned about the Pennsylvania AG's activities.

You'd be wrong.

First, keep in mind that we're writing about a press release. Granted, it won't get a lot of play outside of Pennsylvania and that state's immediate environs, but it is posted on the AG's website, and it will draw some attention (after all, I found it, didn't I?).

More important, the AGs don't operate in isolation. They meet regularly and trade war stories (you won't be far wrong if you think about their gatherings as a big 20 group meeting for the consumer protection cops).

At the next such meeting, the Pennsylvania AG will be crowing about his latest dealership enforcement trophy. The other AGs in attendance will have a lot of interest in this enforcement action and will be sure to ask for all the details.

You can bet that some of them will return to their home states and tell their folks to peruse their complaint files for eBay-related auto complaints.

That's a list where you don't want to see your dealership's name.

New York DMV Weighs in on Dealer Internet Sales

March 2008

By Geoffrey C. Rogers

Just when you think you've caught a break . . . In these days of government regulations that are increasing at a staggering rate, you get a decision from an agency saying that the regulations don't apply. "Why, here," you say to yourself, "is a cause for celebration!"

Let's say, for example, that rules applicable to "in person" sales don't apply to Internet sales. You are elated. But, not so fast. For, what the government giveth, the government can taketh away. That's what happened recently in an opinion issued by the Counsel's Office of the New York State Department of Motor Vehicles.

Orest Grechka, doing business in New York as Extraordinary Auto Sales, was registered as a dealer in New York. An administrative law judge (an employee of the DMV) found Grechka guilty of violating six counts of the DMV regulations for his vehicle sales activities on the Internet. Grechka appealed the decision of the administrative law judge to the DMV Appeals Board, as was his right. The Appeals Board reversed the administrative law judge, dismissing all the charges, saying, "Those who sell vehicles via the Internet are not required to register in New York State, nor are they required to have an established place of business in New York."

Therefore, there were no violations for sales conducted over the Internet. So, does this mean that from now on anyone in New York selling vehicles over the Internet doesn't have to worry about the laws and regulations applicable to "in person" sales?

Did we catch a break? Read on . . .

On March 19, 2008, the Counsel's Office of the DMV issued an opinion saying that the Appeals Board erred in its Extraordinary Auto Sales decision. The Counsel's Office stated that any person located in New York who meets the very broad definition of "dealer" under New York law must register as a dealer regardless of whether sales are transacted in person or over the Internet.

The opinion also says that Internet sales are governed by all of the laws and regulations applicable to "in person" sales and that dealers, Internet or otherwise, located in New York are subject to enforcement actions by the DMV for violations.

So, if you are a registered dealer in New York and you have an Internet sales program, you should be certain that your Internet transactions comply with all the laws and regulations that apply to "in person" sales. If you are located in New York and not registered, and are engaging solely in vehicle sales through the Internet, better check with counsel.

eBay Buyers and Sellers Beware!

September 2008

By Dana Frederick Clarke

We often wonder about the allure of a collectible suddenly appearing in the midst of an eBay search, particularly when it's a car the buyer has dreamt of delivering to the waiting arms of his garage. Nothing, however, substitutes for a physical inspection before plunking down money, as a recent case proves.

The U.S. Court of Appeals for the Ninth Circuit has handed down a warning to both eBay buyers and sellers. In the case of *Boschetto v. Hansing,* the court rejected the buyer's argument that his purchase of a motor vehicle advertised as "a 1964 Ford

Galaxie 500 XL 427/425 hp 'R Code' in awesome condition" through eBay subjected the out-of-state sellers to personal jurisdiction in his home state of California.

Paul Boschetto was the winning bidder for the car, agreeing to pay more than $34,000 to the seller, Paul D. Hansing (who happened to be an employee of one of the Wisconsin dealers named as defendants). Boschetto arranged for the car to be shipped to California from Wisconsin. Viewing the car in California, Boschetto did not agree with the seller in Wisconsin that the vehicle was "in awesome condition," concluding, instead, that it was a lemon. Boschetto attempted to rescind the purchase, without success. He then sued the Wisconsin defendants in a California district court, alleging that they had violated the California Consumer Protection Act and that they were also liable for breach of contract, misrepresentation, and fraud.

The Wisconsin defendants argued that they were not subject to personal jurisdiction in California because Boschetto could not establish that the transaction was more than a "one-shot affair." Under California's long-arm statute, Boschetto needed to demonstrate that the Wisconsin defendants had "purposefully availed themselves of the privilege of doing business in California." Citing the Supreme Court's precedent in *Burger King Corp. v. Rudzewicz*, the court noted that "a contract alone [cannot] automatically establish" personal jurisdiction over the defendants.

The court also was not persuaded by Boschetto's argument that the selection of eBay as the conduit for the sale altered the jurisdictional outcome. However, as a warning to sellers over Internet auction sites, the court colorfully explained that its ruling "is not to say that the use of eBay digs a virtual moat around the defendant, fending off jurisdiction in all cases." Indeed, the court observed that "[w]here eBay is used as a means for establishing regular business with a remote forum [rather than, as in the instant case, a one-time transaction] . . . a defendant's use of eBay may be properly taken into account for the purposes of establishing personal jurisdiction."

When Boschetto filed his complaint, he neither knew, nor alleged, that the Wisconsin defendants used eBay for more than his purchase of the awesome lemon. After hitting the personal jurisdiction roadblock in the district court, Boschetto sought to marshal evidence of the Wisconsin defendants' "regular" California business through discovery. He was again rebuffed in that attempt by the court's agreement with the district court's denial of Boschetto's discovery efforts because he could not demonstrate more than his belief that such efforts would "yield jurisdictionally relevant facts."

Although a good outcome for these out-of-state sellers, this case provides just enough helpful discussion for future plaintiffs to avoid a similar fate. For those sellers engaged in more than one sale to out-of-state buyers in a particular state, it is likely that future plaintiffs who have been educated on Boschetto's hurdles will allege (in an attempt to satisfy the jurisdictional requirements of the buyer's home state or, at least, to convince the court that it is entitled to some discovery on the issue) that some portion of the seller's business was regularly conducted through eBay.

As for Californian Boschetto, we can only assume his case is on to the Wisconsin courts for the next round of his legal battle. *Boschetto v. Hansing*, 2008 WL 3852676 (9th Cir. (N.D. Cal.) August 20, 2008).

Point-Click Compliance
November 2008
By Maya P. Hill

Several years ago, in what we think was a smart and necessary move, many dealers decided to set their inventory loose on the information superhighway and began advertising on the Internet. What a wonderful way to reach potential buyers who wanted to do their price, color, and gas mileage comparisons from the comfort of their living rooms!

Subsequently, dealers took the next step and decided to offer vehicles for sale via the Internet. We've seen this, not just on Internet auction sites such as eBay, but also on individual dealerships' websites. These days, a buyer can hop online, compare vehicles in a dealer's inventory, negotiate prices and credit terms, sign sale documents electronically, and become the proud owner of a vehicle with just a point and a click of the mouse. We've noticed that on their websites, some dealers make statements such as, "Complete your entire transaction over the Internet," or, "Do your shopping online and complete your purchase with us over the telephone." Some dealers also offer home delivery of newly purchased vehicles. Talk about convenience!

While Internet sales are a great way to reach buyers and offer them the option of not having to make a trip to your dealership, these sales raise a number of compliance issues that dealers should be aware of when considering an online sales strategy. These issues fall under the umbrella of what we like to call "Point-Click Compliance." Some are of a federal nature, and some vary from state to state. We suggest consulting with your attorney before implementing an Internet/telephone sales strategy and checking in periodically to make sure your program complies with the host of laws that apply.

The list of issues we provide below is intended to be a starting point, and chances are your attorney will be able to flag other concerns that are specific to your state or locality.

Point-Click Compliance Checklist

1. Home solicitation sales and door-to-door sales. Many states have what are called "Home Solicitation Sales Acts" or "Door-to-Door Sales Acts." Now, likely you don't go knocking on random doors like a Girl Scout trying to sell thin mints and peanut butter patties. But these laws may be misnamed because they aren't always limited to sales you make at someone's home going door-to-door. While state laws vary, many of these statutes apply to sales conducted or consummated at a place of business other than your dealership—not just at someone's house. They can also include sales you make via telephone or electronically. Some laws exclude sales that are entered into via telephone or electronically if you don't have any other contact with the buyer. And some laws apply only to sales where you make the phone call and exclude sales that result from the buyer's initiative.

Why should you care about these laws? Generally, they impose a permit requirement, either on your dealership as an entity or on the individual salespeople who conduct the sales. They also generally impose certain disclosure requirements, including notice to the buyer that she has three days to cancel the sale. Additionally, some laws require you to provide the written disclosures in the same language in which you conducted the sale transaction. So, if you conducted the transaction in Spanish, for example, your written disclosures have to be in Spanish. This is the case even if you don't have to provide the retail installment contract and other sale documents in Spanish.

2. Red Flag compliance. By now we're all familiar with Red Flag compliance. You know—the act of verifying your customer's identity as part of your dealership's written identity theft prevention program, which you're required to maintain by federal law. There are a number of "red flags" out there—anything from a discrepancy between the address your customer provides on the credit application and the address that pops up on the credit report to a discrepancy in the customer's Social Security Number or date of birth. When your customer comes to your dealership, you can see her in person, you know what she looks like, you can match her photo to that on her driver's license, and so on. But when conducting a sale over the Internet or the phone, how do you know that the person you're dealing with is the person she claims to be? Online or on the phone, a customer can be whoever she wants to be—and she could be a perpetrator of identity theft. Of course, your written identity theft prevention policy should take into account various means by which to detect identity theft, not just comparing someone's physical appearance to the picture and description on her driver's license.

Another issue that pops up when transacting business over the Internet or on the phone is pulling a credit bureau report. If you don't know for sure whom you're dealing with, then how can you represent to the credit bureau that you have the customer's permission or other authorization to pull credit for that person?

3. State laws. One of the main reasons to expand your sales program to include selling cars online or over the phone is, at least in part, to reach a broader market, including people who live far from your dealership. If you're a Virginia dealer, you might sell a car via the Internet or on the phone to a Maryland resident. What state's laws will govern that transaction? Can the customer sue you in Maryland? States usually impose something called the "minimum contacts" rule. Depending on what kinds of advertising activities you engage in and how actively you engage in business in other markets, you could be hauled into court in a state other than your own. Keep in mind that "advertising" doesn't just mean print, television, and radio ads. If your website reaches customers in another state, and if a customer can show that you had sufficient contacts in that state—if you directed your actions toward that state—it's possible that you'll find yourself in that state's courtroom.

There's nothing wrong with offering vehicles for sale online or completing a transaction online or over the phone. In a climate where technology is king and people are short on time, you almost have to implement some sort of Internet/telephone sales strategy to stay competitive.

Just remember that doing so is not without risk. Consider putting a "Point-Click Compliance" program in place to help ensure that you're in line with any applicable state and federal laws.

Your Internet Buyer Sues You in His Home State— Can He Do That?
November 2008
By Emily Marlow Beck

Resident of State A buys a car over the Internet from dealer in State B. Car develops problems. Buyer sues in State A. Do the courts in State A have jurisdiction over the dealer, permitting them to hear the case?

You might think I'm subjecting you to one of my law school exam questions, but this is a real question that the courts in many states have had to grapple with. Courts faced with these cases are forced to look at all of the facts and circumstances surrounding the sale. Seemingly slight variations of the facts can send the court down differing paths in determining whether jurisdiction exists. Need some examples? Let's look at a couple of recent cases.

The first case involved Carl Dawson, a Texas resident. Dawson bought a car online from Choice Auto Brokers, Inc. Choice Auto delivered the car to Dawson in Florida.

The car suffered from mechanical problems, and Dawson was unable to drive it home to Texas. Dawson sued Choice Auto in a Texas court.

Choice Auto claimed that it was not subject to personal jurisdiction in Texas. Dawson argued that Choice Auto was subject to Texas jurisdiction because it had sold 43 cars to Texas residents in the previous three years, 19 of which it had delivered to the buyers in Texas, and offered legally binding contracts to Texas residents through the Internet. That level of activity is what we lawyers would call a "bad fact." The Texas trial court found that Choice Auto was subject to Texas jurisdiction. Choice Auto appealed.

The Court of Appeals of Texas reversed the trial court. It found that Choice Auto did not have enough contacts with the state to allow for jurisdiction. The appellate court found that Dawson accepted delivery of his car in Florida and that the malfunction occurred in Florida. While Choice Auto solicited sales business from Texas residents and exchanged data with Texas residents via its proprietary website, it did not use its website to enter into contracts with Texas residents. Rather, it routed its Texas customers to an eBay auction site to complete the purchase agreement. Finally, there was no indication that Choice Auto targeted Texas customers, had an office in Texas, or otherwise performed business activities in Texas. Accordingly, the court held that Choice Auto's activities did not establish a pattern of activity sufficient to support personal jurisdiction in Texas.

The dealer should be very pleased with this result. Other courts in other states might have come down on the other side of this one.

Case two involved Paul Boschetto, a California resident, who was the winning bidder for a 1964 Ford Galaxie sold on eBay by Jeffrey Hansing, a Wisconsin resident and an employee of Frank Boucher Chrysler-Dodge-Jeep. Boschetto arranged for the car to be shipped from Wisconsin to California, but, upon arrival, it failed to meet Boschetto's expectations or the advertised description.

Boschetto sued in a California federal district court, where his complaint was dismissed for lack of federal jurisdiction. The district court reasoned that an eBay sale consummated with a California purchaser was insufficient to establish jurisdiction over Hansing and the dealership and that "the eBay seller does not purposefully avail himself of the privilege of doing business in a forum state absent some additional conduct directed at the forum state." Unhappy (again), Boschetto appealed.

[Editor's note: Forum: Latin. Court of justice: place where legal remedy can be sought.—Gilbert Law Dictionary]

The U.S. Court of Appeals for the Ninth Circuit affirmed the lower court. The court explained that the formation of a contract with a nonresident is not, standing alone, sufficient to create jurisdiction. Furthermore, the fact that eBay was used as the conduit for the sale did not affect the jurisdictional outcome considering the particular facts of the case.

The court explained that Boschetto did not allege that Hansing or the dealership was using eBay to conduct business generally or that they conduct regular sales in California or any other state. Instead, this was a one-time contract for the sale of a good that involved the forum state only because that is where the purchaser happened to reside. The court concluded that the sale of one automobile via the eBay website, without more, did not provide sufficient "minimum contacts" to establish jurisdiction over a nonresident defendant in the forum state.

In comparing these two decisions, it's hard to shake the thought that the California court would have come out differently if the facts in front of it were more like those before the Texas court. As it happened, Californian Boschetto's suit was dismissed against Wisconsin's Frank Boucher Chrysler-Dodge-Jeep. Choice Auto, claiming that it was not subject to personal jurisdiction in Texas, lost the first round, but won at the Texas Court of Appeals level. In both cases, the dealers were not subject to out-of-state prosecution. However, as we said, these cases are very fact-specific, with seemingly small differences leading to different results.

As dealers sell more and more cars to out-of-state buyers over the Internet, expect to see more cases like these, but expect to see the courts landing on both sides of the jurisdiction question, depending on the facts in front of them. Maybe that's something to think about when developing your online sales program.

Choice Auto Brokers, Inc. v. Dawson, 2008 WL 4367837 (Tex. App2008). *Boschetto v. Hansing,* 539 F.3d 1011 (9th Cir. (N.D. Cal.) August 20, 2008).

The Internet, Pricing, and Discounting

April 2009

By Thomas B. Hudson

I was reviewing reports of court cases recently and ran across something that sounded familiar. It also sounded a few warning bells I'd like to share with you.

Dolly saw a 2006 Nissan Murano advertised on the Internet. When she contacted the dealer about the car, a dealer representative quoted the purchase price as $15,500. When Dolly drove to the dealership to pick up the car, a second representative told her the purchase price was actually $21,500. Molly, Dolly's sister, agreed to act as a co-signer so that Dolly could get a better rate. A dealership representative drove to Molly's house and had her sign a blank retail installment contract. A month later, Molly received the completed documents. The contract showed the amount financed as $23,800. The contract also showed Molly as the sole buyer and borrower. Molly and Dolly sued the bank that bought the contract from the dealership. The sisters argued that the bank violated the Truth in Lending Act, the Equal Credit Opportunity Act, and state unfair trade practices and consumer protection laws. The bank unsuccessfully moved to dismiss.

It's too early in the course of this lawsuit to make any judgments about who did what to whom—that will come later after some discovery or, if it comes to it, after a trial. For now, I want you to focus on Dolly's claim that the car was advertised on the Internet at $15,500, but when she arrived at the dealership, the price was $6,000 higher.

It is possible that the price discrepancy was simply an error on the part of whoever did the Internet ad or that there is some other innocent explanation for the extra $6,000. It's also possible that the tooth fairy is real. When I hear facts like this, alarms go off, and I start asking myself questions.

What if this dealer was advertising the vehicle on the Internet at $15,500, and what if the Internet ad said something in small print like "for cash and good credit customers"? I've actually seen Internet ads like that.

And what if Dolly or Molly's credit wasn't strong enough to qualify for purchase by a nondiscounting sales finance company? And what if the only sales finance company willing to buy Dolly or Molly's deal was a deep-discounting buyer that would buy the contract only if the dealer agreed to a $6,000 haircut? And what if the dealer simply tacked the expected $6,000 haircut onto the car price to recoup the haircut?

I read this case a week after I was in the offices of a sales finance company that buys retail installment contracts from dealers at a discount. The compliance officer of the company described to me a problem he was wrestling with. It seems that his company had just bought a contract financing the sale of a Chevrolet pickup truck, showing a cash price of $15,000. The compliance officer, however, had gone to the dealer's website and had found the very same truck advertised at $11,000. Was it just coincidence that the contract had been bought at a $4,000 discount? The compliance officer wanted to know what, if anything, the company could do about the deal.

Now, either these two situations just happened to pop up at the same time, or they illustrate a more-common-than-I-thought dealer practice that is (1) illegal and (2) dangerous.

If practices like these are occurring at your dealership, write this on a piece of paper and post it on the breakroom bulletin board: "YOU CANNOT INCREASE THE PRICE OF A CAR TO COVER A DISCOUNT YOU TAKE ON THE SALE OF A FINANCE CONTRACT FOR THAT CAR."

Why not, you ask?

Because when you increase the price of the car to cover the discount, the amount of increase in the purchase price suddenly becomes a finance charge for federal disclosure purposes, that's why. And, unless you disclose the price increase as a finance charge (and no one does), you've violated federal disclosure laws.

Along the way, you've probably also violated the maximum finance charge rate provisions of your state's retail installment sales law, state advertising laws that require you to sell cars at the price at which you've advertised them, and state laws that prohibit "unfair and deceptive" acts and practices. You've also, no doubt, violated the terms of the dealer agreement between you and the sales finance company to which you have sold the discounted contract, subjecting you to the potential liability of buying the contract back if the sales finance company demands that you do so.

If your dealership sells retail installment contracts to sales finance companies at a discount, the dealership needs to understand how to do so, and how to price its cars, without violating the law. Although most dealers will probably dislike changing their practices to accommodate those pesky laws, they will find that they will sleep better at night if they do.

Time to schedule another visit to the lawyer's office.

Molley v. Five Town Chrysler, Inc., 2009 U.S. Dist. LEXIS 13765 (E.D. Pa. February 20, 2009).

eBay Buyer Beware!
May 2009
By Catherine M. Brennan

Almost every person has, by this point, either bought something on eBay or has at least heard of eBay, the online auction website.

Indeed, many motor vehicle dealers now use eBay quite effectively to sell used motor vehicles to purchasers all over the United States. Surprisingly, millions of transactions have occurred across state lines—sometimes far across state lines—

with little or no significant litigation. But what happens when something goes wrong?

Several state and federal courts have addressed jurisdictional issues in eBay transactions where dissatisfied buyers have sued sellers, alleging misrepresentation and other claims when the seller failed to deliver goods as promised or described. But recently, an Indiana court considered what happens when the eBay seller sues a buyer for rescission of payment after the buyer picked up the item in the seller's state and then decided to walk away from the deal. The result signals an opening for online motor vehicle dealers seeking to keep their litigation costs down.

Llexcyiss Omega and Dale York of Indiana listed a Porsche for sale on eBay. The eBay listing provided that the winning bidder—not the sellers—must arrange and pay for delivery of the car. Halfway across the country, Richard and Marlene Attaway of Idaho saw the listing online, bid on the car, and won the auction. They paid Omega and York through PayPal, the online payment service owned by eBay. As required in the eBay listing, the Attaways arranged for a transporter based in Washington State to pick up the car in Indiana and deliver it to them in Idaho.

After taking delivery of the car, the Attaways filed a claim with PayPal seeking a refund of the amount they paid for the car, stating that the description of the car in the eBay auction listing did not match the reality of the car delivered to their doorstep. PayPal denied the refund request and told the Attaways to work directly with the sellers to resolve their dispute.

The Attaways apparently did not take the issue up with Omega and York. Instead, they ultimately persuaded the credit card company associated with their PayPal account to refund their money, leaving Omega and York out of payment. The sellers then sued the Attaways in Indiana small claims court, seeking $5,900 in damages. The Attaways filed a motion to dismiss, claiming that the court lacked personal jurisdiction over them. The trial court denied the motion, and the Attaways appealed this issue directly to the Indiana Court of Appeals.

The Attaways claimed that the lower court made a mistake in not dismissing the lawsuit, and that the Indiana courts lacked personal jurisdiction over them. Courts must have personal jurisdiction over parties to a lawsuit in order to balance the significant harm that can come to a party asked to defend a lawsuit in a far away court.

More than 60 years ago, in *International Shoe Co. v. Washington,* the U.S. Supreme Court established that a nonresident party to a lawsuit must have certain "minimum contacts" with the forum state to ensure that the maintenance of a lawsuit does not offend "traditional notions of fair play and substantial justice." Such personal jurisdiction can take two forms: general or specific.

General jurisdiction exists where the party's contacts are so continuous and systematic in a state that the party should reasonably anticipate being brought into the courts of that state, even in causes unrelated to his contacts with the forum state. Specific jurisdiction requires that the party purposefully availed himself of the privilege of conducting activities within the forum state and that the conduct would make the party reasonably anticipate being hauled into court.

The Indiana Court of Appeals first noted that it could not locate any other case in which a seller sued a buyer for rescission of payment after the buyer collected the item from the seller. In reviewing the few cases that have involved eBay auction disputes, the appellate court noted that the majority of courts that have considered the issue of jurisdiction in online auction cases have held that the usual online auction process—that is, the clicking of a button online to buy goods—does not rise to the level of "purposeful conduct" required to assert specific jurisdiction.

The appellate court then reviewed the facts of this transaction. Here, the Indiana sellers, Omega and York, filed suit against the Idaho buyers, the Attaways, after the Attaways took delivery of the vehicle and then rescinded payment.

The court found that the Attaways knew of the sellers' location before bidding—in fact, the sellers' location would impact the delivery price the Attaways would pay for the car, as the sellers stated in their listing that the buyer must arrange and pay for delivery. This was an important consideration, as delivery fees could vary significantly depending on the length of travel required to deliver the car.

Additionally, the Attaways agreed to appear in Indiana—either in person or through a representative—to pick up the car when they submitted a bid. The court found that all of these contacts, taken together, went beyond a single online purchase. Accordingly, the court found that the Attaways "purposefully availed" themselves of the privilege of conducting activities within the state of Indiana such that they could reasonably anticipate defending a lawsuit in Indiana related to this eBay purchase.

The court also determined that this decision was fair and just, finding that the burden on the Attaways is no greater than the burden Omega and York would have if they had to file their lawsuit in Idaho. It seemed more than fair that Indiana courts should be permitted to exercise personal jurisdiction over individuals who have entered into a contract with an Indiana resident for the purchase of property located in Indiana. Thus, the court sent the case back to the lower court for trial.

What does this mean for dealers that sell their motor vehicles online? At a minimum, dealers should review their online listings and indicate that, as a condition of bidding on the motor vehicle, buyers must come to the dealer's state themselves or through a representative to pick up the car and have it delivered to their home state. The addition of this fact to the single online purchase seems to have been just the hook the Indiana court needed to make sure Indiana residents could bring residents of a foreign state into Indiana courts. Clearly, it is far less expensive to bring a lawsuit in your local court than to have to file these actions in a far away state. In these lean days, it pays to review your online listings to cull every advantage you can.

Attaway v. York, 2009 Ind. App. LEXIS 515 (Ind. App. March 13, 2009).

Interstate Internet Car Sales and State UDAP Laws
June 2009
By Thomas B. Hudson

We're back to one of our favorite topics—dealers using the Internet to sell cars to out-of-state buyers. Litigation involving interstate Internet transactions started as a trickle several years ago. Nowadays, it's a rare month that goes by without a report of another case involving this topic.

At first, the cases all involved jurisdiction—the question of whether a dealer could be sued in the car buyer's state. Those cases, which depended very heavily on the facts surrounding the sales, seemed to split about evenly, with dealers winning as many as they lost.

We predicted, though, that plaintiffs' lawyers would broaden their attacks on Internet sales practices. This case illustrates the sorts of attacks that we were concerned about.

Lyle Real, a Missouri resident, bought a used Chevrolet Corvette convertible that he saw advertised on an Internet auction website by Radir Wheels, a company wholly owned by Richard Conklin. The advertisement represented that the motor vehicle was in good condition and drivable.

Real called Conklin to confirm the condition of the motor vehicle, and Conklin assured Real that the car was drivable from Conklin's New Jersey location to Missouri. After Real won the auction, he called Conklin, who told him then that the car might not be drivable. Real thus had the car shipped from New Jersey to Missouri. Real paid for the car with a check payable to Conklin, who held the title.

Real took the car to a mechanic who told him it needed more than $40,000 worth of repairs. Real sued Conklin and Radir under the New Jersey Unfair and Deceptive Trade Practices Act (UDTPA).

The trial court awarded Real a judgment for more than $25,000 against Conklin, representing a tripling of the difference between the amount he paid and what Conklin delivered. Conklin appealed.

The appellate court ruled that the trial court should have dismissed the state UDTPA claim because Conklin was not a "dealer" or a "merchant" to which the Act applied. Real appealed.

The New Jersey Supreme Court reinstated the UDTPA claim for Real. The high court noted that the UDTPA prohibits the use by any person of any unconscionable commercial practice, misrepresentation, or the knowing omission of any material fact in connection with the sale or advertisement of any merchandise. "Person" includes any natural person, company, or business entity.

Conklin claimed that the UDTPA should not apply to an online transaction and that he was not a "person" because he was not a used car dealer. The high court disagreed and noted that even though Conklin did not necessarily satisfy the definition of "dealer," he certainly did satisfy the definition of "person" to which the UDTPA applied. Additionally, the high court found that the UDTPA applies to a transaction where an out-of-state consumer buys a used motor vehicle from an in-state seller over the Internet.

Look for more cases like this one. Plaintiffs' lawyers really like state "unfair and deceptive acts and practices" laws like the New Jersey UDTPA. Such laws frequently provide that a successful plaintiff is entitled to some multiple of the plaintiff's actual damages (double or triple multiples are common) and provide that a successful plaintiff may recover attorneys' fees.

And look for variations on this attack, such as a claim by the car buyer that the UDAP law of the buyer's state applies. The one thing that we can guarantee is that the suits will keep coming.

Real v. Radir Wheels Inc., 2009 N.J. LEXIS 150 (N.J. April 8, 2009).

Internet Marketing, Fraud, and State Consumer Protection Laws
June 2009
By Thomas B. Hudson

Marketing cars by using the Internet, are you? What happens when your out-of-state buyer claims that the car you sold him isn't in the condition you described on your website? Can you claim that any problems with the car were obvious ones that the customer's reasonable inspection would have identified, and that you aren't responsible for them?

A recent case dealing with a California buyer and a Tennessee dealer addresses these issues. Let's look at how the court handled the buyer's complaint.

California resident Mark Bradley bought a car over the Internet from All American Classics of Tennessee, Inc. All American's employees stated that the car "needed nothing" and that the engine was "mechanically perfect." When the car arrived, Bradley noticed that it was not in the same condition as it appeared on All American's website. The car also almost immediately broke down when Bradley drove it.

Bradley attempted to return the car to All American and obtain a refund, but All American refused. Bradley sued, seeking rescission of the contract and damages based on fraud and violations of the Tennessee Consumer Protection Act (TCPA).

With respect to the fraud claim, All American argued that Bradley did not satisfy one of the elements of fraud, i.e., he did not reasonably rely on the misrepresentation. The trial court granted All American's motion for a directed verdict, finding that because the defects in the car were obvious, Bradley or someone acting on his behalf would have found them in the course of an inspection. Bradley appealed.

The Tennessee Court of Appeals reversed the trial court's decision and remanded the case. The appellate court noted that All American was located in Tennessee, almost 2,000 miles from Bradley's residence in California. The appellate court also noted that All American controlled the flow of information through the pictures it sent to Bradley and the representations made by its employees about the car. Any opportunity to discover the defects in the car was minimized by All American's efforts to hide problems with the car in its pictures and the distance between Bradley and the car.

The appellate court stated that, now that consumers are using the Internet to make purchases, it may not be reasonable for a prospective buyer who lives far away to inspect his or her purchase. According to the appellate court, "One cannot be

251

permitted to fill a website with misrepresentations designed to induce a buyer to purchase an item in reliance thereon and remain immune from liability based on the simple fact that the buyer did not inspect the item before purchase." Accordingly, the appellate court concluded that Bradley was not unreasonable in relying on All American's misrepresentations.

The appellate court also concluded that Bradley made a prima facie case that the website statements and other actions of All American were deceptive under the TCPA.

*[**Editor's note:** prima facie: adverb, Latin, 15th century. At first view; on the first appearance.]*

To avoid the problems that this dealer ended up confronting, you might want to do a top-to-bottom review of your Internet sales and marketing process. That review should include some face time with your friendly legal adviser to determine what your documentation looks like, what your website says, and whether your policies and procedures can be changed to reduce your risk as much as possible. Once these steps have been taken, you can then (again, with your lawyer's help) train your Internet sales staff to deal with buyers in ways that don't create liability for you.

Bradley v. All American Classics of Tennessee, Inc., 2009 Tenn. App. LEXIS 138 (Tenn. App. April 16, 2009).

Is Your "Cash Price" a Moving Target?
August 2009
By Thomas B. Hudson

At a recent conference, I sat in on a session where another speaker was holding forth. He was from one of the companies that host websites where dealers can advertise cars for sale, and his topic was "Internet Sales Best Practices." I was listening out of the corner of my ear, and taking a quick glance at each slide as I was catching up on my e-mail, when he suddenly had 200% of my attention. He had posted a slide showing what he had identified as "a very effective Internet posting." The posting under discussion, however, showed a price for the vehicle of "$14,995 (cash and good credit customers)." The obvious implication of this price posting was that potential buyers who were not cash and good credit customers would pay a (presumably) higher price.

That's an enforcement action or a class action plaintiff's lawsuit waiting to happen. "What's the problem?" you ask.

Here's the problem. The federal Truth in Lending Act, Regulation Z, and most state retail installment sales acts require the disclosure of a vehicle's "cash price." "Cash price" is a defined term under federal and most state laws, and it is defined in a manner that doesn't include any charges for the cost of the credit extended in a credit sale transaction. So, a dealer who sets one cash price for credit buyers and a lower cash price for cash buyers has just converted the difference between those two numbers into a finance charge. That's not good.

That's not good because unless the differential is added to the finance charge and included in the APR calculation (and it never is), the dealer has a slam-dunk disclosure violation. An enforcement agency or plaintiff won't stop with alleging a disclosure problem—you can bet that any complaint will also claim that the differential must be considered in determining whether the transaction violates state maximum finance charge rate laws. And you can expect to see the old standby claim—that the practice of quoting different cash prices is a violation of a state unfair and deceptive acts and practices law.

The issue is not limited to Internet pricing. I rarely attend an industry conference at which I don't end up trying to convince a dealer that he cannot increase the price of a car when he determines that he's going to have to assign the retail installment sales contract for that car to a subprime company that buys such contracts at a discount. It's the same issue, albeit in a context in which the enforcement authorities or plaintiff's lawyer might have a difficult time proving those claims.

But the dealer posting "$14,995 (cash and good credit customers)" has just handed the enforcement agency or plaintiffs a winning case on a silver platter.

If you haven't had a sit-down with your friendly local Ben Matlock regarding your dealership's pricing policies, you might want to make a note to self to do so, sooner rather than later. Especially if you're using any Internet ads like these.

*[**Editor's note:** Benjamin Leighton "Ben" Matlock: A fictional character from the television series, Matlock, played by Andy Griffith. Matlock is a renowned, folksy, yet cantankerous, defense attorney who is worth every penny of his $100,000 fee.— Wikipedia, the free encyclopedia]*

Chapter 8

Advertising

State Attorneys General have decided that dealer advertising violations are a source of easy revenue. From ads that we've seen, dealers must enjoy forking over big bundles of cash to the AGs, otherwise, they would be a lot more careful about the things that they let the ad agencies sell them.

In addition to being car lawyers, we are also just plain old citizens who subscribe to newspapers, listen to the radio, watch TV, and empty our mailboxes every day. Consequently, many, if not most, of the dealer ads we see might as well be "Kick Me" signs taped to the dealer's backside. Dealers forget that the AGs and their staffs, in their capacities as ordinary citizens, also are subject to these same advertisements.

Way too many dealers sign up for ad campaigns without doing any due diligence at all. Dealers assume that the ad company has done its legal homework and that the ad company will stand behind the dealer in case the AG comes calling. Some pay a substantial cost to learn the hard lesson that those things are not true.

We have seen AG enforcement actions against dealers that have involved fines or civil penalties of $250,000, $300,000, or more. In addition to the check the dealer has to stroke to the AG, the dealership has to pay its own lawyer, it must divert scarce management time to resolving the charges, and, ultimately, the dealer suffers reputational damage. It wouldn't surprise us if the total fines, costs, and damages in these cases were to approach $1 million.

And in case you think that you can stay under the AG's radar, think again. The AGs of all the states meet regularly and swap stories of their successes. If the Arizona AG stands up at one of these meetings and says that he nailed a dealer's hide to the door for advertising violations to the tune of a quarter mil or so, you can bet that every other state AG in the room will be taking careful notes and making plans to review dealer ads when he or she gets home.

That isn't the sort of attention you were looking for from your ad campaign.

(Another!) AG Advertising Action

October 2007

By Emily Marlow Beck

Fibbing. Fudging. Stretching the truth. Story-telling. A little white lie. Whatever you call it, telling a little lie here or there never hurt anybody, did it? If you ask the Connecticut Attorney General's office, the answer is a resounding "yes."

According to a press release issued by the Connecticut Attorney General's office, the state AG has sued a Subaru and Dodge dealership alleging almost 300 instances of false and misleading advertising that could ultimately result in hundreds of thousands of dollars in civil penalties and could potentially result in criminal investigation.

What kinds of false and misleading advertising, you may ask? According to the AG's office, Attorney General Richard Blumenthal's action charged the dealership with making almost 300 illegal or false claims over a period of three years. Allegedly, the dealership offered "loans with zero or $1 down payments," "payments as low as $37 a month," and "limited time discounts as deep as 70%."

Why did these ads get into the AG's craw? According to the AG's release, virtually no customers received these "special deals." Instead, the dealership buttressed its advertising claims using "made-up" testimonials from "phantom" customers. The AG said the dealership allegedly engaged in additional misdeeds, including:

- Telling customers they could "road test" a "pristine" new or used car for up to four years by paying the dealership $37 a month and permitting the dealership to regularly inspect the vehicle, when, in fact, the $37 a month payment was only for three to six months. After this three- to six-month period, the customer had to make the full payments.
- Claiming to offer discounts to U.S. government employees for a "limited time," when, in fact, the dealership offered no such discounts.

Even keeping in mind that this is an AG press release, and that there may be another side to the story, the AG's claims look pretty bad. All in all, the AG release alleged at least 293 separate violations of the Connecticut Unfair Trade Practices Act, which imposes a maximum $5,000 per violation penalty. The dealership has closed its doors, but the AG release also notes that the AG intends to send a "powerful message to car dealers" and that "a referral for criminal investigation is a distinct and real possibility."

You'll note that the AG's beef in the press release had very little to do with pinheaded and technical violations of regulations or statutes. Instead, the AG focused on the untruthfulness of the ads. So, this headache could have been largely avoided if the dealer had simply adhered to rule number one in advertising— tell the truth and be able to substantiate every claim made.

But, then again, if you're the kind of person who likes to live on the wild side, go ahead and make false claims and use "imaginary customer" testimonials. Just be sure to imagine up some defense lawyers and cold, hard cash to pay all those not so imaginary fines and penalties while you're at it.

"Recall" Mailer Raises Issues

November 2007

By Emily Marlow Beck

I have finally gotten all of our staff trained to bring me any dealer direct mail pieces that show up in their mailboxes. It is absolutely amazing the things they come up with.

The latest ad to hit my desk was supposedly from the "Used Vehicle Recall Notification Center." The ad announced a "vehicle recall event" that, upon further examination, was nothing more than a sales event by a Maryland dealer.

Maybe this Maryland dealer hasn't heard about the Georgia dealer trying to fend off the Georgia Attorney General's $50 million suit alleging that the dealer sent out fake vehicle "recall" notices. I haven't seen the mail piece used by the Georgia dealer, so I don't know how closely it resembles the one used by the Maryland dealer, but I can think of 50 million reasons not to use the word "recall" in a direct mail piece.

The Maryland mailer caused me to raise my eyebrows for a couple of other reasons. Large text in the upper right-hand corner screamed, "Pre-owned vehicles for as much as 70% off original MSRP." Apart from what the cars' original MSRPs have to do with anything, many states expressly prohibit references to MSRP discounts in ads.

Another part of the mailer stated, "Good Credit? Bad Credit? No Problem. We Can Get You Financed Regardless of Your Situation." Statements like these aren't generally a problem, as long as they are completely truthful. This dealer better be prepared to finance every slug that comes onto the lot, or risk an AG's or plaintiff's claim that the ad is unfair and deceptive.

The same thing goes for the ad's statement that "you are pre-approved to receive as much as $5,000 off any pre-owned vehicle or new Hyundai or Mazda in stock." Unless the dealer will be able to prove, if challenged, that customers actually received that sort of discount from the prices at which the dealer customarily sold the cars identified in the ad, the dealer will risk the same sort of "unfair and deceptive" claim.

Are these real worries, or just problems that a pointy-headed lawyer would worry about? I think that they are real, and since I'm writing this on Halloween, maybe even scary real. AGs around the country have made dealer advertisements one of their consumer protection priorities.

Here's a quick dealer checklist for mailers:

- DON'T rely on the mail house or ad agency for legal review. It's your ad, and you will be held accountable for its content.
- DO read the ad and make certain that every statement is not only true, but also not misleading.
- DO stay familiar with the ad requirements imposed by your state's general advertising laws and regulations, as well as special requirements imposed by your state motor vehicle administration, consumer protection agency, or other agencies.
- DO stay familiar with the advertising restrictions imposed by the Truth in Lending Act, the Consumer Leasing Act, and Federal Reserve Board Regulations Z and M.
- DO have your dealership's lawyer review the ad.
- DO get the ad company or mail house's assurances, in writing, that the ad it mails will be the exact ad you and your lawyer reviewed.
- DO keep a file for each mailer, containing the ad, the lawyer's OK, and the agreement with the ad company.
- DO figure out a way to keep up with federal and state legal developments that will affect ad compliance. What was legal last year may not work this year.

If you take these precautions, chances are you'll never have to defend your mailers, and, if you do find yourself called upon to defend them, you will be in much better shape to do so. Don't forget, the AG and all of his or her staff members have mailboxes, too.

But Your Honor, the Plaintiff Has No Damages . . .
January/February 2008
By Thomas B. Hudson

We have frequently written on the topic of state "unfair and deceptive acts and practices," or UDAP, laws. Nearly every state has a version of a UDAP law, and these laws are the most powerful tools in the hands of plaintiffs' lawyers suing dealers on behalf of car buyers.

The laws are popular with the plaintiffs' lawyers because they are vague (after all, what IS an unfair practice anyway?), because they often provide for a multiplier of twice or three times the actual damages incurred by the consumer, and because they provide for the award of attorneys' fees to a successful plaintiff. All that together adds up to Christmas 12 months of the year for plaintiffs' lawyers.

In some states, the UDAP law will even permit a plaintiff to sue when he or she has suffered no actual damages. Those laws aren't typical, though—most states require that the plaintiff actually prove that he or she has been damaged.

That leads to the question of how damages are measured. A recent California opinion deals with that issue. Here's what happened in that case.

Terry Anderson saw an advertisement in the newspaper regarding a specific vehicle. Interested in buying that type of vehicle, she called Riverside Chrysler Jeep, where an employee told her that the vehicle was for sale.

Anderson drove to the dealership to look at the vehicle with the intention of buying it. The vehicle was not yet prepared for sale, but Anderson indicated that she would return to buy it the next day. When she returned, she negotiated a final price with the salesperson who, after consulting with someone, told her that the vehicle was not for sale as it had not yet been through a safety inspection.

Anderson asked to be notified when the vehicle was ready for sale. Four days later, Anderson called the dealership and was told the vehicle had been sold. However, the same vehicle was later advertised for sale.

Anderson sued Riverside Chrysler, alleging that it had violated the California Consumer Legal Remedies Act (CLRA) and the state's Unfair Competition Law (UCL). Riverside Chrysler filed a demurrer (a "demurrer" is a legal pleading by a defendant that says, essentially, "Judge, even if everything the plaintiff has alleged is true, she still doesn't have grounds for a suit."), asserting that Anderson had failed to plead facts demonstrating that she suffered an injury in fact and lost money or property as a result of the alleged unfair practices by Riverside Chrysler. The trial court agreed with the dealership and sustained the demurrer. Anderson appealed.

The California Court of Appeals reversed the trial court's ruling in part, finding that Anderson pled sufficient facts by alleging that she lost time and money as a result of having to drive to the dealership twice and, therefore, suffered an injury in fact. The appellate court noted that lost leisure time and mileage costs were sufficient damages to serve as the basis for standing under the UCL and CLRA.

Furthermore, the appellate court determined that it was not

necessary that a transaction be consummated in order for Anderson to state a cause of action for violation of the CLRA. In other words, Anderson could bring her suit even though she hadn't bought the car!

The dealership was partly successful in defending itself, however. Anderson had not challenged the trial court's ruling that she failed to plead sufficient facts under the CLRA. The appellate court concluded that she had thus failed to meet her burden of demonstrating the existence of reversible error as to her claims under the CLRA. Because of her failure to raise this CLRA issue on appeal, the appellate court only reversed the trial court's ruling with respect to Anderson's claim under the UCL and affirmed the trial court's judgment with respect to the CLRA.

The lesson here? The threshold level for damages under these UDAP laws is very low. Evidently, just the loss of time and the cost of gas used to drive to the dealership is enough—at least in California.

Is it any wonder that plaintiffs' lawyers love UDAP laws?

Anderson v. Riverside Chrysler Jeep, 2007 WL 3317819 (Cal. App. November 8, 2007).

Massachusetts AG Penalizes Dealers for Misleading Advertising

January/February 2008
By Nicole F. Munro

Was it really a happy New Year for eight Massachusetts auto dealers? Probably not. On January 2, the Massachusetts Attorney General's office imposed civil penalties in the amount of $290,000 on eight Massachusetts dealers for engaging in false and misleading price advertising. In addition, those dealers agreed to refrain from engaging in advertising that might mislead consumers about the actual prices of motor vehicles.

In response to an overall initiative by the Massachusetts AG's office targeting false and misleading advertising practices in that state, the AG found that eight auto dealers misled consumers about the prices of vehicles in their print advertisements. In an Assurance of Discontinuance filed with the Suffolk County Superior Court, the Massachusetts AG alleged the dealers had committed the following wrongs:

1. They used "Asterisk Pricing" to represent the price of a motor vehicle.

2. They displayed prices artificially lowered to reflect cash or trade value.

3. They misrepresented rebates reflected in displayed vehicle prices.

"Asterisk Pricing" is defined as advertising of a prominently displayed, artificially low price for a vehicle ("prominent price"), where the material terms and conditions that must be met to receive the advertised price are listed in small print separate from the prominent price, and include a "Cash or Trade" reduction. The AG contended that the advertising practices misled consumers concerning the actual prices of motor vehicles.

Keep in mind that the releases related to this dust-up are from the AG's office. It isn't unusual for dealers to have "another side of the story," but often they settle claims like these anyway in order to avoid the cost of further litigation.

Without admitting liability for the alleged misconduct, the dealers agreed to cease the challenged activities and pay a civil penalty ranging from $20,000 to $75,000 per dealer. Specifically, the dealers agreed to stop displaying the pricing of vehicles where the prices are reduced by applying cash or trade-in values, if the cash or trade-in values are not displayed in a form of equal prominence to the prominently displayed price. The dealers agreed not to display the MSRP of a vehicle reduced by applying a rebate or other discount, unless they provided the criteria necessary to receive a nonuniversal rebate or clearly and conspicuously described a universal rebate or discount. The dealers further agreed to display any material term modifications of an advertised price clearly and conspicuously and to refrain from generally misrepresenting the price of any vehicle or advertising price where the dealer knows, or should know, that the advertisement could mislead a reasonable consumer.

Massachusetts is only one of many states where Attorneys General are concentrating on practices that appear unfair or deceptive to consumers. For example, in the January issue of the *Maryland Bar Journal*, Maryland's Attorney General calls his office "the biggest and best law firm in the state." He champions consumer protection as the "bread and butter" of the AG's office and states that the Maryland AG's office plans to actively pursue consumer complaints to "right wrongs" and to "protect the public." In an election year where consumer protection is at the forefront of the political agenda and credit providers are on the chopping block, car dealers are a big target for up and coming elected officials. You should beware of your Attorneys General (a/k/a aspiring governors), but be aware of your advertising practices first.

Do You Know What Your Mailers Say?

January/February 2008

By Thomas B. Hudson

My mailbox is a never-ending source of entertainment. Several times a month, dealership "mailer" advertisements appear among the catalogs and bills. I always open them first, because I'm interested in the text of the mailer that some ad company has created for the dealership—text that I can assure you the dealer's lawyer has not seen.

The latest mailer professed to involve a "GMC Owner Loyalty Program." Even though the GMC and GM logos were prominently displayed in the mailer, the ad appeared to involve only the dealership.

What entertaining things did this mailer contain? The first sentence that caught my eye was, "Now, as part of General Motors, [dealership's name] has the distinction of extending this GMC Owner Loyalty Program to customers in the [city] area." Now, I can tell you, it will come as a surprise to General Motors that this dealership is a "part of General Motors." Ill-informed lawyers around the country who mistakenly believe that dealerships are sales outlets owned by manufacturers have filed many lawsuits based on that mistake. When a dealership holds itself out like this as "a part of" the manufacturer, courts may be reluctant to let the dealer argue that it is a separate corporate entity and should be treated as such.

Next appeared the statement, "Now is your chance to experience Employee Pricing at [name of dealership]." Now, there's nothing inherently wrong with that sentence as long as it is true. If, however, the customers who buy during this event pay more than the dealership's employees, the dealership's mailer becomes Exhibit 1 in an "unfair and deceptive acts and practices" lawsuit by a customer or in an enforcement action by the Attorney General.

Further in the ad were bullet points about the details of the dealership's offer. Two of those bullet points were "no money down" and "no inception fees." I'll bet that the dealership will be imposing a documentation fee of some sort. Will a customer claim that the doc fee makes these claims fraudulent? And what on earth is an "inception fee" anyway?

Another bullet point said, "0% FINANCING AVAILABLE FOR 60 MONTHS ON SELECTED MODELS." That statement of the payment period for financing is likely a "triggering term" under the Truth in Lending Act and Regulation Z that requires the dealer to make certain other disclosures. Often dealers satisfy this requirement by using an example, a technique that TILA and Reg. Z permit. Sure enough, an example appeared at the bottom of the mailer, but it was labeled "Lease example" and didn't contain the legally required information.

A fourth bullet point offered, "12 MONTHS FREE VEHICLE MAINTENANCE." Any lawyer who has reviewed advertisements for longer than 15 minutes will break out in hives when he or she sees the word "free," because what "free" really means is "if you buy a car, we'll provide something else 'at no additional cost.'" The "something else" isn't "free" if you must buy a car to get it. The Federal Trade Commission regularly warns against the use of "free" in this way, and the practice can run afoul of state law as well.

It also made me laugh that the "Program" was available for "THREE DAYS ONLY"—Thursday, Friday, and Saturday. As to which Thursday, Friday, or Saturday, your guess is as good as mine. No dates were mentioned.

Finally (and my personal favorite line in the mailer), at the very end of the ad, just above the signature of the dealership's representative, was the statement, "Note: Due to the special, invitation-only nature of this event, this letter plus a valid ID is required for admittance." Call me a cynic, but I'd bet both my dogs and my favorite rod and reel that anyone with a pulse who walks on the dealership's lot during this "invitation-only event" will be welcomed with open arms. Several enforcement actions by AGs around the country have attacked statements like this that create a false sense of urgency.

My overall reaction was that the ad copywriters who prepared this litigation time bomb had no training in auto dealership advertising legal requirements, and that no knowledgeable compliance professional or lawyer had laid an eye on it. If you let your ad company operate in a similarly unsupervised way, maybe your ad will entertain me next time.

"Free" Products Weren't Free; FTC Sets $200,000 Penalty
March 2008
By Thomas B. Hudson

There's a nifty organization called the National Association of Dealer Counsel (NADC) made up of lawyers who represent car dealers. NADC has a "listserv" that permits its members to chat about new legal developments.

From time to time, one of the lawyers will lament that he or she cannot get the dealerships that he or she represents to quit using the word "free" in their ads. The typical ads say things like "free tires for the life of your car" or "a free $500 gas card" when you buy a car.

A recent FTC enforcement action on exactly that sort of

issue might get those dealers to focus on the serious risk of the use of "free" in their ads. The $200,000 penalty imposed by the Federal Trade Commission should really serve as the proverbial two-by-four.

An online advertiser that drove traffic to its websites using spam e-mails with misleading subject lines agreed to settle FTC charges that it failed to disclose that consumers have to spend money to get the so-called "free" items it touts. That follows a long-standing and consistent FTC position—if you have to buy something to get something else "free," the something else isn't "free."

The settlement, filed by the Department of Justice on the FTC's behalf, requires the defendants to disclose the costs and obligations to qualify for the advertised products or services and bars them from sending e-mail that violates the CAN-SPAM Act. The settlement also requires that the company pay, I repeat, $200,000 in civil penalties.

According to the FTC's press release, Member Source Media LLC, d/b/a ConsumerGain.com, PremiumPerks.com, FreeRetailRewards.com, and GreatAmericanGiveaways.com, as well as the company's principal, all used deceptive spam and online advertising to lure consumers to its websites. For example, Member Source Media used e-mail subject lines such as "Congratulations. You've won an iPod Video Player"; "Here are 2 free iPod Nanos for You: confirm now"; "NASCAR Tickets Package Winner"; "Confirmation required for your $500 Visa Gift Card"; or "Second Attempt: Target Gift Card Inside." The company's web-based ads contain similar representations: "CONGRATULATIONS! You Have Been Chosen To Receive a FREE GATEWAY LAPTOP."

The FTC charged that when consumers arrived at Member Source Media's web pages, they were led through a series of ads for goods and services from third parties. To "qualify" for the "free products," consumers first had to wade through pages of "optional" offers. If they cleared this hurdle, they discovered that they must "participate in" a series of third-party promotions that required them to do things such as buy products, subscribe to satellite television service, or apply for multiple credit cards.

The FTC alleged that Member Source Media's failure to disclose material facts—such as the fact that consumers had to pay money or provide some other consideration to get their "free products"—was deceptive and violated the FTC Act. In addition, the agency charged that deceptive subject lines in Member Source Media's spam e-mails violated the federal CAN-SPAM Act.

The settlement requires that Member Source Media clearly and conspicuously disclose in its ads and on its web pages that consumers have to spend money or incur other obligations to qualify for a free product or service.

The settlement also requires the company to provide a list of the obligations a consumer is likely to incur to qualify for a chosen item—such as applying for credit cards or purchasing products. In addition, the settlement bars future violations of the CAN-SPAM Act and requires the defendants (I repeat) to pay the aforementioned $200,000 civil penalty.

Finally, the settlement contains bookkeeping and record-keeping provisions to allow the agency to monitor compliance.

The DOJ filing is a stipulated final order for settlement purposes only. The stipulated final order does not constitute an admission by the defendants of a law violation and requires approval by the court. It has the force of law when signed by the judge.

Dealers may note that the business charged with sinning by the FTC was an Internet business; they may want to assume that the auto business is immune from enforcement actions like this. That would be a really, really bad idea.

And did I mention that $200,000 fine?

MythBusters! (Now You Know Better!)

March 2008

By Emily Marlow Beck

Can a penny dropped from the top of the Empire State Building really be deadly? Can you survive a multi-story elevator fall by jumping right before the elevator hits the ground?

If these questions sound familiar or interesting to you, you might watch my new favorite TV show. I'm talking about "MythBusters," where two scientists conduct wild and crazy stunts, testing the validity of modern myths, rumors, and urban legends. Some of my favorite episodes are, "Is yawning contagious?" and "How many balloons does it take to lift a three-year-old off the ground?"

Have I given you a frightening peek into the window of my soul? Perhaps. Do I have a point? Absolutely. Here it goes.

As a compliance lawyer, I spend a bunch of time "busting" the compliance myths that grow like toxic mold out in Dealer-ville. Fortunately, unlike the TV "MythBusters," I don't have to conduct any wild and crazy stunts to disprove these "myths"— I've got brave dealers to do it for me. With that in mind, here are two of the biggest myths floating around out there when it comes to dealer ads.

Myth #1: I've got people who take care of that stuff for me.

Do you remember the story back in 2004 about the Minnesota dealer who paid $250,000 to the state Attorney General's office because of noncompliant mailers? The story ran in *Automotive News,* which quoted the dealer as saying that he relied on the representations of his marketing company when it promised him that the ad complied with all applicable laws. Unfortunately, the dealer learned about my Myth #1 the hard way.

We hear the same tune sung by dealers far too often, as many dealers routinely rely on marketing companies for advertising compliance. In 2007, our firm reported on a number of advertisement enforcement actions by state Attorneys General. Many of these targeted dealers were simply following the lead of third-party ad companies.

Just ask the Washington State dealer who, along with a Louisiana advertising company, had to cough-up tens of thousands of dollars in fines in 2007 for allegedly sending mailers that, among other things, contained misleading price information and used envelopes that resembled official certified mail. While I don't know for certain, I'd bet dollars to doughnuts that the dealership relied on the ad company's promises that the materials were compliant.

At other times, we hear tales about various "mercenary" sales outfits that come to a dealership and run special sales "extravaganzas." Sadly, we usually hear about these crews long after the last balloon has shriveled up. We hear about dealers facing citations from the local authorities because the sales outfit failed to obtain the required sales permits that it promised the dealer it would get. We hear about dealers being forced to buy back the deals it sold to the bank because the third-party sales crew assigned contracts that didn't comply with the reps and warranties in the dealership's agreement with the bank. The worst stories we hear are about dealers facing the potential of criminal fraud charges because the rent-a-salesmen falsified information they submitted to the bank on behalf of the dealership. In almost all of these situations, the dealer relied on the promises of members of the sales crew, who, incidentally, are nowhere to be found when things go wrong.

Myth #2: I can take off my "dealer hat" when running ads.

Because I don't like being ignored at parties, I usually don't introduce myself as a lawyer when I go out. But, no matter where I go and how I'm known, I keep some basic "lawyering" rules in mind. ('Cause being the hit of the party is usually not worth getting disbarred, right?) It works much the same way with dealer advertising—it's very difficult for dealers to escape their legal requirements when it comes to ads. Which brings us to Myth #2.

We sometimes hear stories about dealers who are, shall we say, not particularly forthcoming about their identities when advertising to customers. Often, this can be as simple as when a dealer (or zealous salesperson) runs an ad in a local newspaper without identifying the dealership (i.e., "Call Nate at 555-1212."). I've even heard of dealers using more sophisticated techniques and blind advertisements to accomplish the same goal—to attract customers who wouldn't otherwise respond to a dealership's ad.

At other times, dealers let go of their compliance savvy when they cross over into the brave new world of online advertising. Dealers who impose a strict vetting process for radio and print ads often stand by as their online ads fall prey to their in-house cyber geek's fancy.

While your ad obligations will vary from state to state, you typically can't "take off your dealer hat" to circumvent the restrictions under the dealer laws. Instead, you'll need to know how those laws will apply to all of your ads.

For example, does state law require you to disclose your dealer number? The stock number of the vehicle? Must you include the price of certain fees and charges in the advertised prices? Is an "Internet-only price" permitted? Depending on your state laws, these sorts of requirements may follow you wherever and however you advertise.

So, there you have it. Two advertising compliance myths busted, and two rules to help keep you out of the AG brag book for 2008.

Special Events Companies and Your Dealership's "Good Name"
April 2008
By Thomas B. Hudson

According to a recent report from the *Portsmouth Herald,* a Portsmouth, New Hampshire, woman claimed in a lawsuit that, after she responded to a flyer from a Mazda dealership touting a Memorial Day weekend sale, temporary salesmen provided by a promotional company (which was hired by the auto dealer), duped her out of a dinner, suggested she have sex to keep a promotional television, stole her Nissan, and then sent a collection agency after her for $4,000 in alleged depreciation for the Mazda she had for two days.

The dealership's owner said he's "still trying to figure this mess out," adding he hired the promotional company and its out-of-state salesmen to help him during the weekend sale. He also suggested that New Hampshire follow California's lead by requiring auto salesmen to be licensed only after a police background check.

"That would cut a lot of this riff-raff out," he said. "I'm a small dealer and if I didn't do a good job, I wouldn't be here."

The woman's suit claimed that she responded to a flyer that

promised to pay off auto "loans" for trade-in customers who bought new Mazdas. A $4,000 rebate and a 20-inch flat screen TV sweetened the pot, according to court documents. The woman went to the dealership, traded in her Nissan, and signed a $4,750 loan for the new Mazda.

The woman claimed that the next day, she accepted a dinner invitation from a temporary Mazda salesman named "Will." She picked Will up at the dealership. When Will wouldn't spring for dinner, she drove him back to a motel. There, she claimed, he suggested trading the dinner tab for sex. When she balked, Will threatened to take back the promotional television, she claimed.

The woman claimed she returned to the dealership to return the Mazda and take back her trade-in, all within a three-day grace period supposedly promised by the dealer. She left the Mazda on the lot, but the Nissan was gone. It was later found at an airport parking garage, and a warrant was issued for the arrest of the temporary salesman, who, it turns out, was on probation for an Oregon conviction.

The woman's six-count suit, which asked for a jury trial and triple damages under the Consumer Protection Act, alleged fraud, deceit, misrepresentation, negligence, and violation of the federal Fair Debt Collection Practices Act, and claimed emotional distress, a bad credit rating, and other damages.

The dealer was reported as declining on-record comment about specifics, but saying he expects the next step will be mediation through the state auto dealers association. The reporter's crowning quote? The dealer said, "I just want to clear my good name."

Say what? What good name?

Who hired this promotional company? The tooth fairy?

Did the dealer do any due diligence on the promotional company and the employees that he was all too willing to turn loose on his customers? Did the dealer insist that the promotional company agree to use only properly trained and AFIP-certified salespeople who had received ethics training? Did the dealership ask how long each employee of the promotional company had been employed, and ask to review the promotional company's hiring criteria? Did the dealer determine how long the company had been in business, and how recently it had changed its name to keep potential new dealer customers from finding out its past misdeeds? Did the dealership ask the promotional company to identify the last 10 dealerships the promotional company had worked for, and then make a few "How about these guys?" calls? Did the dealership check to see whether the promotional company carried insurance that would protect the dealer if the promotional company's employees turned out to be a bunch of bad actors? Did the dealer insist that the dealership's own employees closely supervise the promotional company employees to make sure they were not misbehaving?

If the dealer did all of that, or even most of that, I'll gladly concede that he might have a "good name" to protect.

But if the dealer didn't do most of those things, then he entrusted his customers, his dealership's reputation, and, perhaps, if a jury gets mad enough, the viability of the dealership itself to the promotional company without taking the basic steps he should have taken to protect himself and his customers. If he didn't do those things, or most of them, what "good name" does he have?

I suspect that there are promotional companies out there who do a good, ethical job of running these special events sales. But if I'm a dealer, until I know darn well that I'm dealing with one, I'm going to assume that the only thing protecting me, my "good name," my customers, and the future of my dealership is my own diligence in checking out the company and its employees.

States Continue Crack Down on Ad Practices

May 2008

By Patricia E.M. Covington

Unless you live in a cave, you know that it's a dangerous world out there if you play fast and loose with your dealership's ads. State Attorneys General and lawmakers take this issue very seriously, and crackdowns on car dealers' advertising practices happen every day.

Just recently, we told you about the settlement agreement Massachusetts Attorney General Martha Coakley reached with eight car dealers for allegedly using false or misleading prices in their print advertising. In case you forgot, she got civil penalties ranging from $20,000 to $75,000 from each dealer. As if the big money penalties were not enough, the settlement specifically prohibited the dealers from using "asterisk pricing."

What is asterisk pricing? Oh, come on. You know! It's a dealer advertisement quoting a price with an asterisk, which, in small print at the bottom of the ad, indicates that the advertised price is conditional (for example, based on a $1,000 down payment). Coakley's settlement also prohibited the dealers from advertising rebates where the terms are not clearly disclosed, or universally applied, and from hiding terms and conditions in small print where those terms affect the actual price of the vehicle.

Scary though it may be, enforcement actions like the one brought in Massachusetts are par for the course these days. For example, Illinois Attorney General Lisa Madigan recently filed a lawsuit against an unlicensed auto loan broker for allegedly falsely advertising that he would assume consumers' car loans until another buyer agreed to purchase the car. The auto loan broker allegedly failed to make the payments due on the cars, resulting in the broker's customers having their cars repossessed; the customers were left holding the bag for substantial out-of-pocket fees and damaged credit. Attorney General Madigan is seeking to ban the loan broker from selling cars in Illinois, to rescind the contracts entered into by the broker, and to order the broker to pay restitution to the victims. The suit also seeks a civil penalty of $50,000, plus $50,000 for each violation committed with the intent to defraud, plus court costs.

The Oregon Department of Justice also joined the ranks by finalizing amendments to new advertising rules, which took effect on January 2, 2008. Among other things, these new rules require dealers to disclose all fees, add-ons, and payments made on behalf of the buyer and to clarify negative equity. The rules also address auto advertising issues, including misleading business names, Internet advertising, misleading reasons for sale, withdrawals of advertisements, and broker fiduciary obligations. Further, the rules govern the unfair or deceptive use of "free" offers and rebates. Finally, the Oregon DOJ enacted a rule adopting the Federal Trade Commission Used Car Rule, federal Truth in Lending Act, and federal Consumer Leasing Law, which will give the Oregon DOJ the authority to enforce these federal laws in Oregon.

What do these actions mean if you are a dealer? Simply put, dealers need to buckle down and make sure their ads are in tight shape. Pay attention to the nuts and bolts requirements that apply to car ads in your state. Know what message your ads are sending to consumers. Mean what you say, and keep all promises made. Otherwise, you may find yourself paying hugely for your promises.

Lawsuit in a Kit

May 2008

By Thomas B. Hudson

When I was a kid, I was nuts about those plastic model airplanes, cars, and boats that they sold at the hobby shops. Do you remember them? They contained all the parts and pieces that you needed to make a miniature version of the real thing. I sniffed too much of that model airplane glue, messed up my brain, and had to become a lawyer, but that's another story.

I thought of those kits when I opened my mail recently and discovered two solicitations. One was from a mortgage company; the other was from a local (D.C. area) car dealership. They were "lawsuits in a kit."

Meaning? Well, just this: Any Attorney General or plaintiff's lawyer could assemble a pretty good lawsuit just by reviewing the mailers and making a couple of assumptions.

The mortgage mailer came in a government-brown envelope. On the outside, in large caps, appeared "HOUSING STIMULUS REBATE ENCLOSED" (I'm not making this up). Also on the outside was the following: "BUSINESS MAIL— PENALTY FOR TAMPERING. WARNING: There is a $2,000 fine or 5 years imprisonment or both for any person obstructing or interfering with the deliver [sic] of this letter."

Inside was a check for $1,200! Well, actually, no. Inside was a "rebate coupon" for $1,200 for a "closing cost credit" on a mortgage loan. The offer had images of the Statue of Liberty, a simulated check, and the words "OFFICIAL NOTIFICATION: ECONOMIC STIMULUS ACT OF 2008."

Now call me a cynic, but the mailer looked to me like someone told the solicitation's designer to make the piece look as much like an official government communication as possible.

State AGs have levied fines for solicitations that mimic government communications—those arguments would be easy to make with this piece. So, this is lawsuit in a kit number one.

The car mailer was one I'd seen before, and had even written about before. The dealer using it must not subscribe to *Spot Delivery®*.

The white envelope it came in bore a return address of "Administrative Office," with a street and city. That sounds vaguely official, right? The envelope was one of those window jobs, with enough room in the window to permit you to see what looked like an official document inside. Sure enough, when I opened it, the top of the document was a fake certificate of title.

The solicitation offered me "FREE Gas," in the form of a gas gift card, if I bought a new car. These folks obviously haven't gotten the word that the Federal Trade Commission bans the use of the word "free" to describe the cost of something if, in order to get the "free" item, you must buy something else, and that "something else" is sold at a price usually arrived at through bargaining (like a car sale).

The piece also contained the following claims: "Each vehicle will be clearly marked with drastically reduced prices." "Finance representatives will be on hand to offer you special interest rates . . . and help you obtain the best terms." "Used car buyers will be on hand to offer you top dollar for your trade." What's wrong with these claims? Perhaps nothing—if they are true.

But once again, here comes the cynic. What if the prices charged for the cars on the day of the sale are not drastically lower than the dealership's usual prices? What will be "special" about the interest rates? Will they be lower than the rates regularly offered by the dealership? Will the trade-in values for this sale in fact be "top dollar" values? These are all facts that can be determined by looking at information that can be obtained from the dealership in the course of any official investigation or lawsuit. If they are not true claims, here's lawsuit in a kit number two.

Trust me, either of these lawsuits in a kit would be easier to assemble than those model airplane kits were. Now, where's my glue?

Are Your Pants on Fire?
July 2008
By Thomas B. Hudson

If you've ever read any of my articles on advertising, you know that a couple of common dealership solicitation techniques drive me nuts (actually—they are probably advertising company techniques, but more on that in a moment). The ones I really hate are solicitations that are designed to look like correspondence from, or approved by, the government, and ads that offer "special" sales and trade-in terms when the actual deals completed during such sales aren't "special" at all.

In article after article, I've warned that those practices are an engraved invitation for an Attorney General to bring a charge against the dealer for engaging in unfair or deceptive acts and practices. If any dealers are reading these warnings, they better read especially carefully if they are from Arizona.

Arizona Attorney General Terry Goddard announced a $225,000 settlement with a large Scottsdale dealership. The AG's press release says that the settlement resolves claims of deceptive advertising and sales practices and requires future advertisements to be clear and not deceptive.

According to court documents, the dealership failed to disclose important terms and conditions of offers advertised in newspapers, through direct mail, or on the Internet. In some instances, the dealership included a "[Dealership's name] discount" as part of the vehicle's advertised price but did not always give the discount to the consumer. In other cases, the dealership refused to sell advertised vehicles to consumers consistent with the terms of the ads.

The AG groused: "New and used car sales complaints ranked high once again this year in the top 10 complaints filed with my office. This is unacceptable. Arizona consumers should expect truthful advertising from all businesses, including car dealerships, and my office will continue to pursue these complaints until all car dealers understand they must advertise truthfully."

As is customary in such proceedings, the settlement, in the form of a consent judgment, does not constitute an admission of wrongdoing by the dealership. The settlement requires the dealership to:

- "Stop engaging in false and deceptive advertising and selling vehicles for more than their advertised price;
- "Ensure that its ads accurately identify vehicles available for sale, the price of the advertised vehicles, and which options are included in the advertised price;
- "Ensure it has advertised vehicles in inventory and available for sale, or that a fair substitute is available;
- "Stop using ads that appear to include a check or come from a governmental entity;
- "Stop using newspaper ads that exaggerate the number of vehicles available for sale;
- "Stop using direct mail letters that claim to offer a variety of 'special' discounts or programs, but in fact deliver no real benefits to consumers who received them;
- "Adopt policies and procedures to implement the specific terms of the consent judgment;

- "Provide training to its employees and enact procedures to discipline employees who fail to comply; and
- "Ensure that all parties involved in its advertising, including independent marketing companies, are aware of the settlement."

Additionally, the settlement provides a mechanism for consumers to file complaints with the Attorney General's office for their interactions with the dealership occurring on or after March 1, 2007. The settlement requires the dealership to review the complaints and resolve them according to the terms of the settlement, but the dealership is not necessarily required to pay refunds.

The dealership will pay $225,000 to the Attorney General's office for civil penalties, attorney's fees, and costs of investigation. When you consider that the dealership had to pay its own lawyer (we bloodsucking lawyers ain't cheap), and when you consider the cost to the dealership to create and enforce the advertising procedures that it has agreed to adopt and the amount of management time to deal with this mess, you can bet that the cost to the dealership for this one is pushing half a million.

I said at the beginning of this article that I would get back to the subject of advertising companies. From the car dealer ads and solicitations I see day-in and day-out, most advertising companies don't seem to know squat when it comes to the laws and regulations that govern dealer ads and solicitations. They offer these programs to dealers, and dealers seem to buy them without any sort of critical review.

That doesn't excuse the dealers who hire these advertising companies, though. The first rule of dealer ad and solicitation compliance is, "IS IT TRUE?" If you're trying to make your solicitation look like it's coming from the government, or if you are claiming that just another weekend sale will offer special deals to consumers when you know that it will just be business as usual, then IT AIN'T TRUE.

If your solicitations aren't true, you can bet that you are a fat target for your Attorney General. You probably don't need that half million anyway.

FTC Sues for Deceptive Credit Card Marketing
July 2008
By Thomas B. Hudson

The Federal Trade Commission recently sued CompuCredit Corporation and its wholly owned debt collection subsidiary, Jefferson Capital Systems, LLC, for deceptive marketing practices in selling credit cards to consumers in the subprime market. The action bears watching by car dealers.

The FTC charged both defendants with violating the FTC Act and Jefferson Capital with violating the Fair Debt Collection Practices Act (FDCP). The FTC and the FDIC had engaged in a coordinated investigation of the defendants' marketing practices. The FDIC also has issued notice of administrative charges against CompuCredit and two banks that issued credit cards marketed by CompuCredit.

The FTC's Lydia Parnes said, "It is important for all consumers—including those in the subprime market—to have access to credit card products. But the marketing of these products must be truthful; it should not—and cannot—be misleading about the true costs and terms of the credit card." As stated in the FTC's complaint, CompuCredit markets credit cards, primarily through direct mail solicitations, under various brand names.

The FTC claims that CompuCredit violated the FTC Act by

misrepresenting the amount of credit that would be available immediately to consumers, failing to disclose up-front fees, failing to disclose that certain purchases could reduce a consumer's credit limit, and misrepresenting a debt collection program as a credit card offer. Jefferson Capital allegedly sinned by misrepresenting a debt collection program as a credit card offer. It was charged with using abusive collection tactics such as making debt collection calls to individual consumers more than 20 times per day, including before 8 a.m., after 9 p.m., and on Sundays.

A paragraph from the FTC's complaint will give you an idea about what had the FTC's shorts in a twist:

25. In a typical and illustrative direct mail solicitation package, CompuCredit also has represented, in the cover letter, at the top of the page, set aside from other text, and in bold:

- You're Pre-Qualified*!
- Unsecured Visa card!
- Credit line increase within 6 months when you make your payments on time**!
- No deposit required! Rebuild your credit+!

After the heading described above, CompuCredit further states, "You have been PRE-QUALIFIED* for the Aspire Visa card with a credit limit of $300*. . . . And unlike a secured credit card, your Aspire Visa does not require a deposit." (Emphasis in original.) At the bottom of the page, in a smaller font than the representations described above and included in the main text of the letter, CompuCredit had several disclaimers, including one after the "*" symbol instructing consumers to "[s]ee the enclosed insert which is incorporated here by reference, for a Summary of Credit Terms and Terms of Offer." The ad copy continued, "This offer is subject to further review of financial information. Your available credit line may be reduced by certain fees that will be billed directly to your account, including an annual fee, an account opening fee, and an account maintenance fee, as described in the Summary of Credit Terms."

The disclaimers after the "**" and "+" symbols explain, respectively, that consumers who make four minimum monthly payments on time and remain in good standing will receive a credit line increase and that CompuCredit will report the consumer's account balance to the three major credit bureaus. CompuCredit makes no other mention of fees in this typical and illustrative cover letter.

Part of what the FTC is saying is that it believes that it's a violation of the FTC Act to create advertisements in which an advertiser takes back in "mouse type" what it appeared to give away in big type. If you are a car dealer, or a lawyer or compliance professional reviewing ads for a car dealer, the appropriate reaction should be, "Yikes!" or "Holy Asterisk, Batman!"

Why? Pick up any weekend newspaper and turn to the car pages, or, worse yet, take a walk with me down to the mailbox and open the solicitations from the local car dealer. You'll see that the FTC will not run short of targets for these charges in the near future.

Yep, this one bears watching.

Dash for Cash!

August 2008

By Emily Marlow Beck

Ahh, the dog days of summer. Hot dogs. Balloons. Face painting. Whatever it takes to get folks on the lot, you're up for it. Right? Right?

Maybe not, if you ask the New York Mitsubishi dealer who recently got a visit from the Attorney General's office.

Attorney General Andrew M. Cuomo's office recently announced that a car dealer in New York will have to pay $115,000 in restitution and $35,000 in penalties and costs due to a slew of misdeeds, most of which stemmed from its "Dash for Cash" marketing program.

According to the AG's press release, the New York dealer will pay customers for "persistently using misleading promotions intended to lure them into the dealership." Once "baited" into the dealership, the customers were subject to other fraudulent and unfair sales practices.

So, what did the dealership do to get the AG's office in a fit?

Allegedly, the dealership mailed a scratch-off ticket called "Dash for Cash" to thousands of Nassau County consumers. The scratch-off ticket claimed that customers could win a cash prize, a free vehicle, a vacation, a free gas voucher, or a $1,000 shopping spree. A winning ticket contained three symbols in a row, but it did not explain what, if anything, the consumer won. Instead, the scratch-off required the customer to bring the ticket to the dealership in order to claim the prize.

Once at the dealership, said the AG's office, the customers learned that almost everyone won the vacation or shopping spree. However, because of "blackout" periods or expenditure requirements, including shipping and handling costs, the prizes had minimal value.

As if that wasn't enough, the dealership also allegedly deceived customers by

- getting signatures from customers on sale and financing documents while leading customers to believe that they were filling out paperwork for vehicles they had won as part of the "Dash for Cash" sweepstakes;
- offering false discounts off the sales price of cars by selling the cars at higher retail sales prices, which essentially

nullified the value of the discount offered;

- having customers sign documents with blank terms and then later filling the papers out with terms that were not agreed upon;
- failing to give all necessary documents to customers at the time of purchase;
- promising consumers that they could refinance at a better interest rate after making several car payments or promising to pay one or more months of the insurance payments for the vehicle—and then reneging on those agreements; and
- inserting additional cost items without consumers' knowledge or consent, including VIN etching, service warranties, theft deterrent systems, GPS devices, and other expensive options.

To top it all off, the dealership repeatedly sold consumers used cars without informing the customers that the vehicles had been used as rental cars—a violation of New York law.

Now, there are a couple of things that struck me in this press release.

First of all, it struck me how there is no shortage of proof that AGs take dealer advertising seriously. The press release noted that the AG's office received more than 50 complaints from citizens of New York and that it is urging other harmed citizens to step forward and be counted. More than 50 consumers versus one car dealer—it's an AG no-brainer.

Second, if these allegations are true, this dealer violated the number one rule in advertising—tell the truth, tell the truth, and tell the truth. (The rule is so good, I have to say it three times!) Third, if the press release was any indication, it sounds like compliance wasn't particularly high on this dealer's priority list. But, had this dealership been compliance-savvy, it would have known that most states regulate sweepstakes and other games of chance. Some require registration, while others impose disclosure and other substantive requirements. It is very likely that the dealer featured in this AG press release was aware of none of those things.

Finally, many of these violations, if true, were not technical violations of nit-picky statutes and regulations. Most of these violations involved the dealer engaging in deceptive, low-ball behavior. In other words, the dealership's tactics didn't pass the "smell test," and most of the trouble from the AG's office could have been avoided if someone had bothered to give this sales event a sniff.

So, a word to the wise in Dealer-ville! When you're whipping out those hot dogs and balloons this summer, don't let the ABCs of advertising turn into an AG nightmare.

Wanna Bet?

September 2008
By Thomas B. Hudson

It seems like nearly every issue of *Spot Delivery®* contains yet another story of a dealer hammered by an Attorney General for using an advertising program alleged by the AG to violate state prohibitions against unfair and deceptive acts and practices or other state laws. This month is no exception.

Illinois Attorney General Lisa Madigan has sued two car dealers for deceptive sales and advertising practices. The AG's complaint names Orland Park Nissan and Infiniti of Orland Park as defendants, and alleges that the dealers sent direct mail advertisements in April 2007 to Chicago-area consumers describing an "exclusive credit amnesty event" and urging consumers to call the dealers to arrange a private appointment.

The mailer indicated that targeted consumers might have filed bankruptcy in the past but that the "amnesty" would permit consumers to qualify for affordable auto financing, despite their credit ratings. The direct mailer envelope claimed that "important vehicle recall information" was enclosed and that the consumers' response was required.

However, no recall by the National Highway Traffic Safety Administration existed, and the mailer didn't contain recall information. Both the AG's office and the Better Business Bureau had received complaints against the dealerships. "These deceptive mailers purposely and unfairly targeted consumers who may have struggled at one time to manage their finances," Attorney General Madigan said. "This lawsuit should send the message to auto dealers that my office won't tolerate using deceptive marketing practices to lure unsuspecting consumers into risky loans."

*[**Editor's note:** It's discouraging when the state's top legal officer evidently doesn't know the difference between "loans" and "credit sales."]*

The AG's complaint alleges that the deceptive mailer violates several Illinois laws, including the Consumer Fraud and Deceptive Business Practices Act, the Loan Advertising to Bankrupts Act, the Uniform Deceptive Trade Practices Act, and the Illinois Administrative Rules on Motor Vehicle Advertising.

The AG's suit asks the court to prohibit the dealers from

- violating these consumer protection laws;
- offering incentives and free prizes;
- using the term "recall" in advertisements;
- offering coupons with sales agreements; and
- advertising that a loan would be made to a consumer who has declared bankruptcy.

The suit also seeks restitution for consumers and asks the court to assess civil penalties of $50,000 per violation, an additional $50,000 statutory civil penalty, and a $10,000 civil penalty for each violation committed against a person over 65 years of age. Madigan's suit also asks the court to order the defendants to pay the costs of the investigation and court proceedings.

Keep in mind that, at this point, the AG's charges are just that—charges. The AG hasn't proven anything, and the dealerships have yet to respond in court.

I might end up eating crow after the dealers file their responses in court, but I couldn't help but entertain some suspicions about the dealerships' use of this direct mail program as I read the AG's press release. Here are some "I'll bets:"

- I'll bet that the dealerships bought this direct mail program from some advertising company.
- I'll bet that the advertising company did not run the program by lawyers familiar with auto dealer advertising laws and restrictions.
- I'll bet that no one at the dealerships gave the program the "smell test" (goodness knows, this one reeked!).
- I'll bet that the dealerships' lawyers never reviewed the program.
- I'll bet that the dealerships didn't ask the advertising company to produce a legal opinion that the program complied with all federal and state laws.
- I'll bet that the dealerships didn't contractually require the advertising company to indemnify them in case authorities challenged the program or in case consumers sued the dealerships.
- I'll bet those dealerships don't buy our books!

Big in Trouble

September 2008

By Thomas B. Hudson

When I was a young parent, I swapped stories with other young parents about the cute things our kids would say. Now that I'm officially (according to the Sociable Security folks) an old toot, I swap stories about grandchildren with my grandparent friends.

One of those buddies is a graphic artist friend. Her granddaughter, Abigail, has a cute saying when she wants to say that someone has gotten into hot water. She says that they are "big in trouble."

That was the first phrase that came to mind when I read the report of an action filed against a Kansas Suzuki dealer, Chad Franklin Suzuki, by Kansas Attorney General Steve Six. According to the complaint filed by the AG, the dealership's radio and television advertisements promised customers one of two things—the customer could either drive a new Suzuki for life with no payments or drive a new Suzuki for a fixed period at a fixed price.

The dealership has also been the subject of a local TV investigative story that alleged that the dealership submitted doctored credit applications to banks and finance companies, inflating incomes, residence periods, and the length of job experience. A Google search turns up scads of consumer complaints, mostly dealing with a promotion that offered $49 per month car payments.

If you take the time to read the Internet postings, your likely reaction, like mine, will be, "How could these customers be stupid enough to fall for this stuff?" Don't people who agree to a deal that is way too good to be true have some culpability themselves? But that question is one for another time. The AG will tell you, and I'd agree, that a swindler couldn't argue the gullibility of his marks as a defense to his fraudulent actions.

The AG's six-count suit claims that the dealership's actions constituted unconscionable and deceptive acts or practices and seeks restitution to consumers affected by the allegedly tainted program, the release from their obligations of all customers who request it, reasonable investigative fees, and civil penalties payable to the state. Yikes!

If the allegations in the AG's suit, the Internet postings, and the TV reports turn out to be correct, you can bet grandma's garters that a wave of civil, class action lawsuits will follow. Double yikes!!

Keep in mind that, so far, all we have are allegations, and that's why we build courthouses. It's possible that the dealership will have a defense to these charges.

If the dealership ends up fighting the AG's charges and civil lawsuits, it will likely end up spending hundreds of thousands of dollars, even if the fight is successful. If the AG and the plaintiffs' lawyers win, the damages awards, attorneys' fees, and related court costs will probably total a staggering amount, and it will be "bye, bye, dealership."

That's what I'd call a dealership "big in trouble."

Use of the Word "Free" in Ads Just Might Cost You

September 2008
By Patricia E.M. Covington

Some may say, "There ain't nothin' for free." We're not so sure about that, but in the world of business and selling cars, there is a whole lot of truth to this adage. If a dealership isn't careful about how it uses the word "free" in an advertisement, that ad could cost a whole lot more than the price of print space in the local newspaper.

Dealers should know that the Federal Trade Commission regulates the use of the word "free" in advertisements. FTC regulations provide that if a product or service is usually sold at a price arrived at through bargaining, as distinguished from a set or fixed price, it is improper to represent that another product or service is being offered as "free" with the sale. Since the sale price of a car is usually established through a bargaining process (some more lively than others), extreme caution should be employed when using the word "free" in advertisements.

Now, let's look at some of those "free" offers being advertised. We're talking about the idea of "free gas cards" with the purchase of a new car. According to the FTC, there is nothing "free" when the sale price is derived through bargaining.

If a dealer uses this four-letter word, "free," it just might end up with more than the mouth full of soap a mother threatens her "young 'uns" with for saying other four-letter words. Yep, "free" can be a bad word and a costly one. How much? How about $200,000?

The FTC recently chased down an online advertiser for misusing this four-letter word. In its spam emails, the online advertiser used the enticement of "free" gifts to drive traffic to its website. The online advertiser failed, however, to disclose a critical fact—that consumers had to spend money to receive the so-called "free" gifts. The "free" gifts advertised included $500 gift cards, an iPod video player, and a laptop computer.

To qualify for the "free" products, consumers had to scroll through pages of "optional" offers and participate in a series of third-party promotions, such as purchasing products or applying for credit cards. Not so free, huh? The FTC didn't think so either. It sued the online advertiser for violating the FTC Act. It alleged that the online advertiser's failure to disclose that consumers had to pay money or provide some other consideration to get the "free" product was a deceptive practice. Bottom line—the online advertiser had to pay $200,000 in penalties. Ouch!

Lest dealers forget state law enforcers, their enforcement actions could also be costly. State Attorneys General have added deceptiveness in advertising, along with other consumer protection issues, to the forefront of their agendas. For example, in January of this year, the Massachusetts Attorney General imposed $290,000 in civil penalties on eight Massachusetts dealers for engaging in false and misleading advertising.

Using words like "free" in ads just might get dealers more than they bargained for, like "free" unwanted publicity on the front page of the local Sunday paper.

Did I Forget to Pay a Traffic Ticket?

October 2008

By Thomas B. Hudson

Every month in *Spot Delivery*®, we seem to have yet another story about a dealer's advertising that has resulted in trouble with the law, usually with the Attorney General. Every time we see another awful ad, we think, "It can't get any worse than this."

Last month, it was the "fake recall" mailer, the one that implied that the customer's car had been the subject of a recall notice. Some dealer, who evidently doesn't get out much and had not picked up on the fact that the Georgia AG was suing a dealer in that state for millions for using such a mailer, decided that fake recalls were a swell way to increase traffic.

This month, we report on an Indiana dealer's latest variation on the "see-if-we-can-make-them-open-the-envelope" scheme. So far, this one hasn't turned into an AG investigation, but these sorts of mailers draw AGs like extra-ripe peaches draw yellow jackets.

· The Indiana dealer's mailer came in a government-brown envelope. In the upper left return address area appeared, "TRAFFIC DIVISION, DEPARTMENT OF TICKET DISBURSEMENTS," with an address. Directly above the clear address window was printed, "IMPORTANT: TICKET ENCLOSED." Inside the envelope? You guessed it—an advertisement for the dealership.

So, the addressee gets the thing in the mail and either pitches it because it is immediately identifiable as junk mail, in which case it is ineffective, or, fooled by the government look of the thing, opens it to discover the dealer's ad. What do you suppose the addressee's response will be?

Perhaps some will say, "How clever. I think I need to buy a car from these sly people." But we'll bet that most will say, "What a sleazy trick!"

This stuff must be effective at bringing in enough traffic to satisfy the cost of the mailing and the fee charged by the marketing company, or we wouldn't keep seeing it. But the cost-effectiveness of such programs has to be weighed against the legal risk that such programs carry.

AGs around the country have brought actions against car dealers who have tried to make ordinary mailers appear to be something from the government. The AGs' claims usually call these mailers unfair or deceptive. That's usually enough ammo to pin an offending dealer to the wall, but I think that a dealer using an envelope like the one above could also be charged with violating a "doing business as" law (most states have them) by identifying the sender as "Traffic Division."

We usually suggest that dealers run ad programs that vendors are trying to sell them past the dealer's lawyer, but sometimes it isn't necessary to incur that expense. A dealer can save that legal fee simply by employing the good old "smell test." If it reeks, like this one does, save those legal fees and pitch it.

A $37 Acquisition Fee, Then Take Over the Payments!
January/February 2009
By Thomas B. Hudson

My friends know that I collect dealer advertising like some people collect coins or stamps. And why not? The ads are a source of constant entertainment.

I get some real doozies, but a recent one from a South Carolina dealer really piqued my interest. Let me share some of the ad content with you. As I do, I'll tell you why the ad is the front-runner for my Boneheaded Ad of the Year Award.

First, the ad described the dealer as an "Outlet Store." I'd be interested in whether the Attorney General would claim that characterizing a car dealership as an "outlet store" is an unfair or deceptive act or practice. After all, most people think that outlet stores are places where manufacturers sell their merchandise at especially low prices. If that isn't happening at this dealership, the term might be a dangerous one to use. I Googled this dealership, and, sure enough, it is located near some outlet stores. If I were the AG, that wouldn't fly as an excuse to characterize the dealership as an "outlet store."

Next, the ad trumpeted, "Payments start as low as $199.00 per month." Stating the amount of a payment in an advertisement is a "triggering term" under the federal Truth in Lending Act and Regulation Z. When an ad uses a triggering term, the ad must also disclose the amount or percentage of any down payment, the terms of repayment, and the annual percentage rate, using that term or APR. Whoever wrote this ad had not been introduced to the federal law and regulation.

Then came that perennial favorite, "Top Dollar On All Trade-Ins." That's bad enough, but elsewhere in the ad was, "You will never receive more money for your trade! Special appraisers will be on hand!" What do you think the chances are that this dealer, if challenged, could back those statements up? I also wonder if this dealer is planning on making up any money it loses on offering generous trade allowances by jacking up the cash price of the cars it sells (a little "fuzzy math" trick that sharp AGs and plaintiffs' lawyers are onto).

Another statement that we see all the time in ads caught my eye: "All credit applications will be accepted." That's an attempt to fool customers into hearing, "Everyone's application for credit will be approved." On the reverse side of the page, I ran across, "Bank approval required on all credit applications." Shame, shame on the ad writer and the dealer for trying to fool the ad readers.

The ad claimed, "[Name of city], South Carolina has been selected as the exclusive site for this $37.00 Acquisition Sale." That makes it sound like some third party has "selected" this dealership to offer this great sale, when all that has occurred is that the dealer has bought a lousy ad campaign from an ad company.

But the icing on the cake was, "A $37 Acquisition Fee, Then Take Over the Payments." I almost don't know where to start with that one. First, there's the implication that these cars have somehow already been financed for someone else and that the new buyer is simply paying a small sum to "take over the payments." Call me cynical, but I'll bet that these transactions will be straightforward credit deals between the dealer and the customer that are assigned to banks or sales finance companies. If that's the case, the attempt to describe them as something they are not is likely to be challenged as an unfair or deceptive act or practice. I'd also like to get a look at how that $37 gets disclosed in the retail installment contracts that this dealer has its customers sign. The $37 is almost certainly a finance charge, and probably a prepaid finance charge at that. Any finance charge has to go into the disclosed finance charge and is used to calculate the APR. If it is a prepaid finance charge (and assuming that state law permits a prepaid finance charge), it needs to be disclosed in a particular way.

It should really steam this dealer that an ad company charged it money for an ad that has the potential to land the dealer in a great deal of hot water. It should also concern this dealer that its managers signed off on an ad with as many problems as this one has.

To paraphrase a Midwest Attorney General who laid a very large dollar fine on a dealer for a deceptive ad campaign, "Dealers cannot simply say whatever they want to say to get people into a dealership."

Or, stated another way, dealers' ads need to be truthful. What a concept!

Puffery in Advertising
March 2009
By Michael A. Goodman

A basic guideline of unfair or deceptive acts or practices analysis is this: What you say in your advertising must be true. Dealers cannot pull claims out of thin air and stick them in ads simply because they sound good or because someone else is doing it.

Certain kinds of claims, however, are not held to this standard. These claims are called "puffery."

The Federal Trade Commission has explained that it "generally will not pursue cases involving obviously exaggerated or puffing representations, i.e., those that ordinary consumers do not take seriously." This is the Commission's way of saying that it prefers to spend its resources on advertising claims that consumers rely on to make purchasing decisions. The FTC tends to disregard those claims that the reasonable consumer is sophisticated enough to ignore.

It won't always be easy to figure out which of your claims consumers might rely on. In one case from 1966, the Commission explained that puffery refers generally to an expression of opinion not made as a representation of fact. In 1979, however, the Commission concluded that the claim that a television antenna was an "electronic miracle" could not be dismissed as puffery. Although the Commission agreed that advertisers throw around the term "miracle" to describe "situations short of changing water into wine," the Commission was concerned that consumers might see this claim as a representation that this antenna was superior to others.

Given the subjective issues at play here, let's ask a couple of questions: (1) How would a reasonable consumer interpret a claim? and (2) When does an opinion become a representation that a consumer might rely on? Advertisers must proceed with caution before reaching for the puffery defense.

Countrywide Home Loans is currently learning how tricky this can be. According to an article on MSNBC.com, Countrywide stated repeatedly in marketing, advertising, and Congressional testimony that it was working hard to modify mortgages of borrowers having trouble making payments. Two Countrywide customers sued Countrywide, claiming that such claims constituted a breach of good faith, fraud, negligence, and misrepresentation because Countrywide repeatedly told the customers that it would work with them on a modification and then refused to follow through.

One of Countrywide's responses to the suit has been to argue that all of its promises regarding loan modification were, in effect, puffery. Countrywide has also pointed out that its specific loan documents for these customers do not mention the prospect of loan modification.

The customers, on the other hand, point to Countrywide statements in the general media touting their dedication to assisting borrowers in trouble, including then-CEO Angelo Mozilo's testimony before Congress in which he said, "I want to underscore . . . what is perhaps the most important goal going forward—to keep families in their homes."

The customers who sued Countrywide want to hold the company to the standard set in its public statements. Countrywide wants to stick with the specific details of its relationship with these customers.

The outcome of this debate remains unpredictable; but meanwhile, many dealers might prefer to keep this kind of uncertainty out of their operation. If you want to say that your dealership is "amazing," "excellent," or "the best known to mankind," the FTC probably isn't going to bother with you. As you inch closer to claims that might influence a consumer's decision making, you also inch closer to being held responsible for what you say.

Remember the Golden Rule of advertising: What you say must be true.

Think Twice Before You Hand Over Those Keys!

April 2009

By Emily Marlow Beck

My husband and I live just a short walk away from the Capitol Building in Washington, D.C. So, when all the plans for the Presidential Inauguration started brewing, many of our friends and neighbors encouraged us to rent our home to out-of-towners who were traveling in for the event. After all, we heard tales of folks renting out itty-bitty studio apartments for hundreds or thousands of dollars a night, and we seriously considered hopping on the bandwagon.

We ultimately decided against it. It's not that we have a particularly valuable home or that we own anything that anyone would want to steal. Call us a couple of wimps, but we just couldn't get past the idea of handing over the keys to our home and letting strangers take it over for a few days. To be honest, it kinda creeped us out a bit.

So, it always comes as a bit of a surprise to me when I hear stories about dealers who willingly turn over the keys to their dealerships to third-party sales outfits and let them take the reins and run willy-nilly through the dealership for days or weeks at a time.

Take the recent story of a dealership in New York. According to the press release issued in late January by the New York Attorney General's office, the dealership will have to pay $20,000 in restitution and fees for defrauding customers. Attorney General Cuomo's office entered into an agreement with the dealership, which allegedly deceived customers through misleading advertisements and promotions and failed to inform customers that cars purchased were previously used as rental vehicles. All of these deeds were in violation of a 2005 agreement the dealership already had with the AG's office.

In one promotion, the dealership allegedly included an instant savings certificate in the form of a check worth $2,988 off the price of a used car, and, in another promotion, the dealership allegedly included a "Customer Cash Back Savings" voucher worth $4,000 off the price of a vehicle. The dealership then allegedly increased the retail sales price of the vehicle to account for the certificate or voucher. To top it all off, several of the consumers bought cars they did not know were previously used as rental vehicles.

According to the release, the Attorney General also alleged that the dealership engaged in other deceptive acts, such as

- using footnotes that contradict, modify, or limit the principal message of an advertisement;
- including deceptive sweepstakes offers in marketing materials;
- implying that a sale was a liquidation or public sale, when such was not the case;
- engaging in deceptive credit sales advertising;
- including deceptive photographs and artwork; and
- increasing the retail price of an automobile to allow for a rebate or discount—thus saving the consumer no money.

Now, these allegations were pretty strong, but that wasn't what caught my attention. What really got me were some comments made by the dealership's lawyers.

A local news outlet, Central New York News, reported the dealership's attorney's explanation for the alleged misdeeds. The dealership's lawyer said that the advertising and sales violations were conducted by an out-of-state marketing company as part of two special sales held at the dealership in 2007 and 2008.

Under a contract with the dealership, the marketing company handled all advertising and promotions for the sales and brought in its own staff from out of state to negotiate with customers and transact the sales. According to the dealer lawyer, some of the dealership's staff were present during the sales but were not privy to all of the details of the transactions. "These are negotiations that go back and forth with the customer," said the dealer lawyer. "We are not 100% sure what the out-of-state salesmen said."

Stop the presses!

Let me get this straight. You spend years, not to mention gobs of money, to develop and build your dealership's reputation. You're in one of the most highly regulated industries in the country, where lawsuits and enforcement actions against car dealers are as common as muck. Yet, with all this at stake, you hand over the keys to your dealership to a third-party, out-of-state marketing company and let it take your store for a spin. You've clearly got more nerve than I do.

But, this article makes me think about a whole bunch of things. I wonder if the third-party marketing company offered compliance or ethics training to its employees. I wonder if the marketing company made any efforts to familiarize itself with the nuances of New York laws and regulations. I wonder if the company offered to indemnify the dealership for any fines or penalties that the marketing company racked up in the dealership's name.

I also wonder (but think I know) whether the dealer did its due diligence on the marketing company by asking the marketing company these and a few other pretty basic questions.

Unfortunately, I was unable to find answers to any of my questions. I struck out when I Googled the name of the marketing company and tried to find its company website. It was nowhere to be found. Instead, I pulled up tales of a dealership picking up the pieces.

Something to think about the next time you're considering handing over those keys.

You Don't Even Have to Open the Envelope!

May 2009

By Thomas B. Hudson

A friend who is a consultant to auto dealers regularly supplies me with examples of direct mail advertisements from his dealer clients. Almost always, the ads he forwards to me are mailers that have been sold to the dealers by an ad company. And, almost always, the level of noncompliance of these mailers, and the legal risk to any dealer using them, is very high.

The latest batch of mailers arrived yesterday. After reviewing them, I was struck by one particular problem common to several of the pieces. The problem I noticed was that an Attorney General would not even have to open the envelope to suspect that the mailer contained violations.

One mailer showed in the return address area of the envelope the name "Program Headquarters." Of course, what was enclosed was not a letter from Program Headquarters, but rather an advertisement from a dealer. The obvious intent of using "Program Headquarters" instead of the dealer's name was to avoid a prompt trip to the round file. Other mailers used return addresses such as "Main Office" or (my particular favorite) "Disbursement Headquarters." Another mailer had a similar return address using initials next to a federal-looking eagle. Inside the clear window on the front, you could get a glimpse of something that might just be a check. "Hey, a check from the government—I've gotta open that!"

Another mailer was gussied up in a red-and-white color

scheme to resemble a U.S. Postal Service priority letter. The envelope actually said "Priority Documents," "Express Delivery," and "Return Receipt: REQUESTED" on the outside. For knowledgeable eyes, the "Presorted Standard" postage gave this one away, but many consumers wouldn't notice that. Inside? Nothing but a one-page flyer announcing a dealer's sale.

Then there are those envelopes that bear stern warnings about the punishments for interfering with or obstructing delivery of the mailer, or stealing it. The warnings apply to all mail, including that birthday card you just got, but no one except people who peddle direct mail finds it necessary to print these warnings on the outside of the envelope.

So what's wrong with these little direct mail tricks, you ask? Maybe nothing—I was told that the purveyor of these materials said he'd been using them "without a problem" for 20 years.

But maybe he's just been lucky. In the last couple of years, we've seen intense interest by AGs in dealer advertisements of all kinds, including direct mail ads. The AGs target ads that they deem to be "unfair or deceptive." In at least a couple of the enforcement actions that have been reported, the allegations involved mailing envelopes that were made up to look like official correspondence of some sort. I think that an AG would have the same problem with the sorts of misdirection I saw on the outside of many of these envelopes.

Even if these disguised ads didn't turn out to be practices an AG would target, they are still dangerous, in my view. AGs don't like deceptions like these—when they see them, they wonder whether there might be other deceptions inside the envelope, too. It's ironic—the ad companies use tricks to get consumers to open the mail, only to find that those same tricks are very effective at getting the AG to pore over the direct mail advertisement looking for other deceptions.

We Finance Anyone! Really?

May 2009

By Nicole F. Munro

"Low credit, no credit, we finance anyone."

While dealers probably haven't been making these claims lately, as the recession fades, and the economy brightens (yes, it will happen—eventually), dealers may be inclined to throw themselves back into the subprime financing arena. In an effort to get people in the door and into cars, one or two may be tempted to advertise that the dealer can "finance anyone."

Before a dealer boldly makes that statement, or any other statement in connection with offers of credit, the dealer should check his or her state's credit advertising rules. Don't forget that the Truth in Lending Act also governs credit advertising, and dealers should not ignore federal law requirements in their advertising compliance efforts.

Generally, a dealer who advertises specific credit terms must state only those terms that actually are, or will be, offered by the dealer. While this restriction appears under federal law, a dealer also could be sued for its violation under a state's unfair and deceptive acts and practices law. Further, most states prohibit unfair or deceptive acts and practices, including deceptive credit advertising. Many states also provide specific disclosure requirements and limitations applicable to credit offers. Just a flavor of some of those states' laws follows.

A dealer located in Alaska may not advertise that the dealer finances any person or does not reject any person's credit. A dealer located in Arkansas may not claim a buyer may "take over payments," and Arkansas law limits the manner in which a dealer may offer extended first payment periods. Like Alaska, Arkansas law also limits a dealer from claiming that everybody gets financed unless it is absolutely true and without qualification.

Some states, like California, not only require compliance with the Truth in Lending Act's Regulation Z advertising requirements for all credit sales, but also impose significant disclosure requirements and restrictions on credit advertising. California law also prohibits a dealer from using claims in advertising such as "everyone financed," "no credit rejected," or similar claims unless the dealer is willing to extend credit to any person under any and all circumstances. Kentucky, Louisiana, Mississippi, and more than a handful of other states also place limitations on unrestricted credit offers.

If a dealer in Connecticut advertises in a language other than English, all required disclosures or limitations on the offer advertised must appear in the advertisement using the language principally used in the advertisement. Illinois dealers may not advertise or imply in advertisements that rates are approved or set by the state of Illinois or the Department of Financial Institutions.

Iowa dealers may not advertise add-on or discount rates of interest (federal law prohibits this as well). Regulations in Maine require advertisements to be in plain language, and Massachusetts and Missouri laws require conditions or terms relating to qualification for credit to be clear and conspicuous. The Office of the New York Attorney General has published advertising guidelines for automobile dealers in connection with both the sale of vehicles and the offer to provide credit financing for those sales. Ohio, Texas, Virginia, and Washington also heavily regulate credit advertising, and the list can go on and on!

When the economy recovers, and when dealers begin spending money on advertising again, we advise that it's better not to be penny wise and pound foolish. A wise dealer will have its attorney review not only the advertisements for the sale of vehicles, but also its offers for credit.

Chapter 9

Arbitration

When we get around to the next book, the chances are pretty good that it won't include a chapter dealing with arbitration. Our newly elected Democratic Congress is in full consumer protection mode, and will likely try to do away with the ability of businesses to use pre-dispute mandatory arbitration provisions as a means of reducing the risk of ruinous class action lawsuits. It probably doesn't dampen the anti-arbitration ardor of these elected representatives that eliminating arbitration agreements is high on the agenda of the so-called "trial lawyers," who so generously contribute to Congressional campaigns. Furthermore, it hasn't helped matters that one of the top national arbitration organizations has been pilloried for potential conflicts of interest and has exited the consumer arbitration business.

But for now, dealers need to give some serious attention to the question of whether, and how, they will use mandatory pre-dispute arbitration agreements. We aren't aware of any studies, definitive or otherwise, dealing with whether dealers who employ these agreements are better off than those who don't, but there is plenty of anecdotal evidence that suggests that arbitration agreements are a net benefit for dealers. This anecdotal evidence suggests that,

- arbitration proceedings are generally less expensive than lawsuits;
- they take considerably less time and management attention to resolve; and
- lawyers who represent consumers against dealers are less likely to be interested in representing consumers in arbitration proceedings that they are in dragging a dealer to court.

Other evidence, also anecdotal, indicates that some plaintiffs' lawyers (perhaps seeing the writing on the wall) have learned how to "game the system" and are happy to press their clients' claims in arbitration. Other reports have indicated that arbitration fees and charges can mount quickly, rivaling or exceeding the costs of a lawsuit. Although it would seem that the deterrence effect noted above would offset these disadvantages, we haven't seen any research that indicates to what extent that happens.

Dealers will want to involve their lawyers, and perhaps their insurers, in the decision to arbitrate or not arbitrate. The articles in this chapter, most of which deal with challenges to the enforceability of arbitration agreements or the class action waivers that they typically contain, should help with the decision.

Public Citizen's Arbitration Report Misses Mark

November 2007
By Thomas B. Hudson

Public Citizen is a Washington, D.C., consumer advocacy group that seems to have a talent for misleading the public with information that is either wrong or intellectually dishonest. They've done it again.

This time, the topic is arbitration, a subject that is important to dealers because a dealer's use of a fair and well-drafted arbitration agreement is the dealer's best first line of defense against class action lawyers and other predatory litigators.

On September 27, 2007, Public Citizen issued a press release that railed against credit card companies that have begun to use the arbitration process in collecting the debts owed to them by consumers. The release also criticized the National Arbitration Forum, one of the largest arbitration organizations in the country, and claimed abuses in the arbitration process.

The foundation of the report is Public Citizen's claim, based on its study of nearly 34,000 collection cases that arbitrators found for businesses in 94% of the arbitration proceedings. That 94% number evoked the following quote from Joan Claybrook, Public Citizen's President: "People shouldn't have to give up their legal rights just to get a credit card. This is a system that is unfair to consumers, many of whom are struggling financially, and a huge gift to big business. We need to ban arbitration clauses in consumer contracts now."

Really? Evidently the press thought so. Public Citizen's report was picked up by many news sources, and quoted from liberally (no pun intended) and uncritically.

It's the "uncritically" part that really steams me.

Remember that Public Citizen tells us that these 34,000 arbitration proceedings were "virtually all" collection cases. What Public Citizen doesn't bother to tell us is how courts treat consumers in collection cases. If consumers do about as well in such cases in arbitration as they do in court, wouldn't you think any honest analysis would point that out?

Remember that collection cases are nearly always pretty straightforward. Consumers understand that they owe the balance claimed, and so they do not bother to contest the claim, and indeed often do not even show up for the trial. I do not know how consumers fare when defending collection lawsuits in court, but am aware of at least one Georgetown University Law Center study that indicates that the percentage of courtroom outcomes in favor of businesses is as high as, if not higher than, the 94% number that causes Public Citizen such anxiety.

Isn't the real question to be addressed the question of whether arbitration outcomes are more or less favorable for the consumer than litigation outcomes? Public Citizen doesn't even hint that it might be appropriate to compare courtroom outcomes with litigation outcomes before jumping to unfounded conclusions. And, as far as I know, no reporter even bothered to ask the question!

That's the intellectual dishonesty in the Public Citizen report. What if someone actually bothered to look, and the litigation figures turned out to be essentially the same as the arbitration figures? Will Joan Claybrook call for the abolition of the court system because businesses win 94% of their collection lawsuits? Don't hold your breath.

Sanity Strikes in Ohio
December 2007
By Thomas B. Hudson

This case will remind you of why they call the middle of the country the "Heartland." It's the home of sensible, levelheaded people who aren't afraid to exercise a bit of common sense, even when they're wearing black robes.

In this arbitration decision, a court came up with two shockers. First, the court decided that a warranty company had no obligation to explain an arbitration agreement to a consumer. Then, lo and behold, the court concluded that a consumer is bound by a contract she signs, even if she doesn't read it. Let's look at the court's opinion.

Steve and Amy Khoury sued United Service Protection Corporation (USPC) and Denney Motors Associates, Inc., for breach of contract, breach of express and implied warranties, violation of the Ohio Consumer Sales Practices Act, violation of the Magnuson-Moss Warranty Act, rescission, and fraud. The suit was filed after the Khourys had problems with a 1999 Corvette that Mrs. Khoury bought from Denney Motors on May 29, 2004, and after USPC denied coverage for the problems under a vehicle service warranty that Mrs. Khoury purchased when she bought the 'vette.

After an unsuccessful attempt to move the matter to federal court, USPC moved to stay proceedings pending arbitration, citing a binding arbitration clause in its warranty booklet. The Khourys filed a memorandum in opposition to the motion, arguing that the arbitration terms were unconscionable.

The trial court denied USPC's motion, stating that it "would be unconscionable to enforce an arbitration clause which a seller failed to make a buyer aware [sic]. Because defendant has failed to show that it is entitled to arbitration, the Court declines to stay proceedings in this case pending arbitration." The trial court denied USPC's motion to stay proceedings pending arbitration, "finding such arbitration terms 'substantially unconscionable.'" Unhappy with this result, USPC appealed.

On appeal, the Khourys again argued that the arbitration terms were unconscionable. The Khourys also claimed that they were unaware of the arbitration clause until USPC filed its motion to stay.

USPC argued that the trial court erroneously determined that it presented no evidence that the Khourys received a copy of the arbitration clause. The appellate court noted, however, that the record contained the affidavit of Charles Pullins, the President of Denney Motors, which indicated that Mrs. Khoury was given a copy of the booklet containing the arbitration clause when she bought the vehicle and warranty. The court determined that this evidence refuted Mr. Khoury's affidavit, which indicated that neither he nor his wife was provided with the booklet containing the arbitration provision. The appellate court concluded that the trial court erroneously failed to consider the Pullins affidavit when it found that USPC presented no evidence that plaintiffs received a copy of the arbitration clause.

USPC also argued that the trial court erroneously implied in its decision that USPC had a duty to explain the arbitration provision to the buyers, and argued that knowledge of the contents of the arbitration provision must be imputed to the Khourys. In support of these arguments, USPC asserted that one who signs a contract is presumed to know its contents.

The appellate court noted that the law does not require an arbitration agreement to be orally explained to a party prior to obtaining the party's signature, that "parties to contracts are presumed to have read and understood them and . . . a signatory is bound by a contract that he or she willingly signed."

I think I'll move to Ohio.

Khoury v. Denney Motors Associates, Inc., 2007 WL 3149174 (Ohio App. October 30, 2007).

The Arbitration Wars, Continued

March 2008

By Thomas B. Hudson

Plaintiffs' lawyers have had some limited successes in the far west and in a few other states in their efforts to convince courts that mandatory arbitration provisions, used by dealers and other creditors as a first line of defense against class action lawsuits, should not be enforced. Now, the North Carolina Supreme Court has bought the same arguments that have been rejected by many courts. The case involves mortgage credit, but car folks shouldn't quit reading—the concepts apply across the board. And don't stop reading if you don't do business in North Carolina—there are lessons here for you as well.

Fannie Lee Tillman and Shirley Richardson got mortgage loans from Commercial Credit Loans, Inc., and bought single premium credit insurance in connection with their loans. The loan agreements contained a standard arbitration clause. Later, North Carolina outlawed single premium credit insurance.

Maybe the North Carolina prohibition led Tillman and Richardson to file suit—we don't know. But in any event, they brought a class action lawsuit against Commercial Credit for violating North Carolina's Unfair and Deceptive Trade Practices Act, unjust enrichment, and breach of the duties of good faith and fair dealing. The plaintiffs claimed that they did not want or need single premium credit insurance and that Commercial Credit did not tell them that the insurance was optional. They claimed that Commercial Credit failed to provide the required disclosures regarding the credit insurance and charged "fees that were deceptive, unfair, duplicative, imposed without commercial justification or disclosure, and in excess of the fees permitted by North Carolina law."

Commercial Credit moved to compel arbitration. The trial court found that the arbitration clause was unconscionable because of prohibitively high arbitration costs and the "loser-pay" fee-shifting provisions. The trial court also found that the arbitration clause was excessively one-sided and lacked mutuality because it preserved access to the courts for Commercial Credit but prohibited class actions and restricted access to the courts for the borrowers.

Commercial Credit appealed. The appellate court reversed the trial court's decision and remanded the case to the trial court for entry of an order granting Commercial Credit's motion to compel arbitration. The plaintiffs appealed.

The North Carolina Supreme Court reversed the appellate court's decision. The high court concluded that the oppressive and one-sided substantive provisions of the arbitration agreement and the unequal bargaining power between the parties rendered the arbitration agreement procedurally and substantively unconscionable. The trial court did not explicitly conclude that the facts supported a finding of procedural unconscionability, but the record indicated that the plaintiffs were rushed through the loan closing, they were not told about the credit insurance or the arbitration clause at the closing, and Commercial Credit admitted that it would not make the loans without the arbitration clause. The high court found that the bargaining power between the parties was unquestionably unequal and that the plaintiffs provided sufficient evidence to establish procedural unconscionability.

The high court agreed with the trial court's finding that the lender's arbitration agreement contained features regarding the costs of arbitration that would deter consumers from seeking to vindicate their rights. Commercial Credit argued that the cost analysis was irrelevant because the American Arbitration Association's Consumer Rules superseded the terms of the agreement. The high court disagreed, stating that the arbitration agreement itself provided that the terms of the agreement controlled in the event of any inconsistency with the AAA rules. The high court also stated that it was inappropriate to rewrite an illegal or unconscionable contract. The high court concluded that it must consider the agreement as drafted because the underlying concern was whether borrowers would be deterred from bringing claims based on the terms of the agreement.

The plaintiffs' next argument concerned the one-sidedness of the agreement. The plaintiffs argued that the arbitration agreement preserved Commercial Credit's ability to pursue claims in court, while denying borrowers that same option. The agreement allowed foreclosure actions and actions in which the total damages, costs, and fees would not exceed $15,000 to be pursued in court. The high court found that, since 1996,

Commercial Credit brought over 2,000 collection actions with an average payout of under $7,000 and had not initiated a single arbitration in North Carolina.

The plaintiffs' final argument was that the arbitration agreement was unconscionable because it prohibited joinder of claims and class actions. The high court concluded that the limitation on joinder or class actions contributed to making the arbitration procedure financially inaccessible, because it would deter potential plaintiffs from bringing cases with low damages amounts and costs that cannot be shared with other plaintiffs. The high court also determined that this limitation contributed to the one-sidedness of the agreement because the ability to join claims or bring class actions would only benefit the borrower.

[Editor's note: joinder: the uniting or joining together of distinct causes of action or persons in a legal proceeding. Joinder of causes of action: Under modern rules of civil procedure a party asserting a claim to relief may join as many claims as he has against an opposing party whether they are legal or equitable.— Gilbert Law Summaries, Law Dictionary.]

So, where does this analysis leave a North Carolina car dealer or creditor? Because the court's opinion is very fact-specific, it's hard to say. Anyone using an arbitration agreement in North Carolina will need to review, and possibly revise, the agreement. We suggest the following:

- Any revision should pay particular attention to the cost and fee-sharing language. Any such language should be as consumer-friendly as possible.
- The review should also target any "carve outs"—things that the consumer is required to arbitrate but the creditor is not obligated to arbitrate. Even though many courts around the country have rejected challenges by consumers based on the presence of such carveouts, this one didn't.

The fewer such carve outs, the better.

- While the high court's opinion pointed to the waiver of class relief as a contributing factor to the expense argument posited by the plaintiffs, the opinion doesn't seem to go so far as to ban class waivers, and pro-consumer fee-sharing provisions might reduce or eliminate this factor.

- The arbitration provision itself should be prominently featured in the credit documents, and the creditor's written procedures should require time for the consumer to review and consider the terms of the arbitration agreement.

With all of these changes, can I tell you that North Carolina arbitration provisions would be enforced? Nope, but they'd stand a better chance of enforcement than the arbitration agreement trashed by the North Carolina Supremes in this case.

Tillman v. Commercial Credit Loans, Inc., 2008 WL 201750 (N.C. January 25, 2008).

Snoozing and Losing

April 2008

By Thomas B. Hudson

I am frequently asked whether dealers' use of mandatory arbitration agreements as a defense against class action lawsuits and as a way to escape potentially crippling damages awards by courts is a tactic that actually works. Since I am a lawyer, my standard reply is, "It depends."

What does it depend on, you say?

First, you need a well-drafted arbitration agreement that bends over backward to favor the consumer. The terms of the arbitration agreement that deal with the consumer's obligation to pay the costs and expenses of arbitration, the place where the arbitration will take place, so-called "carve outs" of issues that the dealer or finance company is not required to arbitrate, the prohibition against class relief, and the election of the Federal Arbitration Act are all provisions that are frequently attacked by plaintiffs' lawyers who are trying to convince courts not to enforce arbitration agreements. These provisions need to be addressed in ways that will improve the likelihood that a court will enforce the arbitration agreement.

Second, the arbitration agreement needs to be conspicuous. I don't have a dog in the fight when it comes to whether the arbitration agreement needs to appear in a document by itself, except in those few states that have so-called "single document" rules. If the arbitration provision appears in a buyers order, retail installment sales contract, or lease, I always recommend that it appear in bold type, all caps, boxed, or some combination of all three, and that the acknowledgment that appears above the customer's signature contain a reference to the fact that there's an arbitration agreement in the document.

Third, the dealer needs to avoid dumb mistakes. In a few instances, we've seen cases where the dealer has failed to sign the arbitration agreement. In other instances, dealers have documented a transaction with separate documents that have contained "dueling" arbitration agreements with different provisions. A dealer-hostile court will seize on such mistakes as a reason to refuse to enforce the arbitration agreement.

And last, when a dispute arises, don't wait too long to elect arbitration under the agreement. A recent case illustrates what can happen when you snooze.

Ernesto Radillo sued Superior Nissan of Mission Hills and Nissan Motor Acceptance Corporation, alleging that Radillo, who does not speak English well, was assisted by a Spanish-speaking employee in buying a new vehicle from the dealership. Radillo alleged conversion, fraud and concealment, violation of the Consumer Legal Remedies Act, rescission, and restitution.

The dealership answered the complaint in April 2006 and raised 23 affirmative defenses, none of which mentioned arbitration. NMAC answered and cross-complained against Radillo, but did not seek arbitration of the claims raised in the complaint or the cross-complaint.

The defendants later executed a case management conference statement that demanded a jury trial and also requested meditation. The parties participated in mediation on December 14, 2006. During the time the action was pending in superior court, the parties, including the defendants, used discovery methods applicable to civil litigation.

[Editor's note #1: arbitration: The submission of a dispute between two parties to a third, impartial party (arbitrator) with the agreement that the decision of the arbitrator will be binding and final. It is a quasi-judicial procedure that avoids the formality, delay, and expense of a normal trial.

Editor's note #2: mediation: Intervention; settlement of disputes by an objective third person who attempts to work a compromise.—Gilberts Law Summaries, Law Dictionary.]

On December 20, 2006, Radillo moved for leave to file a first amended complaint. The amended complaint raised issues of whether Radillo's name had been forged on documents used to finance the purchase of the Nissan. On January 25, 2007, nine months after first answering the complaint, the defendants for the first time demanded arbitration of the claims. The trial court found that the defendants had waived the right to compel arbitration. The defendants appealed.

The appellate court affirmed the trial court's judgment with regard to whether the defendants had waived their right to compel arbitration under California waiver law. The defendants also claimed that the Federal Arbitration Act should govern the waiver analysis. Applying a three-step analysis, the appellate court determined that the defendants had a known right to compel arbitration, that they acted inconsistently with that right, and that Radillo was prejudiced by the inconsistent acts. Consequently, the appellate court rejected the FAA argument as well, leaving Radillo free to press his claim in court.

So, as I said, it depends. Get yourself a good arbitration agreement, don't try to hide it from the customer, watch out for rookie mistakes, and make the decision to invoke the arbitration agreement as quickly as you can. If you do all of these things, it's likely that a court will enforce your agreement.

Radillo v. Superior Nissan of Mission Hills, 2008 WL 444439 (Cal. App. February 20, 2008).

Florida Dealer Prevails in Internet Arbitration
June 2008
By Thomas B. Hudson

Two of my favorite topics are interstate Internet sales and arbitration, so I perked right up while reading a court opinion that dealt with both topics. I immediately wondered how well the dealer had handled the Internet sale and whether his arbitration agreement would hold up under the consumer's challenge. Here's what happened.

Genuine Motor Cars, Inc., advertised on eBay to sell a Ford van located in Florida. The advertisement indicated that the van had genuine leather seats. Raymond Ewers contacted Genuine by phone and confirmed that the van in fact had genuine leather seats.

Based on these representations, Ewers negotiated to buy the van. Ewers and his wife, Mayra Coughlin-Ewers, agreed to exercise the "buy it now" option on eBay for a total of nearly $32,000. Before viewing the vehicle, the plaintiffs wired the money to Genuine's bank in Florida. The plaintiffs indicated that they would take delivery of the van in Florida (making delivery in Florida is a good fact for the dealer).

When the plaintiffs arrived in Florida, the purchase documents, including a pre-printed agreement to arbitrate, were presented to Coughlin-Ewers, since the van was to be titled in her name. She signed the documents, including the arbitration agreement.

After the sale was completed, the plaintiffs discovered that the upholstery in the van was not leather. They then sued Genuine and others in Ohio state court, and the defendants removed the matter to federal court and moved to compel arbitration.

The plaintiffs argued that the arbitration agreement was unenforceable. Specifically, they argued that the arbitration agreement suffered from "procedural unconscionability." Time for a short law school lesson here—"unconscionability" can be "substantive," when the actual terms of an agreement are very unfair, but it can also be "procedural," when some element of the transaction's completion is unfair. An arbitration agreement that required a Florida car buyer to arbitrate his dispute in Anchorage, Alaska, would be substantively unconscionable, while procedural unconscionability might be argued if the dealer's salesman required the buyer to sign documents without reading them.

In arguing procedural unconscionability, the plaintiffs pointed out that the defendants did not inform them of the purchase documents, including the arbitration agreement, until they arrived in Florida. Rather, upon their arrival, the defendants presented the documents to Coughlin-Ewers in a stack. The documents, including the arbitration agreement, were pre-printed form documents. At no point did anyone explain the contents or terms of the arbitration agreement or advise her that she had time to review the documents. The plaintiffs also pointed out that, although Ewers holds a law degree and is currently a judge, Coughlin-Ewers has no legal background and did not review the arbitration agreement with her husband prior to signing it.

The U.S. District Court for the Northern District of Ohio found that the plaintiffs failed to establish procedural unconscionability. The court found Coughlin-Ewers to be sufficiently capable of understanding the arbitration agreement. The court noted that she admitted she was a teacher and thus presumably possessed a college education. Moreover, her husband was an attorney and a judge. Although not present in the "office," he was in the showroom at the time she signed the documents. Thus, she had access to counsel if she had any concerns about the contents of the arbitration agreement.

Dealers and their counsel should pay close attention to some reservations expressed by the court. The court expressed some concern that the plaintiffs were informed of the arbitration agreement only after they agreed to buy the van, wired the money, and arrived in Florida. The court concluded that its concern was allayed (or diminished in strength) by the fact that the arbitration agreement was a contract separate and distinct from the purchase of the van and that the defendants never informed the plaintiffs that they would not receive the van unless they signed the arbitration agreement. The court granted the motion to compel arbitration.

If, like me, you think that a judge who hauls a car dealer into court over seat coverings is abusing the legal system, I don't think you'll be alone. It's probably my imagination, but, reading between the lines, I think the judge deciding this case probably thought so too. And if that thought led in part to the dealer's victory here, maybe there's some justice after all.

Ewers v. Genuine Motor Cars, Inc., 2008 WL 755268 (N.D. Ohio March 19, 2008).

Consumer Fails High Standard for Vacating Arbitration Award

September 2008

By Thomas B. Hudson

OK, your customer sues you, arguing that you violated one or more of the couple of dozen laws that apply to a typical consumer credit sale or lease of an automobile. You've been smart, though, and have listened to Spot as over the years he has barked about using arbitration agreements. You move the court to order the matter to arbitration, and the arbitrator decides in your favor. You've won, right?

Maybe not. The wheels of justice may grind slowly, but sometimes it seems like they never stop. Your customer's not done yet, and he files a motion to vacate the arbitrator's award. Let's see how such a scenario plays out.

When Angela Maguire leased a vehicle from Freehold Subaru, LLC, the parties entered into a buyers order and a lease agreement. Each document contained a provision broadly compelling arbitration in the event of a dispute.

Maguire's lease included optional charges for an extended warranty service contract and an "etch" insurance policy. Maguire later sued Freehold in state court, alleging several state consumer protection law violations. The trial court granted Freehold's motion to dismiss the complaint and compel arbitration.

In arbitration, Maguire argued that Freehold had violated the New Jersey Consumer Fraud Act in the lease transaction. Because the appointed arbitrator had represented automobile dealers, Maguire requested a new arbitrator. The American Arbitration Association denied that request.

The arbitrator's award rejected all of Maguire's claims. In response, Maguire filed a motion in the trial court to vacate the award and remand the matter to a different arbitrator. She argued that the award was against public policy and made in manifest disregard of the law, and that the arbitrator was not impartial. The trial court rejected Maguire's claims as unsupported by evidence, explaining that applicable law sets a high standard for vacating an arbitration award. Maguire appealed.

The New Jersey Superior Court, Appellate Division, affirmed the trial court's decision for Freehold. The appellate court explained that arbitration awards are presumed valid and listed the grounds for vacating an award under state and federal law. In sum, under either standard, courts will uphold an award absent fraud, corruption, or similar wrongdoing. Because the appellate court concluded that either standard supported upholding the arbitration award, it did not establish whether the state or federal standard applied.

The lesson for dealers here? First, if you've gotten a favorable result in arbitration, it will be pretty difficult for your customer to challenge it.

The second lesson? If that arbitrator's award is in favor of your customer, you'll have a hard time yourself if you want to try to challenge it.

Maguire v. Freehold Subaru, LLC, 2008 WL 2796393 (N.J. Super. App. Div. July 22, 2008).

Throwin' Stuff Against the Wall . . .

October 2008

By Thomas B. Hudson

Plaintiffs' lawyers REALLY hate mandatory arbitration agreements because such agreements deprive the lawyers of their most formidable threats—class action lawsuits and juries that don't like car dealers. So when a lawyer's client shows up with paperwork indicating that the client has signed an arbitration agreement, the lawyer's first task (if he wants the case to stay in court or settle, in either case resulting in a big fee) is to convince a court that the arbitration agreement should not be enforced.

Because most courts will reject arguments that a well-drafted arbitration agreement shouldn't be enforced, the lawyer, faced with an uphill fight, will typically start throwing arguments at the court, hoping one will stick. This case involves such a tactic.

Before we address the opinion, I'll note that this opinion doesn't involve auto finance, but it illustrates the sorts of challenges to arbitration that car dealers frequently face, and the ways that at least some courts deal with those challenges.

Back to the opinion, let's look at the facts. Mark Cronin entered into a loan agreement with CitiFinancial Services, Inc. When CitiFinancial reported the loan to credit reporting agencies, it reported the full amount of the loan, including the five years' worth of unmatured interest, instead of the unpaid balance of Cronin's loan.

Cronin contested the account balance with the credit reporting agencies, and each agency performed a reinvestigation. CitiFinancial continued to report the accelerated balance of the loan.

Cronin, an attorney representing himself, sued CitiFinancial in a putative class action, claiming that CitiFinancial violated the federal Fair Credit Reporting Act. CitiFinancial moved to compel arbitration and stay all proceedings pursuant to an arbitration agreement the parties signed as part of the loan transaction.

*[**Editor's note #1:** putative: Reputed; supposed; commonly esteemed; believed; assumed. E.g., a putative father is the man believed to be the father of a child born out of wedlock.—Gilbert Law Summaries, Law Dictionary. When a plaintiff files a class action, but the court has not certified a class, the action is referred to as a "putative" class action.]*

*[**Editor's note #2:** putative: commonly accepted or supposed.— Webster's Ninth New Collegiate Dictionary.]*

Cronin started lobbing his arguments. He came up with four. First, he contended that the arbitration agreement was invalid because it was a contract of adhesion (he had no say as to its terms) and lacked mutuality of obligation (CitiFinancial's promises were unequal to his). Then he argued that the agreement imposed unconscionable costs on him. Next, he contended that the arbitrators who would hear his claims (from the American Arbitration Association or the National Arbitration Forum) were not neutral because they did much arbitration for CitiFinancial and would be disposed in favor of such a frequent customer. Finally, he argued that the arbitration agreement did not apply to his claims under the Fair Credit Reporting Act, because the FCRA claims were not contemplated by the parties when they entered into the agreement, and because arbitration conflicts with the goals of the FCRA.

The U.S. District Court for the Eastern District of Pennsylvania dealt with Cronin's claims in order. The court found that even if the arbitration agreement constituted a contract of adhesion, it was nevertheless enforceable because there was no evidence that the agreement's terms unreasonably favored CitiFinancial or that Cronin lacked meaningful choice in accepting the terms of the agreement. The court also found that there was mutuality of obligation even though CitiFinancial could foreclose on a loan without arbitration. The court noted that the exception of foreclosure from arbitration does not render an arbitration clause unconscionable.

The court also found that the arbitration agreement did not impose unreasonable costs on Cronin, the agreement placed most of the costs on CitiFinancial, and provided for reimbursement of those costs by Cronin only if the arbitrator determined that Cronin's claim was filed in bad faith.

Finally, the court found that Cronin's claim that the arbitrators were biased was "speculative," that the arbitration clause was broad enough to cover Cronin's FCRA claims, and that there was no evidence that Congress intended to preclude FCRA claims from being arbitrated.

The court rejected Cronin's arguments and granted CitiFinancial's motion to compel arbitration.

The case provides a lesson, and we have a couple of warnings to go with the lesson. The lesson is that the arbitration agreement that CitiFinancial used here was one that was well drafted by someone familiar with typical challenges to the enforceability of arbitration agreements and was pretty consumer-friendly. By anticipating what the plaintiff would throw against the wall, the drafter put CitiFinancial into a position to win its motion.

The warnings? First, note that this was a federal court opinion. In my experience, federal courts are less receptive to plaintiffs' unenforceability arguments than are state courts. Second, some courts have actually bought into the argument that an arbitration agreement that carves out foreclosure or repossession claims by creditors is not enforceable. If you're using an arbitration agreement with such carve outs, you might consider whether it would be prudent to remove them.

Cronin v. CitiFinancial Servs., Inc., 2008 WL 2944869 (E.D. Pa. July 25, 2008).

Pigs Get Fat, Hogs Get Slaughtered
November 2008
By Thomas B. Hudson

One sure-fire way to make sure a court won't enforce your arbitration agreement is to ask it to do more than get you in front of an arbitrator. I can't tell you the number of arbitration agreements that I've seen that indicate that the drafter got piggy, trying to use the arbitration agreement as a means of tipping the balance in a dealer or creditor's favor.

Even though this case involves mortgage credit rather than car credit, it illustrates the point nicely.

Donald and Roxanne Abner signed a promissory note held by Bank of New York secured by a mortgage held by Mortgage Electronic Registration Systems, Inc. The mortgage contained an arbitration clause stating: "If the appointed arbitrator should award any damages, such damages shall be limited to actual and direct damages and shall in no event include consequential, punitive, exemplary, or treble damages as to which the borrower and lender expressly waive any right to claim to the fullest extent permitted by law" (hint to the drafter—you just drew a big bulls-eye on your client).

MERS and Bank of New York filed a foreclosure action, and the Abners counterclaimed, alleging violations of the Home Ownership and Equity Protection Act, usury, and breach of contract. The Abners also sought to rescind the mortgage.

MERS and Bank of New York moved to compel arbitration. The trial court denied the motion, finding that the arbitration clause was unconscionable. MERS and Bank of New York appealed.

The Kentucky Court of Appeals affirmed the trial court's decision. The appellate court found that the Abners could be entitled to statutory damages for any Truth in Lending Act disclosure violation, as well as statutory damages for violations of the federal Home Ownership Equity Protection Act. The appellate court also found that if the Abners proved their claim for usury, they could be entitled to remedies including forfeiture of all interest on the note and recovery of damages in the amount of twice the interest paid. Finally, the appellate court found that the Abners were seeking punitive damages for unfair and deceptive practices under the Kentucky Consumer Protection Act.

The appellate court concluded that the mortgage's arbitration clause was unconscionable and unenforceable, stating that it prevented the Abners from meaningfully pursuing any of their statutory claims because it disallowed recovery for statutory damages.

The creditor here was left without the protection of an arbitration agreement, because the drafter of the agreement got piggy and tried to pick the consumer's pocket. Remember that the two reasons that dealers and creditors should use mandatory arbitration agreements are to avoid class actions and to stay away from juries, which typically don't like creditors and dealers. Don't try to use the agreements to limit the consumer's remedies or expand on the creditor's rights.

You'll get slaughtered.

Mortgage Electronic Registration Systems, Inc. v. Abner, 2008 WL 2852433 (Ky. App. July 25, 2008).

Yo No Comprendo Arbitration

March 2009

By Nicole F. Munro

Dealer advertises in Spanish. Dealer negotiates a transaction with non-English-speaking buyers in Spanish. Dealer explains an English version of a retail installment sale contract in Spanish. Dealer fails to explain, or at least mention, a stand-alone arbitration clause. In Florida, that results in the dealer's inability to enforce the arbitration clause. The dealer in the following case apparently had the buyers sign a blank contract, which possibly motivated the court's refusal to enforce arbitration. That being said, a look at the Hialeah case indicates that dealers who negotiate and explain a transaction in a foreign language should explain all documents to be signed and potentially enforced against a buyer in that language. The failure to do so could result in the unenforceability of the terms contained in the unexplained form.

Responding to an advertisement on Spanish-language television, Roberto Basulto and Raquel Gonzalez bought a 2005 Dodge from Hialeah Automotive, LLC. Hialeah employees dealing with Basulto and Gonzalez understood that the buyers did not speak or read English. Consequently, the entire transaction was conducted in Spanish. When the deal went south, the buyers sued Hialeah, alleging fraud in the inducement and violation of the Florida Deceptive and Unfair Trade Practices Act (FDUTPA). They sought rescission of the arbitration agreements they had signed and rescission of the retail installment sale contract. The dealer moved to compel arbitration. The trial court ruled that the arbitration agreements were unconscionable and that the request for public injunctive relief under the FDUTPA was not a remedy an arbitrator could enforce and oversee.

At trial, the dealer's personnel testified that, although the contracts were written in English, they reviewed the content of the contracts with the buyers in Spanish. The buyers testified that in their conversations with the dealer's personnel, arbitration was never mentioned. The trial court found the buyers to be credible and concluded that arbitration was not mentioned, or, if mentioned, was not explained in an understandable way. The dealer appealed to the Florida District Court of Appeal.

The appellate court noted that the dealer's personnel undertook to explain the contracts to the buyers in Spanish, and that, having done so, they were obliged to do so accurately. In addition, the appellate court affirmed the trial court's ruling that an arbitrator is not suited to enforce and oversee injunctive relief claimed under the FDUTPA.

What's the moral of the story? As a dealer, if you choose to negotiate in a foreign language, ensure that you accurately explain the obligations of the borrower contained in all documents you intend to enforce. ¡Adiós y buena suerte!

Hialeah Automotive, LLC v. Basulto, 2009 Fla. App. LEXIS 566 (Fla. App. January 28, 2009).

Arbitration Agreements—Stand Alone or Include in Another Document?

April 2009

By Thomas B. Hudson

When I speak to dealer groups, one of my topics is usually the use by dealers of mandatory arbitration agreements in their consumer contracts. I am a strong proponent of such use, because arbitration agreements provide a very effective defense against two of the biggest legal risks that dealers face—class action lawsuits and out-of-control juries.

When I finish my prepared presentation and ask for questions, I frequently am asked, "Should my arbitration agreement be part of my buyers order or retail installment contract, or should it be a stand-alone document?" I usually answer by saying that, unless the dealer is located in a state with a so-called "single document" law requiring that all the agreements with the customer appear in the same document, I really don't have a preference. I point out that if the arbitration language is included in the buyers order or retail installment contract, the dealer has one less document to lose or forget to have signed. On the other hand, including the arbitration language in a separate document keeps the customer from arguing that it was "buried" in small print in the buyers order or retail installment contract and that he or she didn't know it was part of the deal. In other words, there are advantages to both approaches.

A recent case suggests that use of a stand-alone agreement might have an added advantage, at least under certain circumstances. Here's what happened.

Earl Scott visited Napleton's Nissan to buy a car and ultimately chose a 2005 Nissan. On the same day, he signed a retail installment sale contract.

The transaction was a typical "spot delivery" deal, in which the dealer delivered the Nissan to Scott, subject to acceptance of the retail installment contract. The retail installment contract contained an arbitration clause. Scott also executed a separate stand-alone agreement to arbitrate.

According to Scott, within days after the contract was executed, the dealership, presumably unable to sell it to a financing source, rescinded it and advised him that the Nissan must be returned to the dealership immediately. After

Napleton's took possession of the Nissan, Scott sued the dealership in state court, alleging violations of the Florida Motor Vehicle Sales Finance Act, the Fair Credit Reporting Act, the Equal Credit Opportunity Act, and the Florida Unfair and Deceptive Trade Practices Act and breach of contract. The defendants removed the case to federal court and moved to compel arbitration pursuant to the stand-alone arbitration agreement. The trial court granted the motion to compel arbitration and dismissed the case. Scott appealed.

The U.S. Court of Appeals for the Eleventh Circuit (which has jurisdiction over federal cases originating in the states of Alabama, Florida, and Georgia) concluded that Scott had agreed to arbitrate his disputes with the dealership. The appellate court rejected Scott's argument that, because the dealership had rescinded the retail installment contract, it had also rescinded the stand-alone arbitration agreement. Finding that there were no legal constraints external to the parties' agreement that would foreclose arbitration, the appellate court affirmed the trial court's decision.

So, for dealers who engage in spot delivery transactions using documents that permit the dealer to rescind the agreement (usually a retail installment contract), the use of a stand-alone arbitration agreement might be the way to go, state law permitting.

As always, be sure to check with your lawyer before deciding one way or the other.

Scott v. EFN Investments, LLC, 2009 U.S. App. LEXIS 3035 (11th Cir. (S.D. Fla.) February 17, 2009).

"Waive" Goodbye to Your Arbitration Agreement
April 2009
By Thomas B. Hudson

So you took our suggestion and included an arbitration agreement in your buyers order or retail installment sale agreement, and then an unreasonable customer with an unreasonable complaint (who just wouldn't be satisfied) sued you. The customer's lawyer, wanting to gain some leverage in pressing his client's claim, has asserted that his client is suing on behalf of a class and has demanded punitive damages in an amount that seems to have no end of zeroes.

No problem. After all, you've heard us say for years that an arbitration agreement with a class action waiver is the best initial defense against a class action lawsuit or a big dollar punitive damages claim, so you're in good shape, right?

Maybe yes, maybe no. Having your arbitration agreement in place is the first step in defending your dealership, but you have to know how to use the thing.

Plaintiffs' lawyers have a bagful of tricks that they employ to convince courts that a dealer's arbitration provision is invalid or that something the dealer has done has resulted in a waiver by the dealer of its right to enforce the arbitration agreement against the consumer. A recent case dealt with such a waiver argument.

Don Wahls leased a car from Ed Voyles Jeep-Chrysler, Inc. The lease agreement, ultimately assigned to DaimlerChrysler Financial Services Americas, LLC, included an arbitration provision.

Wahls eventually sued Ed Voyles and DaimlerChrysler Financial for breach of contract and fraud. Ed Voyles and DaimlerChrysler Financial moved to compel arbitration. The trial court denied the motion, finding that, by engaging in certain litigation procedural maneuvers, Ed Voyles and DaimlerChrysler Financial had waived their right to arbitration. Ed Voyles appealed.

The Georgia Court of Appeals agreed with the trial court that Ed Voyles and DaimlerChrysler Financial had waived their right to arbitration. Generally, a party waives its right to arbitration if "under the totality of the circumstances, the party has acted inconsistently with the arbitration right, and, in so acting, has in some way prejudiced the other party." Courts look to how far into the litigation process the parties are and whether any party has taken advantage of judicial discovery, which is not permitted under the Federal Arbitration Act.

In this case, the appellate court found that the parties had not progressed too far into litigation—DaimlerChrysler Financial invoked its right to arbitration within four weeks after filing its answer, and Ed Voyles invoked its right within eight weeks. However, DaimlerChrysler Financial had served Wahls with discovery requests and received responses to those requests before moving to compel arbitration. Ed Voyles had scheduled and then cancelled Wahls' deposition before invoking its arbitration right. The appellate court concluded that both DaimlerChrysler Financial and Ed Voyles took actions inconsistent with their arbitration rights, which could have prejudiced Wahls.

Not good.

If you find yourself on the pointy end of a lawsuit, and you're looking to your arbitration agreement for your first line of defense, you should direct your defense lawyer not to take any steps in connection with the litigation that would tempt a court to conclude that you had waived your right to invoke arbitration.

Of course, that doesn't assure that a plaintiffs' lawyer won't find other inventive ways of arguing to the court that your arbitration agreement shouldn't be enforced, but it at least makes that plaintiffs' lawyer work a bit harder.

Ed Voyles Jeep-Chrysler, Inc. v. Wahls, 2008 Ga. App. LEXIS 1343 (Ga. App. November 26, 2008).

Dueling Arbitration Agreements

June 2009

By Thomas B. Hudson

John Adamson, a deaf man, bought a Dodge Caravan from Cherry Hill Dodge. Adamson financed the Dodge by signing a retail installment contract that was subsequently assigned to Triad Financial Corporation.

The retail installment contract contained an arbitration agreement. Adamson also signed a freestanding, separate arbitration agreement that contained terms that were somewhat different from the arbitration terms in the retail installment contract.

Adamson sued the dealership, Triad, and DaimlerChrysler Financial Services, alleging that the defendants violated the Americans with Disabilities Act, the Equal Credit Opportunity Act, the New Jersey Law Against Discrimination, the New Jersey Loan Broker Act, the New Jersey Consumer Fraud Act, and the New Jersey Truth in Consumer Contract Act, and claiming conversion. Adamson also sought declaratory relief. Adamson alleged that during the course of the negotiations, he requested a sign language interpreter, but Cherry Hill Dodge refused to provide one. He also alleged various other forms of misconduct by the dealership.

DaimlerChrysler answered Adamson's complaint and brought cross-claims against the other defendants. Cherry Hill

Dodge and Triad moved to dismiss, arguing that Adamson had agreed to arbitrate his claims.

Adamson argued that the fact that he had signed two separate arbitration agreements rendered both of them unenforceable. This is an argument that we've seen used successfully, and in New Jersey courts, no less. Not this time, however!

The U.S. District Court for the District of New Jersey rejected Adamson's argument, finding that an agreement to arbitrate existed. Adamson then argued that the arbitration agreements should not be enforced because they were unconscionable. Adamson offered two arguments regarding unconscionability. He claimed that it was unconscionable of the dealer to have him sign the arbitration provisions without a sign language interpreter, and he said that the costs of arbitration were too high.

The court found that Adamson failed to meet his burden of establishing that the arbitration agreement itself was unconscionable solely because he signed the agreement without the benefit of a sign language interpreter, but concluded that further evidence was required to determine if arbitration would be prohibitively expensive and thus unconscionable. Therefore, the court ordered limited discovery on the sole issue of the costs of arbitration and Adamson's inability to pay those costs, as compared to the costs of litigation.

So, the dealership escaped the "dueling arbitration provisions" argument. Whether the two agreements will be judged to be unenforceable because of the cost to Adamson of arbitration will have to wait for another day.

Adamson v. Foulke Management Corp., 2009 U.S. Dist. LEXIS 30099 (D.N.J. April 6, 2009).

CHAPTER 9

Nonsignatory Party Entitled to
Enforce Arbitration Agreement
June 2009
By Thomas B. Hudson

Usually a party has to sign a contract in order to be able to enforce it. That isn't always the case, however, and that can be good news for parties that have some relationship to a dealer's sale and financing agreements, even though their signatures don't end up appearing on the bottom line.

Joan Lindsley entered into a retail installment contract with Dodge of Blaine, Inc., for the purchase of a 2003 Dodge Stratus. The contract, which contained an arbitration provision, was assigned to Chrysler Financial.

Lindsley fell behind on her payments, and MFR, a repossession company, and its alleged agents, Thomas Kingore and Anthony Cady, repossessed her vehicle. Lindsley sued, alleging that Chrysler Financial, the MFR defendants, and Bramacint, a debt collector, repossessed her car without the required written notice and, in the process, trespassed on her property and assaulted and battered her.

Chrysler Financial and MFR both moved to compel arbitration of Lindsley's claims. Chrysler Financial and MFR asserted that Lindsley's claims against MFR, Kingore, Cady, and Bramacint arose out of the contract between Lindsley and Chrysler Financial and that the broadly worded arbitration clause encompassed all disputes arising out of or relating to the contract.

MFR asserted that even though it had not signed the arbitration provision, it was entitled to enforce it. Lindsley argued that MFR was not privy to the contract and that MFR never signed the contract or agreed to arbitrate potential disputes.

The U.S. District Court for the District of Minnesota

concluded that MFR was entitled to elect arbitration. Referencing another case for authority, the court determined that a nonsignatory to an arbitration agreement can, under certain circumstances, compel arbitration under an agreement. In particular, the court noted, a signatory may be bound with a nonsignatory "at the nonsignatory's insistence" if there is a close relationship between the involved entities and a relationship between the alleged wrongs and the nonsignatory's duties under the contract.

The court, noting that MFR and Kingore had elected arbitration, determined that the claims against them should be submitted to arbitration. Because Bramacint and Cady had not elected arbitration, the court determined that Lindsley's claims against them should remain before the court. The court also granted Chrysler Financial's motion to stay Lindsley's entire lawsuit pending a resolution in arbitration.

So, if you are involved on the edges of a dealer's sales financing agreement with a customer, and if that agreement contains an arbitration agreement you'd like to be able to enforce, don't assume that you are out of luck just because you haven't signed it. There are exceptions to every rule, and your lawyer might be able to convince a court that you're entitled to enforce that agreement you didn't sign!

Lindsley v. Bramacint, LLC, 2009 U.S. Dist. LEXIS 37138 (D. Minn. April 30, 2009).

Buy-Here, Pay-Here; Leasing; and Rental Programs

CHAPTER 10

So, you think that running a buy-here, pay-here dealership would be simple and uncomplicated, huh? After all, with in-house financing, there would no hustling to hang paper. You'd be able to unload all those cars that don't fit in your special finance department mix. Piece of cake, right?

Think again.

Dealers brave enough to venture into the buy-here, pay-here world are subject to the same body of laws and regulations that govern traditional dealers. But, unlike their traditional brethren, they also need to master the laws that govern the servicing and collection aspects of the auto finance world. That means a whole additional layer of compliance complexity, and, frankly, a bunch of additional ways to attract the attention of plaintiffs' lawyers and regulators.

And, if that wasn't hard enough, the buy-here, pay-here market is changing. Fast. Today's buy-here, pay-here operators tend to be highly sophisticated. They use complicated accounting techniques to track the success of the portfolios they hold and service. Many use starter interrupt devices, GPS devices, or other technology in an effort to keep skips under control and to manage collections.

We see all sorts of new players entering the market, with all sorts of backgrounds, such as franchised dealers, and title and payday lenders. Each of these players brings its own experiences, shaping the face of buy-here, pay-here.

Quick to jump into the mix, many vendors are offering dealers alternatives to the traditional buy-here, pay-here framework, such as lease-here, pay-here and rent-to-own. Hoping that these new programs will improve collections, reduce regulatory burdens, or expand their customer base, many dealers are spreading out into relatively unknown and unproven territory. The jury is still out on how well these new programs will fare.

These are just a few of the many reasons why we think that compliance issues that arise from buy-here, pay-here and similar leasing or rental programs are some of the more interesting issues around. After you read the articles in this chapter, you just might agree.

Pay Now or Pay Later
December 2007
By Thomas B. Hudson

A few years ago, I attended one of Ken Shilson's Buy-Here, Pay-Here Collections Conferences in Houston. My friend Ingram Walters was playing his usual role as emcee, while I was doing the legal presentation. Ingram was gathering questions from the audience and lobbing them to me for answers.

One of the questions seemed like a real stumper. Ingram asked, "What legal mistakes have you seen dealers make that have put their businesses at risk?"

For a moment, I couldn't think of an apt response. Then I recalled an event a couple of weeks earlier that fit the question pretty well.

A fellow had called me from a sales finance company that we represent. It seems that his company was interested in buying a substantial part of a Georgia buy-here, pay-here (BHPH) dealer's portfolio of retail installment sale contracts. My contact wanted me to look over a few deal files and tell him if the documentation looked good. He faxed the sample deals to me, and, with a quick glance, I saw what I would characterize as a fatal problem with the retail installment sale form the dealer was using. Federal law requires that certain Truth in Lending disclosures that usually are included in retail installment sale contracts be segregated from other TILA disclosures. The Federal Reserve Board staff says that segregation can be accomplished by outlining the disclosures in a box or by bold print dividing lines, by using a different color background, or by using a different type style. Whoever had designed this dealer's forms (they looked like they had been printed by a small business printing company) hadn't taken any of the staff's suggestions, but had decided to surround the disclosures with lines of asterisks.

That was troublesome enough, but one of the required federal disclosures that should be contained in the segregated area was simply missing.

I called my client and explained that, although I'd only spent about three minutes on the forms, I thought the TILA violations were serious enough to be fatal. He agreed.

So, here's a BHPH dealer, at the point in the growth of his business when it's time to liquidate to free up cash for new deals, and he can't do it because his documents have obvious and serious legal problems.

A week or so after the Houston conference, I was presented with another example of a potentially fatal dealer mistake. The same finance company called with a similar assignment, only this time the BHPH dealer was in North Carolina. Again, the dealer needed some cash, and my client was considering a bulk purchase of contracts.

When the documents from this deal were faxed to me, I couldn't believe my eyes. This dealer wasn't using a retail installment sale contract to evidence his credit sales of vehicles. Instead, he had found some business forms company, and he had bought documents titled "Note and Security Agreement." He was using loan documents for his credit sale transactions—that's about as elementary a no-no as you will ever see in this business. Again, here's another dealer stuck with a portfolio that he won't be able to unload, because anyone thinking about buying it will have someone like me look at it, and the portfolio's documentation won't pass muster.

In both of these instances, the dealer could have had an experienced auto finance lawyer look over the forms for a few hundred dollars. If the forms had been found wanting, the dealer could have easily switched to one of the forms providers like LAW or Bankers Systems, or he could have used a form from his state dealer association. Any of those solutions probably would have resulted in a saleable portfolio. To save a few hundred dollars, these two dealers omitted a critical compliance step that you can bet any sales finance company in the market for the dealers' contracts will be sure to take.

Pay now, in the form of a few greenbacks, or pay later, with an illiquid business. Your call.

Run Like Hell

April 2008
By Thomas B. Hudson

I'm from the South, and remember vividly the first time I heard the instructions for planting kudzu: "Throw it on the ground, and run like hell."

I think about the kudzu every time I pick up the phone and talk to a dealer who says that he is in the rent-to-own or lease-to-own business. Why? Because there is more misinformation about these programs than any other independent dealership topic that I know of, that's why.

Occasionally we are asked to actually look at one of these programs before a dealer implements it. There are two tell-tale signs that we look for that almost always spell trouble, one in lease-here, pay-here (LHPH) programs, the other in rent-to-own, or RTO, programs.

The LHPH problem is the so-called "dollar-out" lease. We see these frequently.

In such a lease, the lessee is offered the option to buy the leased vehicle at the end of the scheduled lease term for $1 or for some other nominal amount. The problem with such a provision in a lease is that, depending on the definitions in your state's law, it can turn the "lease" into a retail installment sale contract for the purposes of state law, which means that the so-called "lease" has to contain all of the provisions and disclosures required by the state's retail installment sale act. At the federal level, such a provision has the same effect, making the "lease" subject to Federal Reserve Board Regulation Z (a real lease would be subject to Regulation M, which is a completely different kettle of fish). Because the documents were never intended to comply with these state and federal laws, they are often in flagrant violation of them.

The RTO problem that scares us to death is the RTO program that has an initial rental term of more than four months. The problem with a long initial rental term is that it brings the RTO program within the scope of the definitions of Regulation M. Because the RTO programs that we see seldom comply with Reg. M, the resulting documents are full of federal violations.

These certainly are not the only problems we are seeing in LHPH and RTO programs, but these issues just seem to be the flavor of the month. Usually a program that has one of these problems has plenty of additional problems.

So when the LHPH or RTO salesperson comes calling, be careful. Some companies offering these programs are responsible outfits that have done their homework. Others are, shall we say, not so diligent.

We've developed a pretty good test for determining which is which. We tell dealers that when they are offered any new program (not just LHPH or RTO, but any program) by a vendor, they should request copies of the vendor's legal opinion that says, without too many unsettling qualifications, that the program complies with all applicable federal and state laws.

When the dealer asks for such an opinion, the vendor either provides it or not. If no opinion is available, there's a reasonably good possibility that none exists. In such a case, we advise the dealer to run like hell (that's a legal term that means "run like hell").

If the vendor produces an opinion, we first review it to see who wrote it and if the author's credentials indicate whether he or she is likely to have a clue what he or she is talking about. We then review the text of the opinion itself and see whether it looks like the lawyer has identified and answered all of the important issues that such an opinion needs to address, and whether we agree with it.

It's 10 O'Clock—Do You Know Where Your Collection Letters Are?

May 2008

By Emily Marlow Beck

Do you remember that popular media admonition from years back, "It's 10 o'clock. Do you know where your children are?" I feel the same way about collection letters, particularly in the buy-here, pay-here business.

So, let me ask the question: Do you know what your collection letters say? I mean, really, truly, really? A recent case brought this issue to mind. Here are the facts.

Jeanne Mancuso bought a car from Adams Chevrolet, which assigned the retail installment sale contract financing the purchase to Long Beach Acceptance Corporation. Mancuso defaulted on the contract, and Long Beach repossessed the vehicle.

Long Beach sent Mancuso a "Notice of Our Plan to Sell Property." The notice was substantially similar to the "safe harbor" format provided under the Uniform Commercial Code (UCC), but it informed Mancuso that, in addition to paying the full amount owed on the contract, Mancuso would be required to provide Long Beach with proof of insurance in order to redeem the vehicle. Mancuso did not redeem the vehicle, and Long Beach sold it at auction.

Mancuso sued Long Beach, claiming that the Long Beach notice did not comply with Article 9 of the UCC. She specifically claimed that the "proof of proper insurance" language was misleading and misstated her redemption rights because, if the entire balance were to be paid in full, then Long Beach would have no right to require proof of insurance because, at that point, it would have no interest in the vehicle. The trial court dismissed Mancuso's claim without stating a basis for the dismissal. Mancuso appealed.

The Missouri Court of Appeals held that the inclusion of the insurance requirement was not an "error" in the sense of Section 9-614(5). As such, Mancuso needed to plead that the notice was not "reasonable" as required by Section 400.9-611(b). The court concluded that the notice language may be unreasonable if it causes the debtor to believe that something is required for redemption when it is, in fact, not legally required.

However, Mancuso's contractual obligation to insure the vehicle continued even after the car was in the creditor's possession. Accordingly, reasoned the court, the creditor is allowed to require "proof of insurance" or the reimbursement of the cost of its insurance as a condition of redemption, because it is part of the obligation secured by the collateral. As such, the inclusion of the insurance requirement in the notice was reasonable as a matter of law in view of the fact that the maintenance of insurance on the vehicle was "an obligation secured by the collateral." The appeals court affirmed the trial court's holding.

So, the creditor came out on top in this case. (Only after spending who knows how much on legal fees.) But, this case still concerns me. Why? Because I spend an awful lot of time looking at collection letters, that's why.

You might be surprised to know that many buy-here, pay-here dealers I've worked with do not know that the contents of their letters can be heavily regulated, or that many state laws provide "safe harbors" for certain letters. They also don't realize that the content of their collection letters can vary depending on the terms and conditions of the retail installment sale contract they are attempting to enforce.

Other buy-here, pay-here dealers get this, and some actually ask their legal counsel to review collection letters to ensure the letters don't miss the mark. Unfortunately, many of these same dealers don't have internal controls to ensure that their collections employees don't "modify" the documents to beef up collection efforts. It's easy to see how an overzealous collector could add a few lines to your lawyer-approved collection letters and render them noncompliant (not to mention, waste all that money you spent on legal fees). Don't forget that, in the case discussed above, the letters used by the collector were substantially similar to the statutorily prescribed "safe harbor" letters, but for an additional sentence about insurance.

So, what's a buy-here, pay-here dealer to do? It's time to rein in your collection letters! You should have your letters reviewed (initially and periodically) by competent counsel. Once you've got a set of letters that you feel comfortable with, set up some internal controls to make sure that your well-intended collectors don't modify what you paid your lawyer to put in place for you. Trust me, you'll sleep much better!

Hey Buddy, Can You Spare a Car?

May 2009

By Thomas B. Hudson

An opinion in a recent case started me thinking about dealers and loaner cars. Dealers know that anyone in today's society who is injured assumes that someone else is responsible and starts looking for the deepest pocket in sight. In situations in which dealers provide loaners, often the deepest pocket around is the dealer (along with the dealer's insurer).

One way that a plaintiff's lawyer will try to worm his or her way into a dealer's pocket when a loaner car accident occurs is to argue that the dealer was negligent in entrusting a vehicle to the dealer's customer. Note that this argument isn't a "vicarious liability" argument, with the plaintiff arguing that the dealer is liable for the driver's actions solely because the dealer owns the loaner car. Here, the argument is that the dealership was itself negligent when it turned the keys over to its customer.

First, I'll tell you what happened in this case. Then, I'll tell you why I thought it was worth writing about it.

Shane Reph was in a car accident with Ghron Hubbard. Hubbard was driving a truck owned by Southland Idealease, LLC, when he crossed the centerline and hit Reph, injuring both the driver and the passenger.

Hubbard had rented the truck from Southland to use within

the scope of his employment at CP Louisiana, Inc. Hubbard completed a driving academy course and obtained his commercial driver's license before renting the truck.

Reph sued Southland, CP, and Hubbard for negligence. Southland moved for summary judgment on the grounds that it had no liability to Reph. Southland argued that it properly maintained the truck and that Hubbard was properly licensed to rent the truck. Southland also claimed that the Graves Amendment (a provision in a federal transportation bill passed a few years back that mostly did away with vicarious liability) preempted any state law claim based on vicarious liability.

Reph opposed the motion and argued that Southland negligently entrusted Hubbard with the truck and that Southland had a duty to investigate Hubbard's driving experience before renting him the truck. Reph claimed that Southland was negligent by doing nothing more than merely verifying that Hubbard had a commercial driver's license and confirming that he was not impaired at the time of the lease.

The U.S. District Court for the Eastern District of Louisiana granted Southland's motion. The court found that, under Louisiana law, a lessor (one who leases a vehicle to another) can be liable under a negligent entrustment theory only if the lessor had actual or constructive knowledge that the lessee was incompetent to operate the vehicle or had a disability that was apparent at the time of the lease.

Louisiana courts have held that a "prospective lessee's presentation of a valid license satisfies the lessor's duty of ordinary care and inquiry as to the prospective lessee's ability to operate a motor vehicle."

Reph argued that Southland had a heightened standard of care because it held its own company drivers to a higher standard. The court held that Reph failed to provide any legal support for that argument. As a result, the court concluded that Southland met its duty by verifying Hubbard's license and confirming that he was not impaired at the time of the lease.

The court also noted that Southland had no duty to investigate Hubbard's past driving experience. Further, the court concluded that Southland engaged in the business of leasing, it leased the vehicle to Hubbard, and the accident occurred during the lease term. Accordingly, the Graves Amendment would preempt any potential state law claim for vicarious liability.

So, the dealer got to skate on this one. OK, but why do we care about this dealer's experience?

I think that this case should serve as a bit of a wake-up call for dealers to examine their loaner policies and documents. The examination will require help from the dealership's lawyer.

The examination should determine what standards, if any, courts or laws in the dealership's state have adopted for those who entrust cars to others. Perhaps the standard in your state will be the same as in Louisiana, but you can't count on that.

Once the standard is determined, the dealership should develop a written policy dealing with loaner cars. Along with the written policy, the dealership should work with its lawyer to develop an agreement for each customer receiving a loaner to sign as a condition of receiving the loaner.

This agreement will address many matters of importance to the dealership, but it will likely contain representations and warranties by the customer regarding the customer's qualifications to operate the car. Other issues that such an agreement might address include limitations on things the driver can do with the car, a list of any other authorized drivers, liability for damage to the loaner, recitations regarding insurance, limitations on mileage, indemnification provisions, remedies for various breaches of the loaner contract, and damages available for such breaches. Once the agreement is completed, it might be worthwhile to run it by the dealership's insurer.

Reph v. Hubbard, 2009 U.S. Dist. LEXIS 19266 (E.D. La. March 10, 2009).

Look Before You Lease—Things to Consider Before Starting a Leasing Program

July 2009

By Thomas J. Buiteweg

Leasing might be a terrific alternative for your dealership. But, you need to know what you are getting into before you start leasing. Here are few things to consider.

Licensing. Your existing licenses might cover leasing, but some states require a separate lessor's license, so you need to check.

Take a fresh look at advertising. The legal rules for advertising a lease are very different from the rules for advertising a credit transaction. You'll need to learn the leasing rules before you take out that ad for your first lease promotion.

Familiarize yourself with lease disclosures and terms. Lease contracts look very different from the credit sale contracts you use now. For example, you won't see any mention of an Annual Percentage Rate or a lease rate in a consumer lease. Lease disclosures focus principally on the amount due at lease signing, the computation of the periodic payments, and the amount due at lease end. You need to be familiar with these disclosures so you can help your customers understand them. You can find a helpful pamphlet called *The Keys to Vehicle Leasing* on the Federal Reserve Board's website—www.federalreserve.gov/pubs/leasing/.

Lease terms are also different from credit sale terms. Most leases provide for a charge for excess wear and mileage at the scheduled end of the lease. How you compute the amount due if the lease ends early is also usually very different from how you figure the remaining balance under a credit sale contract. You need to understand the terms of the lease form you use and make sure you follow them. You also need to make sure your computer system is programmed to properly complete the lease form you choose.

Evaluate servicing and collections. Servicing leases also offers new twists. You might find yourself collecting sales taxes at a different time and/or rate or on a different basis than you do for credit sales. You may also be dealing for the first time with lots of owner issues like registration renewals, parking tickets, unpaid toll-pass fees, and red light camera fines.

Even payoff quotes get more complicated because the payoff amount differs depending on whether the customer is buying or returning the leased vehicle. You also need to be on the lookout for vehicles returned with odometer rollbacks by lessees looking to avoid excess mileage charges.

The legal rules for collections and repossessions can also be different for leases. For example, some states require a cure notice before repossessing a vehicle subject to a security interest, but do not require one before repossessing a leased vehicle. Another big difference—the lessor keeps any surplus after sale of a leased vehicle after repossession, unless the lease contract says otherwise.

Before you decide the grass is greener on the leasing side of the fence, consider that some states require lessors to send the equivalent of a notice of sale to lessees who end their leases early, even without a default. Other states require lessors to send an itemized bill for excess wear charges, regardless of default.

You need to examine your entire servicing and collection process and make adjustments to deal with these and other unique requirements for leases.

Establish owner liability. A few years ago, federal law ended unlimited owner liability for lessors for property damage and physical injury in most circumstances (although some personal injury attorneys are still trying to challenge the law). However, lessors in most states must still satisfy some form of financial responsibility requirements. This means you might still have to pay some amount on these claims (typically $25,000 to $75,000). You need to make sure you have the proper insurance in place.

Make sure the lease is a lease. There are legal, accounting, and tax rules for deciding whether your lease is really a lease versus a credit sale or lending transaction. For example, if your leased vehicle has a $1 residual value and the customer automatically becomes the owner at the end of the lease after making all the payments, the lawyers are going to say your lease is really a credit sale. If your advertising, disclosures, servicing, and collection activities were all based on the assumption that it was a lease, you will probably have done everything wrong. You need to make sure you structure your lease to avoid this result.

Get professional help. The list above is just a quick summary of the issues to think about in deciding whether leasing is a good fit for your dealership and, if it is, putting together a good lease program. Don't try to do it alone. You need help from qualified accounting, insurance, tax, and legal professionals. If you are going to use a vendor's leasing program, make sure the vendor obtained this kind of help with its program. Ask your vendor to show you the accounting, tax, and legal support for its programs.

If you are tempted to take shortcuts with your leasing program, just remember what happens to people who cross a busy highway without looking both ways.

Before You Take the Plunge

August 2009

By Thomas B. Hudson

So you just had your Chrysler dealership shot out from under you, and you're scratching your head, wondering how you are going to occupy your time and keep food on the table while staying in the car business, right? Then you remember hearing about the used car, "buy-here, pay-here" racket. "Hey!" you say, "How tough can that be? I've always had a used car lot; now, all I need to do is sell the cars and collect the money."

We've seen a number of dealers who have had that reaction and who have quickly set up a buy-here, pay-here (BHPH) operation only to discover, after they've gone off the high board, that there's no water in the pool. Let me explain.

Until now, you have been involved in what we at our law firm casually call "the front end" of the car finance deals you have done. You've advertised, gotten the customer to the lot, sold the car, and then arranged for the financing of the car, meanwhile selling additional stuff like service contracts, Guaranteed Auto Protection (GAP), and all those other finance and insurance (F&I) products. You've then taken care of the paperwork with the state and rolled the car.

Now you're about to meet the "back end" of the car finance business, which is where folks like General Motors Acceptance Corporation (GMAC), AmeriCredit, Ford Motor Credit Company (FMCC), and others ply their trade.

For tax reasons, most BHPH dealers do not keep and service the retail installment contracts that result from the credit sales they make to their customers. Instead, they form a "related finance company," which is a separate corporate entity from the dealership. The dealership creates the retail installment contracts, just as it has always done, but then assigns them to its own related finance company (RFC) rather than to GMAC or some other unrelated finance company.

Let's focus for a minute on that RFC. What will that company need to have in place before it starts buying contracts from its related dealer? Here are a few of the things it will need.

Dealer agreement. The RFC and the dealership need to maintain an arms-length relationship. Consequently, they should have written agreements about the business they transact together. One such business is that of buying and selling the retail installment contracts that the dealership creates. The RFC and the dealership should have a "Dealer Agreement" that sets forth the terms and conditions of the RFC's purchase of contracts from the dealership.

License. Many states require a company buying retail installment contracts from dealers to be licensed as a sales finance company (some states might use a different term). The RFC will need such a license in these states. Hint: Do not call the state and ask whether the RFC needs a license "to make car loans." That's not the business the RFC is in—it is buying retail installment contracts from dealers.

Privacy policy and safeguarding policy. Like the dealership, the RFC is a "financial institution" under the federal Gramm-Leach-Bliley Act and the FTC's Privacy Regulations. It will need its own versions of privacy and safeguarding policies.

Red Flag policy. Like the dealership, the RFC will need its own Red Flag policy. Hint: Photocopying the dealership's policy probably won't work since the duties of sales finance companies and dealerships are somewhat different under the FTC's rules.

Underwriting Manual. The RFC should maintain an Underwriting Manual setting forth the criteria that it uses to determine whether to buy the retail installment contracts that the dealership will present to it for purchase. These Underwriting Manuals serve several important business purposes, such as ensuring that the contracts being purchased are of a consistent quality, but they are also important in assuring that the credit criteria and the credit application process employed by the RFC comply with the federal Equal Credit Opportunity Act and any state anti-discrimination laws.

Collections Manual. It is difficult to overemphasize the role of collections in a BHPH operation. BHPH dealers who do not collect effectively don't remain in business long. The Collections Manual provides a blueprint for effective collection procedures but, like the Underwriting Manual, also has a legal function because it will be constructed to guide collectors in accordance with the collection laws that apply to them. Hint: The federal Fair Debt Collection Practices Act (FDCPA) doesn't apply to assignees that acquire retail installment contracts that are not in default at the time of the assignment, but we nevertheless advise such assignees to follow the FDCPA's requirements as "best practices." The Collections Manual might also contain the collection letters that the company uses. Often, state law dictates the content of these letters, and the requirements for collection correspondence can be very extensive. In addition, the Collections Manual will set forth the RFC's repossession policies and procedures. The RFC's lawyers must review the Collections Manual, and especially the collection letters and the repossession policies and procedures.

Those are just the major topics that come to mind. Add to these such requirements as OFAC, IRS cash reporting rules, do not call, do not fax, do not e-mail, the Americans with Disabilities Act, the Fair Credit Reporting Act, and any number of state laws, and you'll have some sense of the structure the RFC needs to have in place before it buys the first deal from the dealership.

A final hint: This is not a job for a do-it-yourselfer. Get yourself a qualified lawyer and a qualified accountant. You are going to need them.

So, go ahead and take that dive off the high board. But first, make sure that there's some water in the pool.

CHAPTER 10

Chapter 11

Bankruptcy

Unless you are a bankruptcy lawyer, you will need to get your head around a few basic concepts before the things we discuss in this chapter will make a lot of sense. The best way to think about bankruptcy is to imagine a bunch of vultures (the creditors) circling a carcass (the "estate" of the unfortunate bankrupt person), with each vulture trying to snatch anything it can. Unlike avian vultures, however, carnivorous vultures as creditors have rules to follow. Here are a few of them.

The vultures all have claims against the bankrupt estate. The claims, however, are not all equal.

Some claims are "unsecured." A typical sort of unsecured claim is a credit card debt. All the credit card company can rely on is the cardholder's promise to repay the balance due. There is no "security" for the debt if it isn't paid; thus the debt is "unsecured." Unsecured debts in consumer bankruptcies are usually worthless, or, at best, worth a few cents on the dollar.

Other claims are "secured." This means that the creditor has some "security" in addition to the consumer's promise to repay the debt. Usually, in this book, that security is an interest in a car, and the creditor is said to have a "security interest" in the car.

Some security interests are better to have than others. When, for example, the creditor finances the purchase of a car, the creditor's security interest is a "purchase money security interest," or PMSI. The bankruptcy rules give the holder of a PMSI some rights that the holder of a non-PMSI doesn't have.

A security interest can be "perfected" or "unperfected." In broad terms, a perfected security interest will prevail over claims by third parties, such as those by vultures who have not "perfected" their interests, and, very importantly, by the trustee in bankruptcy, whose job it is to marshal as much property of the debtor as possible to permit the payment of as many claims as possible. Usually, a creditor "perfects" its security interest in a debtor's car by noting the security interest on the car's title.

Most bankruptcy cases are fights between creditors and the trustee over which one has the best claim to the debtor's property that is the subject of the security interest. When more than one vulture, er, excuse me, creditor, has a security interest in a car, it is necessary to determine which one will prevail. Generally, when the security interests are of the same type, the first vulture to be granted the security interest will have priority over others whose security interests were created later. When one vulture's security interested is perfected, and another vulture's interest is unperfected, the vulture with the perfected security interest will prevail. Even the trustee will lose a priority fight to the vulture with a perfected security interest.

The articles in this chapter deal with a number of these concepts. You will see how the courts grapple with these concepts as they apply the bankruptcy rules to determine how all of the competing interests in a bankruptcy proceeding are treated. In other words, when the vultures fight, who wins?

Read on . . .

Early Bird Avoids the Loss

September 2008

By Thomas J. Buiteweg

Title applications are taking longer than you like because of too much paperwork? Didn't get that title paperwork quite right, so it came back? Do you need to worry? You bet—if it takes more than 30 days for you to file the right paperwork, and your customer files for bankruptcy.

Generally, a bankruptcy trustee can avoid any lien granted on the debtor's property within 90 days of the bankruptcy.

There is an exception if the lien secures the vehicle's purchase price and it is perfected within 30 days after the buyer takes delivery of the vehicle. In most states, "perfection" occurs when the application for the certificate of title with the lienholder information is filed with or received by the state titling agency.

If, as a dealer, you don't file a proper title application within 30 days of the sale, the bankruptcy trustee can, and probably will, avoid the lien on the vehicle if the bankruptcy filing was within 90 days of the date you filed the title application. If that happens, whoever owns the contract will be an unsecured creditor in the bankruptcy and isn't likely to get paid more than pennies on the dollar.

If you sold the contract, your finance source agreements probably make you responsible for any losses resulting from your failure to perfect the finance source's lien in time. If the customer filed a Chapter 13 bankruptcy, in many cases the finance source would have been paid in full, if its lien were perfected. If that is the case, you may have to pay the full balance owed on the contract. If you find yourself in that situation, take a look at your insurance policy—you might have errors and omissions coverage that will pay the loss.

Let's consider the predicament of the dealer in a recent Illinois bankruptcy case. The dealer bought a used Grand Prix that had a certificate of title issued by Hawaii. On April 6, 2007, a customer bought the Grand Prix and financed it with a third party. The dealer delivered a title application that included the lienholder information, an assigned Hawaii certificate of title, and the required fees to the Illinois Secretary of State within 21 days of the sale. The Secretary of State returned the documents saying the dealer needed to get title to the Grand Prix in its own name before it could sell it. The dealer corrected the paperwork, received a title in its name, and resubmitted a new title application for the customer reflecting the lienholder information. The Illinois Secretary of State received the new title application on July 19, 2007, or about two and a half months after the sale. The customer filed for bankruptcy on September 25, 2007.

The bankruptcy trustee successfully avoided the third party's lien because the proper paperwork was filed more than 30 days after the customer took possession of the vehicle.

The lesson here? If you wait too long to file the title and registration application, you might find yourself in trouble with the state or your customer. Many states require dealers to apply for registrations and titles within a specific amount of time after the sale.

For this reason, you might think about bumping up a couple of inches the filing of that paperwork on your "to do" list.

In re Meyers, 2008 WL 2782748 (Bankr. C.D. Ill. July 15, 2008).

Floor Plan Fraud or Breach of Contract?
September 2008
By Thomas B. Hudson

The purpose of our bankruptcy system is to permit debtors to have their indebtedness discharged so that they can get a new start. Not all debts can be discharged in a bankruptcy proceeding, however. If the debtor has engaged in bad acts, it's possible for a creditor to get a court to declare the debtor's debt, or a part of the debt, as "nondischargeable." That's what this recent case was about.

Clayton Cline owned Mountain Chevrolet. Mountain Chevrolet obtained floor plan financing from General Motors Acceptance Corporation. Cline executed a personal guaranty to

GMAC in connection with the floor plan arrangement.

[Editor's note: Floor plan is industry jargon describing the financing of a dealer's inventory.]

Mountain Chevrolet sold 131 vehicles subject to the floor plan arrangement but did not pay any of the proceeds to GMAC. Mountain Chevrolet then filed a Chapter 11 bankruptcy petition that was subsequently converted to Chapter 7.

GMAC filed a proof of claim for $2,486,699.77 against Mountain Chevrolet. Cline then filed a personal Chapter 7 bankruptcy petition and listed GMAC as an unsecured creditor for $2,400,000.

GMAC asked the bankruptcy court to classify Cline's personal obligation as nondischargeable. Cline failed to answer the complaint, and the bankruptcy court entered a default judgment for GMAC.

The bankruptcy court held an evidentiary hearing (conducted so that evidence might be presented) to determine the amount of the debt that was nondischargeable. The bankruptcy court found that Cline spent $444,105.94 of the proceeds to satisfy personal obligations and spent the remaining amounts to pay debts owed by Mountain Chevrolet. The bankruptcy court first determined that, when Cline used the sale proceeds to pay personal debts, he committed larceny against GMAC, and those amounts were not dischargeable.

The bankruptcy court then found that, when Cline used the proceeds to satisfy corporate debts owed by Mountain Chevrolet, he acted in breach of his contract with GMAC but did not commit embezzlement or fraud. Therefore, the bankruptcy court concluded that the amount of the debt related to paying Mountain Chevrolet's obligations was dischargeable. GMAC appealed.

The U.S. District Court for the Northern District of Ohio noted that the bankruptcy court's focus on whether Cline applied the sale proceeds to pay his corporate debt or his personal debt was not relevant. The issue was whether Cline defrauded GMAC. The district court found that Cline had an obligation under the floor plan documents to hold any vehicle sales proceeds in trust in order to pay GMAC; therefore, when Cline used those funds to pay other debts, he violated the trust relationship.

The court then noted that the only issue left to establish fraud and to render the entire debt nondischargeable was whether Cline acted with intent to defraud GMAC. The district court noted that there were no facts on the record that could be applied to determine Cline's intent. Accordingly, the district court remanded the case to the bankruptcy court to determine whether Cline had the requisite intent to commit fraud.

Note that the court has not found that Cline did anything wrong—that's the purpose of sending the matter back to bankruptcy court. If the bankruptcy court determines that Cline intended to commit fraud, GMAC will almost certainly get the ruling of nondischargeability it is after, and Cline may find himself out a few hundred thousand dollars.

General Motors Acceptance Corp. v. Cline, 2008 WL 2740777 (N.D. Ohio July 3, 2008).

Creditors Win on the Treatment of Negative Equity in Chapter 13 Bankruptcy

September 2008

By Tom Buiteweg

You thought bankruptcy was always bad for a creditor. Well, it is. Sometimes the only good news is that it could have been worse.

Take, for example, the recent line of bankruptcy court cases concluding that a vehicle creditor's secured claim gets "crammed down" to the vehicle's current value in a Chapter 13 bankruptcy just because the creditor included the customer's negative equity as part of the purchase financing. If the creditor's secured claim is reduced to the value of the vehicle, the creditor's claim for the rest of the amount due under the finance contract is unsecured and unlikely to be paid.

That's a really bad result considering how hard vehicle creditors fought to get Congress to pass a bankruptcy reform provision in 2005 designed to stop just that kind of cramdown from happening. Under this provision, creditors financing the vehicle's purchase price were supposed to get paid in full in the debtor's Chapter 13 plan, as long as the financing transaction was within 910 days of the bankruptcy filing and the car was purchased for the debtor's personal use. This provision is now known as the "hanging paragraph." (It was originally named for how it "hangs" by itself in the bankruptcy statute. Given the dozens of cases it has spawned, the name seems to be taking on a new, ominous, meaning.)

Some bankruptcy courts have found that negative equity is not part of the purchase price and that a creditor that finances it is not eligible for protection from cramdown under the hanging paragraph. Other bankruptcy courts disagreed. They found that "price" is a broad enough concept under retail installment sales acts and the Uniform Commercial Code to include negative equity. These courts have found that the creditor that finances negative equity is still eligible for protection under the hanging paragraph.

The good news is that the U.S. Court of Appeals for the Eleventh Circuit recently weighed in on the issue on the vehicle creditors' side. In this—the first—federal appellate court decision to address the question, the Eleventh Circuit concluded that price was a broad enough concept to include negative equity. As a result, a creditor's secured claim is still eligible for protection from cramdown under the hanging paragraph, even if the creditor finances negative equity. That's good news for dealers when they hold their own paper and also good news when they sell it, because it makes contracts that include negative equity less risky to purchase.

Sometimes you find yourself cheering when you just get to keep something you already had.

[Editor's note: "Negative equity" is the phrase used to describe a circumstance in which the debtor owes more on his or her vehicle than the vehicle is worth. When a dealer accepts for trade-in a vehicle with negative equity, the dealer often finances the negative equity as part of the new credit transaction.]

In re Graupner, 2008 WL 2993570 (11th Cir. (M.D. Ga.) August 6, 2008).

Take the Bad News With the Good

November 2008

By Shelley B. Fowler

A couple of months ago, we brought you really good news on the bankruptcy front. Tom Buiteweg shared with you that the U.S. Court of Appeals for the Eleventh Circuit, the first federal circuit court to weigh in on the issue, concluded that financing of negative equity could not hurt a creditor in the event a car buyer eventually filed for bankruptcy.

Before the Eleventh Circuit's opinion in *In re Graupner,* some bankruptcy courts found that negative equity is not part of the creditor's purchase-money obligation because it is not part of the price of the collateral or value to enable the buyer to acquire rights in the collateral. These courts concluded that a creditor that finances negative equity is not eligible for protection from cramdown under the Bankruptcy Code.

Other bankruptcy courts disagreed. They found that "price" is a broad enough concept under retail installment sales acts and the Uniform Commercial Code to include negative equity. Also, they determined that the purchase of the new car and the financing of negative equity on the buyer's trade-in are one transaction. These courts found that the creditor that finances negative equity is still eligible for protection from cramdown under the Bankruptcy Code.

Thankfully, the Eleventh Circuit came down on the side of the second group of courts.

However, often good news comes with bad news; so, here's the bad news . . . Vehicle creditors had hoped that the Eleventh Circuit's decision would end the issue once and for all. Well, no sooner had the ink dried on the circuit court's order than at least one bankruptcy court declined to follow the Eleventh Circuit's lead.

The U.S. Bankruptcy Court for the Southern District of Mississippi agreed with the bankruptcy trustee that the financing of negative equity, although "increasingly commonplace," is not part of a creditor's purchase-money security interest. The court concluded that the financing of negative equity and the purchase of a new car are two distinct transactions and that "Congress could have enacted specific language . . . in order to protect the negative equity as PMSI," but did not do so. Therefore, the bankruptcy court concluded that negative equity is not part of a creditor's purchase-money security interest and the claim of a creditor that finances negative equity is subject to cramdown.

The bankruptcy court distinguished the Eleventh Circuit's opinion in *Graupner*. It concluded that language in the Georgia Motor Vehicle Sales Finance Act, which is not present in Mississippi's Motor Vehicle Sales Finance Law, dictated the Eleventh Circuit's conclusion that negative equity is part of a creditor's purchase-money security interest.

In this court's view, the question of whether negative equity is or isn't part of the creditor's PMSI turned on definitions found in the state's finance laws.

But, all is not lost. Another bankruptcy court, this time the U.S. Bankruptcy Court for the Northern District of Alabama, relied on *Graupner* in concluding that the "inclusion of negative equity on a trade-in vehicle does not destroy the creditor's purchase-money security interest in the entire transaction."

So, are we back to the drawing board on this issue? Not exactly. There is still only one federal circuit court opinion out there right now, and that one sides with creditors. (Note: Federal circuit courts are the second-highest federal courts, with only the U.S. Supreme Court above them.) But we've learned that there is at least one court willing to reject that decision as based upon state law. What we need are more circuit court opinions that follow the Eleventh Circuit's lead. The Second Circuit recently heard argument in the case of *In re Peaslee*, in which the creditor lost at the bankruptcy court level but won at the district court level, but decided to certify the question to the New York Court of Appeals.

Keep your fingers crossed and stay tuned!

In re Busby, 2008 WL 4104184 (Bankr. S.D. Miss. August 28, 2008). *In re Harless*, 2008 WL 3821781 (Bankr. N.D. Ala. August 13, 2008).

Physical Possession of Vehicle Title, Without More, Does Not Perfect Security Interest

November 2008

By Thomas B. Hudson

Marvin Moye was a used car dealer. Hardy Rawls Enterprises loaned Moye money under a "handshake deal" to pay for the purchase of motor vehicles for Moye's inventory. Hardy Rawls contended that, because it supplied the money to enable acquisition of the vehicles, and because it held physical possession of the vehicle titles, it held a first lien on the vehicles.

A lot of people in the car business believe that a seller who holds on to a vehicle's title somehow has a perfected security interest in the vehicle when it is sold to a dealer. That's evidently what Hardy Rawls thought because the lender did not file a financing statement, cause its lien to be listed on the certificates of title, or give the requisite legal notice of its financing to other lenders.

Automotive Finance Corporation also lent money to Moye, but filed a UCC-1 financing statement that covered vehicle inventory.

What happened next? Surprise, surprise—Moye files for bankruptcy. Goes down like the Titanic. Hardy Rawls and AFC end up with competing claims to the vehicles, each claiming its interest is superior to that of the other.

The Chapter 7 trustee in Moye's bankruptcy case conceded that Automotive Finance held a first lien on these vehicles and consented to relief from the automatic stay to allow Automotive Finance to exercise its rights under state law. The trustee proposed to deliver the vehicle titles to Automotive Finance to permit it to realize on its collateral, but Hardy Rawls objected, arguing that its possession of the vehicle titles created and perfected a superior security interest.

The U.S. Bankruptcy Court for the Southern District of Texas observed that, under Texas law, a security interest in a vehicle may be perfected by (1) noting that security interest on the vehicle's title or, in the case of inventory, by (2) filing a financing statement. As such, the court concluded that Hardy Rawls did not have a perfected security interest and directed the Chapter 7 trustee to deliver the vehicle titles to Automotive Finance.

So, why do we so often see cases that involve lenders and credit sellers holding on to titles, thinking that the possession of the titles is a means of assuring that—no matter what the circumstances and including bankruptcy—they get paid? Perhaps that was the law at one time, and having learned the car trade from folks "who have always done it that way," they simply assumed that a strategy that once worked would always work.

Or perhaps the practice was never really intended as an ironclad perfected security interest, but rather was considered as a relatively easy and practical way to enforce the seller or lender's rights against the borrower or buyer, as long as no other party's interests were involved, including those of a bankruptcy trustee.

Whatever the reason, before you rely on merely possessing a vehicle's title as a means of perfecting a security interest in the vehicle, make sure you run your plan by your friendly local lawyer.

As this case demonstrates, sometimes that plan doesn't work.

Stay? Sure—For the Duration
March 2009
By Daniel J. Laudicina

In hard times, we can expect to see an increasing number of consumers turn to bankruptcy protection to alleviate personal financial crises. That being the case, we think it is a great time to remind you of the cardinal rule of bankruptcy law: stay = stay away.

While a bankruptcy is pending, the law grants the consumer an automatic stay from creditors' collection efforts. Think of a bankruptcy filing as a consumer's personal Secret Service detachment—while the bankruptcy is pending, the consumer is just as untouchable as President Obama. And the consequences of trying to prove otherwise are just as steep. (OK, I exaggerate, the Secret Service won't come rough you up for violating an automatic stay, but I'm trying to make my point.)

"OK, we get it," you say. "Stay = stay away." Simple rule. But there are hidden pitfalls that can get you in trouble.

One such hidden pitfall comes into play with starter interrupt devices. In recent years, dealers and finance companies desiring to improve their collections, particularly with respect to less creditworthy consumers, have increasingly turned to starter interrupt devices to lower their risk. These devices, when used properly, can greatly decrease the amount of Advil you keep around the office. They allow a dealer or creditor to disable a vehicle's starter if the consumer fails to make timely payment. If you are not careful, however, they can cause you headaches that will have you blowing through that Advil in no time.

In a recent bankruptcy case, a finance company repossessed Mikasa Crawford's 2001 Chevrolet Prism for nonpayment. After Crawford filed a Chapter 13 bankruptcy petition, the finance company returned the vehicle to her, but she began having problems starting the car due to a malfunction in the disabling device installed by the creditor.

Crawford sued the finance company, alleging that its failure to repair the disabling device was a willful violation of the automatic stay. The U.S. Bankruptcy Court for the Southern District of Illinois agreed. The court concluded that the finance company willfully violated the automatic stay by failing to ensure that the car "operated free from any interference from the disabling device installed at [the finance company's] behest."

The court awarded Crawford $2,220 in actual damages, $2,860 in attorneys' fees, and $1,000 in punitive damages, noting that it took the finance company almost 10 months to fix the problem. Talk about headaches.

As the *Crawford* case makes clear, when a consumer has filed for bankruptcy, the creditor must ensure that any vehicle equipped with a starter interrupt device remains functional for the duration of the bankruptcy and that the consumer does not need to take any steps to ensure the car's continued operation during that period.

In a similar case from several years ago, the court addressed a claim that a creditor violated the automatic stay by requiring a consumer to continue to call the creditor while her bankruptcy case was pending to obtain codes to enter into a starter interrupt device, which, in turn, would allow her continued use of her car.

The court concluded that the creditor violated the

automatic stay by failing to take appropriate action to ensure that the debtor always had correct codes to start her car (i.e., by requiring her to call in). The court further suggested that the creditor could have avoided liability for failure to honor the automatic stay by removing the starter interrupt device when the stay took effect.

In light of these two cases, creditors that rely on starter interrupt devices to improve their collections can avoid problems associated with automatic stays in bankruptcy by following another simple mantra, which incorporates the "stay" reference for ease of memory: If the car stays operable for the duration of the bankruptcy, I stay out of trouble. Simple rule and easy to apply.

In re Crawford (Crawford v. Credit Acceptance Corporation), 2008 WL 5427713 (Bankr. S.D. Ill. December 24, 2008). *In re Hampton (Hampton v. Yam's Choice Plus Autos, Inc.)*, 319 B.R. 163 (Bankr. E.D. Ark. 2005).

Two Federal Circuit Courts = One Answer on Negative Equity Financing
May 2009
By Shelley B. Fowler

About six months ago, I wrote with some dismay about a few negative equity cases. And I concluded that what we really needed were more circuit court cases to follow the Eleventh Circuit's lead.

The Eleventh Circuit opinion I was referring to was *In re Graupner.* That case, the first federal appellate case to address the issue of whether the claim of a creditor that financed negative equity could be crammed down, held that a creditor does not lose its status as the holder of a purchase-money security interest by financing negative equity. Thus, its claim must be paid in full under a Chapter 13 plan. This is clearly a much better resolution than cramdown, where the creditor's secured claim would be reduced to the value of the vehicle. Remember that this protection from cramdown, part of the 2005 bankruptcy amendments, was designed to protect creditors that finance vehicle purchases for personal use within 910 days of the car buyer's bankruptcy filing.

Well, my wish came true. Recently, the U.S. Court of Appeals for the Fourth Circuit came out with its own creditor-friendly decision based on fairly common facts. Let's see what happened.

Telephius and Shawana Price bought a 2001 Lincoln LS from a North Carolina dealership and financed it through Wells Fargo Financial Acceptance. The total sale price of the Lincoln included the negative equity on the 1997 Nissan Maxima that the Prices traded in. When the Prices filed a Chapter 13 bankruptcy petition, they proposed in their plan to bifurcate, or cram down, Wells Fargo's claim into secured and unsecured components. Wells Fargo objected, arguing that its claim could not be modified because it was secured by a purchase-money security interest in the Lincoln that the Prices bought for their personal use within 910 days before their bankruptcy filing. A North Carolina bankruptcy court determined that Wells Fargo did not have a purchase-money security interest in the negative equity portion of the debt. The district court affirmed the bankruptcy court's decision.

Following *Graupner,* the Fourth Circuit concluded that a creditor has a purchase-money security interest for the portion of its claim relating to negative equity. Reversing the district court's decision, the appellate court relied on Section 9-103 of the Uniform Commercial Code and its Official Comment 3 in determining that negative equity financing that is "executed at the same time and in the same contract as the car purchase" is an expense that is incurred in connection with acquiring rights in the collateral and is therefore a purchase-money obligation. The appellate court agreed with the *Graupner* court that the "negative equity financing enabled the purchase of the new car because the negative equity financing and the purchase were a 'package deal.'"

So, are we home free? Not entirely.

Two circuit court cases are certainly better than one, but we can't be sure that other circuit courts (or even these same circuit courts) won't come down on the other side of this issue in the future. That's because the determination of whether a creditor is the holder of a purchase-money security interest depends on state law (Georgia law in the *Graupner* decision and North Carolina law in the Price decision). Certainly, the fact that the Uniform Commercial Code governs purchase-money security interests is helpful, but many bankruptcy courts, even post-*Graupner*, have found that language in a state's motor vehicle sales finance law impacts their decisions on the purchase-money security interest issue.

So, all you can do is keep your fingers crossed that the circuit court trend endorsing the "package deal" approach in favor of creditors continues!

In re Price (Wells Fargo Financial Acceptance v. Price), 2009 U.S. App. LEXIS 7750 (4th Cir. (E.D.N.C.) April 13, 2009).

Trouble in Texas—
Mischief From the Bankruptcy Court

June 2009

By Thomas J. Buiteweg

I suppose we should understand by now that judges are human and they make mistakes. However, a judge in the bankruptcy court for the Western District of Texas made a doozie in a recent case that is causing a big stir in the vehicle financing industry throughout Texas.

[Editor's note: doozer or doozy or doozie, noun (ca.1230): an extraordinary one of its kind; humdinger. —Webster's Ninth New Collegiate Dictionary]

The case seemed simple enough. Clark Contracting Services, a construction company, bought six big specialized trucks that happened to need certificates of title under the Texas titling law. CIT Equipment Financing financed Clark's purchase of the trucks, with the trucks serving as collateral subject to lien in favor of CIT. Then CIT got its name shown as lienholder on the six certificates of title.

About a year later, Wells Fargo Equipment Finance bought the financing contracts from CIT. As part of the deal, Wells took an assignment of CIT's lien on the trucks, but it didn't retitle the vehicles to show its name as lienholder instead of CIT's. About a year after that, Clark filed a Chapter 11 bankruptcy petition.

In the bankruptcy, Clark asked the court to void Wells Fargo's liens on the trucks. Clark argued that the Texas titling law required Wells Fargo to retitle after the liens were assigned to it. The bankruptcy judge agreed with Clark, and that left Wells Fargo with no collateral and an unsecured claim in the bankruptcy proceeding. Not what Wells Fargo had in mind when it got involved in the deal.

So, Wells Fargo loses six specialized construction vehicles. Why should you care about that? Turns out that the decision, if upheld, exposes the holders of millions of ordinary Texas motor vehicle financing contracts to big losses if the customers who owe the money under the contracts file for bankruptcy protection.

"How's that?" you say. Because the decision has serious, negative implications for a common process in the vehicle financing industry known as "securitization." Many sales finance companies and banks bundle up the financing contracts they buy from dealers and sell the bundles to something called a securitization trust. The trust sells securities to investors that represent ownership of a piece of the payment streams due under the bundles of contracts the trust bought. This process is a critically important source for the funds finance companies and banks need to buy more financing contracts from dealers.

As part of the process, the securitization trust takes an assignment of the liens on the vehicles that serve as collateral for the individual financing contracts in the bundles. In Texas and elsewhere, it is common practice not to retitle the vehicles to show the securitization trust as lienholder. First, it would be hugely expensive to retitle thousands of vehicles as part of the process. Second, listing the securitization trust on the title would likely confuse the customers who owe the money under these contracts because the finance company or bank usually continues to service the contracts in its own name after they are securitized.

Of course, if state law required retitling, people would either retitle or not engage in securitizations. But nobody thought Texas law required the securitization trust to retitle. Now, the judge in this case says it does. If the judge is right, securitization trusts holding millions of these "securitized" Texas contracts could have their liens voided if the customers who owe the money under the contracts file for bankruptcy protection.

Fortunately, most people familiar with this area of the law are pretty confident that the judge is wrong and the verdict will probably be overturned on appeal. In addition, as I write this article, Texas is on the verge of changing its titling law to undo the judge's decision. Unfortunately, until these things happen, the risk and uncertainty caused by this decision will probably hamper efforts to raise money through securitizations in a market where money is already tight.

In re Clark Contracting Services, Inc. (Clark Contracting Services, Inc. v. Wells Fargo Equipment Finance), 399 B.R. 789 (Bankr. W.D. Tex. November 28, 2008).

Finance Companies May Not Terminate Agreements With Dealership in Bankruptcy Absent Court Approval
June 2009
By Shelley B. Fowler and Maya P. Hill

With all the talk about bankruptcies these days, it's good to know that courts are looking out for dealerships that file Chapter 11 bankruptcy petitions in an effort to reorganize their businesses.

In order to continue operating in Chapter 11 and thereafter, dealerships need to be able to sell to finance companies the retail installment sales contracts they enter into with customers. In a recent case, seven finance companies tried to walk away from contract purchase agreements they had with a dealership after the dealership filed for bankruptcy, but the bankruptcy court refused to allow them off the hook. Here's what happened.

Ernie Haire Ford, Inc., is an auto dealer in Florida. Ernie Haire Ford entered into retail installment contracts with people who bought cars on credit. The dealership sold the contracts to several sales finance companies pursuant to individual contract purchase agreements with each company. Just days after Ernie Haire Ford filed a Chapter 11 bankruptcy petition, each of the sales finance companies terminated its agreement to buy retail installment sales contracts (RISCs) from Ernie Haire Ford. None of the sales finance companies sought relief from the automatic stay, and the only reason given for termination was that it was the company's "policy" (reading between the lines, this means that they don't like doing business with dealerships in bankruptcy).

*[**Editor's note:** RISC: a retail installment sales contract. This contract is used to document a credit sale from a dealer to a buyer. Then the dealer usually sells the RISC to a finance company or bank. Buy-here, pay-here dealers hold RISCs and collect payments from buyers, unless they have created an affiliated finance company to assign them to.—**CARLAW®: F&I Legal Desk Book**, Hudson, et. al.]*

The sales finance companies argued that they were permitted to terminate the agreements. They claimed that because the agreements were contracts to extend financial accommodations to Ernie Haire Ford, those contracts could not be assumed by the Chapter 11 trustee. They argued that even if the trustee could assume the agreements, the agreements contained provisions allowing them to terminate the agreements at will.

Ernie Haire Ford filed an emergency motion to compel the finance companies to comply with their contract purchase agreements. The U.S. Bankruptcy Court for the Middle District of Florida granted Ernie Haire Ford's motion.

According to the court, the contract purchase agreements would have to be considered "financial accommodations" to avoid the automatic stay. A "financial accommodations" contract typically involves the extension of debt financing to a debtor. However, the contract purchase agreements involved nothing more than the circumstances under which a sales finance company would buy a RISC from Ernie Haire Ford. The contract purchase agreements did not include a promise to make debt financing available to Ernie Haire Ford. Consequently, the agreements were subject to the automatic stay and could not be terminated absent bankruptcy court approval.

Next, the court held that while the sales finance companies had a right to terminate their agreements with Ernie Haire Ford, that right was tempered by an obligation, under Florida law, to act in good faith and in accordance with the parties' reasonable commercial expectations. According to the court, a decision to terminate an agreement based solely on the other party's bankruptcy was not a decision made "in good faith" and also violated the Bankruptcy Code's prohibition against termination of contracts solely because of a debtor's bankruptcy filing. As a result, the court found that the sales finance companies did not have a sufficient reason to terminate the contract purchase agreements.

Last, the court addressed the finance companies' argument that even if they are not allowed to terminate the contracts, they could "functionally terminate" the contracts by using their discretion to reject every RISC Ernie Haire Ford submits to them. The court cautioned that "[r]ejecting every [RISC] that Ernie Haire Ford generates, while accepting similar contracts meeting certain objective standards from other dealers, effectively terminates the agreements in violation of the automatic stay" and also violates the implied covenant of good faith and fair dealing.

So, the dealership wins round one. Don't assume that the finance companies will stop fighting—the court left the door open when it said that the finance companies may bring an "appropriately filed motion for relief from stay" if they believe they have "acceptable grounds for termination of the contracts." But, "acceptable" is the key word!

In re Ernie Haire Ford, Inc., 2009 Bankr. LEXIS 834 (Bankr. M.D. Fla. April 8, 2009).

Chapter 12

Litigation

Some things you can just bank on. The sun will rise. The rooster will crow. And the plaintiffs' lawyers will be back at it, working hard to bring bigger and bolder claims against car dealers. Quite frankly, after our many trips around the sun, we can't help but be awed and amazed by the mental acrobatics that are often used to bring claims against dealers. The cases addressed in this chapter illustrate the point.

Do you charge a doc prep fee? Well, then you must be practicing law without a license.

Did you commit an itty-bitty technical violation of some statute that doesn't provide for a private right of action? Well, then you must have committed an unfair and deceptive trade practice in violation of state law.

Your customer got a raw deal? Well, there must be at least a gazillion more just like them that we could round up into a class action!

Think this is all too scary to be true? The articles in this chapter involve real dealers who struggled with these very issues in the courtroom. We should warn you that this stuff isn't for the faint of heart or the weak of stomach. Read on, brave friends!

Punitive Damages— How Much Is Too Much?
November 2007
By Thomas B. Hudson

Nury Chapa sued Tony Gullo Motors I, L.P., and its sales representative for breach of contract, fraud, and Texas Deceptive Trade Practices Act violations in connection with her purchase of a car. Chapa alleged that Gullo Motors made fraudulent representations, delivered a lower-end model car rather than a higher-end model, made promises it did not keep, and forged various documents.

The jury found in favor of Chapa on all her claims and awarded $7,213 in economic damages, $21,639 in mental anguish damages, and $250,000 in exemplary damages on the fraud claim.

The Texas Court of Appeals affirmed the trial court's findings of liability. The appellate court also found that the amount of the exemplary damage award for the fraud claim was excessive and suggested a remittitur of $125,000. "Remittitur" is a $5 word that means "reduction." When a jury gets out of hand and awards a plaintiff a sum that is unreasonable, the defense lawyer can file a "motion for remittitur." That's what happened here, and both parties disliked the suggestion of $125,000 in punitive damages. Both parties appealed.

The Texas Supreme Court found that Gullo Motors' fraudulent actions merited exemplary (punitive) damages, but that the $125,000 figure exceeded the constitutional limits on exemplary damages. The U.S. Supreme Court has on several occasions addressed the question of whether a punitive damages award can be so large that it violates the defendant's constitutional rights. The court also has made noises about the relationship that punitive damages awards should have to the award of actual damages.

The trial court's award of punitive damages was about nine times the plaintiff's actual damages award. The appellate court halved the award, but that reduction wasn't enough for the high court, which remanded the case to the appellate court to determine a constitutionally permissible remittitur.

In this decision, the appellate court first examined the degree of reprehensibility of Gullo Motors' conduct. The appellate court found that there was no physical harm to Chapa, only an economic harm caused by fraud; no reckless disregard of health or safety; no extreme financial hardship as a result of Gullo Motors' conduct; and the fraud did not involve repeated acts.

The only reprehensible aspect of Gullo Motors' conduct was that Chapa's harm was the result of deceit. Evidence of the deceitful conduct included forged signatures, a misrepresentation by the dealer that it was unable to take the car back upon Chapa's request, switching of contracts, alteration of documents, and threats.

The appellate court then examined the disparity between the actual harm suffered and the exemplary damages award. The appellate court found that such a high ratio of exemplary damages to actual damages should be reserved for "cases with facts demonstrating the most egregious level of reprehensibility."

Finally, the appellate court compared the exemplary damages to civil penalties authorized under the Texas Occupations Code and the Texas DTPA in comparable cases. Based on these findings, the appellate court suggested an exemplary damage award of $50,000, thereby reducing the ratio of exemplary damages to actual damages to less than 2:1. So, this dealer dodged a bullet, if you can call having to pay a punitive damage award of "only" $50,000 dodging a bullet.

If you are a Texas dealer, you can take some comfort in this decision. The court's award of punitive damages—less than twice the actual damages award—should help keep Texas jury awards under control. The decision isn't binding in other states, but you can count on seeing defendants in other states arguing that courts should adopt the Texas court's reasoning.

But don't take too much comfort—the exact relationship between punitive damages and actual damages necessary for a finding of unconstitutionality is still a bit murky. The best protection against large punitive damage awards is to avoid all that reprehensible and deceitful behavior in the first place.

Chapa v. Tony Gullo Motors I, L.P., 2007 WL 2127139 (Tex. App. July 26, 2007).

High Line Damages?

September 2008

By Thomas B. Hudson

Dealers who sell "high line" cars sometimes end up forking over "high line" damages. First, it costs more to fix those expensive cars when something breaks or goes wrong, but that isn't the end of it. Many states have lemon laws or general consumer protection laws (often called "unfair and deceptive acts and practices laws" or, for brevity's sake, UDAP laws) that permit plaintiffs to recover a multiple of their damages. Here's a case in point.

Bruce Tammi leased a car from U.S. Bank. The car's rear spoiler malfunctioned, which prompted warnings and chimes inside the cabin. Tammi took the car in for service more than four times without successful repair.

Tammi sent Porsche Cars North America, Inc., the requisite lemon law notice asking for a refund and costs. Porsche responded that it understood that the car had been fixed. Tammi sued Porsche. After the jury found for Tammi and awarded him $26,600 in damages, Tammi moved to alter the verdict on damages. The trial court granted Tammi's motion and awarded damages of $266,000.

The trial court included the lease payments, as well as the purchase price Tammi paid for the car at the end of the lease, in the damages award. The trial court then doubled the sum of these two amounts as provided by the lemon law, which allows for pecuniary loss to be doubled. Porsche appealed.

The U.S. Court of Appeals for the Seventh Circuit noted that the lemon law permits a customer to recover twice the amount of any pecuniary loss but does not define pecuniary loss. After affirming the jury's liability determination, the appellate court stayed the case and certified questions to the Wisconsin Supreme Court regarding the issue of what constitutes pecuniary loss under the lemon law.

So, we aren't done yet. When the top state court defines the term "pecuniary loss" for the federal court, the federal court will come up with a final damages award, assuming the parties don't settle this one first.

Even though the case isn't finally resolved on appeal, it does illustrate the fact that trial courts aren't at all reluctant to swat manufacturers, dealers, and creditors with stiff damages awards. And another point to remember is that the $266,000 doesn't include the amounts Porsche had to pay its own lawyers.

This consumer litigation stuff can get pricey.

Tammi v. Porsche Cars North America, Inc., 2008 WL 2955577 (7th Cir. (E.D. Wis.) August 4, 2008).

Dealer Defeats Class Certification Motion in "Unauthorized Practice of Law" Case
December 2008
By Thomas B. Hudson

In several jurisdictions around the country, dealers have been hit with rather imaginative class action lawsuits. These suits allege that dealers' actions in completing legal forms, such as buyers orders and retail installment contracts, constitute the practice of law, and that, because the dealers and/or their employees are not lawyers, the actions constitute the unauthorized practice of law.

In the world of class action lawsuits, a defendant usually files a motion to dismiss the lawsuit, arguing that the plaintiff hasn't stated a sufficient claim, and the plaintiff files a motion asking the court to certify that the matter can proceed as a class action.

If the dealer defendant can win the first motion, the matter goes away. If the dealer defendant wins the second motion, the lawsuit continues, but not as a class action, making it much less dangerous to the dealer. If the dealer defendant loses both motions, usually the only question left is how many zeroes will appear on the check the dealer writes to settle the case. In this case, the dealer won the second motion.

Robert and Stacy Baker bought a vehicle from Go Toyota Scion Arapahoe and agreed to pay a "dealer handling fee" that represented, according to the retail installment sales contract, "costs and additional profits to the seller for items such as inspections, cleaning, and adjusting new and used vehicles and preparing documents related to the sale." The contract also included a provision for mandatory arbitration with a class action waiver, but the Bakers did not sign that provision.

The Bakers sued Go Toyota Scion and other dealerships, alleging that the defendants charged them and other car buyers "an illegal fee for preparing legal documents necessary to effectuate the sale of a motor vehicle and that the [d]efendants engaged in the unauthorized practice of law in connection with the purchase or lease of the motor vehicle," in violation of the Colorado Consumer Credit Code, the Colorado Consumer Protection Act, and common law.

The Bakers moved to certify a class of Colorado consumers who financed their vehicle purchases and who paid a dealer handling fee to any of the defendants through a retail installment sales contract. The District Court for Adams County, Colorado, denied the motion for class certification.

The court first concluded that the plaintiffs did not satisfy the "numerosity requirement" (class action rules require that there be enough potential class members to justify proceeding as a class) for class certification. The court stated that the plaintiffs could not use the defendants' sales volume alone to support numerosity.

The court also found that the plaintiffs did not have standing to contest the provisions of the arbitration agreement and class action waiver because they did not sign that provision in their contract. In other words, the plaintiffs couldn't represent others unless their experiences reflected the experiences of the others.

Next, the court concluded that the plaintiffs did not satisfy the "commonality requirement" (the situations of the class members needed to be similar) for class certification. With respect to the unauthorized practice of law claim, the court found that each consumer would have to be contacted to determine whether the consumer sought independent legal advice, whether the dealership provided the legal advice, and whether each consumer relied on the advice. With respect to the arbitration agreement, the court found that it would have to examine each transaction to determine which consumers signed the agreement and, therefore, individual issues of fact existed that precluded class certification. The court also found that certain class members were not eligible for inclusion in the class because they were not "consumers" under the Colorado Consumer Credit Code. Finally, the court concluded that the plaintiffs did not assert sufficient evidence showing that their claims were typical of the proposed class members' claims, and that the plaintiffs were not adequate class representatives.

Dealers in other jurisdictions in which unauthorized practice of law claims have been filed should find this opinion very helpful.

Baker v. Go Toyota Scion Arapahoe, Case No. 07 CV 543 (D. Colo. October 11, 2008).

Arkansas Court Preserves
Interest Rate Exportation Case

January/February 2009

By Alicia H. Tortarolo

Almost 10 years have passed since we reported on the innovative Arkansas Supreme Court case, *Evans v. Harry Robinson Pontiac-Buick, Inc.,* that provided a glimmer of hope (and increased revenue) to out-of-state sales finance companies that buy (or would like to buy) paper from Arkansas dealers.

In the *Evans* case, the court held that a motor vehicle retail installment contract was not usurious under Arkansas law, even though the contract was between a dealership and a buyer that were both located in Arkansas, because the transaction had a sufficient relationship to Texas for the court to enforce the contract provision choosing Texas law to govern the transaction.

The court held the contract would have violated Arkansas' usury law but for the contract's assignment to a Texas entity and the choice of law provision stating that Texas law applied. The court reasoned that the contract had a sufficient relationship with Texas because the credit evaluation, credit approval, contract acceptance, and funding all took place in Texas; the contract contained language that it was simultaneously being assigned to a financing company in Texas; and the buyer was to mail all payments to a Texas location.

The *Evans* court stated that without the sales finance company, Evans could not have purchased the automobile from the dealer. It was confirmed during oral argument that the money for the purchase came from the Texas-based sales finance company and was transferred to the dealer. The court concluded that, while Evans and the dealer initiated the contract in Arkansas, final execution of the contract occurred in Texas. Further, the court appeared to mistakenly categorize the dealer as an agent of the finance company. Based upon these conclusions, the *Evans* decision is imperfect to the extent that another state's court may not render a similar opinion. Through the years, I have even questioned if another Arkansas court may render a similar opinion or look for something to distinguish a case before it to fashion a different outcome. Finally, the court's decision in *Cannon v. AmeriCredit Financial Services, Inc.*, answered my question.

On October 20, 2008, the Arkansas Circuit Court for Washington County granted summary judgment and dismissed a motor vehicle retail installment contract usury claim on the basis that the case facts were virtually identical to the facts presented in the precedent-setting *Evans* case.

In the *Cannon* case, Tina Cannon, an Arkansas resident, purchased an automobile from Valley Motors, Inc., an Arkansas entity. However, the motor vehicle retail installment sales contract stated twice that Texas law governed the transaction. The contract also identified AmeriCredit Financial Services, a Texas entity, as the assignee of the contract. Like the sales finance company in the *Evans* case, AmeriCredit reviewed and approved the financing decision in Texas and disbursed the contract funds to Valley Motors from Texas. AmeriCredit handled all billing and accounting services in Texas. The *Cannon* court concluded "the acceptance and approval of the Contract by [AmeriCredit] in Texas was a necessary predicate to the plaintiff's purchase of the vehicle from Valley Motors."

The court opined that the holding in *Evans* controlled the *Cannon* usury dispute and held that the contract's choice of law provision calling for the application of Texas law was binding and enforceable. Consequently, the contract was not subject to Arkansas' usury law because the court found that the transaction had a substantial relation to the state of Texas.

While an out-of-state choice of law provision appears to be a safe haven for exporting another state's interest rate (and all the state's other legal bells, whistles, and disclosures) into Arkansas, I suggest you tread with caution and make sure that the credit transaction has a relationship to the chosen state as substantial as Texas did to the transactions and sales finance companies in both the *Evans* and *Cannon* cases.

Cannon v. AmeriCredit Financial Services, Inc., No. CV-2008-1255-5 (Ark. Cir. October 20, 2008); *Evans v. Harry Robinson Pontiac-Buick, Inc.*, 336 Ark. 155 (January 28, 1999).

Watch Out for Those Little Things
March 2009
By Emily Marlow Beck

I'm a horrible speller. I always have been. Determined not to be the first eliminated in the elementary school spelling bee one year, I memorized the spelling of the biggest and most complicated words that were on the second-grade syllabus. I quickly met my fate, however, by misspelling a little two-letter word that any first grader would know. (Give my mother a call if you want to know what that little word is. She's already told everyone else, and she'd be happy to tell you, too.) I guess you could say that I learned the hard way that getting all the big things right isn't always enough, especially when getting little things wrong can take you out of the game.

Unfortunately, legal compliance can work much the same way. It doesn't matter how good you are at the big things if you haven't put the little things in order. Even the littlest mistakes can pack a pretty big punch. This is especially true if you live in a state that treats the violation of other state or federal laws as a violation of the state unfair and deceptive trade practices, or UDAP, law. These state UDAP laws can make even the smallest technical violations of state and federal laws fatal, when they might not be otherwise.

A recent case out of Ohio gives us just the example we need. In this case, a woman bought a used Jeep Liberty from a dealer in Ohio. As was required under the federal Used Car Rule, a Buyers Guide was affixed to the Jeep when she bought it (check plus for the dealer). Even better, the Buyers Guide contained the warranty information required under the Rule (check plus, plus for the dealer). So far, so good.

Unfortunately (you knew there was a catch, right?), the Buyers Guide did not contain the name and address of the dealer and the name and telephone number of a person for the customer to contact in case she needed to make a complaint. (Oops!) As you might guess, the customer sued the dealer, alleging that because the dealership violated the technical requirements under the federal Used Car Rule by not including the required contact information, it committed a deceptive or unfair act under the state UDAP law, the Ohio Consumer Sales Practices Act.

The court agreed with the customer and granted her motion for partial summary judgment. The court found that, even though the failure to include the name and address of the dealer was not an unfair or deceptive practice under the federal Used Car Rule, the dealership technically violated the Consumer Sales Practice Act by failing to comply with the Used Car Rule.

Did you catch that little trick? This is what we consumer lawyers like to call "bootstrapping." The plaintiff's lawyer claimed that the dealer violated the state UDAP law by violating some other federal law. These "bootstrapping" cases can, in some circumstances, create causes of action where they otherwise wouldn't exist. That's exactly what happened here.

So, what can we learn from this case?

First, don't forget that, when it comes to compliance, the tiny details can be just as deadly as the big picture. Just think about it—no one in this case claimed that the customer didn't know whom to contact in the event she had any complaints or that she didn't know the dealership's address (after all, she went there to buy the car, didn't she?). The claim was simply that the dealer did not technically comply with the rule.

Second, think about asking your friendly consumer lawyer to walk through your forms and procedures to look for those "little things" that can get you hung up. It's amazing what a fresh set of well-trained eyes can do. He might just be able to pick out a thing or two that you haven't noticed.

Finally, talk to your lawyer about using an arbitration agreement with a class action waiver. In the event that your local plaintiff's lawyer comes a-knocking with his bootstraps on, a well-drafted arbitration agreement with a class action waiver could mean the difference between a one versus one case and a one versus 1,000 case. After all, it's the little mistakes that seem to hurt the most.

Brown v. CincyAutos, 2009 WL 88736 (S.D. Ohio January 12, 2009).

Silk Purses and Sows' Ears

April 2009

By Thomas B. Hudson

Lawyers. You gotta love 'em. They have a client with a $1,000 case, and they immediately start searching for a way to turn the case into a big payday.

How do they do that, you ask? Well, we see a number of strategies, but a common one is to try to elevate a common breach of contract claim into a tort claim. You see, a successful breach of contract suit permits a plaintiff to recover only his or her actual damages. A tort claim ups the ante, because a plaintiff can often recover punitive damages in addition to actual damages. If the plaintiff can get a jury sufficiently incensed at the defendant by showing really bad behavior on the defendant's part, sometimes those punitive damages awards can be eye-popping.

A recent opinion illustrates an unsuccessful attempt to turn a sow's ear into a silk purse. Here's what happened.

Len Stoler, Inc. (LSI), entered into three contracts with National Auto Care Corporation (NACC). Under the contracts, NACC agreed to underwrite and administer limited warranties and insurance for LSI's used vehicles, enabling LSI to market those vehicles as "certified." NACC agreed to provide certain profits on the insurance premiums it collected to LSI.

LSI sued NACC, claiming that NACC breached the contracts and made intentional misrepresentations regarding the profits that LSI would receive. The "intentional misrepresentation" claim is a tort claim that would, if proven, open the door to the plaintiff's recovery of damages beyond actual damages. Including the tort claim ratchets up the danger of the case to the defendant and is a tactic used to drive up the ultimate damages award at trial or the settlement value of a case that doesn't go to trial. NACC, in an effort to get rid of the most dangerous aspect of LSI's case, moved to dismiss the intentional misrepresentation claim.

The U.S. District Court for the District of Maryland granted the motion. The court noted that the intentional misrepresentation claim failed because LSI pled "failure to disclose" and "concealment" but not "false representations," and concealments and failures to disclose are not treated as false representations unless there is a separate duty to disclose. In this case, the court found no separate duty to disclose, because the contracts were arm's-length transactions between two corporations. The court noted that even if it were to find that the nondisclosures constituted false representations, the claim would fail, because LSI submitted no evidence that the concealments and nondisclosures were done knowingly.

So LSI's case remains alive, but, for NACC, it is now reduced to a much-less-dangerous breach of contract claim. That is, at least until LSI's lawyer can come up with another creative claim.

Len Stoler, Inc., v. National Auto Care Corporation, 2009 U.S. Dist LEXIS 9340 (D. Md. February 9, 2009).

When Punitive Damages Are Too Punitive

May 2009

By Thomas B. Hudson and Maya P. Hill

For years, courts, including the U.S. Supreme Court, have wrestled over the question of the relationship, if any, that punitive damages awards must bear to whatever actual damages a plaintiff has suffered. The answer matters to dealers because customers who sue them nearly always claim punitive damages, and any judicially imposed caps on such damages can dramatically reduce the settlement value of these cases.

The latest court to address this issue is an Oregon appellate court. Let's see how that court handled the question.

Shawn Yovan bought a used car with 98,000 miles on the odometer from Lithia Motors. Lithia assigned the related retail installment contract to TranSouth.

Once he started driving the car, Yovan suspected that something was wrong with the car and ordered a CARFAX report. The report led Yovan to believe that the car actually had more miles on it than the odometer showed and that the odometer had been rolled back at some point.

Yovan took the report to Lithia. There was no evidence that Lithia knew about the odometer discrepancy. Yovan and Lithia tried to decide how to fix the situation.

Yovan's lawyer sent Lithia a letter telling Lithia that Yovan had decided to keep the car, to continue making payments, and to sue Lithia for damages, unless they could reach a settlement. Lithia proposed a variety of settlement offers, but Yovan rejected each one. Additionally, a dispute arose between Lithia and Yovan over who had legal authority to negotiate the terms of a settlement or take any action with respect to the car as between Lithia and TranSouth.

Lithia sent a repossession agent to Yovan's house to try to repossess the car, and Yovan refused to let him take the car. The agent allegedly told Yovan that Lithia would take criminal action against him if he did not return the car.

Lithia eventually repurchased the retail installment contract from TranSouth and tried to rescind the transaction with Yovan, telling Yovan in a letter that he had no legal right to keep the car. Lithia then sued Yovan to rescind the transaction and recover the car.

The trial court found that Lithia was entitled to rescind the sale based on language in the retail installment contract, and the jury awarded Yovan $500 in damages for emotional injury and $100,000 in punitive damages.

Lithia moved for remittitur (legal-speak for "judge, please reduce this award to a reasonable amount") to reduce the punitive damages award on the grounds that the award was grossly excessive, and the trial court reduced the award to $2,000. Yovan appealed, and the Oregon Court of Appeals affirmed the trial court's decision to reduce the award.

The appellate court noted that a determination of whether a punitive damages award is "grossly excessive" requires an analysis of (1) the degree of reprehensibility of the conduct giving rise to the award, (2) the disparity between the actual or potential harm and the punitive damages award, and (3) the difference between the punitive damages awarded and the civil penalties authorized in comparable cases.

The appellate court found that although Lithia had sent a repossession agent to Yovan's home and allegedly threatened to take criminal action against him if he did not return the car, Yovan was not a particularly vulnerable victim. The appellate court noted that Yovan had worked in the car industry and knew how the process worked. Further, Yovan had a lawyer who could advise him about what legal actions Lithia could take.

The appellate court found that although Lithia's actions may have been reprehensible, the actions were not reprehensible enough to justify an egregious punitive damages award.

The appellate court then considered the disparity between the actual or potential harm and the punitive damages award. It found that the jury's award of $500 for emotional harm was not proportionate to its $100,000 punitive damages award. Finally, the appellate court noted that with respect to the difference between the punitive damages awarded and the civil penalties authorized in comparable cases, an award of $100,000 was excessive.

The appellate court reached this conclusion after reviewing the Oregon statutes authorizing damages awards that came closest to resembling a case like this. The appellate court found that those statutes only authorized a civil penalty of up to $200, and this amount was not proportionate to a $100,000 punitive damages award. Accordingly, the appellate court affirmed the trial court's decision to reduce the punitive damages award to $2,000, noting that the reduced award represented a proper 4-to-1 ratio of punitive damages to civil penalties. Anything greater than a 4-to-1 ratio, the appellate court noted, would be "grossly excessive."

That is at least one court's take on what the permissible ratio of punitive to actual damages should be. Your state's court may have spoken on this topic recently, or may do so in the future. It might be worth asking your lawyer whether there is such a test yet in your state that could provide you with some exposure guidance.

Lithia Motors v. Yovan, 2009 Ore. App. LEXIS 152 (Or. App. March 19, 2009).

Lemon? Or Just a Car With Problems?

May 2009

By Thomas B. Hudson

When is a car with problems a "lemon" and when is it just a car with problems? A federal appellate court (the only higher federal court is the U.S. Supreme Court) recently addressed that question and delivered up a (gasp!) sensible answer.

Ron Benit sued Mercedes-Benz USA, LLC, under Ohio's Lemon Law, claiming that the Mercedes S55 AMG that he bought 5-1/2 years earlier was a "lemon." A jury found in favor of Mercedes-Benz.

On appeal, the U.S. Court of Appeals for the Sixth Circuit concluded that any errors the trial court could have made were harmless because no reasonable jury could have found that Benit's vehicle was a "lemon."

In reaching its conclusion, the appellate court noted that the car was safe, and Benit drove it for 53,000 miles. The appellate court also noted that, although Benit made many complaints over the years about the vehicle, Mercedes-Benz made the necessary repairs, and Benit never took his vehicle to any of the other authorized Mercedes-Benz dealerships that were nearby.

The appellate court concluded that Ohio's Lemon Law requires a consumer to "demonstrate substantial impairment to the vehicle within the first year or 18,000 miles that the dealer is unwilling or unable to fix." The appellate court stated that Benit failed to meet these requirements and instead drove the car a substantial amount of miles over the years and "took full advantage of the warranty and [Mercedes-Benz's] goodwill." Therefore, the appellate court affirmed the judgment in favor of Mercedes-Benz.

The statement that no reasonable jury could have found that Benit's car was a lemon is a very helpful one for anyone fighting a Lemon Law claim made by a customer who has driven the car a substantial amount. As long as the defendant has performed its duties under any applicable warranties, it should be able to withstand a lemon law claim.

Cars don't have to be perfect to avoid being lemons. Go figure.

That is, as long as the court is as sensible as this one.

Benit v. Mercedes-Benz USA, LLC, 2009 U.S. App. LEXIS 6369 (6th Cir. (S.D. Ohio) March 23, 2009).

Class Certified in Rebate Disclosure Case Against Dealer

July 2009

By Thomas B. Hudson

Must manufacturer rebates be separately disclosed to car buyers? At least one class action lawsuit against a dealer—this one in Louisiana—makes that claim, and, at least so far, the dealer has been unable to make the lawsuit go away. In fact, the Louisiana Court of Appeals, in this recent opinion, upheld the trial court's certification of a class of plaintiffs.

George Conrad sued Lamarque Ford, Inc., for fraud. Conrad claimed that Lamarque pocketed manufacturer rebates that Ford Motor Company offered on new car sales. The trial court certified a class of all persons who bought cars in the rebate program, but whose purchase documents failed to disclose they received the rebate. Lamarque appealed.

The Louisiana Court of Appeals affirmed the trial court's decision. Lamarque challenged the trial court's conclusion that the class satisfied the numerosity requirement on the grounds that each class member would have to be questioned regarding whether he or she received the rebate in order to determine whether a sufficient number of customers were aggrieved in the same manner. The appellate court found that whether a member received a rebate went to the merits of the case and was not proper for determining class certification. The appellate court noted that establishing a definable class satisfies the numerosity requirement, and that class membership hinged on whether the loan documents disclosed the rebate, not whether a person actually received the rebate.

The appellate court also held that the class satisfied the commonality requirement because each member had the same common complaint: Lamarque did not disclose the right to a rebate from the manufacturer. Lamarque argued that the class claims were not typical because fraud claims require fact-intensive and individualized inquiries. The appellate court disagreed, concluding that the class claims were typical because the overriding claims were that Lamarque intentionally failed to disclose the existence of the rebates. The appellate court found that the class representatives were adequate because they had first-hand knowledge of the alleged conduct and had suffered an actual injury. Their stakes in the litigation were typical of the class, and there was no indication of a conflict.

There are a couple of things worth noting about what this opinion says and doesn't say. First, most courts will not entertain class actions when the underlying claim by the plaintiff is one of fraud. Courts will usually say that fraud claims require too much of an individual-by-individual inquiry into such things as the representations made to each potential class member, the reliance by each potential class member on those representations, and the like. This court sidestepped that analysis by focusing only on whether the rebate was disclosed in the documents.

The other thing worth noting here is something the plaintiff did not allege, and that is a violation of Louisiana or federal disclosure laws. It's possible that the plaintiff considered such claims but concluded that they were not winners, or that the plaintiff elected to proceed with his strongest claim, or that, perhaps, the plaintiff simply wanted to avoid stating claims that might permit removal of the case to a potentially more dealer-friendly federal court.

Conrad v. Lamarque Ford, Inc., 2009 La. App. LEXIS 795 (La. App. May 12, 2009).

Sometimes Doing the Right Thing
Still Gets You in Trouble

August 2009

By Shelley B. Fowler

Most of the articles we write for *Spot Delivery*® encourage dealers to do things the right way. However, a recent case proves that, even if you try to do everything right, you still aren't immune from a lawsuit. Here's what happened.

Midway Motor Sales, Inc., leased vehicles to Modern Building Supply, Inc. The leases were assigned to General Motors Acceptance Corporation, and GMAC became the owner of the vehicles. At the end of the lease periods, Midway retrieved the leased vehicles from Modern and altered the odometers to indicate that the vehicles had less mileage than they actually had.

GMAC sold the vehicles at dealer-only auctions and, without knowledge of the odometer tampering, completed odometer disclosure affidavits stating what it believed were the accurate odometer readings. Once GMAC discovered that the odometers had been rolled back, it reported the information to the Ohio Attorney General's office and compensated the owners of the affected vehicles. It seems that GMAC did the right thing by informing government officials of the tampering and compensating affected buyers, right? So, it shouldn't get sued, right? Unfortunately, that's not what happened.

The AG turned around and sued Midway (I don't have a problem with that because Midway was the entity that rolled the odometers back). However, the AG also decided to sue GMAC under the Ohio Consumer Sales Practices Act and the Odometer and Rollback Disclosure Act. The AG claimed that GMAC violated Ohio law by failing to provide true odometer disclosures. The trial court granted the AG summary judgment, concluding that the statute is a strict liability statute. The intermediate appellate court affirmed, but the Supreme Court of Ohio, thankfully, reversed.

The affidavit that a transferor must sign requires the transferor to list the mileage of the vehicle "to the best of [his or her] knowledge." The Ohio high court determined that because the odometer disclosure affidavit "calls for a knowledge-based certification of the odometer reading," it must construe the affidavit together with the relevant statutes and, therefore, reached the conclusion that the "legislature intended for transferors to be liable only for knowing violations of the odometer disclosure statute." Moreover, the high court found that a previous owner would have protected GMAC from liability under the "previous owner" defense for violations, even though the previous owner did not own the vehicles at the time of the violation.

So, GMAC ended up winning, but not after being forced to spend huge amounts of time and energy—and paying huge amounts of legal fees—to get through a trial and two appeals. Seems unfair when all GMAC did was try to do the right thing!

State v. Midway Motor Sales, Inc., 2009 Ohio LEXIS 1590 (Ohio June 10, 2009).

The Curious Case of the Mileage Being Too Low
August 2009
By Dana Frederick Clarke

In Massachusetts, when court proceedings begin, a court officer bellows, "God save the Commonwealth of Massachusetts and this honorable court." Well, after this next story, we might suggest an additional refrain: "and save us from ridiculous claims brought by plaintiffs with no evidence!"

Cherise Roach bought a used truck from Middleton Auto Sales, Inc. The truck had a checkered past; it had disappeared from its original owner and had thereafter been repossessed from a service lot by CUNA Mutual Insurance Company, Inc., as the assignee of the original secured lienholder.

After repossessing the truck, CUNA's repossession agent filed an application for a new title and certified the truck's mileage as being 66,728 miles. However, the repossessor had not actually gained entry to the truck to read the odometer, but simply copied the truck's mileage from the service lot's invoice without any verification of the amount.

Later, after gaining entry to the truck, the repossessor discovered that the actual mileage according to the truck's odometer was significantly lower, reading 31,245 miles. As a result, the repossessor re-filed its title application to correct its previous odometer certification. CUNA then sold the truck to a Massachusetts-based auto wholesaler, Fedele Auto Sales, which in turn sold the truck to Middleton and then to Roach.

When Roach began experiencing mechanical problems with the truck, she sued CUNA, its repossession agent, and others. She alleged, among other things, that CUNA violated the Federal Odometer Act. Specifically, Roach argued that the Act requires persons transferring ownership of a motor vehicle to disclose the actual mileage registered on an odometer if known and that CUNA failed to do so with respect to her truck. Curiously, Roach based her claim, in part, on the incorrect higher mileage certification, as opposed to the corrected lower certification, even though there was no evidence indicating the she either knew about, or relied on, the higher mileage certification prior to purchasing the truck.

The U.S. District Court for the District of Massachusetts disposed of Roach's claim, holding that Roach failed to prove a violation of the Act because there was no evidence that the defendants intended to misrepresent the odometer or acted in reckless disregard of the erroneous mileage reading. In fact, the court noted that CUNA "did not close its eyes to the truth," but instead moved to correct the discrepancy after discovering that the actual mileage on the truck was lower than the amount that it had originally certified as being accurate. Roach also argued that the condition of the truck should have put CUNA on notice that the mileage showing on the odometer was inaccurate. Indeed, Roach stated, "Even a minimal visual inspection of the truck . . . would have alerted [the defendants] that the low mileage indicated on the odometer did not match the truck's condition." Again, the court rejected Roach's claim, holding that Roach offered no admissible evidence that CUNA "reasonably should have known that the odometer reading was incorrect."

If you are like me, you are probably asking yourself—why would Roach buy a truck that she argues looked like it was in such poor condition, and then complain about its poor condition? That question, however, and the reason why Roach would bring a claim on the higher mileage certification that she never relied on when purchasing the truck will remain one of those too frequent litigation mysteries.

Roach v. Middleton Auto Sales, Inc., 2009 U.S. Dist. LEXIS 48590 (D. Mass. June 8, 2009)

F&I Products, Procedures, and Policies

The finance and insurance department. Sure, we can think of a few more hazardous places to work. A nuclear reactor, maybe. Or, how 'bout a rattlesnake farm? But, working in the F&I department? Now, that takes nerves of steel.

You don't believe us? Just think about how much goes on in a car deal—from the up, through the first pencil, through the financing, and to the final delivery. And, yet, this whole song and dance will usually end with the customer walking out of the F&I office with a stack of papers and (hopefully) a set of keys. Talk about pressure!

But, add 'em up here—layers and layers of federal and state regulations governing most of the on-goings in the F&I office, increasing the pressure even more.

Selling ancillary products? Maybe you need to get a license or modify your disclosures. Charging any fees? Better check to make sure the fees are legal and disclosed properly. Spot delivering cars? Don't forget to make sure your state laws permit it, and that you've disclosed it properly. Can't get your customer financed? Maybe an adverse action notice is required. Feeling the pressure to make more money? Don't even think about roasting credit apps, packing payments, power booking, or other slippery deeds (even if no one will notice)!

It's quite a lot to keep up with.

And, as complicated as all this sounds, plaintiffs' lawyers have become increasingly educated about the laws and regulations that govern the credit sale of cars. Many are taking advantage of the dealers' "business as usual" attitudes and becoming experts on the common gaffes made in the finance department. In fact, in our world, it's not unusual to see a consumer's lawyer who knows more than the dealer about the legal requirements that apply to these transactions.

But, plaintiffs' lawyers don't get the last laugh here. Smart dealers are developing compliance-friendly policies and procedures to help keep their finance offices in line. They intend to provide a strong defense in case they find themselves on the receiving end of a lawsuit.

The articles in this chapter deal with some of the hot issues and cases coming out of the finance office. They also provide some tips and best practices to help dealers keep their finance departments on the up and up.

So, grab your hazmat suit and read on!

Dealer's Etch Program Survives Attack

October 2007

By Thomas B. Hudson and Emily G. Miller

Selling cars while complying with all the applicable legal requirements is tough. Financing cars, as dealers do when they have customers sign a retail installment sales contract, is tougher still. When a dealer decides to sell additional goods and services along with the financed vehicle, he faces still an additional layer of complexity. Often, the situation gets to be a bit like three-dimensional chess.

One of the services we see fairly often is something called "etch." This case illustrates how plaintiffs' lawyers can attack the sale of such services. While in this case the attack was unsuccessful, the court's opinion provides a cautionary tale for dealers who sell such products and services.

Michael Pope bought a used truck from Lake Norman Dodge. Pope's retail installment sales contract included a charge of $349 for a window etching system known as Secure Etch Silent Guard Security System. The etch program consisted of a number applied to the window of a vehicle and a guarantee by

415

Fidelity Warranty Services, Inc., to pay $5,000 to any customer whose car is stolen and not recovered within 30 days.

Evidently unhappy with his purchase of etch, Pope sued the dealer, claiming that the etch program was insurance and that the dealer sold the program without an insurance license. Pope also claimed that the "amount financed" and the "finance charge" were miscalculated and that the dealer failed to make insurance-related disclosures. Pope claimed that the dealer violated the federal Truth in Lending Act, the North Carolina Motor Vehicles Dealers and Manufacturers Licensing Law, the North Carolina Retail Installment Sales Act, and the North Carolina Unfair and Deceptive Trade Practices Act (NCUDTPA). He also claimed that the dealer's sister was ugly (just kidding).

The dealer moved to dismiss for failure to state a claim. That's a response that says, "Even if all the facts you state are true, you still don't have a case."

After referring to an Attorney General opinion addressing a similar product, the U.S. District Court for the Western District of North Carolina concluded that the etch program satisfied the definition of a warranty and was not insurance as a matter of law. The court dismissed all of Pope's claims to the extent the claims were based on allegations that etch was insurance.

Pope asserted that his NCUDTPA claim was also based on the dealer's practice of requiring etch. The court found that there was no allegation that the dealer failed to disclose the etch program or misrepresented whether it was required. The contract showed the charge for the etch program, and Pope was told by the salesperson that the program was required. Pope further claimed that he was deceived because the etch form that customers are required to sign stated that the purchase of the etch program was optional, but the dealer required all customers to buy the program. The court refused to allow the claim to continue because the NCUDTPA permits a claim only if the consumer suffers an injury to himself or his business. In this case, Pope failed to allege any causal connection between the statement on the etch form and any purported injury. Pope knew the dealer's policy of requiring the product, and Pope bought the car anyway.

If your similar goods and services programs are challenged, the court's decision for this dealer may prove helpful. As always, though, be cautious in relying too heavily on one favorable opinion. The laws of the various states vary in ways that could be critical to the court's analysis, and a couple of changed facts could have driven the decision in a different direction, in which case, you'd be in danger of being checkmated.

Your move.

Pope v. TT of Lake Norman, LLC, 2007 WL 2480242 (W.D.N.C. August 28, 2007).

More Unauthorized Practice of Law Claims!
October 2007
By Emily Marlow Beck

Spot is a loyal dog that knows how to sniff out the important issues that impact folks in the car business. But, Spot is also a smart dog that knows that sometimes he can learn a lesson or two from the mortgage lenders and "dirt lawyers" out there.

Take, for example, a recent Missouri case. Although the case involved a Missouri bank making residential mortgage loans, it could have applied just as easily to dealers, and Missouri dealers should take note.

So, what caught Spot's attention?

The Missouri Supreme Court recently held that a Missouri bank that charged borrowers a fee to complete various pre-printed loan documents, including promissory notes and deeds of trust, engaged in the unauthorized practice of law. In doing so, the court upheld the Missouri lower court's class action judgment, which awarded the plaintiffs over $1,100,000. In a footnote in the decision, the court made direct reference to a section of the Missouri law, which provides: "No bank or lending institution that makes residential loans and imposes a fee of less than two hundred dollars for completing residential loan documentation for loans made by that institution shall be deemed to be engaging in the unauthorized practice of law."

The court advised that this section "may be applicable to preclude penalties under [the Missouri law that sets forth the penalties that attach to the unauthorized practice of law in Missouri], but does not affect this Court's ability to enjoin or otherwise punish such fees if they constitute the unauthorized practice of law." The court also contained a strong admonishment regarding the judiciary's power to define and control the practice of law in Missouri, claiming, "the judiciary is necessarily the sole arbiter of what constitutes the practice of law."

In other words, the Missouri Supreme Court thinks it is the court's job, and not the job of lawmakers, to determine what is, and what isn't, the unauthorized practice of law in Missouri.

There are a few important things worth noting in this case. First of all, the bank in the case wasn't doing anything particularly "lawyerly"—it didn't hang out a shingle or roll up its sleeves and draft complicated legal documents or wear tasseled loafers. Based on the facts of the case, all it did was fill in the blanks on some pre-printed loan documents. (Sound familiar, car folks?)

Second, this case didn't suggest that the fee the bank

charged was prohibited under state lending laws. It just suggested that nonlawyers who collected such fees were engaging in the unauthorized practice of law.

So, what does this mean for Missouri dealers? Well, for starters, dealers in Missouri should think carefully before charging any fee for the preparation of documents unless that fee will be paid to a licensed attorney (fat chance, right?).

Dealers in other states aren't totally off the hook. Plaintiffs' lawyers can be pretty creative critters, but most of them would be just as happy to avoid firing their own neurons and poach an idea or two from a colleague. So, these types of claims may be coming soon to a theater near you.

Eisel v. Midwest BankCentre, 2007 WL 2367591 (Mo. August 21, 2007).

Are Your Spot Delivery Procedures "Customer-Friendly" Enough?

October 2007

By Thomas B. Hudson and Maya P. Hill

Spot delivery transactions occur when a dealer requires the customer to agree that the deal will be rescinded, or will not become effective, until a financing source agrees to buy the customer's contract. Spot delivery transactions raise a host of legal questions, and they are hard for dealers to do correctly. Consequently, plaintiffs' lawyers find these transactions attractive to attack. A recent Florida case—this one in federal court—illustrates how a dealer can structure a spot delivery to reduce the risk of a successful attack.

Alisa Jones bought a car and financed the purchase. In connection with the sale, Jones signed several documents, including a retail installment contract and a "Bailment Agreement for Vehicle Spot Delivery."

The Bailment Agreement provided that, pending credit approval of the buyer, the car would remain the dealership's property even though it was in the hands of the purchaser. Jones left the dealership with the car on the same day that she executed the documents.

Several days later, the dealership notified her that her financing agreement had been rejected and demanded that she return the vehicle. Here's where it gets interesting.

Take a look at the dealer's policies as reflected in the unwind of the deal. Jones returned the vehicle, and the dealership refunded her down payment. The dealership did not ask her to sign any further documents with different terms and did not ask her to reapply for credit at a higher interest rate. Jones was not charged any additional money in rental fees, and she was not charged by her automobile insurer to insure the car for the days during which the car was in her possession. All in all, the dealer's policies were very customer-friendly.

After returning the car, Jones sued the dealership, claiming that (1) the spot delivery violated the federal Truth in Lending Act; (2) she was entitled to recover damages under Florida's Motor Vehicle Retail Sales Finance Act; (3) the dealership had pulled her credit with no real intent of financing her purchase, thus violating the Fair Credit Reporting Act; and (4) the spot delivery agreement violated Florida's Unfair and Deceptive Acts and Practices Act.

Jones also moved for class certification and partial summary judgment on her claims. The dealership moved for summary judgment as to all claims and argued that Jones was an improper class representative. The U.S. District Court for the Middle District of Florida denied Jones' motion for class certification and her motion for partial summary judgment, and granted the dealership's motion for summary judgment as to all claims.

The court found that in order to recover under Florida's Motor Vehicle Retail Sales Finance Act, a plaintiff has to suffer some economic injury. Jones did not suffer any economic hardship because the dealership refunded all of her money upon return of the vehicle and her insurance company did not charge her for coverage during the few days she had the car. In addition, no finance charges were assessed, and Jones did not have to pay any use or mileage fees.

As to the FCRA claim, the court found that the dealership clearly intended to seek financing for her vehicle and pulled her credit for this specific purpose. The court noted that when a prospective buyer signs a retail installment contract in which the seller makes clear that it may attempt to assign the proposed financing arrangement to a third party, no FCRA violation occurs if the seller pulls the buyer's credit report for this purpose.

The court went on to find that the spot delivery agreement did not violate TILA because TILA does not apply to vehicle credit transactions in which the amount financed exceeds $25,000. The court did not address the broader issue of whether spot deliveries in general violate TILA.

The court found that the spot delivery agreement did not violate Florida's UDAP provisions because the documents Jones signed clearly stated that the delivery was contingent on the dealership's ability to secure a third-party financer and specifically provided that the dealership could legally cancel the sale if certain conditions were not satisfied.

Finally, the court denied Jones's motion for class certification. The court noted that class certification requires a class representative who is part of the class and, because Jones's claims were all dismissed, she could not be a member of the class.

You will need to be careful interpreting this opinion. What works in one state won't necessarily work in another. If you're reviewing your spot delivery procedures in light of this case, make sure your lawyer is involved.

Jones v. TT of Longwood, Inc., 2007 WL 2298020 (M.D. Fla. August 7, 2007).

Congratulations! You Are Now a Lawyer!

November 2007

By Thomas B. Hudson

The latest class action lawsuit craze is to allege that car dealers who charge a document fee (or an administrative, origination, or other fee) for the completion of legal documents—literally, filling in the blanks of those contracts—are engaging in the "unauthorized practice of law."

Presently, by my count, several of these class action cases are pending in several states. The top state courts in Arkansas and Missouri have rendered opinions in favor of the plaintiffs. (The Missouri case involved the completion of mortgage documents, but auto plaintiffs will claim that the legal concepts in the mortgage case would apply to auto finance.) Arkansas legislators have thrown a patch on the problem in that state, but it's too soon to know whether their fix will work. The Missouri court concluded that the completion of forms for a fee could be the unauthorized practice of law, despite a state law that expressly permits such a charge. So, if your state credit and dealer laws expressly permit a doc fee, you could still be at risk. The court announced that the judiciary, and not the legislature, was the final arbiter of what constituted the unauthorized practice of law.

I'd be willing to bet that every state has an "unauthorized

practice of law" (UPL) statute. These laws stem from a desire by the states to make sure that the public is protected from those who would pass themselves off as lawyers without actually having been admitted to the bar.

Those who are a bit more cynical will say that the UPL laws are just another way of keeping legitimate competitors from poaching on the domains of lawyers. The cynics will point to bar association attempts to ban the sale of "do-it-yourself" wills, tax forms, and the like in book stores and over the Internet, and to attempts to prohibit paralegals from doing tasks that the lawyers claim that only they should be permitted to do. But I digress.

If you are a dealer, what can you do to protect yourself against class claims like these? That answer will vary, depending on what your doc fee practices and other contracting practices have been and what your state law says about the unauthorized practice of law. If you haven't been charging a doc fee, give yourself a gold star and head for the golf course.

If you have been charging a doc fee, but it's clear from your documentation that no part of the doc fee is for the completion of documents, but is instead for other tasks involving the documents, like filing them with the appropriate authorities, your position may be somewhat stronger.

If you have been charging a doc fee, and the description of the fee does not make it clear that it is not a fee for document completion, you may well have a problem. Whether you do or not will depend on what your state's UPL law looks like, and how lucky you are.

Finally, if you've been using a mandatory arbitration agreement with your deals, and that agreement prohibits class relief, you may be able to divert the potential class action into a much-less-dangerous individual arbitration proceeding.

So, if you have been charging a doc fee that might be

vulnerable to these attacks, batten down the hatches, because there's some rough weather ahead. Also, this is dangerous stuff, so on a going forward basis, make sure your doc fee practices get a serious review from your lawyer.

Spots on the Spot

November 2007

By Michael A. Benoit

As most of you know, spot deliveries are a common practice in many dealerships around the country. Where they are permitted by law and properly executed, spot deliveries are a valuable sales process. However, there are many things that can go wrong in a spot delivery, and dealers need to be vigilant in their training and policies to make sure they don't find themselves in a "spot." A recent case (I couldn't make this up) brings the point home once again. See if you can "spot" the errors this dealer made.

Betty Buyer purchased New Car in a spot delivery transaction from Danny Dealer. Betty traded in Old Car as a down payment. She and Danny Dealer signed a retail installment sales contract, contingent on Danny's ability to find a finance source to purchase it. Betty brought New Car back the next day to get the fuel gauge fixed and saw Old Car being vacuumed and cleaned. Unbeknownst to Betty, Danny sold Old Car later that day to a fellow we'll call Dummy.

Spot #1: If you think that Danny should have held onto Old Car until Betty's deal was sold, give yourself a gold star.

Dummy enjoyed Old Car for a few days before law enforcement discovered him in it enjoying certain unlawful vegetable matter. Soon after, Dummy was residing in the pokey, and Old Car found itself at the police impound.

A few days later, Betty dropped back by Danny Dealer's to obtain some additional equipment, which Danny had promised to install on New Car. Much to her surprise, Danny Dealer demanded she return New Car. He told her that her financing had been denied and tried to talk her into different financing terms (Danny never before this instance had provided Betty any notice that Betty's financing application had been denied). Danny also told Betty that Old Car had been impounded because certain unlawful (and aromatic) vegetable matter had been found in it.

Spot #2: In this case, we're not sure if Danny Dealer ever forwarded Betty's application to a finance source. Danny didn't provide any evidence that he did. If he didn't, denying Betty's application for credit was an adverse action that would require Danny to provide written notice under the Equal Credit Opportunity Act. If he had pulled her credit report, he'd also have the obligation under the Fair Credit Reporting Act.

Although he had cleaned and vacuumed Old Car before selling it to Dummy, Danny blamed Betty for the errant vegetation that was in it during the unfortunate visit from law enforcement. He called her a "drug dealer" in an angry exchange in front of other customers and threatened to call the police and "report" Betty if she did not surrender New Car and leave the premises.

Spot #3: This really isn't a spot delivery issue, but Danny is really shooting himself in the foot. Calling Betty a drug dealer in public, if not true, could be slander. That's an actionable offense. And why get into it in the first place? Threatening to report her to the police on those grounds as a means of getting New Car back isn't too cool either.

Shaken, angry and hurt, Betty handed over the keys and demanded Danny return Old Car to her. God bless him, Danny told her she would have to pay the impound charges and get it back herself. Of course, she couldn't do that because Danny had the title and Dummy actually owned Old Car.

About a week later (after several irate phone calls from Betty), Danny towed Old Car to Betty's house and left it on the street, leaving the keys and the title on her front stoop. Old Car was in much worse shape than it had been when Betty traded it in—it wouldn't start, had substituted tires, was dented and scratched, and had numbers carved into the finish. Its trunk had bad water damage, too.

Spot #4: See Spot #1. If you take a trade on a spot delivery, in addition to keeping it until the financing transaction is complete, give it back in the same condition as when you received it when the financing goes south.

As a dealer, your people are your greatest asset, but if not properly educated, they can be your greatest liability. Betty is going to get her rightful day in court, largely as a result of inadequate training of personnel (and plain ole "jerk" behavior). A solid compliance-training program (and there are a number out there) can help everyone spot the "spots" in the organization, and keep the back-end mess to a minimum. Invariably, the dollars you spend up front can save you a hundred fold on the back. And that's not counting attorneys' fees!

Pickin' on Picks

December 2007

By Emily Marlow Beck

If all your customers show up with big, fat wads of cash when they buy a car, don't bother reading this. And, if all your customers can come up with huge down payments, carry on—

you don't need to go further. If you only deal with "A" credit customers, go ahead and turn the page. But, for the rest of you, read on.

"Picks." "Pups." "Dips." "Side Notes." "Pick Up Payments." Whatever you call them, if you work in special finance or buy-here, pay-here, deferred down payments are very likely a big part of your game plan. But there are some rules that govern this complicated practice, and, if you're not careful, little ol' pick payments can cause big, fat problems.

How so?

First of all, federal law is very specific about what can be considered a deferred down payment for federal disclosure purposes. Regulation Z of the Truth in Lending Act provides that a deferred portion of a down payment may be treated as part of the down payment if it is payable not later than the due date of the second otherwise regularly scheduled payment and is not subject to a finance charge. In other words, if your pick payments accrue interest, or if they are scheduled to be paid throughout the term of the contract, they don't qualify as part of the down payment under federal law.

But, there's more. Regulation Z gives some pretty clear guidance about how deferred down payments may be disclosed for federal purposes. In fact, the Federal Reserve Board's Commentary to Reg. Z provides that dealers may treat the deferred portion of the down payment in different ways, as long as certain rules are followed. For example, if the pick-up payment is treated as part of the down payment, it must be subtracted from the amount financed. Further, it may, but need not, be reflected in the payment schedule. But, if the payments go in the payment schedule, they must be included in the total of payments.

Easy enough, right?

Not quite. Don't forget that Reg. Z is nothing more than a federal disclosure law. You still need to look to state law to determine whether deferred down payments are permitted and how they must be disclosed on the contract. Sometimes, state law gives strong guidance on picks; other times, picks are just flat out prohibited. And sometimes, state law is mum on the topic.

Are you still with me? Now that I've confused all you guys, here are the most frequent issues I see with dealers using pick payments.

"Side notes" and other creative documents. Too often when I review dealer operations, I see dealers concocting all sorts of ways to document the deferred down payments. Sometimes I see dealers asking customers to execute "side notes"—like "mini loans"—to keep the customer on the hook for the payment without disclosing the payment on the installment contract.

You've heard us say it a million times—even the slightest changes to your forms can open a Pandora's Box of compliance issues, and deferred down payments are no exception. For example, would this separate agreement or "side note" be treated as a loan under state law? If so, do you need a lender's license to originate it? What disclosures would be required? Further, does your state have a "single document rule" that requires that the entire agreement live in the four corners of the retail installment contract?

Bank representations. Remember that dealer agreement you signed with your finance companies? It probably contained a bunch of reps and warranties that you make to the finance company when you assign a contract to them. Some of those reps and warranties probably include a promise that the dealer has actually received all down payment amounts. Hiding the deferred down payment from your finance sources could be a violation of your dealer agreement, or, worse yet, it could be flat out fraud (yeah, I mean fraud, fraud as in jail-time fraud).

So, what should you do if deferred down payments are a big part of your operations? It's time to start pickin' on the little guy! Ask yourself: Are your deferred down payments Regulation Z compliant? If so, do they comply with any applicable state laws? Think twice before drawing up any side notes or creative documentation, and involve your lawyer when you do. And, follow up with the agreements you have with your finance companies to make sure you don't run afoul of your representations to them.

Dealers, Official Fees, and Shakespeare
March 2008
By Thomas B. Hudson

Dealers regularly pass on "official fees" to their car-buying customers. Done correctly, the practice is generally legal and poses few concerns beyond accurate disclosure of the fees. But, as Shakespeare said in Hamlet's soliloquy, "To be or not to be: That is the question . . ." Let's take a look at a dealer who might not have gotten the question quite right.

Rhonda Bosland bought a car from Warnock Dodge, Inc. As part of the sale, Warnock Dodge charged Bosland a $117 registration fee. The sales contract didn't indicate that the dealer would retain a portion of that fee.

Three years later, Bosland learned that the actual official registration fee was only $97. The legal term for this development is "Oops."

Evidently unable to take a joke, Bosland brought a class action, claiming the $20 overcharge violated the New Jersey

Consumer Fraud Act (CFA) and the Truth-in-Consumer Contract, Warranty and Notice Act (TCCWNA), and that Warnock Dodge was unjustly enriched. Specifically, under the Automotive Sales Practices Regulations, a dealer may charge a documentary service fee on the registration of a vehicle, but the amount must be separately itemized. Because the $20 dealer fee was not itemized, Bosland claimed Warnock Dodge violated the CFA and TCCWNA.

Warnock Dodge moved to dismiss the claim. Warnock Dodge argued that the fee charged was not a documentary service fee and that Bosland could not bring suit because she did not demand a refund first. The trial court granted Warnock Dodge's motion. Evidently still annoyed, Bosland appealed.

The Superior Court of New Jersey, Appellate Division, reversed the trial court's dismissal of the CFA and TCCWNA claims. The appellate court noted that under the CFA, strict liability is imposed for a regulatory violation. Bosland alleged that she was charged a $117 registration fee; that the dealer did not specify that a documentary service fee was included in that amount; that the registration fee charged was $20 greater than the sum of all the official registration fees; and that the $20 difference constituted a documentary service fee, which was required to be disclosed.

The appellate court found that Bosland was not required to prove, at that early stage, that the fee was actually a documentary service fee. Rather, she only had to state a claim upon which relief could be granted, which she had done. Further, the appellate court stated that demand for a refund was not required in order to suffer an ascertainable loss under the CFA. Therefore, the appellate court concluded that Bosland stated a sufficient claim to survive a motion to dismiss.

The appellate court also found that Bosland had sufficiently alleged that Warnock Dodge was liable under the TCCWNA for violating the Automotive Sales Practices Regulations. The appellate court stated that Bosland did not need to allege that the contract was unclear or confusing in order to state a claim under the TCCWNA. The appellate court found that allegations of confusion are only required for claims under the Plain Language Act, not the TCCWNA. However, the appellate court upheld the dismissal of the unjust enrichment claim, finding that no benefit was conferred upon Warnock Dodge that was separate and distinct from the written contract.

The mumbo jumbo from the appellate opinion is judge-speak for the simple concept that Bosland's complaint was sufficient to keep her in court. Bosland still has to make her case before the court, and the jury or judge has to make some factual findings before there is a final judgment that the dealer did things incorrectly.

But, to this point, the dealer's likely already out a lot of money defending the matter. He will be out even more if the case doesn't settle quickly. He faces the risk of a significant class award. He has his business interrupted. His executives are focused on stuff other than selling cars.

Do you suppose Warnock Dodge asked its lawyer the correct way to disclose the official fees? That, after all, was the question.

Bosland v. Warnock Dodge, Inc., 2007 WL 3085857 (N.J. Super. App. Div. October 18, 2007).

Credit Fraud: The Wrong Kind of Favor

April 2008

By Emily Marlow Beck

While many of my colleagues and I earn our bread by picking apart and analyzing the laws that govern motor vehicle dealers and finance companies, a good chunk of our firm's practice deals with the laws and regulations that govern mortgage lending. We (more or less) affectionately refer to the mortgage crowd as "dirt lawyers," and they call us "motor heads." And, even though I've got motor oil running through my veins, I know better than to turn a blind eye to the goings on in the dirt law world. A recent AG claim against a mortgage broker caught my attention.

In early March, the office of Massachusetts Attorney General Martha Coakley sued a mortgage broker, alleging that it "fraudulently procured mortgage loans by submitting to lenders asset and income information for loan applicants that was fabricated or inflated."

The complaint asserted that the broker violated the Massachusetts Consumer Protection Act by, among other things, submitting loan applications to lenders that the broker knew, or should have known, contained false or inflated asset and income information. The complaint argued that the broker falsified information to secure loans for consumers who would not otherwise have qualified and, as a result, received fees from lenders it otherwise would not have received had it submitted accurate information.

It's not clear what, if any, penalties the mortgage broker will ultimately have to pay. The AG's office is seeking civil penalties and reimbursement of legal fees from the broker and also wants to forbid the broker from "brokering" loans in the future.

A press release quoted the AG as saying that "[i]rresponsible behavior by mortgage brokers has directly contributed to the foreclosure crisis that has devastated communities across the state. Our office will continue to hold businesses accountable for their role in fraudulent mortgage lending."

Mortgage loans? Foreclosures? What does any of this have to do with the car business?

For starters, it's easy to see how the misdeeds that got the AG's office up in arms could just as easily occur in a dealership—particularly a dealership that deals heavily in special finance. It's also interesting to note how the AG connected the dots between brokers overstating income and asset information and the "foreclosure crisis." In doing so, the AG suggested that an increase in foreclosures in the state is due, at least in part, to lenders who loan money to folks who simply don't qualify based on the false information provided by brokers.

So, what lessons should your dealership take from this AG claim? Here are some thoughts. While employees may be tempted to fudge income or asset information a tad here and a smidge there to help your customers get approved, misleading the assignee of your contract is serious business.

Remember that dealer agreement you signed with your finance companies? It probably contained a bunch of reps and warranties that you make to the finance company when you assign a contract to it. Some of those reps and warranties probably include a promise that all information provided to the assignee is accurate. Misleading your finance sources is, at a minimum, a violation of your dealer agreement, but is more likely flat-out fraud (as in, jail-time fraud). If the outfit that buys your contracts is federally chartered or federally insured (categories that include nearly all banks), that flat-out fraud is a federal felony.

Also, it's important to note how the AG complaint focused on how overstating income information could lead to foreclosures. Every once in a while we'll see a similar claim on the "car side"—a claim that a customer would not have had his or her car repossessed and his or her credit ruined but for the fact that the dealership put the customer in a payment that the customer couldn't afford. Allegations of falsified income make these sorts of claims even more dangerous.

So, how do you reduce these risks at your dealership?

First, train your employees that monkeying with credit application information is a crime and a violation of your dealer agreements. Then train them some more.

Then consider periodically auditing your deal files to make sure the income and asset information is consistent with any stipulations provided. Track down any inconsistencies with the responsible employee. Develop a "zero tolerance" policy for falsifying credit application information.

There are also some procedures you could implement to reduce claims that employees are falsifying income information. For example, consider requiring customers to complete all credit applications in the customer's handwriting. If this isn't practical in your dealership, consider asking customers to initial income and asset information provided in the credit application. The customer should also initial any changes to this information.

I, for one, am happy to take this little lesson from the dirt lawyers of the world.

A Double-Edged Sword

May 2008

By Thomas B. Hudson and Maya P. Hill

As we read the court's opinion in a recent case, it occurred to us that perhaps a bad practice had resulted in a favorable decision for the dealership. See what you think.

Bill Walker bought a car from Sunrise Pontiac Buick GMC Truck, Inc. John Haynes was his salesperson. As part of this transaction, he paid a $400 fee labeled "Dealer Incurred Costs (DIC)." It was only after he signed the final buyer agreement that he signed a worksheet that showed the breakdown of the costs and fees, including the DIC.

Some time after Walker bought the car, Haynes called him to tell him that the dealership was looking into some of the fees that were charged to customers, including the DIC, and asked if Walker wanted to get his money back for that fee. Walker said yes, and that is how Haynes introduced him to Causey, the attorney working with Haynes (in case you think there's something rotten in Denmark here, we don't think there's anything wrong with your sense of smell).

Walker sued Sunrise under the Tennessee Consumer Protection Act for common law fraud and misrepresentation, arguing that Sunrise illegally included the DIC in the vehicle's selling price and fraudulently misrepresented the nature of the costs to him during the transaction. He moved for class certification on both grounds.

At trial, Sunrise employees testified that the DIC amount varied by transaction and that customers were told that the fee represented various different services. Sunrise employees also testified that the fee did not represent any real costs incurred by the dealer and were pure profit for the dealership.

Sunrise moved for partial summary judgment, arguing that the claims were not proper for class certification. The trial court denied Sunrise's motion, and Sunrise appealed. The appellate court denied Sunrise's applications for permission to file an interlocutory appeal, and Sunrise appealed again.

The Supreme Court of Tennessee reversed the trial court's ruling and held that neither claim was proper for class certification. As to the TCPA claim, the court noted that the statute expressly provided for an individual's right of action, but did not provide for a class or cumulative right of action. In cases where the statute is unambiguous, the court explained, the plain meaning of the statute should control.

As to the common law fraud and misrepresentation claim, the court held that such claims are typically not proper for class certification because of the nature of the claim. Rather, the court continued, each alleged instance of fraud and misrepresentation usually varies by transaction, making the claims more suitable to pursue in an individual capacity. The court was persuaded by Sunrise's evidence that there was no uniform representation regarding the fee to customers and that, according to dealership employees, statements made to customers regarding the fee varied from negotiation to negotiation.

Now, we think it's not a good practice to charge any fee or charge, and especially something like this one, that sounds like a doc or administrative fee, without first determining what the fee is to be charged for and determining whether the fee is a reasonable charge for the services identified. Failing to provide the buyer with a disclosure (reviewed by counsel, of course) is also, in our humble opinion, a bad practice.

So, here the dealer imposes a charge for who-knows-what, described to each customer as the salesman sees fit, and what happens? The dealer dodges a class action claim!

We have to believe that if the dealer had "good" practices in place, however, Walker would not have sued the dealership in the first place.

Walker v. Sunrise Pontiac Buick GMC Truck, Inc., 2008 WL 375257 (Tenn. February 13, 2008).

Hickory, Dickory, and Doc Fees

June 2008

By Thomas B. Hudson

My partner Emily Beck has suggested that I climb down from my high horse when I talk about doc fees, and I've concluded that she's giving me good advice.

My antipathy toward doc fees comes from the fact that plaintiffs' lawyers are attacking them more frequently and in ever-more innovative ways. Content at first to argue that doc fees were not permitted by state law, the attacks morphed to allegations that doc fees were improperly disclosed under federal (and also sometimes state) law. Then we saw claims that doc fees, when imposed only (or more frequently) in financed deals, were required to be included in the finance charge and in the APR. Next, the plaintiffs' lawyers charged that by placing doc fees close to government-required fees, or by labeling them in a way that made them seem like official fees, the dealer had committed an unfair or deceptive practice under state law. The plaintiffs' lawyers' crowning achievement came when they convinced courts in several states that the charging of doc fees for completing contracts constituted the unauthorized practice of law.

Those attacks got me up on my high horse. Emily, who hails from a Virginia dealership family, argues that doc fees are a fact of life and have become an income stream for dealers. Her feeling is that doc fees aren't likely to go away soon.

She's probably right about that, so, assuming that your dealership is going to charge a doc fee, let's take a look at the steps you should take to reduce the risks that you will meet one of these inventive plaintiffs' attorneys face-to-face. Here's a checklist that you can start with.

- Determine whether state law permits doc fees. Some do, some don't. Some states' laws are silent on the topic. Some allow doc fees if the dealer goes through a few extra hoops. Get a legal opinion on the question from someone knowledgeable in dealer legal issues—this isn't a place for do-it-yourself legal work.
- Don't assume that because a state's law permits a doc fee of, say, $195, that you can necessarily charge that amount without risk. Plaintiffs will argue that if you are charging $195 for $25 worth of work, you have violated the law in a variety of ways.
- Have a written policy regarding doc fees. The written policy should state when doc fees will be imposed, the amount of the doc fees, and the estimated cost of the various chores for which the doc fee is imposed. The time to create this policy is when you decide to charge (or continue charging) doc fees, not after a suit is filed. You should have this policy reviewed by counsel—see the admonition above against do-it-yourself legal work.
- Comply with your own policy. If your policy is that you will charge a doc fee in every deal, don't agree to drop it for the buyer who is a hard bargainer.
- Have your policy reviewed periodically by counsel. Laws change and plaintiffs' theories of attack change. What works and can be defended today may not work and may be indefensible tomorrow.

- Consider using a mandatory arbitration provision in your deal documents as a first line of defense against class actions and large punitive damages awards. When a policy creates as many avenues of attack for plaintiffs as the charging of doc fees does, you need every defensive advantage you can get.

The bottom line? If you are going to charge a doc fee, do it right. The imposition of such a fee makes your dealership a target, and a class action target at that, for those inventive plaintiffs' lawyers. OK, I'm off my high horse. But I still have one foot in the stirrup.

Top Five Things You Need to Know About Selling Aftermarket Products
July 2008
By Nicole F. Munro

Standing in the airport, I glanced at the magazine racks. On nearly every cover was a top five or 10 list, which suggested to me that folks understand things better if we put them in a list. So, here is my list of the top five things dealers need to know about selling aftermarket products.

As economic belts tighten, dealers look for alternate ways to increase profits. One such way is the sale of aftermarket products. From etch to GAP to paintless dent services, dealers have become increasingly inventive in the number and types of products sold with a motor vehicle. While it is impossible to label and describe each product, it is clear that product features impact the sale of the product. These features may dictate whether or not the charges for the product can be financed, whether the dealer needs a license to sell the product, how the dealer must disclose the charges for the product, and/or whether additional disclosures are required. Because of feature variability, dealers these days must consider the following five issues before selling an aftermarket product.

1. Classification. States are becoming mine fields of regulation for aftermarket products. A dealer's first concern should be the classification of the product being sold. Is the product a vehicle protection product? If not, an aftermarket product could constitute a service contract, an auto club membership or service, or worse—insurance. Each feature of an aftermarket product must be compared to state laws to determine whether a state regulates the sale of the product and, if so, in what way. If you can't figure out what the product is, call your regulator—and your lawyer.

2. Licensing. After figuring out what the product is, a dealer needs to determine whether it needs an additional license or certificate of authority to sell the product. If it is an insurance product, the dealer may need to get an insurance agent license. If it is an auto club, licensing by a completely different state agency may be required.

3. Financing. Now that the dealer has classified the product and obtained the appropriate license, if necessary, the dealer must determine whether he may finance the sale of the product as part of motor vehicle installment sale transactions. The dealer should look to the statute governing credit sales and determine whether the statute allows a creditor to include the aftermarket product in the cash price of the vehicle. If unable to include it in the cash price, the dealer looks to whether the state expressly allows additional charges, is silent with respect to additional charges, or limits additional charges to those that are expressly provided in the statute.

4. Disclosure. Intimately related to item three, if the law applicable to a credit sale allows the dealer to charge for the aftermarket product, the question becomes where must the cost of the aftermarket product be disclosed in the contract? If a credit sale statute treats the cost of the aftermarket product as part of the cash price, a dealer may likely lump the product into the cash price. (Note that a dealer should still adequately disclose the cost of the aftermarket product outside of the retail installment sale contract to avoid claims of payment packing.) Some states, however, require a creditor to separately itemize the charge for the product. Of course, if the charge is paid to a third party, the Truth in Lending Act requires a creditor to separately itemize the charge and identify the party paid. If TILA applies and it's a third-party charge, the charge must be disclosed separately in the contract, and special TILA rules apply.

5. Laws. Finally, a dealer must look back to federal and state law to determine whether he must provide any other disclosures associated with the sale of the aftermarket product. Federal law may require a creditor to make certain disclosures in order to exclude charges from the calculation of the finance charge. Under some state laws, disclosures must accompany any warranty for a vehicle protection product. Other state laws require auto clubs to provide disclosures to their members. Service contracts and insurance are also heavily regulated.

Like theories on weight loss, my top five issues may be slightly different from someone else's. Nonetheless, I think each of these is an important consideration. And, it doesn't end here. Beyond these origination issues, we've found that buy-here, pay-here dealers and sales finance companies are increasingly worried about what should happen when a buyer prepays a contract, the vehicle is repossessed, or the optional product is cancelled. But, that's a top five list for another article.

Time for a Doc Fee Checkup?

August 2008

By Thomas B. Hudson

One of the more inventive arguments that plaintiffs' lawyers have come up with regarding doc fees is this one: A dealer that completes contractual documents by filling in blanks is engaged in the unauthorized practice of law.

Amazing. Courts in a couple of states actually have bought this argument, so it's refreshing to see a court have an attack of common sense and send the plaintiff's lawyer and this cockamamie theory packing.

Gary Flanary sued Carl Gregory Dodge of Johnson City, L.L.C., alleging that the dealership engaged in unfair and deceptive practices in violation of the Tennessee Consumer Protection Act (TCPA) by charging a $349 "administrative fee" that Flanary alleged was "all profit." Flanary also brought claims for the unauthorized practice of law, intentional misrepresentation/ fraudulent inducement, and unjust enrichment.

The trial court granted summary judgment for the dealership, and Flanary appealed. The Tennessee Court of Appeals affirmed the trial court's decision.

The appellate court first found that the dealership was entitled to summary judgment on its TCPA claim. The appellate court stated that, under the TCPA, an act or practice should not be deemed unfair unless the act or practice causes, or is likely to cause, substantial injury to consumers that is not reasonably avoidable by consumers themselves and is not outweighed by countervailing benefits to consumers or to competition.

The appellate court found that Flanary did not show injury from the imposition of the administrative fee. The evidence showed that Flanary agreed to a $12,000 "out the door" price with the salesman for the vehicle, and that is exactly what he paid. Flanary testified that he simply looked at the bottom line number. Therefore, the appellate court concluded that he did not suffer an "ascertainable loss of money or property" as required by the TCPA.

The appellate court also concluded that the dealership did not engage in the unauthorized practice of law by preparing a power of attorney and arbitration agreement and by charging for the preparation of those documents. The appellate court found that the dealership did not advise or represent Flanary in any capacity or do anything that would require the professional judgment of a lawyer.

The appellate court stated that "[t]he simple act of filling in the blanks on form documents that have been prepared for a business use does not constitute the unauthorized practice of law."

Finally, the appellate court concluded that the intentional misrepresentation and fraudulent inducement claim must fail because Flanary did not show injury or that the dealership was unjustly enriched.

So, chalk one up for the good guys, at least those in the Volunteer State. If you are a dealer elsewhere, you need to know that plaintiffs' lawyers have doc fees in their crosshairs. If you haven't done so already, it would be a good idea to check with your lawyer to make sure your practices are defensible.

Flanary v. Carl Gregory Dodge of Johnson City, L.L.C., 2008 WL 2434196 (Tenn. App. June 17, 2008).

Want a Job Making License Plates?
August 2008
By Thomas B. Hudson

Fraud by dealership employees isn't anything new. Sometimes the fraud targets are the dealership's customers, sometimes the dealership itself is the target, and sometimes the companies that buy retail installment contracts and leases from dealerships are the victims.

You really have to wonder whether the dealership employees know the risks that they are taking when they dummy up credit applications, assist in providing fake "stips" (stipulations), or add phantom equipment to the car's description in order to get the bank or finance company to increase its advance. Any dealership employee considering any such activities might want to pay attention to a recent press release from the feds.

The Office of the United States Attorney for the Western District of Missouri announced that the former general manager of a Kansas City, Missouri, dealership pleaded guilty in federal court to a wire fraud scheme. The scheme involved falsifying paperwork on car leases in order for the GM to obtain higher commissions for himself.

According to the release, Duane C. Clark waived his right to a grand jury and pleaded guilty in U.S. District Court to a federal charge of wire fraud, following an FBI investigation.

Clark, formerly general manager of John Chezik Homerun, Inc, d/b/a John Chezik Honda, admitted that from April 3, 2000, through June 14, 2004, he fraudulently altered car lease worksheets and contracts by adding (or approving the addition of) dealer-installed options that were never actually installed. The altered leases were then assigned to American Honda Finance Corporation.

The altered lease contracts showed an inflated vehicle value due to the nonexistent dealer-installed options, fraudulently added by Clark. As a result, Clark and others received higher commissions from Chezik. The total potential loss, as calculated from the altered lease worksheets, was approximately $62,230.

Clark hasn't been sentenced yet, but the U.S. Attorney noted that under federal statutes, he could be subject to a sentence of up to 20 years in federal prison without parole, plus a fine up to $250,000 and an order of restitution.

Clarke was fortunate that the buyer of leases from the dealership was a state-chartered sales finance company and not a federal financial institution. Federal law (18 U.S.C. 1344) says:

Whoever knowingly executes, or attempts to execute, a scheme . . .

(1) to defraud a financial institution; or

(2) to obtain any of the moneys, funds, credits, assets, securities, or other property owned by . . . a financial institution, by means of false or fraudulent . . . representations . . . shall be fined not more than $1,000,000 or imprisoned not more than 30 years, or both.

Ouch!

In short, playing fast and loose with the companies that buy your dealership's leases and retail installment contracts is not a career-enhancing move. Unless your chosen career is making license plates.

What Happens When Your Customer Isn't Insured?
August 2008
By Thomas B. Hudson

Sometimes it seems like there's just no end to the ways a dealer can get into a legal jam. That's really not surprising, I suppose, considering that dealers lease and sell cars; they also sell service contracts, GAP, etch, various sorts of insurance, and occasionally the kitchen sink. Here's an example of a dealer's problems arising from the sale, or nonsale, of credit insurance.

Beatrice Carr bought a vehicle from Circle S Enterprises, Inc., d/b/a Newbury Auto Mart. Included in the monthly payment was $29 for credit life and disability insurance that Circle required as part of the sale.

Carr's daughter, Linda, made the monthly payments to Circle until Carr, at the age of 81, died, nearly three years after the purchase. After Carr's death, Linda assumed that the credit life and disability insurance paid off the retail installment contract; so, she stopped paying.

Oops. Without informing Carr, Circle never obtained the insurance because Carr was too old to qualify. After the holder of the retail installment contract repossessed the vehicle, Circle refunded to Carr's estate the amount paid for insurance premiums plus 6% interest from the date of the sale.

Carr's estate sued Circle for failing to obtain the insurance, alleging breach of contract, conversion, negligence, violation of the South Carolina Unfair Trade Practices Act, and violation of the Regulation of Manufacturers, Distributors, and Dealers Act. The trial court granted Circle's motion for a directed verdict, stating that the evidence did not support a finding that Carr's estate suffered any loss or had been damaged in any way.

Carr's estate appealed, and the South Carolina Court of

Appeals reversed the trial court's ruling. The appellate court recognized the general proposition that "one who pays insurance premiums is justified in assuming that payment will bring immediate protection." The appellate court found that Carr's estate would have benefited from the insurance because the vehicle would not have been repossessed and found that sufficient evidence existed for each claim to be presented to a jury.

The appellate court rejected Circle's argument that Circle only offered to obtain price quotes for the insurance and that it was not, itself, the insurance provider. The appellate court also found that Circle's refund of the premiums was not dispositive on the issue of whether Circle's continued acceptance and retention of the premiums for insurance it knowingly did not obtain resulted in harm to Carr's estate.

[Editor's note: dispositive, adj. (1613) directed toward or effecting disposition (as of a case), (dispositive evidence).— Webster's Ninth New Collegiate Dictionary]

The lesson here? Dealers need to monitor and audit their insurance sales activities to make sure that they are obtaining insurance on everyone who has elected it. It might also be a good idea to take a look at the dealership's and the insurer's forms to make certain that they accurately reflect the dealer's role and obligations regarding insurance.

Estate of Carr v. Circle S Enterprises, 2008 WL 2404218 (S.C. App. June 10, 2008).

Bulletproof?

August 2008

By Thomas B. Hudson

One of the services we offer at our law firm is a dealership compliance audit. When we do those audits, we actually visit the dealership to observe the practices and procedures that the dealership is using in connection with its credit sale and lease activities, and we also review every scrap of paper the dealership uses.

After we've completed our review and communicated our sometimes-critical conclusions to the dealer, we often get the request from the dealer to address the dealership's documents, policies, and procedures and "make them bulletproof."

There's only one problem. We don't do bulletproof.

If a lawyer tells you that your operation is bulletproof from attacks by plaintiffs' lawyers, we suggest you consider changing lawyers. Of course, it could be the case that your lawyer is just a lot smarter than we are, and that he or she carries around some bulletproof in that alligator hide briefcase, but we can tell you that we have never seen bulletproof, and we don't think it exists.

When I tell dealers that we're fresh out of bulletproof, I go on to explain what I think we actually can do to reduce the dealership's lawsuit exposure. I ask the dealers to imagine that they are out in a field with a bow and a quiver of arrows. Then I ask them to imagine a barn 100 feet away with targets plastered all over the side and to imagine that some of the targets are 4-foot circles, others are 2-foot and 1-foot circles, and some are tiny 6-inch circles. I tell the dealers that what we try to do is to make them the smallest, most difficult-to-hit target for the plaintiffs' lawyers.

How do we do it? Well . . .

We shrink the dealership's target by making sure that all the forms the dealership is using comply with federal and state law, and that the forms work properly together. We rework, if necessary, the dealership's written policies and procedures, and we make sure that the implementation of the policies and procedures doesn't stray from their written description.

We suggest that the dealership have a designated Privacy and Compliance Officer and, if it is large enough, a "Customer Representative" whose job it is to help customers who have complaints. We urge F&I compliance certification and ethics training for those dealership personnel whose duties would benefit from such training.

We recommend that the dealership use consumer education brochures, such as *Understanding Vehicle Finance,* available free from the National Automobile Dealers Association's website, and *The Keys to Vehicle Leasing,* available from the Federal Reserve Board's website, and that copies of these brochures be displayed in the dealership and included with the documents given to every customer.

We suggest that the dealership visit with the appropriate state regulators, both to determine whether the regulators have resources that would help the dealership and to make sure that the dealership doesn't have its first contact with the regulators in connection with a customer complaint. And, finally, we recommend that the dealership incorporate a mandatory arbitration agreement into its contracts with customers as a first, best line of defense against class action lawsuits and outsized jury awards.

Bulletproof? Nope. But a mighty difficult target.

Can Your Dealership Afford to Pack Payments?

September 2008

By Thomas B. Hudson

You would have thought by now that dealerships would have gotten the word on payment packing. I mean, we've carried articles in *Spot Delivery*® pointing out how dangerous the practice is. National news routinely contains reports of enforcement actions (often involving stiff fines) against dealers engaging in the practice. And reputable trainers around the country tout a "true menu" sales process as an antidote to the old, discredited way of doing business. When we speak to dealership groups, we showcase the evils of payment packing, and when we visit dealerships, we look for signs of packing.

Still, you can't kill it with a hammer—there always seem to be dealerships that don't get the word.

The most recent example involves an Oregon dealership, nailed by the Oregon AG for allegedly payment packing and doing other bad stuff. Here's a recap of the AG's press release.

On August 20, Oregon Attorney General Hardy Myers announced a $100,000 settlement agreement with Erling Johansen, Inc., d/b/a Salem Nissan, a Salem car dealership. The agreement addressed several practices the AG called illegal, such as "packing" sales contracts with unwanted aftermarket products, not telling buyers they did not have to buy the additional stuff, and not following the specifics of the "bushing" law when the dealer couldn't find a buyer for the customer's contract within 14 days of the sale and had to unwind the deal.

The dealership was named in an Assurance of Voluntary Compliance (AVC). The AVC admitted no law violation on the dealer's part.

The dealership agreed to pay the Oregon Department of

Justice (DOJ) $100,000 for its Consumer Protection and Education Fund. The first of three payments, $15,000, was due immediately; $15,000 was due by September 1, 2008, and $20,000 by October 1, 2008. DOJ will suspend payment of the remaining $50,000 if the dealership "materially complies" with all conditions of the agreement.

According to the AG's press release, DOJ staff investigated complaints against Salem Nissan and found that in almost every new and used car sale transaction, the dealership was "packing" the contracts with several aftermarket products without the consumers knowing they didn't have to buy the products. The AG claimed that this was done under a program titled "Pride of Ownership," which included extended service warranties, securities products, insurance, and a gas-saving device called a Vortex Fuel Maximizer. (No doubt, this sounds hauntingly familiar to some of you.)

The AG said that its investigators also found that Salem Nissan violated the Oregon "bushing" statute on numerous occasions by having consumers sign new sales contracts without advising them they had a right to walk away from deals if the original offers were no longer available.

Under the agreement, Salem Nissan must make extensive changes to its operating procedures. The dealership agreed that it would not represent that the sale or lease of an automobile is contingent on buying additional products such as extended warranties, that it would describe the difference shown on the extension sticker between the offering price and the Manufacturer's Suggested Retail Price (MSRP) as "additional dealer profit," "additional mark-up," or a similar term, and that the extension sticker would accurately itemize and describe all charges added to, or subtracted from, the MSRP to reach the offering price.

The dealership also agreed to comply with all aspects of the Oregon "bushing" law in unwinding a deal if financing cannot be obtained within 14 days after the contract is signed. The dealership must tell the buyer that he or she did not qualify for financing and is entitled to receive all items of value paid as part of the transaction, including any trade-in, down payment, and monthly payments that might have been made.

The dealership also agreed that its employees would, in good faith, attempt to resolve consumer complaints filed with the Oregon DOJ within 20 days following receipt of the complaint. If at that time the complaint isn't resolved, the dealership will arrange for mediation and, if that fails, arbitration.

The dealership agreed to conduct training for all its sales, finance, and management personnel for the next year, and for all new personnel within 15 days of employment, regarding state consumer protection laws and rules applicable to car sales. (Hint! Hint! AGs like compliance-training programs! Where's yours?)

Finally, the company agreed to make an additional review of any transaction where the buyer's competency to enter into a contract is questioned. The following types of transactions would automatically be reviewed:

- Buyers are under age 18 or over age 70
- Buyers for whom English is not the primary language and a communication barrier may exist
- Buyers who had purchased a different vehicle within the last 12 months
- Buyers without a driver's license
- Buyers with a physical or mental handicap that would hinder their ability to drive

So, at the end of the day, the dealership is out of pocket at least $50,000, and maybe $100,000. It has had to pay its own lawyer probably tens of thousands of dollars, has suffered a serious publicity black eye, and has had to accept operating constraints and training responsibilities that will occupy management's time and divert the dealership's energies away from its business.

And, you thought that menu-selling program you just installed was expensive!

Oops, My Bootstrap's Broken

October 2008

By Thomas B. Hudson

Occasionally, those clever plaintiffs' lawyers will convince a court that a law that was actually intended to address one activity is really a Swiss Army Knife that can be used in many other ways. A recent case illustrates an unsuccessful attempt to bootstrap a general fraud claim onto a specific federal law dealing with odometer disclosures. Let's see what happened.

Mayble Bodine bought a truck from Graco, Inc. Graco gave Bodine an accurate odometer statement but did not give her a copy of the truck's title. Graco assured Bodine that the truck was in good condition.

Bodine registered the truck and learned that it had been classified as a "restored salvage vehicle" under Arizona law and that the truck had mechanical problems that made it dangerous to drive. Bodine attempted to return the truck to Graco, but Graco refused and denied knowing about the truck's status as a "restored salvage vehicle." Bodine sued Graco, alleging violations of the Motor Vehicle Information and Cost Savings Act (Odometer Act). Graco moved to dismiss, and a magistrate judge granted the motion. Bodine appealed.

The U.S. Court of Appeals for the Ninth Circuit affirmed

the trial court's grant of Graco's motion to dismiss. Bodine argued that Graco violated the Odometer Act by deliberately withholding the title to the truck from her to conceal the truck's collision history. The appellate court addressed the issue of whether the Odometer Act allows a private right of action where the intent to defraud relates to something other than the vehicle's mileage. The court noted that Congress enacted the Odometer Act to prohibit tampering with car odometers and to provide protection to vehicle buyers in connection with the sale of vehicles with altered or reset odometers, and that the regulations accompanying the Odometer Act require a person transferring a vehicle to disclose the vehicle's mileage to the transferee in writing on the certificate of title or other document issued by a state that indicates ownership of the vehicle.

The Odometer Act provides for a private cause of action when a person violates the Act with intent to defraud. The appellate court noted that the Seventh Circuit, addressing the issue under similar facts, has held that the Odometer Act creates a private right of action for violations of the Act where the transferor fails to disclose the vehicle's mileage to the transferee on the vehicle's title with the intent to defraud the transferee as to the vehicle's mileage. The appellate court also noted that, although the Odometer Act does not specifically limit the "intent to defraud" to odometer fraud, Congress enacted the Act to prohibit odometer tampering and to protect consumers against the sale of vehicles with altered or reset odometers.

The appellate court further noted that every part of the statutory scheme speaks to odometer fraud and does not suggest that Congress intended to reach additional types of fraud. Thus, the appellate court found that the language and purpose of the Odometer Act suggests that a private cause of action exists under the Act only where the alleged intent to defraud pertains to the mileage on a vehicle. Therefore, the appellate court concluded that Bodine did not have a claim against Graco under the Odometer Act.

This should settle the question in the Ninth Circuit, but you should expect to see the same argument tried in other circuits.

Bodine v. Graco, Inc., 2008 WL 2841160 (9th Cir. (D. Ariz.) July 24, 2008).

Do the Right Thing, and You May Still Get in Trouble

October 2008

By Shelley B. Fowler

Spot Delivery® is our forum to stress how important it is for dealers to learn and to follow the many laws and rules applicable to their business. Most of the time, we assume that when you do the right thing, you won't get in trouble. But not always . . .

A recent case shows that even when a dealer does everything right, it can still get sued by a disgruntled customer. In the end, the dealer came out the winner at both the trial and appellate court levels. But I'm sure the dealer in this case didn't feel like the victor after having to spend time, money, and aggravation over the course of eight years just to get two courts to agree that it did nothing wrong.

Arthur and Linda Tripp signed, among other documents, a buyers order, credit contract, title reassignment form, and application for certificate of title and registration to buy a used 1994 Ford Taurus from Charlie Falk's Auto Wholesale Incorporated (CFAW). Both the buyers order and the credit contract contained a clause allowing CFAW to cancel the transaction in the event Future Finance Company, Inc., the financing company, would not accept the deal. The credit contract also included a $395 processing fee in the total amount financed. The title reassignment form and application for certificate of title and registration contained an odometer disclosure, showing a mileage reading of 67,154.

The Tripps made a down payment and left with the vehicle, bearing temporary tags, the same day. One week later, CFAW informed the Tripps that Future Finance declined the deal. CFAW offered to restructure the deal, but the Tripps declined, and CFAW took possession of the Taurus. The Tripps received a refund of their down payment, less the mileage charges they incurred.

A year later, the Tripps sued, claiming that CFAW violated the Truth in Lending Act, Virginia's Consumer Protection Act, and the Federal Odometer Act, and was therefore liable for statutory damages. CFAW moved for summary judgment, and the trial court granted the motion.

Unhappy with the result, the Tripps appealed to the U.S. Court of Appeals for the Fourth Circuit. The Tripps argued that CFAW violated TILA because it provided the required credit disclosures after the Tripps signed the contract. The appellate court rejected the Tripps' argument and found that the record showed that CFAW explained the documents to the Tripps and gave them an opportunity to read the documents prior to signing them. Therefore, there was no TILA violation, because CFAW provided the required disclosures in a form that the Tripps could keep prior to having them sign the documents.

The Tripps argued that CFAW also violated TILA by failing to label the $395 processing fee as a finance charge that was optional for cash buyers. The appellate court found that CFAW consistently charged the fee for preparing necessary title work to both cash and credit buyers and therefore it was not a finance charge.

The Tripps also argued that CFAW violated TILA, because it failed to inform them that the TILA disclosures were estimates. The appellate court found that the amounts and terms disclosed to the Tripps were not estimates, because, had Future Finance approved the deal, the Tripps would have been obligated to buy the car on the terms disclosed. Therefore, CFAW did not have a duty to disclose that the figures were estimates.

The Tripps argued that CFAW violated the FOA by failing to accurately disclose the mileage in an attempt to deceive the Tripps. The appellate court found that the requirements of the FOA were not triggered because title to the Taurus did not transfer to the Tripps. The court also found that CFAW accurately disclosed the mileage as five miles more than was disclosed on the title when assigned from Crestar to CFAW, taking into account the number of miles the car was driven by the Tripps when they test drove it.

The appellate court affirmed the trial court's decision not to exercise supplemental jurisdiction over the state law claims after dismissing all federal claims.

So, the lesson in all this? Continue to do the right thing, but don't be surprised if you still get in trouble.

Tripp v. Charlie Falk's Auto Wholesale Incorporated, 2008 WL 3992464 (4th Cir. (E.D. Va.) August 29, 2008).

Is Nice Enough?

October 2008

By Emily Marlow Beck

I hear my share of interesting comments and questions when I hang out and perform "booth duty" at dealer conferences. At a recent conference, I met a dealer who shared with me his "secret formula" for avoiding consumer lawsuits. This dealer explained that he didn't need to concern himself about the technical "nuts and bolts" of the laws because by "treating customers right" and "trying to do the right thing," the dealer was able to sleep at night and not worry about lawsuits.

This comment caught my attention. After all, we sure have written enough articles through the years about how consumer-friendly programs can be a great deterrent to consumer claims and class action lawsuits. After all, happy customers don't call complaining to their local Better Business Bureau and state consumer credit regulators.

If you read state Attorney General press releases, you might just agree with this gentleman. After all, state AGs have cranked up their enforcement actions against the sales practices of car dealers, most of whom, if the AG allegations were true, were not adhering to the Golden Rule.

For example, just recently, an Oregon AG accused some local dealers of payment packing, among other things. According to the AG's press release, the dealership included the cost of additional, optional products in the transaction and misled the customers as to the true cost of the products.

A couple weeks later, the AG in next-door Washington State tapped a bunch of dealers for naughty deeds. While the dealership admitted no wrongdoing, it settled claims of all sorts of misdeeds, including credit application fraud and not timely paying off of liens.

Based on these AG reports alone, you might be inclined to agree with my pontificating dealer friend that bad behavior is the cause for disciplinary actions against car dealers, and that by nixing the "bad behavior," a dealer could eliminate her risk of regulatory enforcement. That is, of course, unless you set your sights on the other coast. New Jersey, to be exact.

The New Jersey State Division of Consumer Affairs announced recently that it conducted "unannounced inspections" on New Jersey car dealerships for compliance with the federal Used Car Rule and certain provisions of the Consumer Fraud Act. As a result, the Division issued "notices of violation" to 49 dealerships throughout New Jersey.

The dealerships cited failed to post prices for the used vehicles offered for sale in accordance with the Consumer Fraud Act and/or failed to post a Used Car Buyers Guide on used motor vehicles in accordance with the Used Motor Vehicle Trade Regulation Rule.

Based on the press release, Division investigators found 49 of the 97 dealerships inspected in six New Jersey counties to be in violation. Of the 2,144 used vehicles inspected, 1,492 were offered for sale without a posted price, and 472 failed to contain a Used Car Buyers Guide.

The Division listed the noncomplying dealers by name in the press release—kind of like a teacher writing the names of misbehaving students on the chalkboard. (Certainly not the kind of free advertising they had hoped for!)

The Division explained that, by sending the notice of violation, the Division sought to ensure that the dealerships posted the required information on all used vehicles offered for sale. Named dealers had 15 days to respond to the notice of violation. Oh, and the Division also asked for a civil penalty and "reimbursement of investigative costs." While I couldn't confirm the amount of the penalty, several news articles stated the penalty as $2,000.

This AG press release got me thinking.

First, I think some of the dealerships got off pretty easy. In this case, the state regulatory agency came knocking. Had the Federal Trade Commission paid them a visit, the dealers who violated the Used Car Rule could be facing an $11,000 per violation penalty. *[Editor's note #1: That penalty has since been increased to $16,000.]* That ain't no small change.

[Editor's note #2: Bigger ouch.]

Second, I'd bet you dollars to donuts that most of these dealers didn't see this coming. A local newspaper reporting on the investigations and citations quoted the general manager of one dealership as saying, "In the 33 years I've been a dealer, [the law] was never enforced." My bet is that many of these dealers thought that, because these issues had been overlooked for so long, they'd continue to be overlooked. Unfortunately for these guys, that wasn't quite the case.

Finally, I think the story of the New Jersey dealerships goes to show that, while treating customers right is a great way to stay out of the consumer cops' warpath, there is no substitute for knowing and complying with the nuts and bolts of the law—even the ones that you don't think will be enforced. But, while you figure those laws out, don't forget to be nice!

What Did You Do on Your Summer Vacation?

October 2008

By Emily Marlow Beck

What's your idea of summertime fun? The beach? Hot dogs? Days by the pool, sipping piña coladas and slathering on the coconut delight tanning polish?

How 'bout slapping around a bunch of car dealers? It seems like the attorneys in the Washington State Attorney General's office had quite a bit of fun doing just that this summer.

According to its press release, the AG's office reached a settlement with Washington State car dealerships, which the AG's office hopes will "drive home an important message to all car dealers." The settlement agreement didn't include an admission of wrongdoing, but required the dealerships to comply with consumer protection laws, work to resolve consumer complaints in good faith, and pay $20,000 in attorneys' fees and costs.

According to the release, the AG's Consumer Protection Division launched a joint investigation with the Department of Licensing into the dealers' business practices in 2006 after receiving a complaint from a consumer who said she paid $18,700 for a "new" KIA Optima before discovering that it had been previously sold and titled to another customer. When state investigators took a closer look, they found quite a potpourri of alleged misdeeds.

For example, the AG's office alleged that the dealerships falsified credit applications by inflating salaries and lowering housing costs. As a result, at least four cars were repossessed because buyers couldn't make the payments on cars they should not have been able to buy in the first place.

If that wasn't enough, the dealerships allegedly routinely

failed to pay off liens on customers' trade-ins within two business days, as required by state law. As a result, customers continued to receive bills for cars they no longer owned and, in some cases, were hit with overdraft fees.

To top it all off, the office also alleged the companies improperly certified customer signatures on Department of Licensing documents, failed to maintain advertising records, and violated Washington's "bushing" statute.

Don't forget that the dealers settled these claims with the AG without any admission of wrongdoing. There has not been a trial, and no judge or jury has found that anyone has done any bad deeds. So, these cases may have just been stories of perfectly well-behaved dealers who fell prey to some AGs who got up on the wrong side of the bed. Either way, a visit from the state AG's office is no way to end your summer. But, if you ask me, it could have been much worse.

How so? Well, for starters, the dealers didn't have to pay up any huge fine or penalties. We've seen dealers pay far more hefty penalties than the ones imposed here. In recent months, we've seen dealers ticketed in amounts of nearly $300,000 just for abusive advertising programs.

Second, remember the story about the Massachusetts mortgage broker who was hit by the state AG earlier this year for falsifying credit applications? The AG sought to forbid the broker from "brokering" loans in the future. The dealers at issue here didn't have their licenses placed on the line.

Further, had the dealerships really, truly been falsifying credit applications, they could have been in big time trouble with their assignee finance companies. We've said it before. Misleading your finance sources is, at a minimum, a violation of your dealer agreement, but is more likely flat-out fraud (as in, jail-time fraud). If the outfit that buys your contracts is federally chartered or federally insured (categories that include nearly all banks), that flat-out fraud is a federal felony.

So, all of you who avoided a visit from the AG's office this summer, pat yourself on the back. But, don't be too complacent. Quite a few of your dealer brethren did not fare so well. And, besides, it doesn't look like the AG's office has vacation plans any time soon.

Trade-in Trouble

December 2008

By Catherine M. Brennan

Regular readers of *Spot Delivery*® know that violating the law will get you sued. They also learn that violating the law while failing to respond to your customer's complaints about your bad actions—no matter how unintentional you may later claim they were—will land you in court. What everyone—readers and nonreaders alike—need to realize is that law violations may also land you on your local television news as the lead story in the consumer fraud segment.

Certain practices are more likely than others to raise the ire of your average customer. One example is a no-brainer: A dealer that takes a car with an existing loan balance as a trade-in needs to pay off the debt. This will become increasingly important as the economy continues to struggle and more consumers seek to trade in their higher priced vehicles for more affordable wheels. Even if your state law doesn't require the dealership to pay off the liens on those underwater cars—although many of them do —it is bad practice to leave your customers on the hook for two car payments, without a pay-off plan.

This very issue reared its head recently in Illinois and Utah, two states that explicitly require a dealer in this situation to pay off the lien on the trade-in. In November 2008, Illinois Attorney General Lisa Madigan filed a lawsuit against a Chicago auto dealer for allegedly failing to pay off nearly $50,000 in trade-in vehicle liens in violation of the state's unfair and deceptive acts and practices law. Madigan's complaint alleges that Montell Chevrolet in Chicago failed to pay the outstanding balances on trade-in vehicles that consumers surrendered when they purchased new cars. The state UDAP law expressly requires dealerships to pay off a lien within 21 days.

Madigan's office reportedly received four complaints against Montell, reflecting outstanding balances ranging from $10,000 to more than $30,000. Because Montell failed to pay off the liens on the trade-ins, the consumers remained financially responsible for a traded-in vehicle they no longer possessed. As a result, some consumers became targets for creditors' repeated demands to pay off the liens, while others continued to make monthly payments for the traded-in cars. Consumers who filed complaints with the AG's office said their credit ratings suffered. This is real, significant harm, especially as lenders across the country are tightening their underwriting standards in the face of a dearth of credit.

The kicker here is that Montell already is operating under a 2005 consent decree with Madigan's office, requiring the dealership to pay off trade-in liens within the legal limit of 21 days, and Madigan's office claims that it tried to mediate these current allegations before filing its lawsuit. Therefore, Madigan is asking the court to find the dealership in contempt of court for violating the consent decree and to enter a permanent injunction against the dealership to bar it from engaging in the practice of failing to pay off the liens on trade-ins in the future. The complaint also asks the court to order Montell to pay restitution to consumers, a $50,000 civil penalty, an additional $50,000 penalty for each violation of the Consumer Fraud Act, and all fees associated with the investigation and prosecution of the case.

Meanwhile, across the country, in a separate case, the Utah Department of Motor Vehicles is investigating Grants Auto Sales in Logan for allegedly promising customers thousands of dollars for their trade-ins, and then refusing to pay off the liens on those trade-ins. Like Illinois, Utah law provides that if a dealer takes a trade-in from a retail customer as part of the sale of a motor vehicle and there is an outstanding balance owing on the trade-in, the dealer must, within seven days, notify the lienholder in writing that the vehicle has been traded in. The dealer is required by Utah law to pay the lienholder for the trade-in vehicle within 21 calendar days of the date of sale, or within 15 days of receiving payment in full for the motor vehicle it sold, whichever is earlier. Because Grants allegedly failed to do either, the Utah DMV shut it down. According to local news accounts, the DMV plans to file criminal charges against the dealership for its inaction.

Of course, not all states require the dealer to pay off the balance on a vehicle it takes in trade. However, some of those states warn consumers of the risks of relying on a dealer to pay the balance on a trade-in. In Georgia, the Governor's Office of Consumer Affairs warns consumers about the dangers of relying on the car dealer to pay off the lien on a trade-in. Even if a dealership agrees in writing to pay off your existing lien, the Governor's Office cautions that there is no guarantee that it will do so. In a weakened economy, it is not unlikely that some dealerships would experience financial difficulties or even go out of business before paying off the customer's lien.

So, what is a dealer to do? First, locate the law in your state that requires you to pay off the balance on the trade-in, and implement procedures to make sure you make the payoff within the allotted time frame. Second, make sure your financing documents account for these time frames. Finally, make sure that if you agree to make the payoff in your contracts, you honor those contracts. Nothing will lead to a lawsuit faster than a consumer harried by creditors on a car he or she no longer owns.

And nothing attracts viewers like a "victim's plight" on a television consumer fraud segment.

Power Booking? How About Power Jail Time?
December 2008
By Thomas B. Hudson

"Power booking," when used by dealers, sounds like a cool, successful, macho practice that indicates that the dealer sold the buyer a car and lots of additional stuff. Actually, it's a very uncool, illegal practice that not only violates a dealership's agreements with the companies to which it sells its retail installment contracts, but also state and federal criminal laws.

If you are a dealer, or if you work in a dealership, and are not familiar with the term, that's probably a good thing. If you're in close touch with the practices in your finance department, and you haven't heard the term, then the practice likely is not occurring at your dealership. If you aren't in close touch with your finance department's practices, remember that your finance employees can carry these tricks with them from job to job, so it might be worth an internal audit to make sure your operation is clean.

The term "power booking" actually refers to the practice by some dealers of lying about the car's equipment and accessories to get the bank or sales finance company to pay more for the contract. The practice occurs when the dealer is attempting to sell a retail installment contract. And, no, you didn't misread what I said. I said, "lying."

Banks and sales finance companies typically require the dealer to provide a detailed description of the vehicle and its equipment and accessories so that the bank or finance company can determine what the vehicle is worth. The bank or sales finance company then typically uses that value to determine the amount that the bank or sales finance company will advance to the dealer in connection with a particular vehicle.

A vehicle with, for instance, a sunroof is worth a bit more than one without. The dealer may have accurately described the vehicle to the buyer, who, after all, can tell whether the vehicle has a sunroof, so there is no fraud involved in the transaction between the dealer and the buyer.

The fraud arises in the transaction between the dealer and the bank or sales finance company. When the dealership's representatives misrepresent the vehicle to the bank or sales finance company, they have defrauded the bank or sales finance company and can be sued in a civil court for damages. That's only the beginning of the problem, however. A power booking dealer also violates criminal laws. Most states, as well as the feds, have laws that make this sort of activity illegal. Dealers and dealerships that engage in such activity can expect to face the prospect of being fitted with a bright orange jumpsuit.

"But," some dealers will say, "What's the chance that I'll get caught if I'm power booking? A lot of buyers pay as agreed, and the bank or sales finance company is none the wiser. No harm, no foul."

Well, I can't tell you what the chances are of a power booking dealer getting caught, but I can tell you that those chances are much higher now than they were a couple of years ago. Why so, you ask?

First, banks and sales finance companies have tumbled to the practice. Nearly every company I know of that buys contracts from dealers now regularly calls the buyer and goes through a scripted interview designed, in part, to make sure the vehicle description provided by the dealer is correct. It only takes one buyer saying, "What sunroof?" to cause the fecal material to impact the cooling device.

Second, the practice has caught the eyes of Attorneys General around the country. Although AGs are usually a lot more interested in fraud against consumers, it's fair to say that they are always interested in any flimflamming practice by dealers. It would only take one complaint by a dealer's funding sources to get an AG interested in a dealer's practices.

So, power book if you want to, but just be prepared to do some powerful jail time.

The Devil You Don't Know: How Broad Is Your UDAP Law?
January/February 2009
By Emily Marlow Beck

It can be difficult to follow the rules when you don't know what they are.

When I was about 10 years old, I played on a boys' basketball team, and I took my task of learning the rules and fundamentals very seriously. I learned my bounce pass, my lay-up, and basic dribbling skills. I learned not to travel and to avoid getting caught too long in the paint, and, the brainy kid that I was, I could recite the mathematical dimensions of the entire court by heart. But, when my coach told me to foul my opponent toward the end of one game, I wasn't sure quite what to do. Partly out of desperation and partly out of instinct, I hopped on the back of the boy with the ball and rode him down the court. That day I learned about technical fouls the hard way. Apparently, my "Basketball 101" book didn't warn me not to piggyback my opponent.

This story reminds me of state unfair and deceptive acts and practices, or UDAP, laws. But, before you think I've taken too many elbows to the head, let me give some background.

Many state UDAP laws "spell it out for you" and contain a bunch of enumerated deeds that the state legislature frowns upon. For example, Colorado law provides that it is a deceptive trade practice to knowingly fail to identify flood-damaged or water-damaged goods as to such damages. Idaho law prohibits knowingly making false or misleading statements of fact concerning the age, extent of use, or mileage of any goods. Many other states have their own lists of dirty deeds that run the gamut. This type of UDAP law gives you a list of "do this" or "don't do that."

But, not all state legislatures were so thoughtful as to give you a handy, dandy list. Instead, most UDAP laws contain a very general "don't do anything bad" prohibition that isn't quite as clear. Missouri law, for example, states that the act, use, or employment by any person of any deception, fraud, false pretense, false promise, misrepresentation, unfair practice, or the concealment, suppression, or omission of any material fact in connection with the sale or advertisement of any merchandise in trade or commerce is declared to be an unlawful practice. And that, folks, is pretty darn broad. The lawmakers might as well have said, "Y'all behave, now."

These broad UDAP laws can be a favorite "go to" for plaintiffs' lawyers who bring claims against dealers. After all, state laws don't always contain bold statements like, "Thou shall not payment pack." Instead, many of the more commonly attacked "unsavory" dealership practices often fall within the second, broader "don't do anything bad" type of UDAP statute. This can make preventing and defending against allegedly wrongful practices particularly difficult and can, in some instances, give dealers a false sense of security that they're complying with the law.

To make matters worse, because some UDAP laws are so broad, many plaintiffs' lawyers try to "bootstrap" federal or state law claims into UDAP claims. With this little trick, plaintiffs' lawyers argue that the violation of another law, state or federal, is a violation of the state's UDAP law. Depending on how the state UDAP law is written, this trick can actually work.

So, why should you care? You've heard us say this before, but UDAP laws often permit plaintiffs to recover multiple (usually two or three) times their actual damages. Some permit recovery of statutory damages or permit other relief, even when the plaintiff has no actual damages. If that wasn't enough, UDAP laws typically provide that the customer may recover attorneys' fees and court costs.

What should you do to protect yourself? For starters, if your dealership is in a state where the UDAP law contains enumerated prohibited practices, you should take some time to learn exactly what those practices are. Look at your operations, and make sure you aren't stepping into prohibited territory.

Avoiding the "anything naughty" type of UDAP claim can present more of a challenge. Developing a culture of honesty and transparency in all transactions is a great start. Consider everything from the dealership's advertising to delivery procedures. You'll need to ask yourself some tough questions. Do your ads have a tendency to mislead, or do they give a false impression? Do your sales or finance procedures tend to mislead customers as to the condition of the vehicle or the terms of financing? Do you have clear, customer-friendly policies and programs in place setting forth the proper way to spot deliver vehicles? Sell products? Handle customers' trade-in vehicles?

Don't forget that good, compliance-friendly fundamentals might just keep you from learning about the scope of your state's UDAP law the hard way.

I Love it When a Plan Comes Together

January/February 2009

By Thomas B. Hudson

Cigarettes. Black lung. Asbestos. Breast implants. Plaintiffs' lawyers never seem to run out of reasons to sue people.

Lawyers who make their livings suing car dealers have latched onto yet another way to get their hands into dealers' wallets. A slew of class action lawsuits around the country allege claims against dealers when car buyers have financed credit insurance, GAP, service contracts, and other such products along with the cars that are the subject of the retail installment contracts they sign.

The plaintiffs' lawyers claim that when the car buyers pay their obligations early, the dealer, the finance company, or at least someone other than their clients is obligated to refund some part of the cost of the products. I mean, after all, you gotta blame somebody, right?

The cases, many of them filed as class action suits, are serious business, and dealers defending the cases need all the ammo they can find. A recent opinion may provide them some.

In connection with the purchase and finance of his new Audi, Andrew Massih enrolled in the Total Loss Protection Program (TLPP) for a fee of $499. The TLPP was a typical GAP program that protected Massih against owing a deficiency in the event the car was a total loss.

Jim Moran & Associates, Inc., (JMA) was the TLPP administrator. Massih prepaid his contract in full but received no refund of the GAP premium from JMA. Massih filed a class action against JMA for breach of contract for failure to refund the unearned GAP premium.

The trial court granted JMA's motion for judgment on the pleadings. Massih appealed.

The U.S. Court of Appeals for the Eleventh Circuit affirmed. The court reasoned that, under the terms of the GAP agreement, Massih was entitled to a refund only if he made a request to cancel coverage during the original term of the retail installment sales contract, and because Massih had not sent a notice to cancel coverage during the term of the contract, he was not entitled to a refund.

Now, think about the car buyer's allegations here for a moment. How is the GAP company (or credit life or credit disability insurance company) supposed to find out that the car buyer has prepaid his retail installment contract so that it can make a refund? There are only two parties who will know for certain that the retail installment contract has been paid off early—the buyer and the bank or sales finance company that is the holder of the retail installment contract.

The GAP company probably has no relationship with the bank or sales finance company holding the retail installment contract and is in no position to require the contract holder to go to the trouble and expense of notifying the GAP company of an early payoff. Indeed, the GAP company may not even know who holds the contract because the contract may well have been reassigned.

The GAP company, in drafting the contract, had a better

plan. It put the obligation of the notification of prepayment squarely where it belongs—in the hands of the person whose self-interest would give him incentive to go to the trouble of making the notification. That was good lawyering on the part of the drafter of the TLPP, and, says the court, the language placing that duty on the buyer actually works! Of course, whether this defense will work with other products will depend on how well the documentation for the other products was drafted.

As they used to say on the A Team, "I love it when a plan comes together."

Massih v. Jim Moran & Associates, Inc., 2008 WL 4946213 (11th Cir. (M.D. Ga.) November 20, 2008).

Bad Times and F&I Crimes
January/February 2009
By Thomas B. Hudson

The Washington Post headline read, "Crime Increases When Times Are Bad." I suspect that most people seeing those words immediately imagined more burglaries and convenience store stick-ups.

Not me. The first mental image I had was of several guys gathered in a dealership's F&I office plotting over ways to portray a bad deal as a good one.

These are perilous times for dealers in more ways than I can count. Lenders are pulling floor plans (inventory financing). Sales finance companies and banks have either quit buying paper or have gotten so picky regarding creditworthiness that St. Peter couldn't get financed. Customers have hunkered down to the point that the dealer's postman's arrival counts as an "up." When customers do show up, they are torn between the

Escalade, if they believe gas will stay at $1.59 a gallon, and the Fit, if they see gas going back to $4.39 a gallon. And then there are those minor difficulties with the manufacturers, that, when they aren't talking about bankruptcy, they are discussing discontinuing entire lines of vehicles that all of us have grown up with. Perilous times, indeed.

So, why should dealers, with all of these problems to deal with, care about my mental image of the huddle in the F&I office? Isn't that like worrying about how neatly the deck chairs are stacked on the Titanic?

I would argue that dealers need to be especially vigilant regarding F&I practices when times turn hard. Why?

First, a dealer doesn't need the expense and diversion of an Attorney General investigation, a TV news investigation, a plaintiff's class action lawsuit, or perhaps all three at one time, when the dealership is trying hard just to survive until times get better. Time, money, and other resources spent dealing with these problems can't be allocated to measures that might actually help the dealership survive.

Second, F&I abuse is fairly easy to prevent. I know that this is true, because I have seen it prevented. Some dealerships have a culture of dealing squarely with customers and with their banks and finance companies. Others have a culture of cutting corners and hiding the ball whenever they can make a dishonest dollar. The culture that a dealership develops reflects the ethics, or lack thereof, of the dealer principal and top management. If the guys at the top are dirty, the entire operation is likely to be dirty. It's not enough, though, that the top folks at the dealership have pure hearts. They also have to have in place the training, audit processes, and oversight to make sure that their good intentions get translated into good actions. We see dealers all the time who manage to do things right. I'm not saying that it's easy to do so, but rocket science it ain't.

Finally, under the weight of other problems, the dealership can fold altogether, turn itself into an independent operation, and forget about those pesky franchise problems, or go into some related business. People may lose fortunes, small and large. Absent other ethical lapses, no one will go to jail because the business fails. But people go to jail for F&I fraud. When those guys in my mental image are manufacturing stips (see Editor's note below), "power booking" to inflate the perceived value of financed vehicles, and inflating incomes (and phonying up income documentation to back up the inflated numbers), they might as well be wearing shirts with bulls' eyes on them, because Attorneys General all over the country have these practices squarely within their sights. When the AGs find these practices at a dealership, they trace them, when they can, from the bottom to the top.

The prospect of the shame and expense of defending criminal charges, and the inconvenience of having to spend several years as the guest of the state, will bring your other problems, like the possibility of losing that Pontiac franchise, into perspective.

These are perilous times, all right, but that's all the more reason to keep your business legal and ethical.

[Editor's note: For general readers, "manufacturing stips" is the creation of fake ID documents, payroll stubs, and other documents so that a dealer can defraud a finance company by making the customer look more creditworthy than he or she is. When a deal is subject to stips, it means that the finance company has told the dealer, "I'll buy the deal provided you produce proof that the customer is earning the $30,000 that the application you have given us claims he's earning, and a copy of the customer's

electric bill to show that he's living at the address you've shown in the application, etc. A crooked dealer will create phony documents to satisfy the request for stips.]

It's a Small World Wide Web After All

January/February 2009

By Emily Marlow Beck

Anonymity can be a very good thing. My high school and college buddies and I often joke about how fortunate we are that we made it through our awkward stages before the explosion of the information superhighway. Hopefully, my personal gaffes and bad hairdos will remain dead and buried back in college where they belong. (Don't laugh—that mullet you sported in '87 won't do you any favors today.)

Alas, times have changed. It looks like a Texas car dealership could have used a little bit of that anonymity that we all took for granted. According to a FOX 26 news exposé, a Texas woman sued a dealership for fraud, claiming that the dealership made "material misrepresentations" to her by "charging her a higher interest rate than what she qualified for so they could make more money on the deal."

As if being on the receiving end of a lawsuit wasn't bad enough, according to the news report, after deposing the dealership CFO about the dealership practices, the plaintiff's lawyer posted a video excerpt of the deposition on YouTube for the entire world to see.

So, what did the CFO say in the video? My point-click wasn't quite quick enough to find out. By the time I searched YouTube, the dealership had filed a motion for a protective order, and the judge made the plaintiff's lawyer take the video down. But, according to the news article, the video featured the CFO responding to questions about how the dealership determined the rate of finance charge that it would offer customers on a contract.

Allegedly, the CFO explained what the dealership did with the extra money from the marked-up rate charged to the customer. Per the news article, the CFO explained that the "mark-up" was split between the dealership and the credit union that agreed on the rate, with the dealership receiving 75% of the cut. "It's not a kickback," he said. "It's a fee."

The news article also quoted the plaintiff's lawyer as saying that the dealership promised to find the customer the "best deal," but that it offered the customer a rate that was 3% above the "approved rate of 7.5%."

Now, I have no idea what actually happened in this particular incident, and the only information I have is what I can read in a news article. But, the idea of anyone using YouTube to expose a dealership's alleged misdeeds piqued my curiosity—so much, in fact, that I searched YouTube for similar stories. Using the search terms "dealership fraud," I pulled up 467 videos on YouTube. I don't know how many of these videos are on point, but most of the videos have titles like, "Car Dealership Scams Burn Buyers, Sellers" and "Car Dealer Scams Revealed." Many of these videos began as local news reports. Now, thanks to modern technology, they are available worldwide.

This story also got me thinking about the all too common practice of dealerships telling customers that the contract rate is the "best rate." Dealership employees need to be trained to be as transparent as possible regarding the financing process and avoid those two little words like the plague.

Perhaps most shocking to me, however, was the plaintiff's lawyer and CFO's apparent lack of understanding of the indirect finance process. Folks familiar with how indirect finance works know that dealers often write a retail contract at a higher rate than the wholesale "buy rate" offered by the finance company. This "buy rate" is the wholesale rate at which the finance company will purchase the contract, not the rate for which the customer qualifies.

I'd like to gather all the participants in one room—the lawyer, the dealer, the customer, the press—and hand out copies of *Understanding Vehicle Finance*. It's a nifty little booklet produced by the American Financial Services Association and the National Automobile Dealers Association that accurately describes the indirect financing of motor vehicles. It's so good, in fact, that the Federal Trade Commission reviewed it and slapped its seal on it before the publication was printed in both English and Spanish. It is free and downloadable from the NADA and AFSA websites. It isn't copyrighted, either, so you can make copies for all your employees, the media reporters you deal with, your customers, and anyone else who might benefit from an accurate description of how dealer financing works.

But, then again, you might be the kind of person who likes to see your personal and professional gaffes broadcast all over the world. If so, I hear the Jerry Springer Show is always looking for content.

Don't Be a Paper Pack Rat!
January/February 2009
By Emily Marlow Beck

Some years back I saw a daytime talk show program about "hoarders"—people who have a compulsion to collect and keep the most basic objects. The show highlighted folks who hoarded everything from old newspapers to used appliances. Homes were jam-packed with years' worth of objects that the hoarders just couldn't seem to let go of.

When it comes to the contents of their deal jackets, dealers can be a bit the same way. Many dealers I work with think that, when it comes to papering a deal, "the more the better." I often encounter resistance when I tell dealers that they should remove certain forms from their transaction documents. It's almost as if they feel I'm cutting a little hole in their safety net.

Don't get me wrong—I like paper. I, like my compliance attorney brethren, have a special kind of love for the written word. Nothing makes us happier than massaging the delicate text of the forms and contracts that we know very few people actually read. (Believe me, it's a party a minute, folks!) But, when it comes to paperwork, the more doesn't necessarily mean the merrier.

When I review deal jackets, I'll typically find all sorts of forms, all mixed and matched from a variety of sources. Some forms come from state associations or from finance sources. Others are custom-made for the dealer or are provided to the dealer along with certain products that the dealer will sell to customers.

There is certainly no problem with snagging forms from various reputable vendors. In fact, we represent some of these vendors in developing and maintaining compliant forms and believe that well-made, "off-the-shelf" forms are a great option for many dealers. But, some dealers throw forms into the mix like a high school cafeteria lady making "leftover surprise stew." As you might expect, the results can be just as unsavory and leave me with some serious heartburn!

So, how do you know you've got a problem with paper hoarding at your dealership? If your deal jackets look anything like these, it might be time to get some help.

The Silly Putty Deal Jacket. Some folks think that they can get the customer to sign a bunch of forms, throw them in a deal jacket, smoosh them together, and Presto! All of the forms magically become part of the deal. Unfortunately, this is often just not the case. Quite a bit of wordsmithing and drafting is often needed to make sure that all the forms in your deal jacket are properly integrated. To make matters more complicated, many states impose "single document rules" that can affect the enforceability of certain documents. The result? Just because you put the form in the deal jacket doesn't mean that a court will view the document as part of the deal.

The Double Trouble Deal Jacket. Some dealerships are so afraid of letting go of old versions of documents that they use inconsistent duplicates of the same document. I've seen differing versions of buyers orders, installment contracts, product documentation, etc., crammed into the same deal. I've seen as many as four separately signed arbitration agreements in a deal jacket. All the duplicates raise the question—which version of the document controls? The buyers order with the warranty disclaimers or the one without? The arbitration agreement with the class action waiver or the one without? We know of at least one case where a court refused to allow arbitration where the customer signed two separate arbitration agreements with different terms.

The Broken Mirror Deal Jacket. Some dealers forget to make sure that the forms they use actually reflect their dealership's practices. A document that technically complies with all of the knit-picky requirements of the law just won't cut it if it doesn't line up with your actual practices. Ask yourself: Does that privacy policy you picked up at the auction accurately describe your dealership's privacy practices? Does that GPS disclosure that came with your GPS unit accurately describe what the dealership will and won't do with the device? If these documents don't reflect your practices, they'll be noncompliant at best. At worst, they could be viewed as unfair and deceptive.

So, what's a paper-hoarding dealer to do?

First and foremost, it's time to recognize the importance of the contents of your deal jacket. The deal jacket is the paper record of your deal and will memorialize the terms of the transaction. Think twice (and maybe check in with your lawyer) before you add or delete forms from the mix.

Create a list of documents that need to be in each deal jacket, attach the list to the inside of the jacket, and then check off each item added to the jacket or enter "N/A" for documents not added.

Read your documents. Do they reflect your practices? Do you have inconsistent or duplicate documents? If you were buying a car, would you know what your rights and responsibilities were?

Consider getting help. It's not a bad idea to have your friendly consumer credit lawyer put his or her eagle eye to your forms to make sure you've got a winning recipe.

Don't forget about your state and federal record-keeping requirements. Knowing what you must, and must not, retain will help you feel more liberated to renounce your pack rat tendencies.

Good luck!

How Employee F&I Fraud Can Come Home to Roost

March 2009

By Thomas B. Hudson

So, your dealership's employee dummies up a credit app with bogus income information in order to get the bank to buy the deal, enabling the employee to earn his commission. No one else at the dealership is aware of the fraud. Then, uh oh, the employee's acts are discovered.

That's a real problem for the employee, but the dealership should be off the hook for any liability since no one else at the dealership was in on the scheme or knew anything about it, right?

Wrong! Here's a recent case that illustrates one example of a dealership's potential liability in situations like these.

Rosemary Dillinger and Clifford Mounts bought a vehicle from Rub Chevrolet Buick Oldsmobile, Inc. When applying for credit to finance the purchase, Dillinger and Mounts signed a blank credit application. A Rub employee later completed the application with false income information.

First National Bank of Ottawa, believing the application to be truthful, agreed to buy the financing contract. When Dillinger and Mounts defaulted, and the vehicle was repossessed, First National Bank sued Dillinger, Mounts, and the dealership for breach of contract and fraudulent misrepresentation. The trial court ruled for First National Bank with respect to its allegations against Dillinger and Mounts and found that Rub fraudulently misrepresented their incomes, but the court rejected First National Bank's claim that the dealership breached its contract.

First National Bank appealed that latter ruling. The Appellate Court of Illinois reversed the trial court on this issue, finding that the employee's falsification did constitute a breach of contract by Rub.

Rub's contract with First National Bank contained a warranty that the sale of the vehicle was completed in accordance with federal and state law. First National Bank argued that the sale to Dillinger and Mounts violated a state law prohibiting wire fraud. The state law elements of wire fraud included showing (1) a scheme to defraud by means of false pretenses, representations, or promises; and (2) transmission of a document in furtherance of the scheme.

The appellate court noted that undisputed evidence established that Rub's employee violated the wire fraud provision. The court held Rub liable for breach of its contractual warranty to First National Bank as a result of that conduct because Rub did not establish that the employee acted outside the scope of his employment.

So, at the end of the day, the dealership is liable on a fraud and a breach of contract claim for the illegal actions of its employee.

Perhaps it is time to tighten up on the oversight of your dealership's F&I processes and procedures. Maybe a little compliance and ethics training would be a good idea, too.

First National Bank of Ottawa v. Dillinger, 897 N.E.2d 358 (Ill. App. October 23, 2008).

An Elephant in a Haystack

March 2009

By Maya P. Hill

Ever wonder what the term "conspicuous" means? Some common definitions might include "easy to see" or "noticeable." For example, a needle in a haystack is not conspicuous, but an elephant sitting in a haystack probably is. The term "conspicuous" takes on a more elusive meaning when it's used in a consumer credit statute that requires a creditor to disclose something in a "conspicuous" manner. Some states, like West Virginia, explain that a term or clause is "conspicuous" when it is "so written that a reasonable person against whom it is to operate ought to have noticed it." In other words, if a reasonable consumer should have noticed the term or clause in the retail installment contract or loan agreement, it's "conspicuous."

Some statutes take the whole "conspicuous disclosure" issue one step further—instead of just requiring a creditor to provide conspicuous disclosures, they require the creditor to provide certain disclosures in a way that's more conspicuous than other conspicuous disclosures. The federal Truth in Lending Act is one of these statutes, and it requires that a creditor disclose the APR and finance charge in a more conspicuous way than other disclosures.

Creditors do all sorts of good things to their contracts to make disclosures look conspicuous. They put them in bold face type. They put them in boxes. They use CAPITAL LETTERS. But sometimes, it's not just what you do to the specific disclosure that you're trying to make conspicuous that counts— it's what you inadvertently do to other parts of the contract that take away from the conspicuous nature of your disclosure.

When we do dealership audits, we sometimes see F&I folks review with the customer the various documents that the customer will sign in order to complete a deal. Some of these F&I folks do so with a pen or pencil in hand, and, as they go, they draw circles around or highlight in some other way certain terms of the deal. That's a bad idea, and here's why.

Take the case of Tarran Spinner. Spinner got a title loan from Cash In A Hurry, LLC (CIAH). She later sued CIAH under TILA for—you guessed it—failing to disclose the APR and finance charge in a more conspicuous way than other conspicuous disclosures on the contract.

The U.S. Bankruptcy Court for the Northern District of Georgia concluded that CIAH violated TILA by not disclosing the annual percentage rate in a more conspicuous manner than other terms in the contract. CIAH had put double dashes around the APR and finance charge disclosures to make them more conspicuous than the other contract terms. But the court found that handwritten markings on the finance charge, amount financed, and total number of payments (other disclosures required by TILA) made those terms more conspicuous than the APR because the APR was the only one of the four terms that did not have a handwritten mark on it.

The court stated that the most conspicuous term on the contract was the due date because there was a handwritten arrow pointing to the due date and the handwritten words "DUE DATE," all of which were highlighted in orange. The court found that CIAH was liable for $1,000 in statutory damages for the disclosure violation.

What Spinner teaches us is that creditors have to look at the contract as a whole when determining whether a creditor has made a disclosure conspicuous (or "more" conspicuous, as the case may be). It's possible that other markings that appear on a contract could overshadow the attempts the creditor has made with respect to a particular disclosure, just as how making handwritten comments and using orange highlighting on some parts of the contract rendered the APR disclosure insufficiently conspicuous in the case above.

While there's really no steadfast test as to what it means to be "conspicuous" under certain consumer credit laws, your lawyer is probably the best person to make a reasoned determination. Our firm regularly drafts the kinds of documents that are used in vehicle finance transactions. When we do, we have to parse through the requirements of state and federal law to make sure that the documents comply with the laws' requirements. The TILA provisions this court addressed are examples of the kinds of things we pay attention to when drafting credit documents. We pay attention to type size and font, capitalization, bold facing, boxing, and other ways to make the disclosures either "conspicuous" or "more conspicuous." When the form is printed, you can bet that we've made an effort to meet these requirements.

So, before you use a particular contract in the course of business, it's a good idea to run it past a lawyer well versed in these disclosure requirements. And be careful of making modifications to a form your lawyer has approved, handwritten or otherwise, even if you're doing it in the course of explaining the terms to your customer. Doing so might transform your sufficiently conspicuous elephant into an inconspicuous needle.

In re Spinner (Spinner v. Cash In A Hurry, LLC), 2008 WL 5205967 (Bankr. N.D. Ga. September 29, 2008).

Dealer's Completion of Forms and Charging of Doc Prep Fee Not Unauthorized Practice of Law

April 2009

By Catherine M. Brennan

Dedicated readers of *Spot Delivery*® are fully aware of the claims brought by disgruntled consumers over the last few years relating to so-called "document preparation" by dealer personnel and unauthorized practice of law. The lawsuits generally allege that the individual salespeople who sold the consumers their cars must be lawyers because such salespeople fill out legal forms. The claim is usually raised where the dealer charges a fee for "doc prep," and this is just one of many strategies consumers use to get out from under their retail installment contracts.

Some courts have agreed with these claims, finding—with straight faces, apparently—that salespeople who fill in forms in connection with the sale of a car become unlicensed lawyers simply by virtue of charging a fee for their trouble. Recently, however, one Colorado court ruled—with some common sense—that mere completion of legal documents (and charging the consumer a fee for this service) did not constitute the unauthorized practice of law.

Andrew Newman bought a motor vehicle from Ed Bozarth Chevrolet Company Inc. As part of the credit sale, Bozarth's salesperson prepared and completed certain documents relating to the sale of the vehicle and charged a fee to prepare and complete the documents. Newman sued, claiming, among other things, that Bozarth engaged in the unauthorized practice of law by preparing the sale documents and charging an illegal fee for the document preparation. Bozarth moved for summary judgment, arguing that the court should find as a matter of law that the dealership employees did not unlawfully act as lawyers.

The U.S. District Court for the District of Colorado noted that, in Colorado, it would look to a 1964 Colorado Supreme Court decision—*Denver Bar Association v. Public Utilities Commission*, 391 P.2d 467 (Colo. 1964)—to determine whether the act of filling out forms constituted the practice of law. Under that decision, the practice of law generally includes acting in a representative capacity in protecting, enforcing, or defending the legal rights and duties of another and in counseling, advising, and assisting such person in connection with these rights and duties. One nonlegal activity specifically highlighted by the Colorado Supreme Court included the completion of forms that do not require any knowledge and skill beyond that possessed by the ordinary experienced and intelligent layperson.

The court first noted that Newman presented no facts to indicate that Bozarth acted in a representative capacity in protecting, enforcing, or defending his legal rights and duties or in counseling, advising, and assisting him in connection with these rights and duties. This makes perfect sense, of course, because although motor vehicle dealers and lawyers might share a bad reputation (undeserved, of course), no one could legitimately argue that the two are interchangeable. The court went on to say that although Bozarth may have completed "legal documents," the completion of those documents did not require any knowledge or skill beyond that possessed by the ordinary layperson. Thus, when Bozarth's salesperson, identified as "Cookie," completed the documents pertaining to the sale of the vehicle to Newman, she did not engage in the unauthorized practice of law.

The court also found that the charging of a fee for the document preparation did not transform the document preparation (or, more accurately, document completion) into the practice of law. Bozarth did not dispute that it charged Newman a "delivery and handling fee." Bozarth admitted that it disclosed the fee as pure "profit" to Bozarth and allocated the fee to, among other things, preparation of documents. Newman conceded that no federal or Colorado law prohibited Bozarth from charging the delivery and handling fee. The court thus rejected the idea that Bozarth's document completion—which it concluded was not the practice of law—became the practice of law because Bozarth charged a fee. Accordingly, the court granted Bozarth's motion for summary judgment.

The court's decision in Bozarth is, of course, the right result. We might be biased, as we represent car dealers, but think about it. The charging of a fee should not be the act that transforms everyday transactions into an attorney–client relationship. If that were true, could a lawyer argue that no attorney–client relationship existed because a client failed to pay a fee? That would be, of course, no less ludicrous than trying to paint salespeople as advocates.

Newman v. Ed Bozarth Chevrolet Company Inc., 2009 U.S. Dist. LEXIS 15306 (D. Colo. January 5, 2009).

Spot Deliveries in the Crosshairs of Congress

June 2009

By Jean Noonan

As though dealers were not having enough trouble these days, Congress has thought up a new way to add to dealer pain. It is called the Consumer Credit and Debt Collection Act (CCDCA). This proposed law would direct the Federal Trade Commission to issue new rules to prevent "unfair and deceptive acts or practices" by car dealers. And Congress had a thought or two about just what those practices might be.

First on this list of "unfair practices" are "post-sale changes in financing terms." The bill encourages the FTC to make a rule that would require that the dealer honor the financing terms of any contract the consumer signs before driving off in the newly purchased car—even if the dealer is unable to find a bank or finance company that will buy the contract on those terms. No more "unwind" agreements. No more spot deliveries.

But the proposed law doesn't stop there. Next, it tells the FTC to consider making a rule that would provide a cooling-off period for all car sales. The idea is that the sales contract should let the buyer freely cancel the purchase within a certain number of days.

What??? That's right—the buyer selects a car, signs a purchase agreement, gets approved for credit, forks over a down payment and possibly a trade-in, and drives off in your car. You honor all terms of the contract. But, a few days later, the buyer decides she wants a red car instead of blue, or four doors instead of two, or a Honda instead of a Chevy. Under this plan, the buyer would get back her deposit and trade-in, and you would get back your (slightly used) car.

Are you excited yet? Wait, there is more. The bill next goes after dealer participation fees from banks and finance companies. It tells the FTC to consider a rule that would forbid a dealer from accepting compensation based on the interest rate, the annual percentage rate, or the amount financed. Banks and finance companies would still pay the dealer for the contract, but the payment would need to be a flat fee or an amount not tied to an interest rate markup or amount financed.

As a final kicker, the bill would allow the FTC to sue dealers who violate the rule and collect up to $16,000 for each violation. What if a dealer doesn't put a cooling-off provision in its sales agreements? That's a fine of up to $16,000 for each car sale! For good measure, the bill would also allow state Attorneys General to enforce any rule the FTC adopts.

Where did Congress come up with these ideas? From the FTC. In March, the FTC testified before a subcommittee of the House of Representatives on what it was doing to protect consumers from mortgage scams and other abusive credit practices. It was doing a good job protecting consumers, the FTC said, but having more legal authority would help. Lawmakers asked the FTC what it had in mind, and the Consumer Credit and Debt Collection Act was the FTC's response.

Now, there has been the occasional story about an unreasonable unwind demand, and the Justice Department settled claims of race discrimination involving interest rate markups with two dealers last year. But are these the most pressing problems facing consumers in these tough economic times? Are they widespread problems at all?

In May, there was a hearing on the Consumer Credit and Debt Collection Act. No representative of car dealers was invited to speak. No one talked about the benefit consumers receive from spot deliveries and instant financing. No one talked about how such new rules would hurt sales in a car industry struggling for survival. There was no discussion about the very real problems of a cooling-off rule for auto sales. What are dealers supposed to do with cars consumers return? Clearly, such a rule would require dealers to withhold delivery of the car until the cooling-off period has expired. No one discussed the harm to consumers who need to buy a car and drive it off the lot the same day. No one mentioned the "cooling-off" effect this rule would have on dealers' sales.

There are still many steps before this bill could become law. Although it is likely to be voted out of its subcommittee, the full House of Representatives must vote on it, and the Senate must pass a companion bill.

We hope, before that happens, Congress asks these questions and listens carefully to the answers.

Dealer Granted Summary Judgment in Unauthorized Practice of Law Case

July 2009

By Shelley B. Fowler

In our December 2008 issue of *Spot Delivery®* , we wrote about the Baker case, one of many around the country in which dealers have been hit with class action lawsuits alleging that the dealers' actions in completing legal forms, such as buyers' orders and retail installment contracts, constitute the unauthorized practice of law. A recent development makes the Baker case "news" to dealers once again.

To prompt your memory . . . Robert and Stacy Baker bought a vehicle from Go Toyota Scion Arapahoe and agreed to pay a "dealer handling fee" that represented, according to the retail installment sales contract, "costs and additional profits to the seller for items such as inspections, cleaning, and adjusting new and used vehicles, and preparing documents related to the sale."

The Bakers sued Go Toyota Scion and other dealerships, alleging that the defendants charged them and other car buyers "an illegal fee for preparing legal documents necessary to effectuate the sale of a motor vehicle and that the [d]efendants engaged in the unauthorized practice of law in connection with the purchase or lease of the motor vehicle," in violation of the Colorado Consumer Credit Code, the Colorado Consumer Protection Act, and common law.

When we first wrote about the case, we were pleased to report that the trial court denied the Bakers' motion to certify the case as a class action. Now, in a recent opinion, the same court—the District Court for Adams County—granted the defendants' motion for summary judgment.

First, the court found that the Bakers did not come forward with any evidence that any portion of the dealer handling fee was specifically for the preparation of legal documents in their transaction or that any of the documents referred to are legal documents. Next, the court found that because the nature of the dealer-handling fee was disclosed to the purchasers as profit to the dealer, the charging of the fee cannot be deemed to constitute a deceptive trade practice. Last, the court found that the Bakers lacked standing to allege an unauthorized practice of law where they did not assert an injury to a legally protected interest from the purported violation. The court noted that all prior unauthorized practice of law cases have been brought by a governmental enforcement agency or by attorneys asserting injury to the legal profession.

Our thanks go to Michael J. Dommermuth, with the law firm of McGloin, Davenport, Severson & Snow, PC, which represented the defendants in the case, for bringing this recent decision to our attention. He let us know that, back in December, at the request of Tim Jackson, President of the Colorado Automobile Dealers Association, the Colorado Attorney General modified a 1979 Assurance of Discontinuance to permit dealers to drop the disclosure language about the charge representing fees for "preparing documents related to the sale" in documents and in-store signage and to allow dealers to merely disclose that the dealer handling fee represents costs and additional profits to the dealer, without expressly itemizing cost items.

Baker v. Go Toyota Scion Arapahoe, Case No. 07 CV 543 (D. Colo. July 2, 2009).

Missouri Doc Fees: The Drama Continues!

August 2009

By Emily Marlow Beck

Reality TV? Broadway musicals? "Made for TV" specials? No way, José. I've got all the drama I need right here in the world of consumer finance and dealer compliance. If you've been watching the Missouri legislature and courts battling out their turf war over the "doc prep fee issue," you know exactly what I'm talking about.

Loyal readers will recall how it all went down . . .

Act One: In 2007, the Missouri Supreme Court upheld a $1,100,000 class action judgment and held that a Missouri bank that charged borrowers a fee to complete various loan documents, including promissory notes and deeds of trust, engaged in the "unauthorized practice of law" in violation of Missouri law. *Eisel v. Midwest BankCentre,* 2007 Mo. LEXIS 134 (Mo. August 21, 2007).

Act Two: Sometime between the filing of the claim and the court's ruling, the Missouri legislature passed a law saying that Missouri lending institutions who charge a doc prep fee to complete residential mortgage loan documents in compliance with the law would not be viewed as engaging in the unauthorized practice of law in Missouri.

Act Three: The court didn't think too highly of what it viewed as the legislature meddling in its turf, and used the Eisel case to deliver a strong admonishment regarding the judiciary's power to define and control the practice of law in Missouri. The court blasted the lawmakers, claiming that "the judiciary is necessarily the sole arbiter of what constitutes the practice of law" in Missouri.

Act Four: When there's chum in the waters, plaintiffs'

lawyers taste blood. Oodles of Missouri car dealers faced claims that, by charging "doc prep fees," they too were engaging in the unauthorized practice of law in Missouri.

Act Five: The Missouri legislature rides into town on its noble steed, pen and paper in hand. Remembering how it had its hand slapped in the Eisel case, the legislature used a little trickery of its own.

In late July, the legislature passed a new Missouri law, Section 301.558 (as enacted by 2009 Senate Bill 355), which takes effect on August 28, 2009. The law authorizes dealers to charge an "administrative fee," and provides that an administrative fee of less than $200 that is charged in compliance with the new law and that does not result in the waiver of any rights or remedies will not be deemed the unauthorized practice of law in Missouri. In order to comply with this new law, the administrative fee must be charged to all retail customers, and some very specific disclosures must be made on the buyers order, and possibly the retail installment sale contract or "preliminary worksheet."

And, here comes the magic . . .

The new law provides that if a court determines that a fee charged in compliance with Section 301.558 does not waive any rights or remedies of the buyer or is the unauthorized practice of law, then no person who paid the fee may recover either the fee or damages permitted under the Missouri unauthorized practice of law statute. Further, no person who charged the fee in compliance with the new law will be guilty of a misdemeanor under the unauthorized practice of law section. In other words, the legislature took the "sting" out of the state unauthorized practice of law provisions for dealers who follow the new law.

Will this be the final act in the Missouri doc fee turf war saga? Only time will tell, my friend. Until then, it's time for

Missouri dealers to get their forms and procedures polished up in time for the August 28 effective date!

We'll call that one Act Six. Don't forget the popcorn!

Disclosing Cash for Clunkers

August 2009

By Michael A. Benoit

Cash for Clunkers, officially known as the Car Allowance Rebate System (CARS), is a program under which consumers are encouraged to trade in their low-MPG vehicles for more fuel-efficient new cars in exchange for a credit as high as $4,500 to be applied to their purchase or lease transactions.

By now, most dealers are up to speed with their obligations under the program, but they have probably received conflicting advice from their finance companies regarding how to disclose the credit on a retail installment sale contract (RISC).

Starting with required RISC disclosures, there is no question in my mind that the credit must be disclosed as part of the down payment (it's up there in the last of the five boxes on your Truth in Lending Disclosure). For Regulation Z purposes (that's the regulation that tells you how to comply with the Truth in Lending Act), a down payment is "an amount, including the value of any property used as a trade-in, paid to a seller to reduce the cash price of the goods or services purchased in a credit sale transaction." The CARS credit is intended to replace the ordinary trade-in amount (CARS requires that the trade-in be scrapped), and it is required to be used to reduce the cash price of the vehicle being sold.

Next is the question of how to disclose the credit in the itemization of the amount financed on the RISC. Regulation Z gives you a lot of flexibility in how you do this, but, in general, I think it should be a line item deducted from the cash price (e.g., just like cash and rebates). Given that the intent of the statute is to replace the trade-in with the credit, one could reasonably argue that it should be disclosed as "trade-in amount" in the itemization. Of course, it is not technically a trade-in as one may understand (or as state law might define), and that's where folks have expressed concern, some wondering whether it should be disclosed as cash or rebate, or in some other fashion, in the itemization.

Well, it doesn't seem much like a rebate (and few state laws, if any, define "rebate" for disclosure purposes). While the credit accomplishes the same purpose (reducing the cash price), the same could be said of cash or a trade. So we have a conundrum of sorts.

I'm not sure it matters much for federal law purposes whether the credit is disclosed as trade-in, rebate, cash, or "other." As I said, Regulation Z gives you a lot of flexibility with respect to the information that you provide in the itemization, and as long as the amount is separately itemized in a manner that reduces the cash price of the new car, you're probably OK. Keep in mind, though, that state laws may have more to say about the characterization.

At the end of the day, all of this is probably academic. What will really happen? My tealeaves say this: Sales tax calculations will drive the CARS credit disclosure in the itemization. See, some states impose sales tax on the trade allowance, while others do not. Whether they'll take consistent positions on the CARS credit is a different story. Our intelligence says some states plan to treat the credit the way they treat a trade allowance for sales tax purposes; others will not. So, as a practical matter, the dealer is going to disclose the credit in the itemization however he has to, in order for his DMS to correctly calculate the sales tax. No one will reprogram their DMS to specifically address the sales tax treatment of the credit for this temporary program—they'll simply slot it where it works.

I don't know that this will be readily acceptable to your finance companies, but it seems to me to be the practical result for this short-lived program. It would be nice if the law was clear, but then I wouldn't have much to do. This is an instance for judgment calls, so ask your counsel what you should do.

Do Not Call, Do Not Fax, and Do Not E-mail

Remember that first guy you knew who had a "car phone"? Sure, it was as big as a suitcase, but, was it cool or what? Technology has come a long way since those days, hasn't it? Just think about it all—faxes, the Internet, e-mails, texts, direct dialers, caller-ID, and more. The list goes on and on.

It should be no surprise that the laws and regulations governing the use of this new technology have been in a sprint to try to keep up with the advances in technology. And, to be honest, this regulatory thicket is about as disturbing as your teenage daughter's cell phone bill.

Federal laws, such as the federal Do Not Call Rule, the Federal Communications Commission's faxing regulations, or our personal favorite, the CAN-SPAM Act, provide the regulatory framework governing the use of phones, faxes, or e-mails for marketing purposes. State lawmakers have jumped into the mix, too, developing miniature versions of the federal laws. These laws restrict everything from whom dealers can call, what disclosures must be given, and when the consumer can prevent dealers from calling again.

Complying with these laws would be hard enough if they directly addressed current technology. But, how should compliance professionals interpret these laws in light of the use of evolving technology, like cell phones or text messaging? In this chapter, we observe the struggle to fit the evolving technology (the square peg) into the existing legal framework (the round hole).

We keep hoping that Uncle Sam will start doling out crystal balls to lawmakers so they can anticipate these technological developments before laws go into effect. We're not holding our breath.

Branches of Government Disagree on
Standard for Placing Calls to Cell Phones

June 2008

By Michael A. Goodman

Just when you thought it was safe to use an autodialer or prerecorded message to call your customer's cell phone to discuss an existing account, a federal district court in California fundamentally alters this analysis with its opinion in *Leckler v. CashCall, Inc.*

Under the Leckler court's reasoning, merely collecting a customer's cell phone number on an application or during another communication does not establish the required "prior express consent" to call that number with an autodialer or prerecorded message. This determination constitutes a complete rejection of the interpretation formally adopted by the Federal Communications Commission in January 2008. Let's look at how we arrived at this confusing crossroad.

In 1991, Congress enacted the Telephone Consumer Protection Act (TCPA), which prohibited calls using an autodialer or a prerecorded message to a consumer's cell phone. Not just telemarketing calls, mind you—all calls. The Act included two exceptions: emergency calls and calls placed with the consumer's "prior express consent."

Congress gave the FCC authority to issue rules interpreting the TCPA. The FCC has issued and amended such rules over the years, but it has never defined the "prior express consent" standard. In 2005, ACA International, a collection industry trade organization, filed a petition with the FCC requesting guidance on this standard. Specifically, ACA argued that this prohibition should not apply to debt collection calls.

On January 4, 2008, the FCC released its response, known

as a Declaratory Ruling. In this Ruling, the FCC declined to give ACA the broad exception it requested. However, the FCC concluded that a creditor has a customer's "prior express consent" to call the customer's cell phone with an autodialer or prerecorded message if the customer has provided his cell phone number to the creditor, such as on an application.

The FCC explained that providing this information "reasonably evidences" prior express consent. In an earlier TCPA proceeding, the FCC had indicated that consumers who knowingly release their phone numbers have "in effect" given permission to be called at that number. The FCC applied this reasoning to ACA's petition. This broad interpretation of "prior express consent" gave a lot of breathing room to creditors on this issue. Thanks to the district court in California, however, this freedom may be short-lived.

When Tricia Leckler applied to CashCall for a personal loan, the application requested Leckler's cell phone number and other contact information, which she provided. The application did not state that Leckler was consenting to receive autodialer or prerecorded message calls on her cell phone by providing that phone number. When Leckler fell behind on her monthly payments, CashCall began collection activities on the account, including autodialer and prerecorded message calls to her cell phone. In response, Leckler filed a class action complaint in federal court, alleging that CashCall's calls violated the TCPA because borrowers had not provided valid "prior express consent."

The parties agreed that the validity of the FCC's Declaratory Ruling would settle the dispute. The court first considered whether the FCC had the authority to interpret the "prior express consent" standard. Because Congress did not define that term in the TCPA, and because Congress expressly allowed for the FCC to issue rules interpreting the TCPA, the court found that the FCC could interpret the standard.

The next issue for the court was whether the FCC's interpretation was reasonable. The Leckler court said no.

In reaching this decision, the court started with its dictionary, where "express consent" meant "positive, direct, unequivocal" and "requiring no inference or implication to supply its meaning." In contrast, the court's dictionary defined "implied consent" as "manifested by signs, actions, or facts." Simply put, the court concluded that merely providing a cell phone number on an application, without more, is valid implied consent but not valid express consent.

The court further explained that Congress intended valid prior express consent in this context to mean that the consumer expressly consented to receive autodialer and prerecorded message calls on his or her cell phone. More general consent to be called was not enough.

Because the court found that the FCC's interpretation of consent was so at odds with what the court would consider acceptable, the court refused to give any deference to the FCC's position. The court therefore found, as a matter of law, that CashCall's reliance on the FCC's Declaratory Ruling was improper. As a result, the only issue CashCall can challenge going forward in this case is how much it will have to pay in statutory damages.

Creditors nationwide, not just in the Northern District of California, should therefore take note of this decision. The fact that CashCall relied on the FCC's guidance—a reasonable approach—was not a complete defense.

For readers who want to avoid being the next CashCall, the court did give an example of what valid prior express consent could look like. The court explained that the FCC's Ruling "encourage[d] creditors to include language on credit applications and other documents informing the consumer that, by providing a wireless telephone number, the consumer consents to receiving autodialed and prerecorded message calls from the creditor or its third-party debt collector at that number." The court noted that "[i]ncluding such language on credit applications would likely meet the express consent requirement." Right now, that is the closest thing to a safe harbor for callers looking to collect valid "prior express consent."

Leckler v. CashCall, Inc., 2008 WL 2123307 (N.D. Cal. May 20, 2008).

Leckler v. CashCall Rings in Again

November 2008

By Michael A. Goodman

Back in the '80s, Debbie Harry of Blondie (see the following Editor's note) implored people to call her anytime. Debbie told listeners to call her any day or night for a date. She was unequivocal and very specific. But what if Debbie had told listeners her phone number and nothing more? Let's call the first scenario Debbie Specific and the second Debbie General. Now imagine that your parents will only let you call those who have expressly given their consent to be called. Do you call Debbie Specific or Debbie General, or both? If you recall, that was the issue in *Leckler v. CashCall,* 554 F. Supp. 2d 1025 (N.D. Cal. May 20, 2008).

The Telephone Consumer Protection Act generally prohibits autodialer or prerecorded message calls to cell phones, but expressly exempts such calls that are based on a call recipient's "prior express consent." When last we spoke about

Leckler in the June 2008 issue of *Spot,* the court determined that CashCall did not qualify for this exemption because the consent CashCall tried to rely on was insufficiently "express." The *Leckler* court rejected the Federal Communications Commission's formal interpretation that a customer provides his or her "prior express consent" to call his or her cell phone with an autodialer or prerecorded message when the customer merely provides the cell phone number to the creditor (such as on an application). Under the *Leckler* court's reasoning, the FCC order essentially (and improperly) defined "prior express consent" to include implied consent.

The time between the FCC order and the *Leckler* decision was, obviously, happy times for creditors and collectors. They were allowed to "date" any customer who had given a cell phone number for any reason. These happy times did not last long. In May of this year, the *Leckler* opinion came out, slamming the receiver on calls to Debbie General. The facts of the *Leckler* case were as follows.

Tricia Leckler applied to CashCall for a personal loan. The application requested, and Leckler provided, her cell phone number and other contact information. The application did not state that Leckler was consenting to receive autodialer or prerecorded message calls on her cell phone by providing that phone number. When Leckler fell behind on her monthly payments, CashCall began collection activities on the account, including autodialer and prerecorded message calls to her cell phone. Leckler filed a class action complaint in federal court, alleging that CashCall's calls violated the TCPA because borrowers had not provided valid "prior express consent."

Upon motions for summary judgment, the court ruled that the FCC's order did not deserve any deference and was invalid. The court therefore found, as a matter of law, that CashCall's reliance on the FCC's order was improper. That is, creditors and collectors could call Debbie Specific but not Debbie General.

Dissatisfied with the limited choice of dates, CashCall recently tried to revive its case. CashCall filed a motion to dismiss the case and vacate the court's order, arguing that the court lacked subject matter jurisdiction under the Hobbs Act. That is, the court did not have the right or authority to rule on the FCC's order; the Hobbs Act gives the Courts of Appeal exclusive jurisdiction to determine the validity of final orders of the FCC. CashCall is effectively trying an end run around the *Leckler* court's determination that "express consent" means something more than implied consent.

In her response, Leckler admitted that the court must vacate its prior judgment but sought to substitute a new class representative, Miguel Madrigal. Like Leckler, Madrigal received autodialer and/or prerecorded message calls on his cell phone from CashCall. However, Madrigal asserted that he never provided CashCall with his cell phone number, only his home number. (CashCall asserted that Madrigal did, in fact, provide his cell phone number on his application.) By inserting Madrigal in Leckler's place, the court is no longer being asked to invalidate the FCC's order because CashCall's phone calls to Madrigal would arguably establish a clear violation of existing FCC regulations.

If the court agrees with CashCall, the effect is that creditors and collectors would be able to call Debbie Specific and Debbie General. But can they call Madrigal? Hark back to the glorious '80s. Tommy Tutone wanted to call Jenny after getting her phone number off the bathroom wall. Jenny didn't put her number on the bathroom wall, someone else did. She didn't tell Tommy to call her. Madrigal is Jenny, and the new contention is that Madrigal gave neither prior express consent nor implied

DO NOT CALL, DO NOT FAX, AND DO NOT E-MAIL

consent. Madrigal claims that CashCall simply took Madrigal's number off the bathroom wall.

The court has yet to rule on CashCall's motion or Leckler's response. A hearing was scheduled for November 7, 2008. The court will, in all likelihood, vacate its judgment and toss out Leckler's victory. If the court agrees with Leckler and substitutes Madrigal as the class representative, the case could continue, albeit with a narrowed scope. Those who had provided their cell phone numbers to CashCall would presumably be excluded from the class. The class would be limited to those who did not provide a cell phone number but were still contacted by CashCall on their cell phones using an autodialer or prerecorded message.

Where does that leave creditors and collectors? Our advice remains the same, at least for the time being. Creditors should include language on credit applications and other documents informing the consumer that, by providing a wireless telephone number, the consumer consents to receiving autodialed and prerecorded message calls from the creditor or its third-party debt collector at that number. Even if the *Leckler* court decides the Hobbs Act blocks its prior decision, the court's reasoning remains solid, and we suggest proceeding with caution when using autodialers or prerecorded message calls to contact cell phones. That is, call Debbie Specific. Call Debbie General if you include consent language when obtaining her cell phone number. However, do not call Jenny.

*[**Editor's Note #1:** Deborah Ann "Debbie" Harry (born July 1, 1945) is an American singer–songwriter and actress, most famous for being the lead singer for the new wave band Blondie.—Google]*

*[**Editor's Note #2:** Tommy Tutone is a power pop-rock band, best known for its 1982 hit "867-5309/Jenny," which peaked at #4 on the Billboard Hot 100.—Google]*

Is a Text Message a Phone Call, an E-mail, Neither, or Both?

December 2008

By Michael A. Goodman

Neither Congress nor the Federal Communications Commission had text messaging in mind when they adopted standards regulating telephone calls, telemarketing, and e-mail marketing. The Telephone Consumer Protection Act (TCPA) was enacted in 1991, well before the time when people from ages seven to 77 were getting cramps in their thumbs from rapid-fire SMS repartee ("SMS" stands for short message service, a popular form of text messaging). The primary e-mail marketing law, the CAN-SPAM Act, took effect in 2004, but even that feels like a bygone era as far as mobile communications are concerned.

Today, these same federal standards remain in place, and they apply to evolutions in communications technology in ways you might not imagine. With this intersection of the old and the new in mind, this article provides guidance about the rules of the road for text messaging in your business.

You may be interested in sending text messages to your former and current customers, prospective customers who have expressed an interest in what you're selling, and even everybody else out there who doesn't yet know how great you are. What laws are invoked when your thumbs do your talking? The answer to our question requires another question: Is your text message a "telephone call," an "e-mail," neither, or both? The answer is that a text message may be both—not surprising given that text messaging didn't exist when Congress and the FCC adopted the applicable standards.

The TCPA and regulations from the FCC interpreting the TCPA set standards for "telephone calls" without defining that term. However, the FCC has announced in consumer education material that a "telephone call" need NOT be a voice call; rather, a "call" could also be a text communication. This means that the FCC views a text message as a telephone call under the TCPA and, thus, a text message is subject to certain restrictions.

At least one court has affirmed the FCC's position on this issue. In *Joffe v. Acacia Mortgage Corp.*, 121 P.3d 831 (Ariz. App. 2005), the Arizona Court of Appeals agreed that "calls" subject to the TCPA were not limited to real-time voice communications. The *Joffe* court explained that a "call" could mean any attempt to communicate by telephone.

As a result, both the FCC and the *Joffe* court have concluded that text messages are subject to the TCPA's prohibition on calls to cell phones placed using an automated dialing system unless the caller has the called consumer's "prior express consent." This general ban applies to all text messages sent without consent, including sales pitches, service reminders, "cold-call" messages, and communications with current customers.

The TCPA's definition of "automated telephone dialing system" is broad enough to apply to the use of computers to automate the delivery of text messages. It is defined as "equipment which has the capacity: (A) to store or produce telephone numbers to be called, using a random or sequential number generator; and (B) to dial such numbers."

In addition, FCC regulations restrict text messages transmitting sales pitches whether or not you use a dialer to deliver them. For example, a sales campaign using text messages must comply with the national do not call list as well as the requirement to maintain a company-specific do not call list.

In some cases, your text messages will be considered both an e-mail and a telephone call. The FCC and the *Joffe* court agree that a text message that meets the TCPA's definition of a "call" and the CAN-SPAM Act's definition of an "e-mail" must comply with both sets of laws.

Determining whether a text message is an e-mail depends on whether it is sent to an "electronic mail address" or not. CAN-SPAM defines "electronic mail address" to cover an address that includes an Internet domain name (that is, the part of an e-mail address that follows the "@" symbol), whether the e-mail address is displayed or not.

Many text messages will meet this standard. Some messages, however, are sent from phone to phone without using an "electronic mail address" (including SMS messages). CAN-SPAM does not regulate SMS messages.

Any campaign of "commercial" text messages that satisfies CAN-SPAM's "electronic mail address" definition must comply with the FCC's wireless e-mail rule. This rule imposes a general prohibition on commercial messages sent directly to wireless devices, although there are exceptions, including messages based on the recipient's "express prior authorization." Merely having an "established business relationship" with the recipient is not enough. Where you have the necessary authorization from the recipient, your messages must include a free opt-out mechanism and provide your identity.

In sum, before you begin a campaign of text message communications, whether they are sales pitches or not, you will likely need the recipient's express prior consent or authorization. More specifically, you must consider the technology you will use to deliver the messages as well as the messages' content. If you use a computer, you must consider whether it meets the TCPA's "dialer" definition and whether your method of delivery meets the CAN-SPAM Act's "electronic mail address" definition. You must also consider whether your messages are based on an "established business relationship" or not. If so, that may provide an exception from "do not call" compliance, but not from compliance with the FCC's wireless e-mail rule or its ban on dialer calls to cell phones.

In the end, understanding federal regulation of text messages is tricky at first, but manageable if you proceed with caution.

CHAPTER 14

Title
Lending

We just couldn't put our pencils back in their cases without including a chapter on title lending. Why? It could just be the motor oil that pumps through our veins, or it could be that title lenders need to concern themselves with so many issues covered in this book, we thought we'd invite them to the party too.

After all, title lending has a lot of things in common with traditional indirect motor vehicle finance. Both forms of financing usually result in a creditor having a security interest in a motor vehicle, which often (but not always!) results in similar collection and servicing restrictions. Both title lenders and credit sellers (like car dealers) are "financial institutions" for purposes of several state and federal laws, which govern things such as privacy, discrimination, and identity theft.

But, the differences between the two are important. Unlike credit sales, title loans are actual, honest to goodness, direct loans, and are regulated as such. As a result, title lenders will typically be subject to different licensing requirements and rate and fee limitations. (Note that this area is an example of why it's so important to know the difference between loans and credit sales!)

And, like their car dealer cousins, title lenders have been on state and federal lawmakers' radars in recent years. The article in this chapter provides a sampling of these issues and an overview of title lending in general.

A Beginner's Guide to Title Lending
November 2008
By Catherine M. Brennan and Meghan S. Musselman

As the credit crunch continues to loom in this country, cash-strapped consumers increasingly will seek alternative forms of paying for unexpected financial emergencies such as a sick child, job loss, or a death in the family. One form of lending that consumers may consider is motor vehicle title lending. In title lending, the lender makes a loan to the consumer based on the value of the consumer's vehicle. However, the lender does not take the consumer's car. Rather, the lender will take the title to the motor vehicle and a spare set of keys to the car. Leaving the car with the consumer enables him or her to continue driving the motor vehicle during the term of the loan, which, obviously, is of significant benefit to the borrower.

A dealer who decides to enter into the title lending business needs to uncover how his or her state regulates title lending. Almost all states require a title lender to have a license of some sort—the key question is which license must the lender obtain. At least three potential sources of lending authority exist in a state—a law that expressly regulates title lending, a pawnbroker or pawnshop statute, and a general consumer lending statute.

Title lending. In the last several years, many states have adopted statutes that specifically authorize title lending. One such law is the Utah Title Lending Registration Act (UTLRA), adopted in 2003. The Act does not cap the rates that title lenders can charge, but it does require title lenders to register with the state. The Act also imposes certain operational limitations on title lenders. For example, the Act prohibits title lenders from originating a title loan without regard to the ability of the person seeking the title loan to repay the title loan, including the person's current and expected income, current obligations, and employment. The rationale behind this requirement is to prohibit lenders from originating a loan based solely on the value of the collateral, a common prohibition found in many statutes that regulate so-called "high-cost lending," such as the federal Home Ownership Equity Protection Act, which regulates high-cost mortgage loans. Title lenders operating in states with this type of requirement must ensure they take into account actual ability to repay the title loan in their underwriting, as the regulator will surely challenge them if they solely look to the collateral for repayment.

Pawnshops. Other states have allowed title lending to occur under a pawnshop or pawnbroker statute. For example, title lenders operate under the Alabama Pawnshop Act when lending in that state. The Alabama Pawnshop Act covers the pledge of "tangible personal property," which had raised the question of whether the Act authorized the constructive pledge of an automobile. However, in 1993, the Alabama Supreme Court ruled that pawnshops could engage in title pawn transactions under the Act.

Property secured loans. Still other states permit title lending under a direct lending law that generally authorizes personal property-secured loans. For example, South Carolina regulates the loans made by title lenders under the South Carolina Consumer Protection Code. The Code generally applies to all consumer loans in which the principal does not exceed $82,500, a dollar amount that adjusts every even-numbered year. In 2003, the South Carolina legislature, aware of the growth in the title lending business, amended the Code to impose specific requirements on title loans with an original repayment term of less than 120 days. A lender that originates short-term vehicle-secured loans will have the same license as other consumer finance lenders—the supervised lender's license—but will have to comply with enhanced requirements for the title loans. Similar to Utah, the lender must, before making a short-term vehicle-secured loan, form a good faith belief that the borrower has the ability to repay the loan, considering the borrower's, and any co-borrower's, employment, monthly income, and other monthly expenses compared to the loan's repayment obligation for the original term and permitted renewals. Of course, many title lenders in South Carolina responded by modifying their loans so that the maturity date exceeded 120 days. In so doing, those title lenders can avoid the title loan-specific requirements of the Code and only comply with the Code's general lending requirements.

Once the lender has navigated the maze of state laws that could potentially apply to its business, the lender must be aware of the many federal laws that impact its loan originations. Fortunately, the requirements of the federal Truth in Lending Act apply just as they do to any other direct loan or retail installment contract. In addition, Section 670 of the John Warner National Defense Authorization Act for Fiscal Year 2007 and the regulations promulgated by the Department of Defense (DOD) impose certain limitations on consumer credit, including vehicle title loans made to active duty military personnel and their dependents.

Although the Act appears to prohibit vehicle title loans made to active duty military personnel or their dependents, the regulations authorize, but significantly limit, lending secured by vehicle titles. The DOD does not have authority under the Act to amend its apparent prohibition of vehicle title lending. Thus, notwithstanding the regulations, it remains unclear whether vehicle title lending to active duty military personnel or their dependents is permitted. Without obtaining advice from DOD to the contrary, title lenders should follow the explicit ban in the Act and avoid making vehicle title loans to active duty military personnel or their dependents.

Finally, a not insignificant concern title lenders must confront is the stigma associated with title lending. Consumer advocates and Attorneys General have targeted title lending as a form of "predatory lending," arguing that the title lender "traps" the consumer in a cycle of debt from which the consumer cannot escape, ultimately resulting in the loss of the motor vehicle when the consumer defaults. Many state laws take steps to address these concerns by, for example, limiting the number of times a consumer can refinance or "roll over" the title loan. Title lenders would do well to observe sound underwriting practices in extending these types of loans and to adopt a strict compliance program to catch consumer complaints before they turn into consumer litigation.

Auto
Finance
Lexicon

This book deals with the legal side of auto sales, finance, and leasing. In the articles, we sometimes use jargon or shorthand references to legal terms. Here are some of the terms you will see from time to time and a short description of what they mean.

AG: Stands for Attorney General. Every state has one, essentially the top legal officer in the state. AGs usually enforce consumer protection laws and regulations. When we are being cynical, we sometimes say that "AG" stands for "Aspiring Governor." We also sometimes say the same thing when we are not being cynical.

CLA: The Consumer Leasing Act. The CLA governs disclosures in consumer lease transactions. The CLA is actually Chapter 5 of TILA, but is usually referred to as if it is a separate piece of legislation.

ECOA: Federal Equal Credit Opportunity Act. The ECOA prohibits credit discrimination on the basis of sex, race, marital status, etc.

F&I: The "finance and insurance" department of a dealership is called the F&I department. That's where financing terms are arranged and various products like credit insurance and extended warranties are sold.

FRB: The Federal Reserve Board. The FRB authors a number of credit-related regulations that implement acts of Congress. These include Reg. B (The Equal Credit Opportunity Act), Reg. Z (The Truth in Lending Act), and Reg. M (The Consumer Leasing Act).

FTC: The Federal Trade Commission, a federal agency that enforces several federal laws and regulations (including the TILA, the ECOA, and Regs. Z and B) with respect to car dealers. The FTC is the toughest, most consumer-friendly enforcement agency in Washington, and is the "federal cop" for car dealers.

Reg. B: A regulation of the FRB implementing the ECOA.

Reg. M: A regulation of the FRB implementing the CLA.

Reg. P: An FTC regulation implementing the Gramm-Leach-Bliley Act's privacy provisions.

Reg. Z: A regulation of the FRB implementing TILA.

RISA: Refers to a "retail installment sales act." Nearly every state has a RISA. Some states (about half) have a special version of a RISA for motor vehicle financing, and a separate RISA for other kinds of personal property financing. RISAs typically regulate finance charge rates, late charges, grace periods, bad check charges, disclosures, and the like in auto financing agreements between dealers and customers.

RISC: A retail installment sales contract. This document is used to document a credit sale from a dealer to a buyer. The dealer usually then sells the RISC to a finance company or bank. Buy-here, pay-here dealers hold RISCs and collect payments from buyers, unless they have created an affiliated finance company to assign them to. If you call a RISC a "loan," Spot (the Dalmatian mascot for our legal newsletter, *Spot Delivery*®), has instructions to bite you on the ankle.

TILA: The federal Truth in Lending Act. TILA governs disclosures in consumer credit transactions. This is the "granddaddy" of federal disclosure laws.

Tort: A tort is a "civil wrong." The actions that comprise a tort can also comprise a crime, but a tort is not necessarily a crime. Examples of torts are negligence, fraud, and defamation.

UDAP: Refers to unfair and deceptive acts and practices. The FTC has UDAP provisions, and most states do, as well. Only the FTC can enforce the FTC's version—a consumer cannot bring a private lawsuit to enforce it. Not necessarily so at the state level, since many state UDAP laws permit consumers to sue. UDAP laws are favorites of lawyers who sue dealers because they are very general in their prohibitions and usually provide for a multiple (two or three times) the consumer's actual damages, plus attorneys' fees.

Other terms you may see, and what they mean:

ADA: Americans With Disabilities Act

CLA: Consumer Leasing Act

FCRA: Fair Credit Reporting Act

FFI: Federally Insured Financial Institution

FinCEN: A unit of the U.S. Treasury Department

FMCC: Ford Motor Credit Corporation

GAP: GAP is an insurance or an insurance-like product that, in the event of a total loss of a vehicle, pays the difference between the consumer's insurance proceeds and the amount owed on the car.

GLB: Gramm-Leach-Bliley Act, the federal law dealing with privacy

GMAC: General Motors Acceptance Corporation

HIDC: Holder-In-Due-Course

MMWA: Magnuson-Moss Warranty Act

NADA: National Automobile Dealers Association

Negative equity: When a customer owes more on his or her trade-in vehicle than the amount of the trade-in allowance, the difference is called "negative equity." Such a customer is sometimes called "upside down."

NMAC: Nissan Motors Acceptance Corporation

OFAC: The Office of Foreign Assets Control, a Treasury Department Unit

RICO: Racketeer Influenced and Corrupt Organizations Act

SAR: Suspicious Activity Report, required under certain circumstances

SBCWA: Song-Beverly Consumer Warranty Act

SID: Starter Interrupt Device

UCC: Uniform Commercial Code

UCLA: Uniform Consumer Leasing Act

A Quick Primer on Laws and Regulations

A word about laws and regulations: Laws are passed by legislatures. Congress passes federal laws, and state legislatures pass state laws. "Rules" (such as the FTC's Used Car Rule) and regulations are issued by agencies or other state or federal nonlegislative bodies that have been given rule-making or regulatory authority by the legislative body.

An attempt to change a law requires having Congress or the state legislature pass a new law, a process that can be very difficult. Changing regulations can also be difficult but usually not as difficult as changing a law. Sometimes regulatory authorities don't have the power to change regulations because the laws they are administering won't permit the change. As an example, even if the Federal Reserve Board wanted to amend Reg. Z to apply to auto finance transactions in which the amount financed is over $25,000, it could not do so because TILA—an act of Congress—provides that such transactions are not subject to TILA's disclosure requirements.

Appendix 3

Index